PROPHETS OF REGULATION

Library of Congress Cataloging in Publication Data

McCraw, Thomas K.
Prophets of regulation.

Includes index.
1. Trade regulation—United States—History.
2. Industry and state—United States—History.   3. Adams,
Charles Francis, 1835–1915.   4. Brandeis, Louis Dembitz,
1856–1941.   5. Landis, James McCauley, 1899–1964.
6. Kahn, Alfred Edward.   I. Title.
HD3616.U46M38   1984   338.973   84–296
ISBN 0–674–71607–8 (cloth)
ISBN 0–674–71608–6 (paper)

To Susan, with love

Preface

W HEN I began to write this book, I was intrigued by the mysteries that seemed to surround the history of government regulation in America. Why, I wondered, had regulation so often failed to serve the "public interest," as it had been intended to do? Why, if the commissions had proved so ineffective, did they remain active as apparently permanent parts of the government? Why, if agencies were so often "captured" by interests they were supposed to be regulating, did not other branches of government step in and take away their legislated powers?

Plausible attempts to answer these questions, as it turned out, lay close at hand; for regulation is one of the most written-about subjects of our time. As a topic rich in potential insights about many different themes of American culture, regulation has received concentrated attention from innumerable popular writers as well as from hundreds of scholars based in various academic disciplines: law, economics, political science, sociology, business administration. The theoretical frameworks offered by these scholars, as much as the vast body of their empirical research, have been indispensable to me. I wanted to write a *history*, however, and my book does not resemble most of the existing scholarly literature from other disciplines.

On its surface, this book is about four important prophets of regulation, whose work spans more than a century of experience: Charles Francis Adams, Louis D. Brandeis, James M. Landis, and Alfred E. Kahn. I might have called them architects or innovators of regulation, as all of them were. But the designation *prophets* seems better to express the unusual combination each one represented of both theorizing about regulation and actually doing it, of both design and implementation.

In treating these men, I am interested in what they thought about regulation, what they accomplished, and how things turned out for them and for the agencies they influenced. Curiously, although we have been told a very great deal about regulation, we remain relatively ignorant about the regulators themselves. Furthermore, since the prevailing burden of judgment holds overwhelmingly that regulation in America has been a failure, the necessary corollary suggests that regulators themselves have failed. This assumption makes these men and women seem less interesting, more swept along by this or that historical determinism, and somehow less volitional than other types of public figures.

I am inclined to reject this line of thinking. Individual regulators clearly made an enormous difference. Each of my four major characters represented, in the jargon of social science, an "independent social force." Contrary to the popular image of regulation as a light that failed, most of the four proved historically successful. Yet they achieved their goals only under certain conditions—which I have taken care to identify—and only through a good deal of administrative artistry on their own part. For the core of my concern here is regulatory *strategy:* how the regulators themselves framed or failed to frame their purposes, and how they executed those purposes or failed to do so. In the language of administrative science, I am interested in both the formulation and implementation of policy. But policy remains a work of man.

Why choose these particular men? First, because together their careers cover the historical span of modern regulation in America. I wanted to write about regulation as a problem, not merely as an aspect of one particular period of American history. Surely the problem has been with us ever since colonial times, when merchants and churchmen argued over the idea of a "just price" for merchandise. Yet there has been no single watershed, no one era in which American regulatory policy became set once and for all. In the last hundred years, there have been four periods when regulation as a whole took on enhanced importance: the 1870s, the early years of industrialization; the period 1900–1916, often called the Progressive Era; the 1930s, during the New Deal; and the 1970s, when both regulation and deregulation somehow grew simultaneously. In this book each of these four periods is represented by a single member of my quartet.

Aside from providing inclusive coverage of the problem, another reason for selecting Adams, Brandeis, Landis, and Kahn is that each one profoundly influenced the historical evolution of regulation. One of them (Brandeis) indeed is regarded as a patron saint of the whole regulatory tradition; the other three represent more than twenty years of service on five different agencies—two state and three federal. In addition, three of the four were lawyers by training, and this proportion accords well with the occupational profile of all federal and state commissioners over the last century. Finally, all four men thought and wrote extensively about the complex relationship between business and government in America. In doing so they not only fulfilled their roles as prophets of regulation, but incidentally provided a treasury of primary sources for historical inquiry.

My approach fluctuates between the lives of men, economic theory, and historical incident. Each of the four biographical chapters is followed by a brief historical analysis in which I survey broad themes of regulation for the period under discussion. Together, the different parts of the book are designed to suggest the rich combination of human action and impersonal circumstance that constitutes the fabric of history—here the history of regulation, where the strands of volition and determinism are woven just as intricately as they are in the pattern of any other human activity.

Contents

Illustrations

(following page 152)

ADAMS

Photographs courtesy Massachusetts Historical Society, except as shown.

> Young man about town
> Harvard senior picture (Harvard University Archives)
> Civil War officer (Library of Congress)
> Railroad commissioner, cartoon
> Railroad commissioner, Millett portrait (U.S. Department of Interior, National Park Service, Adams National Historic Site)
> President of Union Pacific Railroad
> In Holland, age 63
> American aristocrat

BRANDEIS

Photographs courtesy Special Collections, Brandeis University Archives.

> Young lawyer
> Louis and his brother
> Urban reformer
> National reformer
> Legal craftsman
> Taking his leisure

LANDIS

> Federal Trade commissioner (Donald Ritchie)
> Securities and Exchange commissioner (National Archives)
> The SEC, 1936 (Securities and Exchange Commission)
> With cigarette holder (Harvard Law School Art Collection)
> In Cambridge with Frankfurter (Harvard Law School Collection)
> Lecturing at Harvard (Harvard Law School Art Collection)
> At age 60 (New York Times Pictures)

KAHN

Photographs courtesy Alfred E. Kahn

> At Cornell reunion
> Age 5, in Poland
> At Ripon College
> In *Yeomen of the Guard* and *Iolanthe*
> Advising an undergraduate
> With President Carter
> Signing the Airline Deregulation Act of 1978

CHAPTER 1

Adams and the Sunshine Commission

THE GRAVESTONE of Charles Francis Adams bears an epitaph, written by his brother Henry, which captures the many-sided nature of Charles's career.[1]

> BORN IN BOSTON MAY 27, 1835
> DIED IN WASHINGTON MARCH 20, 1915
> KNOWN TO HIS TIME IN MANY PATHS
> SOLDIER CIVILIAN ADMINISTRATOR HISTORIAN
> HIS CHARACTER COURAGE AND ABILITIES
> WERE DOUBTED IN NONE
> AFTER EIGHTY YEARS OF ACTIVE LIFE
> IN A RESTLESS AND OFTEN A TROUBLED AGE
> HE LEFT TO HIS DESCENDANTS AN HONORABLE NAME
> WORTHY OF THOSE WHICH HAD BEFORE HIM
> SHONE IN THE ANNALS OF THE STATE

Charles trod so many paths in part because the burden of the family legacy pressed hard on him. For any Adams of his generation, life by definition meant a continual struggle with one's conscience, a fateful quest to fulfill one's responsibilities to stern ancestors and to God. By Charles's time, the family's history had entered the public domain; it was so much a part of the nation's own history as to recall Old Testament dynasties. John Adams, the second American president, fathered John Quincy Adams, the sixth. He in turn begat the first Charles Francis Adams, the Civil War diplomat who prevented British recognition of the Confederacy and thereby saved the Union from its most dangerous foreign threat. This diplomat had four sons: John, Charles Jr., Henry, and

Brooks. John immersed himself in the affairs of Massachusetts and of Quincy, the family seat. Henry and Brooks became important historians and social commentators—blueblood versions of what a later age called "personalities."

Of the four brothers, it was Charles who made the most interesting attempt to weave the Adams tradition of public service into the harsh realities of the Gilded Age. Charles was an aristocrat, a man of refinement who shared brother Henry's distaste for the excesses of the era. Yet he also kept one eye to the main chance and took stock market plunges of the greediest sort. An economic analyst who tried to accelerate industrial change, he still preferred the quiet of the countryside, the comfort of history books. He began his career as a muckraker, brilliantly lampooning railroad tycoons in his classic magazine piece, "A Chapter of Erie." Shortly afterward, however, as the first important regulatory commissioner in American history, he warned against infringing on the prerogatives of business management. He made substantial contributions to public life, and to regulation in particular. But he did not forgo the opportunity for personal enrichment at the "Great Barbecue."[2]

Mistakes

"My youth and education," Charles reflected in his autobiography, "now seem to me to have been a skilfully arranged series of mistakes, first on the part of others and then on my own part." Charles's joyless father tended to think of children in the abstract, and he had difficulty perceiving the different needs of his four sons. "Any exceptionalism or individuality," Charles lamented, "he regarded with aversion." Therefore it was certain that his father would insist that he go to the Boston Latin School, but equally certain what would come of the decision. "I loathed it," Charles recalled, "and John loathed it worse than I." The next lockstep, Harvard College, brought little improvement: "No instructor produced, or endeavored to produce, the slightest impression on me; no spark of enthusiasm was sought to be infused into me." These educational "mistakes" seemed in retrospect only the unnecessary prices of privilege. As Charles viewed the matter, he was justified in finishing below the median of his class at Harvard, just as he had done at Boston Latin.[3]

In the years after Harvard, mistakes continued. Worse still, Charles himself now had to bear the responsibility. Intelligent and able, but drawn to no particular field, he searched almost desperately for a vocation. He finally settled on the law, a profession embedded in the family tradition. Forgoing formal training at Harvard Law School, he read for a couple of years in the Boston offices of Francis E. Parker, whom Charles thought a peerless judge of character; and of Parker's cohort Richard Henry Dana, the author of *Two Years Before the Mast.* He enjoyed working with Parker and Dana, but for the law itself he could generate no affection. To his horror he realized that for someone of his temperament the profession offered the worst possible fit. He was "singularly lacking in what is known as tact" (as he himself put it), too self-centered to adapt to office routine, and too much the dilettante to concentrate on detail. Brusque, petulant, "a good deal of a prig," Charles began to despise himself. He went through the motions of admission to the bar, but soon sat "eating my heart out in a clientless office." Then, as clients continued to stay away, he grew panicky in his effort to maintain the fictitious front of yet another Adams on the rise.[4]

Charles's early and middle twenties slipped by without accomplishment. He gadded about, taking advantage of his access to high social and political circles. As a son of Abigail Brown Brooks, one of New England's wealthiest heiresses, Charles had no material need to work. But uselessness tortured him. Decades afterward, his name long since made, he tried to expunge this period from his own memory by destroying the diaries he had kept between his fifteenth and twenty-fifth years. This act was a type of retrospective suicide, the more striking in view of the family's characteristic devotion to diaries as sympathetic confidants in a hostile world.

At just this point in his life (he was twenty-six), the American Civil War intruded. Charles witnessed the unfolding drama at first hand during a long Washington sojourn in 1861, as his family connection brought him into the company of William H. Seward, Charles Sumner, and other Union leaders. When the break between North and South finally did come, President Lincoln dispatched Charles Francis Adams, Sr., to London. This move lifted the family incubus from Charles Jr. and signaled the onset of his adult life. Yet his appreciation of the new freedom took time to sink in, and for a while Charles remained content to attend to family affairs around Boston, acting as surrogate for his absent parent. At length, against his own first instinct and his father's stern advice, he determined to join the army. He began service in 1862 as an officer in the U.S. cavalry.[5]

By the end of the war, Charles had seen action in Antietam and Gettysburg and risen to the rank of full colonel. For him, the climax of the war came when he led his Massachusetts regiment of black troops into Richmond at the moment of Lee's retreat: "the one event which I should most have desired as the culmination of my life in the Army." As his father wrote proudly from England, "How full of significance is this history, which all of us are now helping to make!"[6]

Charles spent the months after his discharge recovering from the rigors of military life. He also took advantage of the interlude to marry the aristocratic Minnie Ogden of Newport, whom he had met during the war, and to spend a long European honeymoon contemplating his future. The war had been an immensely satisfying experience, but only an episode in his life. The road now before him must not lead back to the emptiness of his earlier experience.

The First Big Business

This time, having learned from his mistakes, Charles approached the choice of a vocation more systematically: "Surveying the whole field—instinctively recognizing my unfitness for the law—I fixed on the railroad system as the most developing force and largest field of the day, and determined to attach myself to it."[7] At about the same time, Emerson was coining his famous aphorism about hitching one's wagon to a star. By hitching himself to the railroads, Charles was joining a force that had begun to revolutionize American life.

Already by the 1860s railroads dwarfed most other institutions in American society. At a time when the federal government employed only 50,000 civilians, rail corporations provided jobs for many times that number. Their capitalizations far exceeded those of even the largest manufacturing companies. Railroading influenced American society in the late nineteenth century as only television would in the late twentieth—or as the Roman Catholic

Church had influenced the life of medieval Europe. Henry Adams, that self-conscious student of such matters, accurately characterized his and Charles's entire generation as "mortgaged to the railways."[8]

At the time, Massachusetts had the densest rail network in the world, and the industry's impact was not limited to the realm of economics and business. Railroads affected consciousness; they influenced life itself. As Thoreau ruefully noted, railway locomotives had penetrated to the very banks of Walden Pond: "They go and come with such regularity and precision, and their whistle can be heard so far, that the farmers set their clocks by them, and thus one well conducted institution regulates a whole country. Have not men improved somewhat in punctuality since the railroad was invented? Do they not talk and think faster in the depot than they did in the stage-office?"[9] New England and the industrial northeast had developed mature rail systems by the time of the Civil War. The giant eastern trunklines—the New York Central, Pennsylvania, Baltimore and Ohio, and Erie—built up feeder systems, pierced the Allegheny mountain barrier, and opened up the West for fast, reliable transportation of an enormous volume of traffic.[10] Huge though the railroad system already was, it actually stood on the verge of still more fantastic growth. In the five years following 1868—the time when Charles Francis Adams began his railroad work—nearly 30,000 miles of new tracks were laid, an enormous total, seldom equaled before or since. Surely Charles picked the right star for his wagon.[11]

But within the giant railroad industry, what might be the appropriate role for an Adams? Even though the affairs of railroading somehow constituted a vast new arena for the affairs of state, it remained unclear just how one might play the part of a statesman. As he began to frame a reply to his own question, Charles decided to draw on the one first-rate talent he had inherited, the talent for good writing. Throughout his life, he preserved a vivid image of his grandfather John Quincy Adams, an image that might have applied as well to Charles himself: "I can see him now . . . with a bald head and white fringe of hair—writing, writing—with a perpetual inkstain on the forefinger and thumb of the right hand." For Charles, as for his Adams forebears, the habit of writing became almost compulsive. By the end of his life he had published the remarkable total of 440 items, not counting an endless series of diary entries, letters to family and friends, and editorials written anonymously for newspapers. It seemed as if his Adams genes had issued standing orders that pen be put to paper. Had he used old John Quincy's quills, his own hands would have worn the perpetual inkstain too, like a family birthmark.[12]

By the time he left military service, Charles's expository skills were already in evidence, both in his one significant publication ("The Reign of King Cotton," which the *Atlantic Monthly* carried in 1861) and in the many evocative letters he wrote to his family from the battlefields. Now, in 1867, married, past thirty, and still frustrated by his law practice, he deliberately set about to build a career on the foundation of his writing ability; he would educate himself in all aspects of the railroad question, publish his analyses and thereby publicize his growing expertise, and use the resulting reputation to gain an official public post.[13] "I want," he wrote his friend David A. Wells, "a war with the [railroad] Rings." By battling the rail corporations, he could achieve the fame that might bring him a franchise to regulate them. From this idea grew an ambition ultimately to be a national ombudsman, the public's representative-at-large in its manifold relationships with the railroad system. But one measure of Charles's early naiveté toward the business world is less obvious here: he failed to see the inconsistency between war, on the one hand, and disinterested mediation on the other.[14]

In pursuing this ambitious line of thinking about a career in public life, Charles followed a pattern already marked out by other young men of his generation. These men, despite the mismatch of their refined tastes with the age's garishness, dreamed of critical national roles for themselves as reformers. Another example was Henry Adams, whose "strike for the press" paralleled Charles's "strike for the railroads." A third was David A. Wells, whose economic writings broke new ground in the perennial debates over free trade and protective tariffs. Still another was Frederick Law Olmsted, the landscape architect who attempted to save American cities from self-destruction through developments such as New York's Central Park. And at the center of this group of friends and allies stood E. L. Godkin, the Irish journalist who had settled in America and built, in *The Nation*, an instrument for the dissemination of the group's views.[15]

With all of these men, Charles remained on familiar terms. He and his circle liked to think of themselves as America's "best men." Yet sometimes their elitism and antidemocratic tendencies could not be disguised, and in one sense most of them were a bit foolish. Deeply involved in the political and industrial struggles of their time, they strove to be simultaneously above the battle and decisive in it. That contradictory combination could not prevail, and the group was doomed to frustration. But, in the meantime, its members left permanent marks on some of the innovative institutions of their time (urban park systems, learned journals, regulatory commissions); and Charles's imprint cut deeper than most. Certainly no ultimate disappointment seemed apparent to him in the hopeful years after the Civil War, as he set his prolific pen to work.

A New Phase of Representative Government

From 1867 until his accession to office as a commissioner in 1869, Charles Francis Adams published numerous articles on railroads, in a variety of periodicals ranging from new quasi-professional journals such as the *American Law Review* and the *Journal of Social Science* to those well-established magazines of opinion, *The Nation* and the *North American Review*. Some of his essays were short and perfunctory, others rigorously analytical. Each of them served Adams' strategy of making first a name for himself and then a place.

From the very first article, one thing was apparent: Adams spoke with the voice not of the lawyer but of the economist. He had rejected the legal profession substantively as well as symbolically. From that point on he persistently emphasized the broad landscape more than closeup details, as he concerned himself more with economic policy than with legal process. In nearly every article, he made four themes explicit.[16]

1. Industrialization in America had acquired a momentum of its own, a thrust and direction essentially independent of human will. Technology was shaping society as it had never done before.
2. This technological determinism applied not only to the general aspects of the case, but especially to one industry—the railroads—whose unique economics of natural monopoly sharply restricted governments' choices in making policy.
3. A serious institutional lag had opened up between corporate

development and the public response to it. As a consequence, private and public interests were out of balance.

4. The best solution to the "railroad problem" (as contemporary writers called it) was not really a *solution* in the final sense, but rather some means of coping with a situation that was inherently fluid and complex. To perform this function, a new instrumentality of government must be created: an expert, permanent, apolitical body—in brief, a regulatory commission.

Though much of Adams' thought was derivative, his articles showed a distinctive understanding of the revolution being wrought by machines. He apprehended well the meaning of industrialization's momentum throughout the western world and the implications it held even for the routine of daily life: "Increased communication, increased activity, and increased facilities of trade destroy local interests, local dialects, and local jealousies." Industrial development brought unprecedented centralization and standardization. "Whatever is homogeneous is combining all over the world in obedience to an irresistible law. It is the law of gravitation applied to human affairs. One national centre regulates the whole daily thought, trade, and language of great nations, and regulates it instantly."[17] In Adams' view, personal preference, individual or collective free will, availed little against the force of the machine: "It is useless for men to stand in the way of steamengines." Industrialization simply transcended ideology and politics. "The progressive may exult, and the conservative may repine, but the result will be all the same."[18]

The industrial revolution had hit with special force in the United States, the nation itself being a "child of steam." The country so depended on steam transportation that "progress at any price is the watchword of the present." With this insight, Adams pinpointed the salient fact about railroads in the Gilded Age. Because they were essential to present prosperity and future development, no sum seemed too excessive to pay for them. Profiteering by their promoters, outrageous behavior by the railroad robber barons, all must be accepted as by-products of an essential service. National priorities resembled those of wartime, when victory—and not cost—controlled every decision.[19]

Like wars, railroads soon proved to be inordinately expensive. Entrepreneurs coming into the business found themselves having to put up immense, sometimes shocking, amounts of money. The purchase of land along rights of way, the construction of roadbeds, track, locomotives, and rolling stock, ate up capital as no industry had ever done before. Moreover, these colossal expenditures preceded the earning of a single dollar by the company, because a railroad must be completed before it can carry even one passenger or piece of cargo. In the language of the modern economist, railroading was a capital-intensive industry. During the nineteenth century, its capital requirements far surpassed those of all other types of business, and in the twentieth were exceeded only by those of the electric power industry. But the unusual economics of railroading went even further than this. The earliest operators of trains found that they could transport enormous numbers of passengers and huge loads of freight at only slightly more expense to themselves than when they carried one passenger and one box of cargo. Each additional person or item carried reduced the average cost to the railroad of carrying every person or item in the entire load. Therefore, if the railroad companies wanted to minimize their customers' rates and fares and their own average costs, they should run their trains as fully loaded as possible, with as many cars as their locomotives could efficiently pull. The principles behind these observed tendencies of costs and prices came to be called "economies of scale." In the twentieth century, the principles were personified by Henry Ford, whose assembly lines turned out one Model T after another, at ever cheaper cost precisely because so many were produced.

From the beginning, railroads exhibited almost unlimited economies of scale. And Charles Francis Adams' fascination with this remarkable characteristic infused all of his early writings on the industry. "It is an undisputed law of railway economics," he observed with excitement, "that *the cost of the movement is in direct inverse ratio to the amount moved.*" But the implications of scale reached beyond mere academic interest and even beyond the balance sheets of individual companies. They went as well to the very heart of the railroad problem. For if scale economies were sufficiently great, then competition in the accepted sense of the word simply did not apply. The basic premise of an direct inverse ratio of cost to traffic, Adams wrote, pointed directly to "a conclusion which is at the basis of the whole transportation problem: *competition and the cheapest possible transportation are wholly incompatible.*"[20]

In nineteenth-century America, to declare competition invalid was to invite derision and attack. Protecting himself, Adams took pains to show just how and why railroads differed from other types of business. "Each new railway," he explained, "involves a new expenditure of capital on which interest is to be paid; a new corps of officials; additional rolling stock, terminal facilities, and construction expense." But none of this additional expenditure need occur, since a single railroad could as easily carry all available traffic as could five or six parallel and competing lines. Therefore, Adams concluded, *"The single chance any given community has of obtaining the cheapest possible transportation is limited by its success in directing the largest possible volume of movement through the fewest possible channels.* This may now be stated as an established axiom in railway economics." In other words, the unusual economic logic of railroading impelled the industry toward a monopolistic structure.[21]

Moreover, because such a structure brought "the cheapest possible transportation," Adams argued that society should not merely accept the railroads' drift toward monopoly, but instead do everything it could to accelerate the tendency. But American culture made such a policy repugnant, if not altogether impossible. Given the nation's past opposition to monopoly, Adams might as well have proposed something as unthinkable as reentry into the British Empire or the restoration of slavery. In the eighteenth century, monopoly had meant exclusive economic concessions like the East India Company's domination of the tea trade. Such royal grants of privilege once symbolized the corrupt, absolutist powers against which the founding fathers had fought their revolution. During the Jacksonian period, monopoly had taken the form of privately owned toll bridges, and of Nicholas Biddle and his hated Second Bank of the United States—new enemies, but guilty of a familiar crime. For Americans, monopoly ultimately implied a foreclosure of those economic opportunities that set New World democracy apart from Old World tyranny. Any argument in favor of any form of monopoly, therefore, bore a crushing burden of negative national prejudice.

Conscious of this cultural obstacle but undeterred by it, Adams outlined for readers the limited number of policy alternatives that the unusual economics of railroading would permit. One logical solution might deal with both illegitimate power and excess profits. This solution was public ownership of railroads, which had been tried with much success in Belgium, Prussia, and France. Would public ownership work in America as well? Adams thought not. For one thing, the very decentralization of the American government, its tripartite division of constitutional authority—not to mention the federal-state problem—raised difficult questions about its ability to manage complex enterprises. Here the issue was not so much that public ownership smacked of socialism, but rather that the railroads had a pressing need for competent and intelligent management. The American political system, despite its many virtues, had been designed with different ends in mind. As Adams noted, "the whole instinct of the people leads them to circumscribe rather than to enlarge the province of government. This policy is founded in wisdom." Then, too, the practice of politics had sunk to a historic nadir during the Gilded Age. "Imagine the Erie [railroad] and Tammany rings rolled into one and turned loose on the field of politics, and the result of State ownership would be realized. This plan, therefore, may apparently be dismissed from consideration."[22]

With public ownership disqualified for practical reasons and monopoly unacceptable on ideological grounds, only one alternative remained: enforced competition among railroads. This policy, Adams reported with regret, had been followed dogmatically in Massachusetts. Though it worked well in regulating most industries, it had brought nothing but grief for the railroads.

To explain how this had occurred, and what the remedy might be, Adams characteristically resorted to historical example. And since the thrust of his strategy aimed at the creation of a state railroad commission, his example focused on Massachusetts. Adams noted that the state's first railroad corporations had sprung up in the 1830s and 1840s, financed with some public assistance but paid for primarily through private investment. Despite this private origin, railroads evolved under special charters from the state legislature, as common carrier corporations wielding the power of eminent domain. Because of the obvious importance of the industry, state lawmakers wrote strong controls into these charters and into other railroad legislation as well. Powerful in principle, these provisions actually came to nothing becuse they were seldom exercised. Not only did the railroads themselves ignore the laws, but the government made little effort to enforce them. Most of the laws had been misguided to begin with, and their disuse reflected wisdom on the part of the state.[23] Still they remained on the books, and "the crude legislative makeshifts of forty years ago had gradually passed unchallenged into the general and permanent law of the state." In Adams' view, this situation not only promoted wrongheaded railroad policy; it also invited contempt for law itself. Accordingly, he proposed a careful, thoroughgoing revision and codification of Massachusetts's railroad statutes. Such a reform would require the expertise of just that kind of regulatory commission on which his personal ambitions centered.[24]

To clinch his argument, Adams undertook to demonstrate the way in which even conscientious legislators could err when they began to tinker with so complex an instrument as railroads. As his leading exhibit of legislative blunder, he pointed to a Massachusetts statute that, in effect, defined 10 percent profit as a fair rate of return for the corporations. In naming the 10 percent figure, the legislature imposed both a floor on profits and a ceiling as well.[25] To Adams, the floor was not a particularly good idea, and in the ceiling he saw a potential conflict between corporate interests and the public interest. His argument had appeal, and the deleterious effects of such a law became a theme that would be struck repeatedly by critics of regulation from Adams' day down to our own. The principle involved in the Massachusetts statute, expressed in modern terminology as "fair rate of return on fair value," became the heart of public utility regulation. It formed the focal point of incessant, and ultimately bankrupt, debates in America over stock watering, physical valuation of assets, and utility accounting systems.

In Adams' view, reiterated by countless other critics over the next century, a profit ceiling must reduce innovation and business growth for any company kept under such a rule. For railroads, the ceiling therefore would injure the public interest at just the point where a more flexible profit allowance would better serve it. Adams' argument implicitly identified the public interest with the maximization of railroad traffic. Because of the industry's huge economies of scale, maximization of traffic would minimize rates. The more work a railroad did—the more persons and freight it carried—the cheaper its unit costs, and so the cheaper the prices it could offer to the public. Because of the industry's critical role in the economy, maximization of traffic would promote general economic growth as no other single policy could.

What, then, was wrong with the 10 percent profit limitation? Adams answered this question by arguing that, if a corporation earns a 10 percent rate of return on its capital by doing a certain amount of work, then it has no incentive to do more than this certain amount, or to do even that same work with greater efficiency. Yet a community might well need the railroad to do a great deal more, and then a profit ceiling can only be counterproductive. "The chief tendency of a clause limiting profits," Adams observed, "would therefore seem to be, in many cases, and more especially in those on which the essential growth of the community depends, to bring into direct antagonism the interests of community and corporation,—to put a period to the instinct of growth of the latter."[26]

As if this passive drag on growth were not bad enough, the profit-ceiling rule worked active mischief as well. For if a corporation were prevented from earning a *rate* of return beyond 10 percent of its capital, then it could increase the dollar *amount* of its profits only by increasing its total capital. If the railroad had to be stuck with a fixed rate, then perhaps it could augment the rate *base*. If it did so by building additional tracks and other physical facilities, so much the better. But a far more tempting method lay at hand: the company could simply print more and more shares of stock—that is, increase its capital, but only on paper. This, of course, was "stock watering," and Adams denounced the practice at great length.

He traced the origins of both profit ceilings and stock watering to a well-known British law of 1844. That statute, a landmark in railroad history, had been the brainchild of William E. Gladstone, who at the time of the law's passage served as president of the Board of Trade. "This particular feature of an otherwise well-considered act,"wrote Adams of the 10 percent profit limitation, "led to results in no way anticipated." It contributed to the British railroad mania of 1845 and, even worse, it introduced stock watering into the practice of finance.[27] What had happened in England turned out to be only a mild foretaste of what lay in store across the Atlantic: "In America only is the process found in its highest stage of development. Here it may be studied as an art now in its mature perfection." Almost everything that occurred in the railroad world, Adams noted, led toward additional stock watering. Prosperous companies printed up new securities because they could afford gifts to their shareholders. Poor companies, on the other hand, issued new stock because they could not afford to pay dividends on existing shares. Some railroads took to the printing presses because they enjoyed monopoly positions, others because they felt the hot breath of competitors. New stock rolled off the presses because existing securities understated a railroad's actual value or because so many shares already existed that more made no difference. In these circumstances, the whole notion of a percentage limitation on rate of return had become nonsense.[28]

To their credit, Massachusetts lawmakers had caught on to the stock-watering game. In 1867, two of the state's major railroads merged and came out with substantially higher capitalization than together they had taken in. The legislature quickly responded. Unfortunately, however, it chose as the instrument for disciplining the offending companies the old standby of enforced market competition. Legislators simply encouraged the construction of new railroads to compete with existing ones. In Adams' view—an economist's view—such a policy made no sense. In words foreshadowing Theodore Roosevelt's presidential campaign of 1912, Adams complained in 1869 that the lawmakers "saw only that a monopoly existed; they failed wholly to realize that it was far easier and far cheaper to regulate than to destroy it." To this basic argument, he added a well-calculated appeal to regional pride and self-interest by pointing out that, in contrast to Boston, other cities had profited by wise inaction with respect to competition. Philadelphia and Baltimore, the promoters of the Pennsylvania and Baltimore and Ohio railroad systems, had understood the principle of natural monopoly in railroads and accordingly had built single, integrated systems stretching from the Atlantic Ocean into the Middle West. Boston, meanwhile, foolishly put its faith in forced competition. Adams sketched out the results:

The lack of an intelligent system and an ill-considered faith in manufactured competition have saddled the trade of the East [New England] with a wholly unnecessary debt, which it cannot shake off, larger than the entire sum expended in the construction and equipment of any one of those thoroughly developed trunk lines . . . Under the system of competition, four roads, with all their costly machinery and corps of officials, must be sustained by Boston, while one each satisfied Baltimore and Philadelphia.[29]

From this example of legislative error, Adams moved to his corrective prescription: the creation of a state railroad commission composed of industry specialists. The legislative branch could not do the job of intelligent regulation. "Knowledge cannot possibly creep into the legislature, because no one remains in the legislature long enough to learn." In order to close the gap between public and private interests, analytical expertise must somehow be made a permanent part of the government. Luckily, the proper institutional innovation lay at hand. "Commissions—advisory bureaus—might scientifically study and disclose to an astonished community the shallows, the eddies, and the currents of business; the why and the wherefore of the shoaling of channels; the remedies no less than the causes of obstructions." Here Adams clearly enunciated the theory of what later came to be called the "sunshine commission," a commission that would shed the cleansing light of disclosure on the hitherto secret affairs of business corporations. But he went well beyond that idea. His argument embraced the entire subject of expertise in a modernizing world, as he took note of the proliferation of specialists throughout government departments in western countries. Reflecting on this new approach to the making of public policy in Europe and America, Adams envisioned

the germs of a new system, springing out of a great necessity—a new phase of representative government. Work hitherto badly done, spasmodically done, superficially done, ignorantly done, and too often corruptly done by temporary and irresponsible legislative committees, is in future to be reduced to order and science by the labors of permanent bureaus, and placed by them before legislatures for intelligent action. The movement springs up everywhere; it is confined to no one country and no one body; it arises from the manifest impossibility of temporary [legislative] committees performing the duties imposed upon them, and from the honest desire of legislatures to be enlightened, and not mystified.[30]

Charles Francis Adams had defined his vocation. Now it remained for him to persuade Massachusetts that it needed a railroad commission as much as he needed a commissionership.

A Classic of Muckraking

Adams' three-pronged strategy for his career—educating himself about railroads, gaining a reputation for expertise, and finding a public office—led him toward success in the summer of 1869, a little over two years after he had begun his quest. In that most satisfying summer, Adams won a position on the new Massachusetts Board of Railroad Commissioners and published his "Chapter of Erie" in the *North American Review*. This article brought him immediate fame and later a small portion of literary immortality.

"A Chapter of Erie," Adams noted in his diary, represented "the hardest piece of work I ever did." It paid off: his article is a masterpiece. Occupying 77 pages of the magazine, it entertained as well as instructed its readers. Yet it exhibited none of the exhortation and didactic analysis typical of Adams' earlier writings on railroads. The Erie Railroad, the subject of the essay, was a vital transportation link between New York City and the Great Lakes. Despite the obvious importance of his topic, the author did not sermonize. Instead he struck, with fastidious disdain, the pose of uninvolved chronicler, a writer bemused by the profoundly saddening events now unfolding beneath his Olympian vantage point. Down below, the "men of Erie"—Daniel Drew, Jay Gould, Jim Fisk—careened around the stage like overgrown clowns who yet possessed enough financial wizardry to outwit the aged and almost equally unscrupulous Cornelius Vanderbilt. At stake in this play was control of the railroad and immense power over the economy of New York.[31]

In relating one of the tactical retreats of the men of Erie, Adams set down an unforgettable scene for the annals of American finance. One night during their war with Commodore Vanderbilt, as Drew and his party lounged comfortably in their Manhattan offices,

They were speedily roused from their real or affected tranquillity by trustworthy intelligence that processes for contempt were already issued against them, and that their only chance of escape from incarceration lay in precipitate flight. At ten o'clock the astonished police saw a throng of panic-stricken railway directors—looking more like a frightened gang of thieves, disturbed in the division of their plunder, than like the wealthy representatives of a great corporation—rush headlong from the doors of the Erie office, and dash off in the direction of the Jersey ferry. In their hands were packages and files of papers, and their pockets were crammed with assets and securities. One individual bore away with him in a hackney-coach bales containing six millions of dollars in greenbacks.[32]

The moral of the tale rang through clearly. If such chicanery could so easily corrupt the operations of a single well-known corporation, then what horrors must lie in store for the national railway network! Drawing an even larger moral, Adams went on to attribute this scandal to the materialistic spirit of the Gilded Age: "Failure seems to be regarded as the one unpardonable crime, success as the all-redeeming virtue, the acquisition of wealth as the single worthy aim in life."[33] Coming from a man of thirty-four, who had tasted personal success only in the fleeting context of military glory, this statement reflects a poignant self-consciousness. But the comment also came at a triumphant moment: in the same month in which "A Chapter of Erie"appeared, Adams won his commissionership.[34]

The Board and the Commissioner

The Massachusetts Board of Railroad Commissioners was not the first regulatory agency in America or even the first state railroad commission. That distinction, such as it is, belongs to the Rhode Island commission of 1839, a modest agency that encouraged rival corporations to work together on joint schedules and rates. The railroads preferred to make their own arrangements, however, and the Rhode Island tribunal passed quickly out of existence. Similar commissions began to spring up in response to particular issues of the moment: powers of eminent domain (New Hampshire, 1844) and railroad safety (Connecticut, 1853). None of these agencies had much influence on subsequent developments, and it remained for Massachusetts to become the most important regulatory pioneer.[35]

In his own right, Charles Francis Adams did more than anyone else to give the state its commission. He took a strong hand in writing the enabling act, and he lobbied for it energetically in the legislature. Trusting his pen, he also wrote pro-commission editorials for the *Boston Daily Advertiser*. In Massachusetts, similar legislation had already been introduced prior to 1869, often at the behest of the Boston Board of Trade. The board's members had sought to use the commission device as an aid in recouping the commerce lost to ports farther south, especially New York. Now the Board of Trade supported Adams' bill as well. The railroad industry on the whole took a neutral stance. Rail executives saw little need for a commission, but in Massachusetts they did not deploy their powerful resources to prevent its founding, as they did in some other states. The creation of the commission simply did not strike the legislature, the railroads, or the Boston press as an event of the first magnitude.[36]

The event did, of course, so strike Adams, as his diary entries reveal:

January 21, 1869: My life just now is utterly barren & devoid of interest; I am going through one of the eras of waiting.

March 13, 1869: Came in as usual and passed the day at my office where nothing was going on, though I saw that the Railroad Commissioners bill was again before the Committee and wrote up offering to appear for it.

March 19, 1869: Addressed the rail-road Committee at the State House,—had a good audience and was, on the whole, very well satisfied.

June 9, 1869: My R.R. Comr bill has gone through and now to see if I am put on it . . .

June 19, 1869: Did a little wire pulling in the Commissioner business,— this by the way is a better office than I thought and I fear my chance is poor.

June 20, 1869: I feel quite nervous at times about this commissioner-ship,—it is such a chance if I could only make it.

June 28, 1869: Judge Bigelow [an old family friend] came in and told me that my nomination had gone in,—I was pleased—a two year chase had brought my game down.[37]

Adams actively pursued the commission post by asking influential friends to intercede on his behalf. For one, his old law mentor Francis E. Parker wrote the governor a particularly candid letter:

[Colonel Adams] has industry, and is absolutely honest, he proposes to make what is called "rail-roading" his business for life. In addition to this, he is a man of general intelligence, and has a good style in writing on business matters. He is, also, a good age—thirty-four. Knowing him, as I do, very well, I will say that, if I were Governor, I should not appoint *three* commissioners like Col. Adams. But if there are two such of sound practical judgment, and acquaintance with the subject, on the commission, I think they would find Col. Adams of great use, and that he would make a good third.[38]

The statute that Adams drafted for Massachusetts resembled regulatory legislation passed elsewhere, not only during Adams' own period but over the next hundred years as well. Right up to the 1970s, when lawmakers began to write extremely detailed environmental legislation, most regulatory laws were brief in length and general in tone. They delegated broad powers to ill-defined agencies designed to deal with specialized industrial problems. Content varied according to the industry concerned, but particular lines of policy and procedure were left to the commissions to decide. So was the crucial question of defining the "public interest." In most laws, a striking definitional uncertainty persisted throughout the text, despite the frequent occurrence of "public interest," "public good," and similar phrases.

The Massachusetts legislation of 1869 was inordinately short (only a few paragraphs), even for a regulatory statute. It outlined decidedly limited powers. It focused not on the agency's authority to issue orders but on the investigatory function, mandating the "sunshine" approach to regulation. Its strongest language required that corporations release information to the commissioners, "at all times, on demand." The commissioners themselves could have no conflict of interest, would serve overlapping terms of three years each, and would receive annual salaries of $4,000. This sum was unusually large; no other existing state commission paid its members nearly so much, and the governor of Massachusetts earned only $5,000 annually. Although the commissioners earned high salaries, however, they had no staff to command. The law authorized only a lone clerk, whose $2,000 pay, like that of the commissioners, derived from assessments on the state's railroads. In substance, the act went no further than these bare-boned details of organization.[39]

This left a host of important questions unanswered. What, for example, should the commission do in the event that the railroads simply ignored the new statute, as they had ignored previous laws? The new tribunal had no direct enforcement powers. The act failed even to specify any procedural machinery for the holding of hearings. In short, the commission seemed a pathetically weak institution to set against the railroad juggernaut that Adams had so vividly described earlier. Certainly, whether drafted carefully or haphazardly (and Adams' recollections varied on this point), the act of 1869 left a great deal to the discretion of the new board.[40]

Even so, in retrospect one can see an essential consistency among Adams' ideas, the spirit of the statute, and the behavior of the commission during its first decade of operation. The act laid heavy emphasis on information, publicity, and written reports. It seemed to call for enlightenment as the essential prelude to action. The very tentativeness of the statute implied an appreciation of the complexity of the tasks that lay before any tribunal concerned with railroads. More than a specifically charted course, the act represented the legislature's formal declaration that the time had come for an intelligent, continuous surveillance of railroads in the public interest. (The phrase "the public good" appears in the text.) As Adams wrote a few years later, using a metaphor that caught the spirit of both the law and the board's sunshine approach to administration: "The board of commissioners was set up as a sort of lens by means of which the otherwise scattered rays of public opinion could be concentrated to a focus and brought to bear upon a given point." Yet, except for its authority to require information from the railroad corporations, the agency had no coercive power. As Adams put it in the ten-year retrospective he wrote in 1879: "The Commissioners have no power except to recommend and report. Their only appeal is to publicity. The Board is at once prosecuting officer, judge, and jury, but with no sheriff to enforce its process." Of course this was just what Adams wanted. And his strategy stands out as one of the most ingenious and calculated self-denials in the entire history of regulation.[41]

Rather than a replacement of the existing regulatory apparatus—the legislative committees, the charters and statutes, the annual reports and returns of the railroads—the commission was a new addition to these older devices. The agency began life as an institutional adaptation called into being because, after a generation of uninterrupted growth, the railroad system had become too much for the old legal machinery to handle. The new controlling principles were the unprecedented scale of operations the railroads represented, their financial and technological complexity, and the increasingly important role of transportation in the Massachusetts economy. But the old regulatory machinery remained. Adams' diary makes that clear, with its frequent references to his conferences with the governor, attorney general, and legislative committees. The new commission only undertook to supplement these powerful political agents. Adams knew that regulation, with or without a commission, would always be an inescapably *political* activity. At his direction, the Board of Railroad Commissioners quietly merged itself with these other parts of the state government. Instead of trying to supplant them, the board endeavored to enlighten, assist, and prod. Thus it sought to bend state railroad policy closer toward rationality—or at least toward Adams' particular version of what made sense.[42]

The same evolutionary process recurred again and again in other states, and ultimately in the federal government. Regulation appeared in almost every industry whose characteristics resembled those of the nineteenth-century railroads: technological and financial complexity, vulnerability to exploitation by unscrupulous promoters, a tendency toward monopoly and a relative unresponsiveness to competitive market forces, and vital importance to the economic health of the community. The Massachusetts board became the model for scores of similar agencies, the Massachusetts Bay Colony of regulation. And even at an early date it exhibited certain characteristics that would become common to regulatory agencies in general.

The first of these traits was its small size. The commission supposedly consisted of three members, but in fact all three did not work full time throughout the year. In addition, the commission's initial staff consisted of a single clerk. The agency's budget, practically all of which went for salaries, amounted to a mere $162,000 for the first ten years of operation. Adams ruefully compared this figure with the gross receipts of Massachusetts railroads during the same period, which totaled $322 million. Putting it more vividly, he noted that *"the entire expense of this Board since its organization if charged to the Boston and Albany Road alone, would not have reduced the amount of a single one of its regular semi-annual dividends by one per cent."* The first modern regulatory agency, therefore, could hardly be called a bureaucracy.[43]

Nor did the Massachusetts board function as a collegial body of three equal members. Adams dominated the agency throughout his decade of service; and atypically for regulatory commissions in the future, the personnel of the Massachusetts board held remarkably stable, at least after the quick departure of Adams' first two colleagues. These were James Converse, the first chairman, whose candidacy had been supported by the Boston Board of Trade (Adams regarded him as "the damnedest fool I have met lately—such an ignorant bag of wind!"); and Edward Appleton, a merchant who became involved in a conflict of interest and was not reappointed for a second term. After Adams became chairman in

1872 and began to participate in the appointment process himself, his colleagues became a more capable, solid lot: intelligent enough not to fetter their young chairman's substantial energies, passive enough to give him full responsibility for the *Annual Report* and other written products of the board. But the agency itself remained a one-man show.[44]

Adams' scrupulous attention to his diary—small, leather-bound volumes with tiny blanks for each day but with those blanks always filled—provides a rare source for reconstructing the everyday routine of the commission. The most conspicuous aspect of the agency's schedule was a highly variable workload. Activities ebbed to nothing in the summer months, then became unbearably heavy during the winter. Throughout the 1870s, Adams' diary entries emphasize "my winter work." This disproportion derived not from anyone's personal preference but from the schedule of the Massachusetts General Court. Like most state legislatures, it met only during the winter months. The commission worked closely with the railroad committees of both houses and habitually marched to the beat of the legislature's drum. Often Adams and his colleagues performed for the General Court the kinds of service functions that in the twentieth century would be done by expert staffs of subcommittees. The Massachusetts commission did not surrender its role of independent study and investigation—the agency never became a mere handmaiden to the legislature—but neither did it exactly fit the modern notion of an "independent regulatory commission."[45]

Nobody except the clerk spent a full workday at the commission's State House offices or, later, at its larger accommodations in a Boston office building. Adams and his colleagues stayed out of the office, even out of the city, much of the time. They went on frequent inspection trips. They held hearings on an endless variety of problems, ranging from labor disputes to the siting of new railroad stations and grade crossings. But the most striking point to emerge from Adams' diary is the overwhelming amount of time he devoted to writing, and in particular to drafting and revising official commission documents. Writing must have consumed at least one half of his total working time. "Busy in my usual way," reads one diary entry, "that is with my pen." Adams wrote reports on hearings, veto messages for the governor, bills for the legislature, letters of exhortation to railroad executives, special reports on controversial events such as accidents and strikes, and, most important of all, the board's *Annual Report*.[46]

The *Annual Report* usually ran to about one hundred printed pages of commentary on the course of railroad finance, management, and reform. It gave special emphasis to Massachusetts, of course, but much of the analysis—particularly what Adams liked to call the "philosophical part"—applied to railroading in general. These sophisticated general commentaries by Adams included some of the best writing on industrialization produced in nineteenth-century America. The reports attained such high quality that the commission received requests for copies from all over the United States. Occasionally the document ran into additional printings. Newspapers republished summaries, and once the Chicago *Tribune* not only carried the entire report as an item of general interest but also reprinted and distributed 10,000 copies on its own initiative. Thus, a literary form which in most states and most later periods became the driest of formal bureaucratic documents, Adams made the focus of his "winter work" and a notable annual event in railroad circles. He also drew freely on these documents in the two books and numerous articles published under his own name during his commission tenure. Many passages reappear verbatim in two or three places, reflecting the single-mindedness of Adams' public and private concerns, his willingness to mix the two, and his determination to multiply the size of his audience. His intent was clear. "I wish to shape a national policy," he wrote Secretary of the Interior Carl Schurz, enclosing a copy of his new book *Railroads: Their Origin and Problems*. The book represented, Adams accurately noted, "the only thing of the kind there is."[47]

Adams was deliberately using the power of his pen to set a high standard of regulatory practice. His pointed emphasis on what might be called regulation by publication accorded perfectly with his own distinctive talent. But it also reflected the state's policy concerning the proper function of a railroad commission. Above all, the Massachusetts agency must shun coercion. Legal process could not be employed merely as a matter of course. Accordingly, the board almost never instituted lawsuits on its own motion. It issued no orders that the corporations were legally bound to obey, except for orders to produce information. Sometimes the commission also specified the form such information must take. For example, the agency often required railroads to submit data in standard accounting forms that would facilitate a comparative statistical analysis of different companies. Adams thought it important to make such comparisons as a basis for policy judgments by both the commission and the legislature. So he was always willing to get tough with any railroad that resisted the frank disclosure of information. In general, though, he and his colleagues exhibited a thoroughgoing and persistent aversion to the use of force, a determination to avoid tests of strength. The board might win such showdowns in its role as the public's champion. But Adams sensed that victories of this sort would be pyrrhic. They would so poison the atmosphere that further influence, beyond the narrow boundaries of the commission's legal authority, might be forever compromised.[48]

In its choice of role as a sunshine commission, therefore, the board successfully avoided confrontation. By so doing, the agency discouraged the accumulation of a body of case law that might have made for greater clarity of policy, but also would have restricted the commission's freedom to maneuver. For Adams, clarity of policy was never at issue anyway. His lengthy elaborations in the *Annual Reports* effectively shut off complaints about fuzzy standards—the target of opportunity for so many future critics of regulation. Far more than most regulatory commissions in American history, the Massachusetts board took pains to make its policies and standards unmistakably clear.

Every regulatory agency, in one way or other, has always had to resolve tradeoffs between making broad policy and following legal due process. Of the two, the Massachusetts board chose policy hands down. Adams and his colleagues were preoccupied much more with framing strategies to serve economic efficiency than with insisting on the observance of legal process. The agency, through its informal approach to regulation, maintained a stable truce with railroads, based on indeterminacy, ambivalence, and cooperation. In one sense Adams' strategy amounted to a precise reversal of the state's traditional railroad policy, which had placed on the books a number of stringent laws that everyone then ignored. The commission, by forgoing the role of adversary, avoided the embarrassing impotence of the early railroad statutes.

It also avoided the troublesome question of constitutionality in the delegation of legislative power to agency discretion. More than any other single problem, this question would trouble future commissions, as they battled repeatedly against restrictive judicial review. Ultimately the problem of constitutionality contributed to those endless delays that came to characterize the regulatory process in the twentieth century. Agency after agency, preoccupied with the requirements of procedural due process, frittered away its energies on trivia, thereby minimizing its role in the formation of substantive economic policy. Adams and his colleagues, however, deliberately chose the opposite course, acting even more wisely than they themselves realized.[49]

Their theme, in a word, was *voluntarism*, promoted by publicity and disclosure, disciplined by the unwavering support of the state legislature. When the question at hand involved general policy, the commission initiated. When the issue had to do with some particular controversy, the commission reacted. In all cases, the agency advised rather than coerced. It served now as broker, now mediator, now ombudsman. This voluntaristic approach benefited from the centrality of the railroad industry to the people of the state, most of whom encountered railroads in their daily lives. It also benefited from the divergence of perspectives among passengers, merchants, manufacturers, farmers, and the railroads, a variety that discouraged any definition of the railroad question as simply a war between carriers and shippers.

Perhaps the best means of illustrating the approach taken by Adams and his colleagues, and of accounting for their success, is to examine the board's behavior in different regulatory situations: first, in a railroad accident; second, in the issue of rates and fares; finally, in New England's only serious railroad strike of the nineteenth century.

Safety Regulation

Railroads brought with them some of the most dangerous conditions that mankind had yet created, outside war. The loading of numerous passengers aboard wood and metal cars weighing hundreds of tons, the movement of those cars at great speed, propelled by huge portable furnaces generating high-pressure steam, and the swift passage of the whole train along unfenced tracks that crossed numerous horse and pedestrian rights of way—all this added up to a spectacular range of hazards. From the very beginning, grisly accidents were the apparently inevitable price of railroad development. With the official opening of the world's first commercial railroad—the Liverpool and Manchester, in 1830—came tragedy. A prominent member of Parliament found himself entangled in the train; and before a stunned crowd in attendance at the celebration, he was dragged to his death. The fate of this man was largely his own "fault," and that type of negligence by victims would prove typical of railroad experience. The occasion of human error seemed to multiply wildly in the presence of trains. In consequence, whatever else state governments might decide to do by way of regulating this new industry, they obviously had to do something about safety.[50]

Massachusetts railroads proved comparatively less hazardous than those outside New England, but they still exacted a heavy toll. Reported deaths averaged 87 per year during the 1860s, 143 in the 1870s, and 209 in the 1880s, even though the rate of fatalities per train mile declined steadily. Most injuries and deaths occurred outside the passenger cars, as pedestrians, tramps, horsemen, suicides, and railroad employees were caught between wheel and track.[51]

As has so often been the case elsewhere for other kinds of regulatory initiatives, the role of the Massachusetts commission in promoting safety derived from one particular crisis: the "Revere disaster" of 1871. Revere, just north of Boston on the shores of Massachusetts Bay, was a popular beach resort. Railroad lines connecting it with the metropolis were heavily traveled. In the summer of 1871, average passenger traffic reached 110,000 per week, and for the week of special events ending the month of August, the total swelled to 142,000. The Eastern Railroad, the corporation that operated along the route, ran 191 trains during that week, all of them on the single track that stretched from Boston through Revere and on up to terminals in Maine.[52]

Operating this system without the benefit of a well-developed telegraph network, the Eastern management decided to rely for safety on a careful spacing of train departures. This decision, along with the very heavy traffic on the day in question, was the first condition underlying the disaster. (The decision also aptly illustrated Adams' point about the institutional lag between corporations' interests and the public interest in the early stages of modern mass society.) A second condition was the absence of a rail siding at an important junction, compounded by the illness of the man usually on duty there. This experienced employee had worked out a way of juggling the traffic, using either the main or branch line as a siding, so that one train would wait while the other passed through the junction. His substitute, however, following the letter of the rules, simply held up train after train for a few minutes each, as the inevitable traffic jams worked themselves out. This procedure eventually caused a chaotic running schedule: special resort trains overlapped into the schedules of regular runs, thereby confusing railroad employees down the line as to which train was which. And, if these mixups were not bad enough in themselves, fog now rolled in from the bay.[53]

The result of all this was a violent rear-end collision at the Revere station, where an onrushing locomotive plowed into a stationary passenger train. As Adams described the scene:

The car was crowded to its full capacity, and the colliding locomotive struck it with such force as to bury itself two-thirds of its length in it. At the instant of the crash a panic had seized upon the passengers, and a sort of rush had taken place to the forward end of the car, into which furniture, fixtures and human beings were crushed in a shapeless, indistinguishable mass . . . The [boiler] valves had been so broken as to admit of the free escape of the scalding steam, while the coals from the fire-box were scattered among the *debris,* and coming in contact with fluid from the broken car lamps kindled the whole into a rapid blaze . . . For the severity of injuries and for the protractedness of agony involved in it, this accident has rarely, if ever, been exceeded. Crushing, scalding and burning did their work together.[54]

Twenty-nine persons died; fifty-seven others were injured. The coroner's inquest dragged on for nearly two weeks, amid swelling popular outcry. "Give us less show and more safety," declared former General Benjamin F. Butler, now a gubernatorial candidate; the erstwhile abolitionist Wendell Phillips, now a freelance reformer, pronounced the Eastern Railroad guilty of "deliberate murder." The Eastern had indeed been guilty of negligence, and it ended up paying out over half a million dollars in claims. For Phillips, however, the issue went deeper than damage claims. "I think," he said, in language foreshadowing Edward A. Ross's book of 1907, *Sin and Society,* "we should try to get rid in the public mind of any real distinction between the individual who, in a moment of passion or in a moment of heedlessness, takes the life of one fellow-man, and the corporation that in a moment of greed, of little trouble, of little expense, of little care, of little diligence, takes lives by wholesale." Helped along by such statements, popular outrage at the Eastern railroad continued to rise.[55]

Into this explosive situation stepped the youthful Massachusetts Board of Railroad Commissioners. For ten consecutive working days following the accident, Adams and his colleagues went out to Revere to survey the wreckage, attend the inquest, and question witnesses and railroad officials. Step by step, Adams pieced together the complex mixture of circumstances that had brought on the tragedy. In the official report, he found the Eastern Railroad guilty of lax discipline and negligent management of its traffic. Yet he also noted that the corporation had broken no existing law. Furthermore, he insisted that the apportionment of personal blame must be done not by the commissioners but by "other public officials." Deliberately avoiding any involvement in lawsuits or other legal processes, Adams instead tried to turn the disaster into a cause for education and reform.[56]

His success in doing so provided one small but impressive example of the crisis-response tactics that would become typical of creative regulation. Rather than simply denouncing wrongdoers, the commission pushed forward a strong program for voluntary reform. Adams sent a long circular letter to all railroads in the state, setting forth the causes of the Revere accident and inviting officers of the roads to a conference on safety. The board saw to it that this meeting took place soon after the accident, while public opinion was still seething. Adams suggested that the railroad representatives elect from their numbers a committee of five, to work with the commissioners in making a careful study of railroad safety in the United States and abroad and in proposing new rules for adoption by the corporations. This "long and difficult" joint effort included several trips outside the state to inspect new safety technologies developed by George Westinghouse and other inventors. It involved numerous conferences, with much give and take between railroad executives and commissioners. The whole affair exemplified the fundamental truth that the heart of successful regulation lay in tough-minded, intelligent negotiation between business and government.[57]

At length, the negotiations yielded two products. One was aimed at public opinion, the other at railroad managers. For the public, Adams wrote a detailed and careful report on the accident.

He provided reassurance that things were no worse in Massachusetts than elsewhere. He showed with comparative statistics that in most categories of safety, Massachusetts excelled. For the railroad managers, Adams' committee of executives and commissioners propounded a list of nine major recommendations for the improvement of overall safety. Many of these suggestions pertained to specific steps to be taken, based either on new technology ("the general use of the telegraph in aid of the present time-table system"), common sense ("the adoption of a uniform dress or cap" so that passengers could recognize railroad employees), or procedure ("a revision of the rules under which the several roads are operated"). This last recommendation led to a jointly prepared codification and standardization of operating procedures for all the state's railroads. The new "Rules and Regulations for Operating Railroads" ran to 105 articles, organized under the general categories of Signals, Telegraph, Train Service, and Employes [sic].[58]

All major roads of the state, and several outside Massachusetts, immediately adopted the new rules, either verbatim or only slightly modified and elaborated. The Eastern Railroad, tacitly admitting its responsibility, not only embraced the new rules, but spent a large amount of money on innovative safety devices such as the Westinghouse brake, the Miller platform, and a system of automatic electric signals. All these actions by the Eastern and other railroads constituted a safety revolution in Massachusetts.[59]

In addition to producing this felicitous outcome, the commission's strategy had a second, procedural significance. This was to set an early precedent of voluntary, cooperative, state-sponsored negotiation. Such a design for business-government relations was particularly compelling in the early decades of industrialization, when no powerful public bureaucracies yet existed to help manage the economy and offset the political strength of corporations. In the federal government, similar patterns of business-government negotiation reappeared in such episodes as President Grover Cleveland's reliance on investment bankers to help him stem the financial crisis of the early 1890s, President Theodore Roosevelt's intervention in the anthracite coal strike of 1902, the mobilization planning by government officials and businessmen during World War I, the trade conferences promoted by Secretary of Commerce Herbert Hoover in the 1920s, and the writing of codes of fair competition under the New Deal's National Recovery Administration in the 1930s.

In the case of Adams and the Revere accident, as in these later federal examples, the road taken by public representatives wound through a tricky obstacle course of suggestion, encouragement, and mutual exploitation. In the nature of such negotiations, it was never precisely clear who was using whom; or who, in the end, had won. But a slight edge by one side or the other in this or that detail mattered far less than the steady movement toward a common goal. And for the railroad managers no less than the public representatives, negotiating in this kind of setting was like picking one's way through a minefield. Always in the background, as the companies well knew, lay the threat of direct interventon by the state.

In the Revere episode, for example, Adams easily could have directed the course of popular anger toward retribution rather than reform. He might have called for swift, harsh punishment of the Eastern Railroad. This might have been followed, in turn, by severe new safety standards enforced by a new corps of state inspectors. Such recommendations would have discharged the duties of the commisson, and at low risk to Adams and his colleagues. Instead, Adams used the incident to work out an administrative solution that in his judgment stood a far better chance of actually improving railroad safety. In effect, he manipulated public outrage to serve the ends of the commission, the railroads, and the public, which he perceived as identical. His approach looked more to the future than the past, typifying his personal preference for policymaking over legal process.[60]

As Adams himself argued in the *Annual Report*, if the commission had recommended direct legislation, the effect would have been to impose criminal and civil liabilities for the violaton of a code jointly written by the commission and the railroad managers. Such liability already existed. "The corporations," he wrote, "can disregard the recommendations . . . only at their own risk, and the occurrence of any accident clearly attributable to a disregard of those recommendations would, in presence of a jury, affect the interests of those involved in a way not to be mistaken." The commission and the legislature, in short, must not go too far. "The extreme injustice of the government assuming practical management, as regards essential details, and yet leaving the whole liabil-

ity for disaster on the private corporations, was pointedly stated."
With this insight, Adams identified what would become a central
problem of regulation in the twentieth century, for both economic
and environmental issues. This was the perplexing question of how
government could shape business policy without stifling private
entrepreneurship and innovation.[61]

Finally, the Revere episode exemplified the tendency of regulation to standardize procedures and practices. The establishment of
across-the-board safety rules provided one standard, the use of
comparative statistics another. And the requirement that all railroad employees wear uniforms epitomized the standardizing
thrust of most regulation.

Rate Regulation

Railway rates and fares were the most confusing of all questions
associated with the "railroad problem." In the long run, they also
became the most important issues at stake in regulation. This held
true not only for railroads but for other industries as well: gas and
electric utilities, trucks and airlines, taxis and telephones. The approach of the Massachusetts commission to the question of rates
therefore represents a benchmark of the early attitudes of responsible regulators toward this controversial issue.

The Massachusetts approach rested on three premises, each of
which could as well apply to twentieth-century utilities as to nineteenth-century railroads. First, any determination of the "reasonableness" or "fairness" of rates must inescapably remain a
subjective undertaking. Scientific precision in rate setting is therefore a practical impossibility. Second, the pricing function is part
of corporate management, a function jealously guarded by all business executives, and with good reason. Third, the rate question
directly reflects the debate over competition versus monopoly. In
the case of nineteenth-century railroads, rates were the means
through which an impersonal market signaled its ability or inability to cope with two conflicting forces: with the economic requirements of railroading in particular and "natural monopoly" in
general; and with the noneconomic requirements imposed by society.

Since the rate issue remains unsettled in our own day, we should
not expect to discover that Adams and his fellow commissioners

resolved it over a century ago. They did, however, use their voluntaristic approach, along with publicity and disclosure, to work out a harmonious compromise between traditional American values and the imperatives of railroad economics. To put it as Adams was fond of doing, they tried to bring the interests of the public and those of the corporations into identity. Through a careful educational process, they sought to clarify for both the corporations and the public the basic principles of railroading's odd economics. For railroad managers, Adams recommended specific rate and fare adjustments designed to promote the simultaneous growth of the companies' business and the state's economy. Most of these recommendations to the companies, and practically all of the discussions addressed to the reading public, derived from the same principles Adams had elucidated during his prior journalistic campaign on behalf of the commission's creation: enforced competition conflicted with the public interest; consolidation was a "law" of the industry's economics, which could be made to serve society; and the particular contours of the Massachusetts economy should in turn shape the rate policies of the state's railroads.

Occasionally in the history of regulation, a commission has been set up early enough to affect an industry's structure in its formative stages. This happened, for example, with the Federal Radio Commission of 1927 and the Civil Aeronautics Authority of 1938. It did not happen, though, with the Massachusetts Board of Railroad Commissioners. Adams and his colleagues had to struggle with a maturing but unsystematic structure that was undergoing gradual consolidation. In 1875, some 62 railroad corporations operated in the state. Most of the track mileage belonged to only eight lines, each of them much larger than any of the remaining 54. By the turn of the century, as a result of mergers, the 1875 total of 62 had shrunk to 11, and the eight giants had become four. The commission did little during this period to discourage consolidation; in fact, several of the agency's policies tended to accelerate it, on the grounds of increased efficiency.[62]

Throughout the period of consolidation, railroading remained the biggest business in Massachusetts. The opulent stations of the Boston & Albany, Boston & Maine, Boston & Providence, and other railroads dominated the capital city's skyline as the spires of cathedrals had dominated the urban landscapes of medieval Europe. During the decade of Adams' tenure, Massachusetts rail roads as a group claimed the following annual averages: employment of 20,000 persons, transportation of 40 million passengers and 12 million tons of freight, gross incomes of $30 million, and payouts in dividends of between $5 million and $7 million. A wide variety of corporations performed different types of services. The trunkline Boston & Albany transported a large volume of freight between the state's major port and the Erie Canal's eastern terminus. Shortlines such as the Old Colony carried in and out of Boston numerous passengers who were pioneering commuters. (One such commuter on the Old Colony was Charles Francis Adams himself; he lived in Quincy but worked in Boston, eight miles to the north.[63])

The commissioners, aware of both the vital role of railroads and the complex circumstances, chose their points of intervention carefully. They customarily acted in two types of situations: the very particular, which might excite a specific complaint or petition; and the very general, involving broad economic issues such as the interindustry effect of rate adjustments. Between these two types of situations lay an important range of middle-management decisions that the board almost never addressed. It deliberately left such issues to the business judgment of the corporations.

Over the last century, most critics of the regulatory process have scolded commissions for concerning themselves with trivia. Such criticism obviously has merit in those cases where an agency, in focusing on particularities, forecloses a policy role for itself. But too often this argument obscures the inescapability of trivia in regulatory routine and also ignores some of the reasons behind the creation of the agencies. As viewed by legislatures, one of the principal functions of commission regulation was to settle assorted disputes trivial to society but important to individuals. The new boards were meant to provide legitimate and continuously available arenas for the resolution of such conflicts. For the early railroad commissions, these disputes swirled around such issues as the location of a new depot, the placement of a grade crossing, the extension of a spur line, or the reasonableness of a rate.

The policy of the Massachusetts board in such matters promoted voluntary adjustment. The commission willingly intervened as mediator, but more readily when the issue had to do with service than when it concerned rates. Surviving records of the agency's activities show that it conducted numerous hearings on disputes over new stations and intersections, in cities and towns across Massachusetts. But the record is bereft of the long-winded "rate cases" that dominate the written reports of twentieth-century utility commissions. In only a few instances during Adams' decade of service did the Massachusetts board allow itself to become enmeshed in controversies over specific rates. And in almost no case did it intervene strongly against excessive freight rates or passenger fares. By avoiding particulars, Adams sought to preserve a more general influence over rate structures. The board emphatically denied any arrogation of ratemaking powers to itself, and it made this point the central tenet of its regulatory ideology.[64]

Adams maintained a keen sensitivity to the importance railroad men attached to rate setting. Time and again he denounced the notion of establishing rates by statute, a practice widespread in nineteenth-century state government. Often railroads paid little attention to such legislation. They did so not to show disrespect for the laws of the state, at least in the first instance, but to follow the economic laws of the market. As Adams argued, a flat, across-the-board statutory rate "ignores certain fundamental principles of railroad economy" because it tends to destroy the connection between price and cost. "Where, for instance, all travel pays at the same rate per mile, all persons do not pay for what they receive,—some paying too much and others too little. Slow and cheap travel is, by a system of averages, made to support rapid and costly travel." As Adams saw it, the infinite variety of terrain, equipment, and cargo with which railroads had to deal imposed an overwhelming obstacle to intelligent ratemaking by the government. And if flat rates based on mileage would not work, then legislatures and commissions would have to concern themselves with thousands of particular situations. Only in this way could they meet the needs of each category of cargo for each route of shipment. Adams recoiled from any such prospect. He accurately sensed that an immense caseload would automatically result. (Such a caseload did indeed materialize in the twentieth century, when the federal Interstate Commerce Commission took on the ratemaking function.)[65] By no means, however, did the Massachusetts commission neglect the rate question. Like the agency's policy toward railway safety, its approach to rates emphasized the future more than the past, preferred the general to the particular, and relied on voluntary compliance. As always, the immediate weapons of battle were publicity and disclosure. Adams used his comparative statistics to enlighten both corporate managers and the public at large, while in the background, as Adams kept hinting, lurked the threat of remedial legislative power. This gun behind the door stood ready as a last resort, but the statutory history of railroading suggested to Adams that the gun was more useful cocked than fired.

The commission tried the cocked-gun approach in a circular letter mailed out to all Massachusetts railroads in 1871. Adams' purpose was to promote rate reductions, by way of both enticement and threat. The letter, carefully worded, ran to several pages. It outlined the reduced costs brought by technological innovation ("The locomotive which formerly cost $30,000 now costs but $12,000"), the unusual opportunity now at hand ("Massachusetts is at this time susceptible of a very great and sudden industrial development"), and the payoff to the railroads themselves ("It is a perfectly well-established fact in railroad economy, that where a community is industrially in an elastic condition . . . a reduction of railroad charges within certain limits does not necessarily involve any loss of net profits"). Then came the threat: if the railroads did not lower their rates voluntarily, the legislature might do it for them. Public knowledge of the roads' diminished costs and increased profits, Adams observed, had "excited a very considerable feeling." He added that the state legislature, in its last session, had nearly passed a ratemaking statute. In case any railroad president had not yet seen the draft bill, Adams attached a copy. He also sent off copies of the bill and his letter to be published in the national railroad press, thereby ensuring that both the board's recommendations and the threat of legislation would reach a wider audience. The *Railroad Gazette* printed the entire letter. The *Gazette* editorialized that Adams' admonitions "may induce the companies to adopt a policy on their own motion to avoid compulsory legislation hereafter, if for no other reason."[66]

The content of the rate recommendations revealed Adams' preoccupation with aggregate economic growth. He emphasized, for example, a form of what economists later called the multiplier effect:

In making any reduction, whether in freight or fares, we would therefore suggest to you [Massachusetts railroad presidents] the propriety of

strongly favoring certain commodities in general use along the line of the
road, and, by so doing, strongly stimulate development, rather than neutralize the whole effect of any concessions you may make by dividing it
among too many objects. Take for instance coal . . . a primary raw material in all manufacturing industry. Cheap coal is cheap power; and cheap
power is cheap manufacturing. A reduction of five per cent. throughout
the charges of tariff would scarcely produce an appreciable effect on the
consumption of anything; a tariff, unchanged in numerous other respects,
which gave a reduction of fifty per cent. on the cost of carrying coal,
would at once communicate an impetus to every branch of industry dependent on power.[67]

Six weeks after this letter went out, Adams followed it with a detailed questionnaire that asked what changes had been made so
far. Most replies were conciliatory. A few sounded resentful notes.
One manager in particular grumbled that the commission's statements, "gone broadcast into the public prints," were for his road
"seriously erroneous." Adams complained in his diary about this
"pettish reply" and wondered how he might frame a temperate
answer.[68]

The most important result of the campaign, however, was that
the railroads operating about half the state's mileage did make selective rate reductions. "It is impossible," the commissioners
wrote, "to ascertain exactly the money value of these reductions,
or the amount of relief which they afford to the community. As
nearly as the commissioners can estimate, they represent between
$400,000 and $500,000 per annum."[69] In addition to these immediate results, the circulars forced the companies into a searching
examination of their own rate structures. The questionnaires compelled rail executives to think carefully about the economic implications of ratemaking and to articulate their companies' policies
in writing. As a by-product, the program yielded a thorough docu-
mentary record from a variety of perspectives, most of which the
board published in its *Annual Report*. The whole process exemplified Adams' strategy of using publicity and disclosure as motiva-
tional tools for progressive business management.

The board also showed a willingness to turn any event to advantage in pushing forward its rate policies. One good opportunity came in 1873, in the form of a state-financed tunnel through
Hoosac Mountain, in western Massachusetts. This large-scale construction project, initiated long before the creation of the commis-

sion, had been portrayed by its promoters as the key to an improved rail link with the West and a means of recapturing commercial traffic for the port of Boston. Other observers regarded such a result from the Hoosac Tunnel as a hopeless dream. Construction costs far outran original estimates. (After years of controversy, wits had started referring to the tunnel as "The Great Bore.") At long last, however, the project was completed and the tunnel ready for operation. Adams now proposed that the state itself operate not only the tunnel but also a publicly owned railroad, passing through the tunnel and stretching out for miles on either side. He wanted to turn the project into what he called, in a pamphlet, "The Regulation of All Railroads Through the State-Ownership of One." His idea was to use the new line as a laboratory, trying out novel rate structures, managerial innovations, and safety devices, all under the supervision of the state, which would assume the financial risks of the experiments. This proposal intrigued the legislature: "To-day I wholly surpassed my own expectation," Adams wrote in his diary. "I was in key all through and got hold of my audience,—the strong wine of success filled my brain till I went to bed." But despite his eloquence, the lawmakers turned the plan down. In its place they adopted a system of tolls, opening the tunnel for use by all private railroads.[70]

Even so, Adams' proposal suggested the lengths to which he and his colleagues were willing to go to achieve low freight rates and other regulatory objectives. The Hoosac public ownership idea foreshadowed proposals made later, in the twentieth century, in such forms as the "yardstick" experiments of the federally owned Tennessee Valley Authority. The TVA's intensely controversial history during the 1930s provided the litmus test for American skepticism toward public ownership, even during a severe economic depression.[71] And whatever the period or century, New England always took a more hostile stance toward public ownership than did other regions of the country. Adams' plan for the Hoosac Tunnel, therefore, represented an even bolder suggestion than he himself realized; in retrospect, it speaks volumes about the ideological flexibility of the Massachusetts commission. In proposing public ownership, the agency demonstrated the same kind of entrepreneurship and opportunism that American corporations themselves so often exhibited. (Over the next century, corporations would take much the same position toward regulation that the Massachusetts board took toward public ownership: opposition to the principle but opportunistic support when the mechanism could be made to serve particular goals.) While Adams himself rejected public ownership in the abstract, as impractical and alien to American culture, he could embrace it readily as a pragmatic means for improving railroad management and for allowing an experiment with reduced rates.

As things happened, railroad rates and fares did decline sharply in Massachusetts over the last third of the nineteenth century. Average freight rates per ton-mile dropped from 3.9¢ in 1870 to 1.22¢ in 1900. During the same period, passenger fares went from an average of 2.7¢ per mile to 1.75¢.[72] The commission's efforts obviously played some role in these dramatic declines, especially in the timing of specific cuts. Precisely how strong a role is difficult to say, since many other forces drove rates down as well. For one thing, technological gains improved the productivity of the industry. Then, too, the extensive railroad consolidations of the period usually resulted in the abandonment of unprofitable business lines and thereby removed the need to subsidize them; this made possible subsequent rate reductions on other routes. In addition, the American economy experienced a steady deflation during this period; the prices of most goods and services dropped along with railroad rates, though at a slower pace.

Still another cause, and the one felt most directly by particular railroads, was competition. The rail systems in Massachusetts and elsewhere had been overbuilt, until too many companies were competing for the available traffic. In these circumstances, pressures from rival companies spurred direct rate cutting and also forced railroads into consolidations and mergers, which in turn permitted further rate reductions. Of course, these kinds of pressures reached peak intensity during hard times. Thus the national economic depression of the 1870s brought an extreme form of competitive warfare among railroads. Bidding for larger shares of declining traffic, many rail companies actually cut rates below costs. To meet their periodic cash crises, they deliberately operated at a net loss in order to take in enough money to pay the fixed interest charges on their huge loans.

The dismay of railroad managers who were faced with the problems of economic depression and competition was felt as keenly in Massachusetts as anywhere else in the country. The management of the Boston & Albany, the state's largest railroad, presented its own analysis of the crisis in the following paragraphs published in its annual reports:[73]

1875: This result [a falling off of cash receipts] is due exclusively to the unprecedented competition that has prevailed during the greater part of the year, by which the rates of transportation to and from the West have been forced to the lowest point known in the annals of railroading.

1876: The general depression which during the last three years has settled upon all the industries of the country, aggravated in the railroad business, by the wildest competition ever known, has carried the rate on through traffic far below the dreams of the most visionary advocate of cheap transportation.

Clearly, in cutting their rates and fares, the railroads responded much more strongly to market forces than to the admonitions of the Massachusetts Board of Railroad Commissioners.

The commissioners recognized this fact and were comfortable with it. They knew they confronted a railroad system that had its own momentum. Overall, the industry's agonies during the 1870s confirmed those four observations that Adams had laid out in his early railroad articles: that the industrial system and the railroad business had certain imperatives beyond the control of human will; that enforced competition inevitably produced rate wars, followed by mergers and other consolidations; that this sequence was working itself out in Massachusetts and throughout the nation; and that practical wisdom called for an advisory and catalytic role for government, not a coercive and deterministic one. Adams knew how powerful an engine the market could be. Unlike so many future regulators in America, he sought to exploit market forces and not to fight them.

Yet, in extreme cases, Adams did not hesitate to lay down the law to the railroads. For example, many companies charged more for short trips over routes they alone served than for longer trips over routes also served by competitors. This "long-haul, short-haul" question, as it came to be called, turned into a persistent theme of railroad regulation in America. For Adams the issue represented still another example of the mischief that ensued when state policy encouraged a natural-monopoly industry to operate competitively. The railroads were using their monopolistic short-haul overcharges to cross-subsidize their competitive long-haul

expenses. The resulting injustice to short-haul shippers could not
be tolerated. Thus Adams promoted the following statute:

No railroad corporation of this commonwealth shall charge or collect for
the transportation of goods or merchandise for any shorter distance, any
larger amount as toll or freight than is charged or collected for the car-
riage of similar quantities of the same class of goods over a longer distance upon the same road.[74]

This law, and many like it passed by other states and ultimately by
Congress in the 1887 Act to Regulate Commerce, effectively responded to public outcry. But Adams and other close students of
the railroad industry realized that no mere statute could solve, by
itself, the underlying problem that arose when monopoly was
mixed with enforced competition. A more thorough solution
would require that all regulatory agencies acknowledge and accept the industry's natural-monopoly structure. Regulators then
could work toward a rate system managed by the railroads themselves but tied closely to actual costs, not to the presence or absence of competition along particular routes. In Massachusetts,
Adams achieved a great deal of success by predicating his strategy
on these principles. In the federal government, later on, public
policy veered off in the opposite direction, with unhappy results.

Labor Regulation

At 4:00 P.M. on the afternoon of February 12, 1877, the 67 engineers who operated the locomotives of the Boston & Maine Railroad walked off the job. If trains were en route at that hour, their
locomotives were abandoned where they stood. No violence accompanied this strike, in contrast to the widespread disturbances
that, later in 1877, marked other railroad strikes in the United
States. But the reaction of Adams and his board colleagues suggested that the Massachusetts method of regulation, despite its
many virtues, did not provide complete solutions to labor-manage-
ment disputes.[75]

The immediate background of the strike lay in the economic
distress of the state's railroads during the 1870s. Rate wars and a
general business depression had squeezed the roads' operating
margins, forcing them to economize at every turn. Like most
companies, the Boston & Maine reduced its dividends to stock-

holders by about 40 percent during the worst years of the depression, cutting its employees' wages at the same time by about
10 percent. This wage cut precipitated the strike by the Brotherhood of Locomotive Engineers. The same union operated in Can-
ada as well, and it had just conducted a stunningly successful strike
against the Canadian Grand Trunk Line. Now, under the direct
leadership of the international Grand Chief Engineer, P.M.
Arthur, the Boston & Maine engineers reenacted the union's Canadian tactics. After brief negotiations with the company, they
gave two hours' notice that a further stalemate would bring a
strike. At the end of the two hours, they walked out.

True to his characteristic method, Adams first undertook to
ascertain and publish the facts of the case. Then, from the problem
at hand, he moved on to a structural analysis of the underlying industrial principles. And from those principles he finally inferred a
set of policies that rail corporations should adopt voluntarily. As in
the past, Adams' analysis postulated an institutional lag between
corporate development and the social response to it. The extraordinary hazards of railway operations, he argued, gave rise to new
categories of human problems. Since the corporations failed to
take the lead in solving these problems, the workers themselves organized benevolent and protective unions like the Brotherhood of
Locomotive Engineers. These groups provided insurance funds to
ease the burdens of injury for members and to cushion the shock of
death for surviving dependents. The only trouble, Adams wrote,
was that the union machinery thus created could also serve less legitimate purposes: "It needed only to fall into the hands of dema-
gogues"; given the boom and bust cycles of the railroad business,
"This was almost sure ultimately to happen."

In past years, the Boston & Maine Railroad had caused Adams
numerous regulatory problems. He had little love for its managers.
Now, however, he saw no choice but to side with the company
against the "demagogue" it confronted. Adams felt outraged that
Grand Chief Engineer Arthur, an outsider, would presume to
enter Boston and proclaim at Fanueil Hall "that he had only to
raise his hand to stop every railroad running out of Boston." The
most arrogant corporation, the most irresponsible robber baron,
could never get away with such behavior!

In railroad strikes, Adams argued, the real loser was the public.
"To a modern community the unrestricted and reliable movement

of trains upon railroads is as essential as the even flow of blood through his arteries and veins is to an individual." He rested his official report on the proposition that the trains, like the mail, must go through. The board's report of its complete opposition to the strike, carefully enunciated and released at once to the newspapers, "cleared the air like a thunderclap," according to one legislator. Public opinion, inflamed by inconvenience and by the commission's rhetoric, now rallied against the strikers. The Boston & Maine brought in substitute engineers, and the strike quickly ended. The union had lost its bid for power, in large part because of the commission's swift and decisive opposition.[76]

In his analysis of the episode, Adams said that the proper approach "did not look at the question of employer and employe—labor and capital—at all." Both were at fault: the strikers as proximate cause, the corporations for their historic nonchalance toward the workers' needs. Corporate neglect had alienated the engineers and other craftsmen from a proper identification with their employers. "The community, however, also has rights in the matter," Adams declared, echoing the language of Chief Justice Taney's opinion in the Charles River Bridge Case of 1837. Any kind of railroad strike, for whatever purpose, he went on, "almost necessarily entails an incalculable amount of loss and inconvenience on wholly innocent third parties. It can only be looked upon as an extreme measure . . . the community is throttled that a corporation may be subdued."[77]

Adams' proposed remedies took two separate tacks: severe penal statutes against railroad strikers and a systematic new program of insurance and other welfare measures paid for by the corporations. In addition, Adams presented a plan for step raises and the protection of workers' seniority. This program would harmonize the interests of workers with those of the corporations and so would remove the need for independent unions that threatened the public welfare. As was his custom, Adams broadcast his views to a larger audience in an article for *The Nation*. The proper course for public policy, he wrote,

is also a very simple one, and one which we wonder some of our rich and powerful corporations have not already adopted. They should constitute their own benevolent and life-assurance associations for the benefit of their employees. They should not leave this work to trade-unions; to do so, and thus invite outside influence, is neither sound policy nor good economy.[78]

Again, Adams was reasoning from a premise of attainable harmony. Under proper institutional arrangements, industrial peace would reign automatically. Conflict, more apparent than real in any case, would simply disappear, as the interests of the corporations, their employees, and the public converged. Unfortunately for Adams, however, neither the legislature, the corporations, nor the union saw the issues as he did. The General Court refused to enact the penal statutes he proposed. The railroad companies, having routed the union, showed no inclination to offer its members a welfare program. The union itself stuck to its strike tactics, moving on to do battle in other states.

In Adams' analysis of the Boston & Maine strike, as in some of his suggestions about railroad rates, one sees the naiveté of the patrician man of reason before the emerging enmities of industrial society. The strike episode laid bare Adams' sometimes excessive faith in the ability of disinterested commissioners to resolve questions involving money and power, and heavily laden with emotion. His proposed remedies represented an attempt—noble, perhaps, but nonetheless doomed—simply to argue conflict out of existence.[79] Adams seemed to assume that, if only the facts could be ascertained and publicized, then all affected parties would agree on some self-evident solution. But, in the first place, no truly disinterested version of the Boston & Maine story, or of any story, was possible to ascertain or to tell. Most people cannot separate their prejudices from their interpretations. Adams' own biased account of the strike demonstrates this very point. (The philosophical issue here is the same one at stake in the German historian Ranke's utopian dream of a purely objective history.) And even if, somehow, everyone could agree on what actually had happened, the conflicting economic interests of "labor" and "capital" would never be fully harmonized. Assuming total consensus on the diagnosis, disagreement would still persist on the prescription for a cure. At bottom, Adams' attitude revealed his aversion to some of the stark realities of politics and power. As industrialization swept over American society during the late nineteenth century, self-conscious interest groups began to demand not harmony, but an independent voice. Each one wanted to participate actively as an autonomous force in the negotiations for new industrial relationships. In such a setting, Adams' version of right reason had much to recommend it—but it could not cover up the underlying conflict.

In his diary entries following the strike, Adams provided hints of the reason why men of his type and class (the Mugwump, the scholar-in-politics, the philosopher-king) had difficulty coming to terms with the deep cleavages of modern economic society. The strike had interrupted his composition of an essay on the origins of his hometown, and now he resumed writing: "Turned with pleasure from strikes and excitement to burrowing in history and went on with my Quincy." Industrial conflict might be an exhilarating experience, but it was hardly something to which to devote one's life. Incessant fighting might be an appropriate vocation for P. M. Arthur and other labor leaders. But it held no permanent attraction for Charles Francis Adams, who gladly escaped into the writing of history.[80]

Withdrawal from the Commission

In 1879, after a decade of service, Adams resigned his commission post. His wish to escape from conflict had something to do with this decision, but an even greater motivation was a desire to influence larger events, beyond the boundaries of Massachusetts. He wanted, as he put it, "to shape a national policy," to duplicate his local triumphs in a larger arena of regulation.

Some scholars of regulation, writing in the twentieth century, hold that the typical agency passes through a predictable life cycle. Starting their existence with determination and youthful exuberance, these analysts say, commissions pass inexorably into middle age and finally into senescence. Of course, the men and women who run the agencies go through a similar cycle. They lose interest in the reform premises that underlay the agency's creation. Under the burden of a large and trivial caseload, they slip into stultifying routine. Next they become friendly with the managers of regulated industries. And they end up, even the best of them, far different in outlook from the idealists who entered institutional service while they were young.[81]

For Charles Francis Adams, however, withdrawal from the Massachusetts commission represented something different. It meant a new ambition, a deliberate quest for a wider stage on which to perform the same kind of role. In a remarkably candid letter, published in *The Nation* not long after his resignation, Adams admitted "that there is but one possible position connected with the working out of this railroad problem which I covet. I should like for the next ten years to represent the United States officially in the discussion which ought to take place; just as, during ten of the last twelve years, I represented Massachusetts."[82] As it turned out, his career proved to be a little out of phase with the rhythm of national regulatory policy. The Interstate Commerce Commission did not materialize until 1887, and by that time Adams had become a railroad manager himself, the president of the Union Pacific.

Adams had always combined his official duties with an active career as a private national journalist and "railroad reformer." This line of work had been pioneered by such men as Henry Varnum Poor, editor of the *American Railroad Journal.* Poor knew Adams and used his ideas about publicity and disclosure as preludes to improved management in messages to readers over the years. But, unlike Poor, Adams held public office. This circumstance, together with the transcendent fact of his being a member of the Adams family, shaped a life style different from any other among the journalistic railroad reformers.[83]

Adams' diaries for the years of commission service show him leading an aristocrat's life: traveling often, visiting political leaders in Washington, taking annual trips West, summering in Newport and Nantucket. His routine gradually evolved into something like that of an English country gentleman. Adams interested himself in library, school, and town affairs in Quincy; trusteeships for organizations such as the Boston Athenaeum; directorships of railroads; stints as July 4th orator. Sometimes he sensed, accurately enough, that he was spreading himself too thin. And retrospectively, in his autobiography, Adams expressed the conviction that his jack-of-all-aristocratic-trades way of life had ensured his mastery of none of the several vocations he successively took up. But since no single career could overcome his frequent ennui, Adams kept up with all of them, always having "too many irons in the fire."[84]

The first evidence of his boredom with the commission came in 1872, three years after he first took office. The old sense of excitement about railroads was abating, and the focus of his interest that year turned to the Liberal Republican movement and his father's abortive candidacy for the presidency of the United States. Then Adams spent nearly half of the following year abroad as American commissioner to the Vienna Exposition of 1873. During his European travels, he met once or twice with continental and English railroad men, but his diaries show nothing like the preoccupation with railroads that had been characteristic of 1869.[85] What troubled Adams more than anything else during the depression of the 1870s was the state of his personal fortune. Throughout his tenure as a public servant, he divided his time between the commonwealth's affairs and his own attempts to become wealthy. At some moments his "financiering," as he called it, obsessed him. Gambling recklessly, he continued to speculate in railroads and real estate long after he had made his first million. On more than one occasion he nearly lost everything. And sometimes his plunges into railroad stocks barely skirted the kinds of conflict of interest forbidden by the commission statute Adams himself had written.[86]

The ideology of regulation in America mandates that commissioners not only avoid conflicts of interest but also keep themselves out of politics. Adams found such a separation impossible. He regularly corresponded with Carl Schurz, James A. Garfield, and other national reform politicians, while he never stopped probing for new ways to multiply the influence of his patrician circle of "best men." For example, he spent much of the winter of 1876–77 trying to broker the Hayes-Tilden presidential election dispute. Characteristically, Adams favored Tilden, on the grounds that his own Republican Party could effect a return to its reform origins only by a cleansing fast in the wilderness. This plan would have left Tilden, the Democrat, to occupy the White House while the Republicans purified themselves.[87]

In 1877, Adams' interest in commission work revived in response to the Boston & Maine strike, which afforded him an opportunity for crisis management. But as the crisis quickly abated, he resumed his hobby of writing history. With no one to challenge his desire for control, with only pen and paper to talk back, the avocation suddenly became irresistible: "There is nothing I enjoy so much as historical composition," he confided in his diary, "—why have I not the sense to devote myself to it!"[88] By 1878, as he began his tenth year on the commission, Adams knew that he had succumbed to a malady endemic to career public officials with genuinely first-rate abilities: alienation from all routine. Escape became imperative, a matter of emotional survival. "How wearisome all of this is!" he wrote. "Can I never get rid of this beastly commissionership?"[89]

Fink and the Trunk Line Association

Even as Adams searched for a way to expand his influence, a possible means of escape from New England and the commission appeared in the form of a job offer from Albert Fink of the Eastern Trunk Line Association. Fink was one of the undoubted geniuses of American railroad history. Born in 1827, he had come to the United States from his native Germany as a "forty-eighter." Benjamin Latrobe of the Baltimore and Ohio gave him his first railroad job, and Fink quickly won renown as a daring civil engineer who could design bridges of unprecedented lengths. Fink easily negotiated the transition from engineer to manager, and in 1859 he took office as chief engineer and superintendent of the road and machinery departments for the Louisville and Nashville Railroad. During the Civil War, he performed a minor miracle in helping to steer his road on a course of steady growth and profit. By the end of the 1860s, when Adams took his seat on the Massachusetts commission, Fink already had gained a reputation as one of the brightest men ever to enter the railroad field.[90]

Like Adams and a handful of others, Fink intuitively grasped the significance, in railroad ratemaking, of the preponderance of fixed costs over variable costs. To Fink, the proper basis for a railroad rate was not only the value of the service (a method critics called the doctine of "all the traffic will bear"), but also the cost of the service to the corporation and a proper allowance for profit. Given the different elements involved in computing costs—such as the terrain over which the line traveled, the size of the load, the availability of freight for the return trip, and the capital structure of the railroad—costs would vary infinitely for different roads, routes, and classes of freight. From these premises Fink, like Adams, inferred an iron principle: rates should never be standardized by legislative fiat or commission ruling. The reason, as Fink put it, was the impossibility of "enacting general laws establishing tariffs applicable to *more than one road.*"[91]

Had public policy followed Adams' and Fink's prescription of pegging rates to cost as well as to value of service, then some of

the problems that later plagued the industry and the Interstate
Commerce Commission might have been avoided. Value of service ratemaking did not appreciably hurt the industry so long as it
dominated freight transport. But when, in the 1920s, motor trucks
brought a new kind of competition, the railroads found themselves
abruptly stripped not only of their natural-monopoly position, but
also of much high-value, high-profit traffic. At the same time, because of regulatory constraints imposed by the Interstate Commerce Commission, they were unable to maximize their
advantages with other freights. Fink's emphasis on cost of service,
therefore, spoke more to the twentieth century than to his own
time.[92]

To make his system of cost accounting work within the Louisville and Nashville, Fink developed a series of equations that facil-
itated the close calculation of costs for different types of cargo
over routes of varying length and terrain. In so doing, he pioneered the modern system of classifying expenses so as to permit
refined statistical analysis. In this field, his writings became instant
reference works. Read a century after their compositon, they still
display the intellectual clarity and force that made Fink the leading railroad mind of the nineteenth century. The fact that he
achieved consensus recognition as the "father of railway economics" is no surprise; his contributions to the discipline remain un-
matched to this day.[93]

Adams and Fink had remarkably similar views. They shared a
primary commitment to economic efficiency, a conviction that
railroads tended toward monopolistic structures, and a belief in
the inevitability of future consolidations. Throughout the 1870s,
while Adams served on the Massachusetts commission, Fink labored to bring order to regional railroad networks. The only instrument available to him, given the excess capacity of these
systems, was an extremely controversial device called the "pool."
This arrangement short-circuited the forces of market competition
by dividing all available traffic among participating railroads according to prearranged percentages; and by stabilizing rates at
levels that would yield decent profits to all. In the language of the
modern economist, Fink sought to "cartelize" the industry. He
hoped thereby to end the disruptive sequence of rate wars, bankruptcies, and receiverships that had so troubled railroads during
the depressed 1870s.

By the force of his personality, together with the soundness of his accounting principles, Fink often made such combines work, at least for a time. In the long run, pools and other cartels usually collapsed because the burden of paying fixed costs represented a constant incentive for managers to cheat by cutting rates. Only in this way could they win traffic from competitors, including their pool partners. The worse the health of the economy, or of the individual railroad, the stronger the urge for a company to betray the pool. Since agreements for price maintenance and division of traffic were "in restraint of trade" under the common law, they could not be enforced as legally binding contracts. Furthermore, speculative owners like Jay Gould disliked pooling because it interfered with their schemes to manipulate railroad rates as a means of manipulating stock prices. And, as if all this were not enough, any mention of collusion among railroad men—however honorable, however wise—inevitably brought vigorous protest from shippers and the general public. No matter how directly the logic of railroad economics might lead to pooling in a time of overcapacity and economic depression, the logic of American politics led in the opposite direction. Yet Fink had enough skill to make pools work, and his successful promotions earned him a reputation as the magician of railroad management.[94]

Pooling, to be sure, was not the sort of pattern that an architect of the ideal railroad system would design. But by the late 1870s, the industry had already gone awry through overbuilding and a series of frenzied rate wars. Pooling may well have represented the best means available at the time to rationalize major parts of the industry—assuming a legitimate mechanism for administering the pools.[95] Certainly Adams thought so. Thus, despite a clear recognition of the flaws in the method, he grasped the opportunity to participate in the largest pooling project yet undertaken. In 1879, he resigned from the Massachusetts commission and accepted Fink's invitation to become chairman of the Board of Arbitration of the Eastern Trunk Line Association. Fink himself headed this huge alliance, which included most of the large rail lines east of the Mississippi. Its purpose was to cartelize the industry by allocating traffic among individual roads so as to prevent rate wars. The resulting stabilization would benefit not only the corporations, but shippers and consumers as well.[96]

That, at any rate, was Adams' view: "a great advance on anything yet devised," and for himself a unique chance to project the work he had begun in Massachusetts onto a national stage. He was joining the association, he wrote Fink,

with the distinct understanding on my part that an honest and harmonious effort is now to be made in the direction of a general clearing-house system through which the relations of railroads, not only between themselves, but with the community can be regulated and reduced to a certain degree of order. In this way and in this way only, as you are well aware, is it possible to do the work of the railroads equably and reasonably.

Adams intended to carry forward the sunshine-commission approach he had pioneered in Massachusetts. As he informed Fink, Adams wished not only "to decide questions arising within the combination," but also "to familiarize the public mind with the justice and economy of the clearing-house and apportionment system." And he was especially gratified that Fink had also secured the services of David A. Wells as another member of the three-man arbitration board. Wells was one of the most insightful economic analysts of the period. "If we hang together," Adams wrote his old friend, "I am satisfied we shall make a heavy enough team to cause ourselves to be felt . . . I think we can show them that specialists can do something to advance a great move." The "best men" now had a rare opportunity to affect national railroad policy.[97]

In the face of its intrinsic disadvantages, however, no amount of talent could make the association work. Despite Adams' handsome salary ($10,000 annually), his three years on the new board brought him nothing but frustration. Part of the unpleasantness was his own fault. Determined to maintain his Massachusetts residence, he accepted the inconvenience of shuttling 200 miles back and forth between his home in Quincy and the association's headquarters in New York. In his work on the three-man tribunal, he had to curb a temperamental inclination, reinforced by his success in Massachusetts, to dominate a board of explicitly divided authority. Worst of all, Adams inevitably clashed with Fink, to whom he had to play a "very second fiddle." Because the board's decisions came on appeals from Fink's administrative rulings, conflict inhered in every situation.[98]

In the history of railroad regulation, the Trunk Line Association's failure represented another instance of trial and error, somewhat like the futile attempts of midwestern state commissions to regulate railroads whose routes crossed half the nation. Nor did the federal Interstate Commerce Commission supply a solution to the problem of enforced competition. To the chagrin of rail managers, the landmark federal legislation of 1887 prohibited pooling and thereby discouraged the development of a federally sponsored cartel. Denied the opportunity to pool their traffic, American railroads devised an alternative method of imposing order on chaos. Each of the major lines began to build, purchase, or acquire through merger what one prominent executive called a "self-sustaining system." Such a system contained, within one corporation, tracks leading in and out of all important centers of commerce from the Northeast to the Midwest, plus extensive webs of feeder lines serving the hinterlands. During the 1880s, a wildly competitive construction program, in pursuit of this strategy, compounded the earlier overbuilding. In turn, the strategy itself, undertaken by every trunkline, brought unprecedented overcapacity. As a consequence, in the 1880s and 90s, the cycle of the 60s and 70s recapitulated itself, with bankruptcies, receiverships, national economic depression, and extensive railroad mergers. At last, in the late 1890s, a series of reorganizations, worked out under the expensive auspices of J. P. Morgan and other financiers, led to a streamlined national network of ten major systems.[99]

The irony in all this was that the characteristic American abhorrence of loose business combinations (pools in the case of railroads) inadvertently promoted the growth of large and very tight combinations. These took the form of individual corporations that grew, through merger, to enormous size. Eventually, the building of "self-contained systems" by the major trunklines resulted in still further internal growth of these companies to extremely large proportions. In the aggregate, this process may well have bloated the railroad industry far beyond its economically optimal size. In seeking to circumscribe bigness, therefore, American policy may have perversely stimulated railroad growth beyond all natural tendencies.

Overbuilding in turn led to numerous bankruptcies, capital writedowns, mergers, and abandonments of unprofitable lines. As the number of corporations involved in railroading shrank, a remaining few companies, now of very large size, came to dominate

the industry. In this way, the prohibition against pooling accelerated the trend toward giantism and led to an unnecessarily tight
concentration of the industry. Of course, a good deal of concentration was probably inevitable. As the economic arguments of
Adams in his early railroad articles made clear, mergers were almost certain to occur; and one way or other, railroading in
America tended powerfully toward something like the shape it assumed by 1900. So in the long run it may have mattered little
whether the industry reached this configuration through the rational, controlled process of pooling or through the more violent
cycles of overbuilding, bankruptcy, depression, reorganization,
and interlocking administration through "communities of interest"—the latter constituting a type of invisible pool. What law
and custom had not allowed Albert Fink to do, subsequent financial distress tendered to the ministrations of J. P. Morgan. And
Morgan, unlike Fink, levied colossal fees for his services.

To Adams, the peculiar history of American railroads over the
closing decades of the nineteenth century served to validate the
arguments about technological determinism that had long per-
vaded his own writings. During these later years, he observed the
unfolding of the railroad drama from a variety of perspectives.
After ten years on the Massachusetts commission, followed by
three in the service of the Trunk Line Association, he assumed in
1884 the presidency of the Union Pacific Railroad. Earlier he had
sat on the board of this perennially troubled corporation as a
"public" director, an appointee of Secretary of the Interior Carl
Schurz.

The Union Pacific constituted the eastern half of America's first
transcontinental railroad. It had been built and operated with
substantial federal land grants and other subsidies. Understand-
ably, Adams regarded himself as the ideal Union Pacific president
for 1884, exactly the right man to work out the complex relationships between business and government interests. But the railroad's problems proved to be too great for him, just as had those of
the Trunk Line Association. At the Union Pacific, Adams made
some progress, but then stayed too long at his post. He finally departed in 1890, under heavy fire, humiliated and forced out by his
old adversary Jay Gould. On the whole, the Union Pacific years
were among the least satisfying in all of Adams' life, even though
they represented the apex of his popular reputation. It was the

bitter experience of those years that inspired his much-quoted characterization of American businessmen:

I have known, and known tolerably well, a good many "successful" men—"big" financially—men famous during the last half-century; and a less interesting crowd I do not care to encounter. Not one that I have ever known would I care to meet again, either in this world or the next; nor is one of them associated in my mind with the idea of humor, thought or refinement. A set of mere money-getters and traders, they were essentially unattractive and uninteresting.[100]

Adams' caustic description of businessmen contained more than a hint of self-reproach, since he himself often behaved like a money-getter. He spent a great deal of time juggling his stock portfolio, shifting bank balances from one account to another, and taking out large loans to cover his losses on the stock exchange. And he constantly worried about the effect all this was having on his character.

Besides looking after his fortune, Adams passed the last twenty-five years of his life traveling and writing history. As time went by, he grew more and more discontented. Year by year he watched incredulously as the world he had known vanished before his eyes. Waves of Irish and Italian immigrants poured into Massachusetts, driving him from the family homestead in Quincy to the pastoral suburb of Lincoln, adjacent to Concord. From Lincoln, he watched as other Americans, native-born but just as alien to his aristocratic vision, asserted their growing political strength. Such upstarts as the populists and the new urban proletariat failed to take their places quietly within the American chain of being. Instead, they claimed autonomy and demanded a share in the country's largesse. For Adams, these were ironic, even tragic developments. The coalescence of interest groups implied resolution through force, by means of political activism and persistent attention to one's own welfare—not through a convergence of the interests of all people into a single "public interest." Evidence of increasing civil disintegration seemed to lie all about him. Railroads battled shippers. Industrialists locked out strikers. Big business swallowed up small competitors. For regulation, this fragmenting of American society doomed to temporary irrelevance Adams' conception of the sunshine commission.

Characteristically, he himself responded by striking back. Even in old age his pen remained as sharp as ever, but now his writings took on a note of frustration. He simply could not understand why the rules of the game kept changing; and in particular, the growth of coercive regulation disturbed him deeply. As the Interstate Commerce Commission grew more powerful, less temperate in its judgments, and much more prejudiced against railroads in favor of shippers, Adams became increasingly querulous and irascible. Repeatedly he tried to explain why regulatory policy was going wrong in substituting the principle of coercion for that of simple exposure. His legacy of fair regulation, he felt, had been betrayed—and he could do nothing about it. Some unknown force seemed to be tearing the country apart, and indeed the world. In 1914, during Adams' eightieth and last year, the Great War began in Europe. That event confirmed his conviction that the world had indeed gone mad. Confirmation, oddly, was a comfort. Charles Francis Adams knew he had been right all along.[101]

Epilogue: Muckraker and Regulator

Of the several ironies in Adams' career, the most instructive for the history of regulation lay in the two goals with which he began: to arouse popular anger and to rationalize the railroad system. Although Adams tended to see the first as an essential precondition for the second—that is, to construe the first as means, the second as end—historically the actual sequence did not unfold as he had planned. In personal terms, the impossibility of waging "a war with the Rings" while simultaneously harmonizing their interests with those of society eluded him. To his surprise, the Adams of "A Chapter of Erie" had a profoundly different impact from the Adams of the first *Annual Report* of the Massachusetts board. Even though these two documents appeared within months of each other, their messages clashed. The economic outrage Adams directed at the Erie war just did not square with the economic determinism of railroad technology as delineated in the commission's *Report*. The muckraking function of "Erie" did not mix well with the administrative function of the *Report*. Adams might as well have harnessed a racehorse with an ox under a double yoke and set off behind the two for utopia.

He was not the first or last American to experience this problem, which is endemic to democratic societies. But in the history of regulation, his example represents the most dramatic human case, a personal metaphor for the confusion inherent in the regulator's role. Uniquely, Adams achieved not merely professional competence as both muckraker and regulator, but genuine distinction. His "Erie" remains an unexcelled model of the muckraker's art. Not Steffens, nor Sinclair, nor, in another time, Ralph Nader produced a tour de force to surpass it in vividness and power. Within the minds of all who have read "Erie," whether in Adams' time or our own, the images of Gould, Fisk, Drew, Vanderbilt—portraits of the robber baron as an ideal type—remain acute and indelible. But the caricature that Adams drew became in the minds of many readers the reality.

Simply put, in "Erie" he did his work too well. For generations of Americans, in successive retellings by Gustavus Myers, Matthew Josephson, and other muckraking journalists, Adams' portraits of stock watering and political corruption became the *norms* of railroad management. And if the robber barons were really that bad, then the solution was not rational restraint by government and the careful preservation of managerial prerogatives. Instead, suitable remedies had to be found in the area of indictments, long prison sentences, and harsh regulation. This, of course, was not at all what Adams intended. But readers could not get his pictures of Gould, Drew, and Fisk out of their minds.

"Erie" remained in print more than a century after its publication in 1869, during that triumphant summer of Adams' life. Such literary fame would please anyone. Adams might have preferred, however, that it spring not from "Erie" but from his writings on regulation. For he was not only the prototype muckraker, but also the first modern regulator—and one of the best ever to serve on a state commission. In that role he sought nothing less than to rationalize the railroad system. And in Massachusetts he succeeded, perhaps as well as anyone could have: by codifying the chaotic railroad laws of the state, by standardizing safety regulations and accounting procedures, and by educating rail managers and the public about the unusual economics of the industry.

On the national stage afterward, he failed to duplicate that impressive performance. Others failed as well. In significant measure, these later failures, by so many regulators, derived from an overheated public atmosphere, from the wrath of a public opinion to which Adams himself had made—as muckraker—an important contribution. Once it had been roused to motivate political action, public opinion became a force not easily controlled. The service

Adams performed for the art of muckraking, and for his own youthful renown, proved disadvantageous in the practical art of regulating.

Little evidence remains to suggest that Adams himself ever grasped the irony of his twin triumph as muckraker and regulator. In his old age, when he thought of his "Erie" at all, he recalled that the wily and patient Gould had turned the tables on him, securing in 1890 Adams' ouster from the Union Pacific presidency, thus settling the score for the acid portrait of 1869. But in later years Adams spent much more time puzzling over the decline of his sunshine commission and the rise of coercive regulation. In retrospect, the forces behind this trend in regulation come into much clearer focus than was possible in Adams' time. The most powerful such force was the growing division of the nation's people into determined interest groups. Each of these groups drove hard not toward a single goal—the reasoned peace and harmony Adams wanted—but rather to acquire the power and autonomy that each group believed it must have. Adams, bewildered and embittered by this development, watched helplessly from the sidelines as his beloved "public interest" broke apart among dozens of quarreling economic and ethnic constituencies.

Adams reached the age of sixty-five at the turn of the twentieth century. By that time, industrialization was proceeding at full throttle, American cities were growing at an unprecedented rate, and European immigrants were entering the United States at the rate of one million a year. The census of 1900 disclosed the remarkable fact that fewer than one American in two was both white and the child of two native-born parents. From his position at the top of the aristocratic class, Adams reacted to this new, divided, pluralistic America with downright hostility. In this response lay a lesson for our own subsequent understanding of the history of regulation: in Adams' bitterness at the failure of public policy to proliferate the sunshine commission he had so carefully modeled; in his extreme alienation from what he began to deride as the "Deer Peepul"; in the blatant exaggeration, perhaps from advancing age, of his inborn sense of elitism into a hateful caricature, not unlike those he had so memorably etched of the robber barons in his youth—in all these signs, one can read the sea change that had occurred in American society and therefore in the conditions for regulation.

CHAPTER 2

State to Federal, Railroads
to Trusts

I N THE LATTER PART of the nineteenth century, Charles Francis Adams' Massachusetts Board of Railroad Commissioners took its place as the national prototype of the so-called weak regulatory commission. It became a model for many other states whose legislatures wished to regulate railroads but, for one reason or another, did not want to assume the power of setting rates and fares. An important alternative to the weak commission appeared in the midwestern states of Illinois, Wisconsin, Minnesota, and Iowa. Beginning in 1871, the legislatures of these states passed Granger Laws, which directly regulated the rates of railroads operating within each state. Three of the four states also created "strong" regulatory commissions and empowered them to prescribe maximum rates.[1]

Although significant as milestones in the history of regulation, this midwestern variety of strong commissions proved unsuccessful. Most of the Granger Laws were repealed within a few years of their enactment, for reasons that suggest a good deal about the overall nature of regulation. One stimulus to repeal was a political counterattack by the railroads. Another, more important reason derived from the severe economic depression of the 1870s, which, in both the Middle West and in Massachusetts, drove rates down faster than regulatory agencies could hope to do. Still a third reason, and the most revealing of all, lay in the very nature of the national railroad network: it simply made no sense for small state agencies to perform pricing functions for giant interstate corporations whose tracks crossed thousands of miles in a dozen different states. In the Granger cases of 1877, the United States Supreme

Court firmly upheld the power of public agencies to regulate railroads and other industries "affected with a public interest." But in practice, the Granger commissions did not achieve as much success as their misnamed weak counterparts to the east.[2]

The model weak agency, that of Massachusetts, continued to enjoy a measure of prestige even after Adams' departure in 1879. Such decline as its reputation did suffer occurred only gradually, as a result of several trends common to state railroad commissions during the late nineteenth century. For one thing, the onset of federal railroad regulation in 1887 reduced the importance of all state commissions. For another, no new commissioners as talented as Adams appeared in Massachusetts—a typical example of the difficulty nearly all regulatory agencies have experienced in consistently attracting the best people. Finally, the Massachusetts agency like other state railroad commissions went through a sharp transition in function. One by one, each agency evolved into a public utility commission.[3]

This shift in function occurred more rapidly in Massachusetts than elsewhere, but the change there was also representative of evolutions in other states. In 1885, Massachusetts created a second regulatory agency, the Board of Gas Commissioners, with supervisory authority over the new gas-lighting companies that were bringing artificial illumination to the state's cities and towns. In 1887, this agency became the Board of Gas and Electric Light Commissioners, as the state took formal notice of the rise of still another vital new industry. The gas and electric commissioners, following the pattern of the Board of Railroad Commissioners, did not wield strong authority over rates but tried instead to regulate more gently, mediating a host of difficult issues between the corporations and the public. In 1909, both the original railroad board and the newer gas and electric commission received important powers over the issuance of stocks and bonds by the companies. Four years after that, in 1913, Adams' original railroad commission was renamed the Public Utility Commission and given additional responsibility for telephone companies, street railways, and steamships. Finally, in 1919, the last institutional consolidation occurred, as the railroad and utility commissions were merged into one body, which was named the Massachusetts Department of Public Utilities. This organization still exists today, having grown over the course of a hundred years from its seed as Adams' tiny agency, with its single clerk, to a small bureaucracy with more than one hundred full-time employees.[4]

Much the same pattern of institutional growth occurred in other states, as the American industrial economy began to mature. Led by New York and Wisconsin (whose commissions were reorganized in 1907), state agencies everywhere, in their efforts to do justice to both companies and consumers, focused their regulatory efforts on the question of rates. Working from the premise that gas and electric utilities were natural monopolies, nearly all commissions inaugurated a complex administrative system that came to be called rate-of-return regulation. This system, over the next several decades, dominated the entire state regulatory process, and the details of that evolution confirmed the earlier prophecies of Charles Francis Adams. As Adams had feared would happen, excessive involvement in the rate question resulted in much controversy and red tape and tended to handicap more important efforts to promote rational adjustment of the general relationship between utility corporations and the public.[5]

Many of the problems of rate-of-return regulation began in a controversial Supreme Court decision in 1898. In this important case, *Smyth v. Ames,* the Union Pacific Railroad challenged a Nebraska statute that specified the maximum rates the corporation could charge for hauling freight. The court ruled that the railroad was entitled to a "reasonable" return on "the fair value of the property being used for the convenience of the public." In setting forth this fair-value doctrine, the court inadvertently started a definitional controversy that for many years afterward plagued accountants, lawyers, utility managers, and regulatory commissioners. At one time or another, particular state and federal commissions, and the Supreme Court itself, have included in their definitions of fair value such considerations as the original cost of the property less depreciation (a view favoring the consumer in periods of inflation); the cost of reproducing the same property (a view favoring corporations in periods of inflation); the market value of the corporation's stocks and bonds; and assorted other factors. No authoritative view has ever met with unanimous acceptance by courts and commissions. Nor was definitional uncertainty the only problem. At bottom, the entire concept of "fair return on fair value" is a cost-plus formula, vulnerable to all the difficulties associated with cost-plus ways of thinking about how a business should be conducted. Some of these problems appeared early in the history of utility regulation, and several of them still trouble state and federal commissions. Such difficulties include:

1. Temptation to pad the "rate base" (the rate base is equivalent to the value of the property being used to produce the service; it provides the arithmetic denominator for the percentage "rate of return").
2. Creation of a strong incentive to emphasize capital equipment rather than labor, whenever the one can be substituted for the other (equipment goes into the rate base and labor does not).
3. Disincentives to cut operating costs—and therefore to promote more efficient operation.
4. The problem of "boundaries," in which one part of a company is a regulated natural monopoly but another part of the same company is not.
5. "Regulatory lag," in which the drawn-out proceedings of the commission consume so much time that the situation being ruled on becomes obsolete and irrelevant to future revenue requirements.[6]

In practice, these problems promoted the rise of ingenious accounting methods by corporations, all calculated to maximize revenues in the face of regulatory limits on percentage rates of return. At worst, they made the process of rate regulation a ritualistic charade, played out in the form of full-scale "rate cases" as part of the routine operations of commissions. Such cases, conducted under elaborate procedural rules, often turned into extremely laborious hearings dominated by lawyers and engineers, incomprehensible to ordinary citizens.[7]

The Rise of Federal Regulation

The movement from state to federal jurisdiction did not occur across the entire spectrum of regulated industries. In many industries, state regulation has continued, with no abatement of importance, down to the present day. Most public utilities, for example, continue to be regulated primarily by state commissions. But for industries in which single companies could grow so large that they spread across several states, thereby making effective supervision by any one state commission impracticable, state regulation yielded to federal. The railroad industry set the pattern here. During the latter part of the nineteenth century, as the "railroad problem" became national in scope, its dimensions also became much more complex. In the East, the major regulatory issue often had to do with excessive competition: too many railroads handled too little freight. In the West and South, by contrast, the problem usually took the form of uncontrolled monopoly, as whole communities came to depend for their very existence on single railroad corporations. In all regions of the country, railroads themselves often exhibited tendencies toward questionable financial practices and discriminatory pricing. Such pricing, in which different classes of shippers were charged different rates for the same type of service, might flow logically from the economics of railroading, but it often violated deep-seated popular conceptions of fairness. And underlying the entire national railroad problem was the political incongruity of a democratic society held in apparent subordination to one of its key industries.[8]

Ultimately, railroads grew so powerful and so vital to the national economy that continued reliance on state regulation alone became futile. Federal entry into the picture was precipitated by an important Supreme Court case: *Wabash, St. Louis and Pacific Railroad Company v. Illinois* (1886). In its decision, the court ruled that commerce originating or ending outside the boundaries of a state could not be regulated by that state, even though the federal government provided no alternative means of regulation. This doctrine partially contravened the court's prior ruling in the Granger cases, and the new *Wabash* rule made some final resort to federal regulation all but certain. In 1883, Senator Shelby M. Cullom, a Republican from Illinois, had introduced a bill providing for a federal commission that would administer a set of general and flexible guidelines for the governance of the railroad industry. The *Wabash* decision attracted majority support to Cullom's bill, and in 1887 the Interstate Commerce Commission was born. By that time, a national consensus had developed. Merchants, farmers, politicians, and even many railroad managers were now convinced, after years of trial and error with other methods, that serious federal railroad regulation must be inaugurated.[9]

From our own perspective a century later, the greatest significance of the 1887 Act to Regulate Commerce lies in its creation of the prototypical federal regulatory agency. Most of the later federal commissions were patterned on the Interstate Commerce Commission, in appointment and tenure of members and in relationships with the existing branches of government—legislative, executive, and judicial. In fact, one measure of the success that the ICC was perceived as having in its first fifty years was its imitation in the creation of later agencies. Even so, the ICC began life with several different missions, not all of which easily accorded with each other or with the economics of railroading. The act of 1887 forbade rebating, pooling, and—with some important exceptions—rate discrimination between long-haul and short-haul traffic. The statute prescribed that rates be "just and reasonable," and it provided a new arena—the ICC—in which determinations of reasonableness could occur. The five commissioners were to be appointed by the president and confirmed by the senate, for staggered terms of six years. No more than three of the five could come from any one political party, and each commissioner was to receive an annual salary of $7,500—a very large sum for the time, greater than the salary of all federal judges except those on the Supreme Court.[10]

After an auspicious beginning under its distinguished first chairman, Thomas M. Cooley, the ICC encountered severe difficulties with the courts. Here too it set the pattern for future regulatory agencies. For the federal judiciary, with the Supreme Court in the lead, sharply restricted the powers of the new commission and reduced it, by the late 1890s, to a mere collector of data. Over the next several decades, a gradual process of adjustment occurred, involving the courts, the commission, and, most important, the Congress. Responding to continual problems within the railroad industry, as well as to jurisdictional squabbles between the ICC and the courts, the national legislature steadily added to the commission's authority. The highlights in this long history included: (1) the Elkins Act of 1903, which gave teeth to the prohibition against rebating contained in the original Act to Regulate Commerce of 1887; (2) the Hepburn Act of 1906, which empowered the commission to fix maximum railroad rates, shifted the burden of proof in rate proceedings from the commission to the railroads, and made ICC decisions effective as soon as they were reached; (3) the Mann-Elkins Act of 1910, which broadened the ratemaking authority of the commission, reinforced the long-haul/short-haul rule, and created the Court of Commerce, a short-lived experiment in specialized judicial review; (4) the Transportation (or Esch-Cummins) Act of 1920, which gave the commission power to set minimum railroad rates, to supervise the issuance of railroad securities, to approve the previously forbidden practice of pooling, and to begin comprehensive planning for a systematic national transportation network; (5) the Motor Carrier Act of 1935, which gave to the ICC regulatory authority over the important new interstate trucking industry; and (6) the Transportation Act of 1940, which added still another industry—domestic water carriers—to the roster of businesses regulated by the ICC.[11]

This litany of legislation underlines an extremely important principle: during the twentieth century—just as in Charles Francis Adams' time—the art of regulatory strategy remains in large measure a political art. In no meaningful sense did the creation of the Interstate Commerce Commission take railroad regulation "out of politics," as so many supporters of regulation thought should be done. It was true of course that Congress, by creating the ICC, relieved itself of a continuing need to attend to innumerable trivial matters peculiar to the railroad industry. Congress did not, however, permanently yield its powers to an "independent" regulatory commission. Instead, the congressional committees stayed in close touch with developments at the ICC. The commission itself often originated proposals for new legislation, and the agency took great pains to develop and nurture political support within Congress. Without this support, the ICC could not have done its job properly, especially since a jealous judiciary often threatened to undercut its authority.[12]

Throughout its history, the ICC has remained controversial. Sometimes, as during the Progressive Era, it became the target of railroad industry protests charging that it favored shippers at the expense of carriers. More often, the commission has been accused by shippers and consumer groups of trying to protect the carriers at the expense of the general public. Sometimes, critics with entirely different viewpoints have joined in blaming the ICC for the long-term decline in the nation's rail service. But the most damning line of criticism has rested on claims that the ICC has worked to impede economic efficiency. Indeed, from the historical record, it is clear that the agency's policies often prevented market forces from allocating traffic according to the individual modes of transportation—whether rail, highway, or water—best suited for particular kinds of freight. The commission appears to have interfered with efficiency unintentionally, at first simply through ignorance, since in its early years the economics of transportation was not very well understood. Later on, most errors derived from the ICC's misguided attempts to be "fair" to all parties. The commission regulated transportation rates in such a way as to ensure that each industry—rail, highway, or water—received not those portions of the total traffic most appropriate to its routes, but instead a fair share. In its concern for fairness at the expense of economic efficiency, as in so many other respects, the ICC typified the practice of most regulatory agencies in American history.[13]

Eventually, the kinds of regulatory problems dealt with by state and federal railroad commissions expanded to include troubles rooted in other large enterprises. Although the profound economic movement that has become known as the "rise of big business" began with the railroads in the 1850s, it continued to move forward, in vastly expanded form, causing revolutions in manufacturing and distribution. These changes occurred between about 1880 and 1920. Prior to this period, no single manufacturing enterprise, indeed no entire manufacturing industry, had attained sufficient size to affect masses of people. Before the 1880s, even major factories customarily employed no more than a few hundred workers. The largest manufacturing companies were usually capitalized at less than one million dollars. Yet, within a single generation after 1880, all this changed. By 1890, each of several large railroads employed more than 100,000 workers. By 1900, John D. Rockefeller's Standard Oil Company had grown into a huge multinational corporation capitalized at $122 million. By 1904, James B. Duke's American Tobacco Company completed a series of mergers and internal expansions that took it to a capitalization of $500 million (up from $25 million in 1890). And in 1901, the creation of the United States Steel Corporation climaxed a $1.4 billion transaction. This sum, which far exceeded the imaginations of most contemporary citizens, became a symbol of the new giantism in the American economy.[14]

With the rise of big business, the term "private enterprise" acquired a different meaning. Whereas once it had signified liberty, freedom, and individualism, it now meant danger as well—the threat of giant corporations. Suddenly, big business seemed to menace America. Large corporations represented that same centralized power against which the founding fathers had fought their revolution. Perhaps inevitably, American big business evoked a powerful regulatory response.

Overcapacity and the Rise of the Trusts

In the popular language of the late nineteenth and early twentieth century, such companies as Standard Oil, American Tobacco, and United States Steel became known as "trusts." Although most combinations did not take the precise legal form of a trust (in which trustees for several different companies hold the common stock of those companies and thereby exercise control over them), all such corporations did share the characteristics of centralized management and very large size. The process by which companies in certain industries did or did not grow to great size is not fully understood, even today. But it is much better understood now than it was in the early twentieth century. Within the past few years, several streams of important research in economics, history, and business administration have converged, to make possible a much fuller understanding of the rise of big business and of attempts to regulate it. This story is not a simple one to tell but, because it is one so rich in importance, paradox, and surprise, it well repays the necessary effort.

The trust movement—that is, the powerful tendency of businessmen to combine with their competitors in associations or mergers—grew out of a particular problem of industrialization. This was the problem of periodic industrial overcapacity, tied to the boom-and-bust cycles of the late nineteenth century. Just as worldwide overcapacity lies behind the periodic "sickness" of such contemporary industries as steel, fibers, footwear, and automobiles, so in the late nineteenth century industrial overcapacity caused serious disruptions in the economies of all industrialized nations.

The underlying cause of overcapacity was the industrial revolution, which initially took the form of a revolution in production and productivity. In the first phase of the industrial revolution, progress in the technology of production far outran similar developments in distribution, marketing, and consumer purchasing power. Cyrus McCormick's reaper, invented in the 1830s, laid the foundation for a national and international system of commercial grain agriculture; but the new system of distribution did not develop until a national railroad network emerged for marketing the grain (there were 23 miles of track in America in 1830 and 208,152 by 1890). Changes occurred at uneven rates, and these different paces of change created serious periodic imbalances between nations' capacities to produce and their abilities to consume. In some respects, of course, the differences were natural and inevitable. The rise of the department store (1870s) could hardly have preceded the invention of the sewing machine (1844). And the vast array of consumer goods that poured forth from the production of thousands of American factories could not flow to their users until a corresponding revolution had occurred in packaging and wholesaling.[15]

Machines that could reap grain, stitch cloth, and wrap consumer goods were but three examples of a profound worldwide revolution in productivity. This revolution substituted machine tools for human craftsmen, interchangeable parts for hand-tooled components, and the energy of coal for those of wood, water, and animals. The rising productivity, in turn, often brought overcapacity. The response, among businessmen in every industrial nation, was to combine with one another in schemes designed to limit the total output of their plants, maintain the price levels of their goods, and discourage the entry of new companies into their lines of business.

Such tendencies are discoverable in all industries, all countries, and all times. Adam Smith's famous description of the phenomenon was already trite when he made it in 1776: "People of the same trade seldom meet together, even for merriment and diversion, but the conversation ends in a conspiracy against the public, or in some contrivance to raise prices."[16] But the tendencies Smith observed seemed mild indeed when compared with the manic compulsions stimulated afterward by the revolution in productivity, which made the potential rewards of industrial success far greater than anything possible in Smith's era. It had the same magnifying effect on the potential cost of failure: the immense capital investment represented by a large modern factory or string of factories raised the penalty for failure beyond anything Smith could have contemplated. The collapse of, say, a large steel company would cost tens of millions of dollars in idled physical plant and would throw thousands of employees out of work. Thus industrialists felt a powerful urge to maintain a market for their products—if necessary by temporarily selling below costs, if possible by cooperating with each other for the mutual protection of capital.

Among European industrialists, this inclination to combine in self-defense against overcapacity led to very different results from those in the United States. Although the response was not precisely the same in every European country, governments there generally accepted business combinations as legitimate. European price and production cartels usually enjoyed official sanction, so that the legal machinery of the state could be used to enforce contractual articles of cartelization against rebellious price cutters. In Europe, therefore, with its large public bureaucracies long established, industrial overcapacity became simply another problem for a mature political state to manage. The official sanctioning of cartels provided a convenient way for national governments to prevent direct damage to individual firms and thus to soften and stabilize the otherwise wrenching process of industrialization.[17]

In Europe, typical political battles during the late nineteenth century pitted a fairly united business community against a powerful labor movement. In America, by contrast, the most conspicuous political warfare of that time matched *one group of businessmen against another:* carriers versus shippers, commodity farmers versus mortgage bankers, small wholesalers and shopkeepers against large firms whose marketing divisions were eliminating the traditional roles of local jobbers and retailers. The small size of the United States government, as compared to its European counterparts, meant that no adequate public bureaucracy existed to manage such industrial conflicts. (In 1871, on the eve of the trust movement, only 51,020 civilians worked for the federal government, of whom 36,696 were postal employees. The remaining 14,424 constituted the national government for a country whose population exceeded 40 million.) Under American conditions, the emerging problem of industrial overcapacity, compounded by the boom-and-bust business cycle, moved immediately into the realm of public controversy. To a degree often underestimated by scholars, overcapacity influenced nearly every major economic issue of the period: not only the trust question, but also the perennial and divisive battles over the protective tariff, the railroad rate problem, and the imperial quest for foreign markets to absorb surplus production.[18]

Even so, the initial response to industrial overcapacity took much the same form in America as in Europe. American businessmen, like their counterparts abroad, energetically combined with each other in loose cartels designed to limit production, maintain prices, and divide markets. These cartels were intended to protect all member companies from the fearful consequences of collective overcapacity. By preventing bankruptcies and by making mergers unnecessary, the cartels could preserve the individual identity of all cooperating companies. During the 1870s and 1880s, the number of formal and informal associations erected for this purpose within the United States numbered in the thousands. Seldom, however, did these early cartels accomplish their purpose because almost every one of them encountered legal obstacles. The national culture was so opposed to "monopoly" and "restraint of trade" that American courts refused to enforce cartel arrangements against recalcitrant members.[19] Thus, unlike their European counterparts, American businessmen participating in cartels were left free to cut their prices in violation of the cartel agreements or to sell their products outside geographic areas determined by the cartel. In 1890, passage of the Sherman Antitrust Act served to formalize the common law's hostility to cartels, as well as to compel the Department of Justice to become an active opponent of cartel-like associations. The Sherman Act soon began to have an enormous, if paradoxical, impact.

The New Vocabulary

To understand that impact, it is necessary to use certain terms of modern economic analysis. Before proceeding further with the story of the trust movement, it will be appropriate to pause briefly and investigate the meaning and application of this new economic vocabulary. It is important to remember that most of these terms did not originate with the trust movement. Instead, they have evolved over the years since passage of the Sherman Act, as part of an enormous effort of research in the fields of economics and business administration.

In applying such terms in historical analysis, we are something like modern astronomers studying the pre-Copernican theories of

Aristotle or Ptolemy. That is, we are testing the assumptions and insights of an earlier generation of observers through the use of methods developed in a subsequent scientific revolution to which they had no access. Although it may seem unfair to judge early twentieth-century observers by standards of economic reasoning they themselves did not fully comprehend, that price must be paid in return for our own understanding of the trust question. Even so, we should remember, in our effort to minimize the unfairness and achieve an appreciation of the problems faced by this earlier generation, that the movements and trends best described by the new vocabulary were not all equally prominent at the same time. At any given moment, some dominated the scene while others were latent. It is only through the double lenses of our own retrospect *and* the contemporaneous view that we are able to reach a mature historical evaluation of the elements involved in the trust question.

For us, the vocabulary essential to an understanding of that question has a minimum of seven relevant terms:

1. *Productive efficiency.* This term refers to the amount of work accomplished in relation to the effort expended. The underlying principle is common in mechanical engineering, as in the comparison that steam engines are more efficient than internal-combustion engines because they deliver more work per unit of fuel consumed. In economics, the meaning of productive efficiency is similar, but much broader. It includes anything that businesses can do to reduce the cost or improve the quality of their products, without any offsetting effect. Such changes may be organizational, technical, or of some other kind. One example of productive efficiency is machine mass production on assembly lines.[20]

2. *Allocative efficiency.* This term relates to the way in which an entire economy operates. In an allocatively efficient economy, no further rearrangement of prices, outputs, or distribution of goods and services can possibly make one consumer better off in terms of his own desires without making another worse off in terms of his. With the highest allocative efficiency, prices are set close to the marginal costs of production—that is, the cost of the last unit produced. Maximum allocative efficiency is equivalent to maximum "consumer welfare"; and in economic theory, any policy that promotes allocative efficiency and consumer welfare car-

ries a very strong favorable presumption. Similarly, any policy tending to diminish them should, if such a policy is to be justified, bring extremely beneficial offsetting effects of a noneconomic nature. Of course, allocative efficiency and consumer welfare apply chiefly to "economic man" and say little—at least directly—about aesthetic values, income distribution, ideological preferences, or any number of other legitimate human concerns. Even so, the concepts have important implications for practical politics as well as for theoretical economics: in modern times, high government regard for allocative efficiency and consumer welfare has been closely correlated with democracy; and low regard, with authoritarianism.[21]

3. *Scale economies.* There are two types of scale economies; in both, the larger the operation, the greater the productive efficiency. The first type is a *physical* scale economy, related to the amount or size of equipment used in a business operation. In the case of railroads, as Adams saw so clearly, the larger the number of cars in a given freight train, the lower the ton-per-mile cost of moving a given item of cargo. In some industries, such as oil refining (and others involving the flow of liquids or gases), economies of scale also derive from certain advantages in geometry. The volume of a pipe, for example, increases with the square of its radius. If the radius is doubled, the volume is quadrupled. Thus the bigger the pipe, the greater the productive efficiency, all other things being equal. The second type of scale economy is not physical but *organizational,* deriving from what Adam Smith called "the division of labor." It focuses on method rather than on equipment. The more particularized an operation is, the more efficiently it can be done by a specialized tool, machine, or skilled worker. The larger the undertaking, the more numerous and specialized its constituent labor force and machinery can be and, therefore, the greater the potential productive efficiency.

4. *Vertical integration.* This term refers to the gathering of many different business functions within a single firm. A company that conducts all of its business operations itself, ranging from the derivation of its raw materials to the selling of its finished manufactured products at retail, is said to have achieved complete vertical integration. A company's movement toward vertical integration almost always takes the form of incremental decisions to extend the functions performed by the existing business. An oil-refining

company, for example, might decide to purchase tank trunks for transporting its gasoline to market; later it also decides to build service stations from which the gasoline will be sold at retail. Both decisions represent vertical integration.

A fully integrated oil company would own exploration and production equipment for the finding and pumping of crude oil; tanker fleets and pipelines to transport it; refineries to turn it into gasoline, kerosene, and heating oil; tank trucks from which to wholesale these products; and service stations for sales to retail customers. The company would pursue this strategy of vertical integration in order to match its organizational scale economies with its physical ones. If the company did not integrate vertically, then the scale-economy potential in refining might be interrupted randomly by a host of unforeseen events: an abrupt stoppage of crude-oil supply, a sharp rise in its market price, the unavailability of transportation at a critical time, a collapse of the distribution system, or some other sudden bottleneck in the movement of the product from one stage to another. With vertical integration, on the other hand, every part of the operation (exploration, production, transportation, refining, wholesaling, retailing) would be matched in size to every other part, and the company's own managers would supervise the flow of oil through the system. A continuous movement of the product at constant speed and at declining costs of production should be assured.

Even so, vertical integration is not necessarily good for all companies. It seems to work well as a business strategy only for firms in those industries that possess a significant scale economy at some stage in the production or marketing process. A business integrates vertically for the purpose of ensuring that its advantage from the scale economy is maximized and not interrupted. But vertical integration can also become dangerous to the survival of a firm, since it has the disadvantage of putting all a company's eggs in one very large basket, and then risking that entire basket to the contingency of a declining market for its products.

5. *Horizontal combination.* This term signifies agreements among producers of a certain item: either to limit production of the item or to maintain its price level, or to do both. (The word "horizontal" refers to all participants' being in the same line of business, producing the same item; as opposed to "vertical," which refers to different business functions—production, whole-

saling, retailing, and so forth.) In the late nineteenth century, when manufacturers began to make use of the new technology and new sources of energy in their factories, shops, and refineries, they discovered to their astonishment that production had suddenly become the least of their worries. They could produce huge quantities of oil, steel, sewing machines, cigarettes, and hundreds of other items. But could they also sell this enormous new production? And, if so, could they still keep their prices up, even as vast quantities of their goods kept flowing onto the market? Many producers found an apparently affirmative answer to these questions in mutual cooperation—that is, one or another type of horizontal combination. On the surface, these associations seemed attractive. Yet horizontal combinations had two enormous flaws. Whereas they might help participating companies, they would hurt non-participating ones; even worse, they would reduce consumer welfare by creating artificial scarcities. Total output of specific products would be restricted, prices kept up, and allocative efficiency diminished.[22]

In practice, a particular horizontal combination might take one of several different forms. At its simplest, it consisted of an informal agreement among, say, all the coal dealers in a single city, who made a mutual promise not to sell a ton of coal below a certain minimum price. A more complex horizontal combination appeared in America as a European-style cartel—ten or twelve steel companies sharing output quotas and price agreements. The ultimate horizontal combination proved to be huge firms such as American Tobacco Company, which represented the final stage in a series of mergers that brought all important cigarette companies into one industry giant. This so-called tight form, involving actual mergers of corporate entities, became known as "horizontal integration." In fact, all horizontal integration involved horizontal combination, but not vice versa. Most horizontal combinations were not tight mergers, but loose associations of corporations that still retained their individual legal identities. The difference between loose horizontal combinations and tight ones turned out to be extraordinarily important.[23]

6. *Center firms.* This term denotes those new types of giant companies—such as Standard Oil, American Tobacco, United States Steel, and a few hundred others—that grew to large size *and remained large.*[24] These center firms tended to have a set of

common characteristics. All were capital-intensive, requiring very large outlays of investment. All were technologically advanced, in the sense that their production facilities were dominated either by continuous process production (Standard Oil, American Sugar Refining, United States Steel) or by some combination of large-batch production with machine mass production (Singer Sewing Machine, American Tobacco, Quaker Oats, Pillsbury Flour, International Harvester). Consequently, all center firms enjoyed some significant scale economy in the production or packaging process, and all were vertically integrated. Planning for the future, center firms also adopted an unusually long-range perspective. Because of the enormous investments required, survival was a far more important goal than was short-run profit. Accordingly, many center firms planned their business strategies on the basis of five-year horizons. In addition, many of them engaged in organized research and the development of new products. To manage their many internal functions, they began to organize complex managerial hierarchies.[25]

7. *Peripheral firms.* This term refers to companies that were small, labor-intensive, managerially thin, and bereft of scale economies. Concerned for survival, they looked more to this year's profits than to five-year plans. Peripheral firms, in other words, represented the opposite kind of company from center firms. The distinction between peripheral and center is not a perfect one, but the two terms may be considered as the polar ends of a spectrum: very pronounced differences are evident from one end of the spectrum to the other, but the differences become less dramatic toward the middle. The major point, however, is that center firms and peripheral firms represent two fundamentally different types of businesses.[26]

To be "peripheral" does not necessarily mean to be unimportant. Many peripheral firms are major sources of employment and thus vital to the national economy. Such industries as textiles, furniture, clothing, food service, building materials, hotels, and automobile repair are characterized by a large number of relatively small firms. These peripheral firms compete with each other very much in the fashion of Adam Smith's classical model, which remains the model of competition described in economics textbooks. Companies in these industries, along with numerous other kinds of peripherals—ranging from restaurants and family retail outlets to specialized parts manufacturers and subcontractors for the center firms—form the backbone of small business in all capitalist economies. These industries, like the companies in them, are also called peripheral, to distinguish them from such center industries as oil, steel, automobile manufacturing, and electrical machinery.[27]

The New Research

As we have noted, the modern discipline of economics has helped us to understand the rise of big business, especially by supplying some of the necessary vocabulary. But economic research has also displayed some important limitations. Despite advances in the subdiscipline of industrial organization, the economic theory of oligopoly is not yet mature. Mainstream theory still tends to assign too little significance to the gains in productive efficiency arising from changes in the forms of business organizations, including vertical integration.[28]

One very important contribution to research on center firms has come not from economics but from history, especially from the world's leading historian of business, Alfred D. Chandler, Jr. In a series of articles and books written from the 1950s to the 1980s, Chandler and his students have systematically examined the evolution of the business system in the United States and in other major capitalist economies. From this study of more than one thousand center firms has emerged an enormous body of information about their evolution, structure, business strategies, and methods of internal governance. The implications of Chandler's work are far-reaching, but its principal message is simple and forthright. The economist Robert Heilbroner described Chandler's Pulitzer Prize book, *The Visible Hand,* as "a major contribution to economics, as well as to 'business history,' because it provides powerful insights into the ways in which the imperatives of capitalism shaped at least one aspect of the business world—*its tendency to grow into giant companies in some industries but not in others.*"[29]

For a better understanding of the trust issue, three of Chandler's propositions are especially helpful. First, the industry structure characteristic of the American center economy evolved largely during the forty-year period between 1880 and 1920. The shakeout of center firms and peripheral firms into a more or less stable configuration did not end abruptly in 1920, but the major phase of this evolution was complete by that time. Evidence of a remarkable industrial stability may be found by comparing a list of the 200 largest U.S. manufacturing companies (measured in assets) in 1917 with a similar list for 1973:

a. In 1917, 22 of the largest 200 companies were in the petroleum business. In 1973, 22 of the largest 200 were still in petroleum. For the most part, they were the same 22.
b. In 1917, 5 of the largest 200 companies were in the rubber business. In 1973, 5 of the largest 200 were still in rubber. Four of these five were the same (Goodyear, Goodrich, Firestone, Uniroyal). The fifth, Fisk, merged with Uniroyal—then called United States Rubber—in 1939.
c. In 1917, 20 of the largest 200 companies were in the machinery business. In 1973, 18 of the largest 200 were still in machinery. For the most part, they were the same companies.
d. In 1917, 30 of the largest 200 companies were in the food products business. In 1973, 22 of the largest 200 were still in food products, and several other food companies remained in the top 200 as parts of conglomerates.
e. In 1917, 26 of the largest 200 companies were in the transportation equipment business. In 1973, 20 were still in transportation equipment (down, partly as a result of mergers, from 26 in 1948).[30]

These numbers suggest that the companies which succeeded initially in center industries later enjoyed a considerable advantage over firms entering the same industries. Their advantages included scale economies and lower unit costs achieved through long production runs. If the companies also rationalized their production process by concentrating operations in their lowest-cost plants— and most did just this—then their advantages increased even more. Finally, when the companies proceeded to integrate vertically, thereby protecting the advantages they already held in production, they became inordinately difficult for competitors to dislodge. Considering the numerical evidence, which shows that the companies maintained their position over a very long period, the fact of their continuing dominance becomes a historical phenomenon of enormous help in understanding the trust question.

A second proposition is that companies in every manufacturing industry attempted the same sort of growth strategy described above. That is, the movement toward horizontal integration was universally attractive. Firms in peripheral industries tried it as often as did those in center industries. Only the outcome proved different: unlike center firms, peripherals almost never succeeded. (*None* of the largest 200 companies in either 1917 or 1973, for example, was in furniture, printing, or similar peripheral industries.) Thus the difference between center and peripheral must be regarded as crucial to understanding the true nature of the trust question.[31]

A third proposition has to do with the evolution of business organizations in other countries. After having established that certain patterns characterized the structure of American industry in the twentieth century, Chandler went on to discover that the very same patterns obtain, with surprisingly few modifications, in other major market economies. These similarities appear despite different markets, political cultures, and sources of supply. The numbers cited above concerning the stable makeup of the largest 200 American manufacturing companies resemble comparable sets of numbers compiled for the same period in Germany, France, Britain, and Japan. Only the pace and timing of appearance vary, and even these do not differ radically. Furthermore, the pattern of industries themselves tends to be similar to that in the United States, as the following list shows:

	U.S. (192 companies)	*Abroad* (187 companies)
Center industries		
Transportation equipment	22	23
Electrical machinery	20	25
Stone, clay, and glass	7	8
Tobacco	3	4
Chemicals	24	28
Rubber	5	5
Petroleum	14	12
Peripheral industries		
Furniture	0	0
Printing	0	0

This list includes all manufacturing companies (worldwide) that as of 1973 had at least 20,000 employees. Approximately one half of the total of 379 were American firms, and half had their headquarters elsewhere.[32]

The striking similarities between industrial experience in the United States and in other market economies suggest strongly that the economic and technological characteristics of certain industries encourage them to assume either a center or peripheral configuration and to maintain that configuration over a long period of time. These characteristics now seem much more important than do differences in legal systems or national cultures; in fact they appear to determine the relative size and organizational structure of firms within the industries represented. This conclusion is of great importance to anyone interested in assessing the historical record of big business in the United States, a record that includes all attempts to regulate monopolistic "trusts."

The Old Assumptions

In the minds of many members of the generation that came to maturity during the 1880s and 1890s, the huge new companies we now call center firms seemed somehow unnatural. This generation, like all its predecessors, had grown up in an era occupied almost exclusively (the railroads being the sole exception) by what I have identified as peripheral firms. With their meager resources and lack of political power, such firms posed no threat whatever to the country's democratic heritage. The sudden appearance of center firms, on the other hand, brought novel and alarming practices: degradation of human labor in such industries as steel (where immigrant laborers put in 72-hour workweeks); unscrupulous manipulation of stocks and bonds in industries such as railroads and utilities (where "frenzied finance" seemed common); and abrupt losses of community control, not only over industries but over individual center firms, whose resources often dwarfed those of city and even state governments.

In the early years of industrialization, the trusts seemed to be mysterious mutations, the consequences of some evil tampering with the natural order of things. They were not merely economic freaks but also sinister new political forces—powers that had to be opposed in the name of American democracy. Such a conclusion seemed especially compelling once the ruthless, inhuman methods used in the formation of Standard Oil, American Tobacco, and other huge companies had reached public attention. Unlike loose cartels, which protected the interests of all participating companies, these tightly organized, horizontally and vertically integrated giants swallowed up numerous competitors and pushed aside traditional wholesalers and retailers. If the low prices of center firms brought unprecedented benefits to masses of consumers, then those same prices also injured large numbers of competing small producers, wholesalers, and retailers.

Yet the central assumption shared by most contemporary critics was simply that trusts were *unnatural*, the bastard offsprings of unscrupulous promoters. Without the benefit of experience and of a vocabulary that could clarify important distinctions in the business revolution—center firms compared with peripheral, productive efficiency compared with allocative, vertical integration compared with horizontal, and so on—those observers had only their personal sensibilities and traditional political ideologies to guide them. Both their personal and political values concerning the nature of liberty, the meaning of opportunity, and the promise of America seemed to be seriously threatened by the new monster trusts.

By about the middle of the 1880s, public sentiment in America had crystallized: something had to be done about trusts. Courts began to be more attentive to violations of common-law prohibitions against the collusive fixing of prices and planned limitations of output. In 1887, Congress created the Interstate Commerce Commission as a new means of dealing with the perennial railroad problem. Three years later, Congress passed the milestone Sherman Antitrust Act, which seemed clear, concise, and to the point. The Sherman Act declared illegal "every contract, combination in the form of trust or otherwise, or conspiracy, in restraint of trade or commerce." It defined as a criminal "every person who shall monopolize, or attempt to monopolize, or combine or conspire with any other person or persons, to monopolize any part of the trade or commerce among the several States, or with foreign nations."[33]

Despite the apparent clarity of the Sherman Act, however, its implementation raised severe difficulties. Unlike the Act to Regulate Commerce of 1887, the Sherman law set up no new regulatory commission or other machinery, but instead relied on the existing structure of government. Enforcement was vested in the federal Department of Justice, but the attorneys general of the 1890s showed little inclination to prosecute aggressively. When they did prosecute, their favored targets were not the feared center firms but local combinations of peripheral firms, whose price-fixing practices were easy to demonstrate. During the Sherman Act's first twenty years, by far the majority of prosecutions were aimed at loose cartels of small companies. The six or seven "big cases" of this period, however, did pertain to railroad combinations and to large trusts in sugar, beef, oil, and meatpacking. But in almost none of these cases did the court decison emerge in the form that antitrust advocates had hoped to see. The apparent clarity of the statutory language became lost in verbal uncertainties. Courts struggled with the meaning of such terms as "restraint of trade" and "monopolization"; and judges' opinions created a semantic confusion that persisted for years afterward. Soon the obvious ineffectiveness of early antitrust policy began to stimulate a new movement to do something more. Meanwhile, the severe economic depression of the 1890s added another note of urgency, and finally both the populists of that decade and the progressives of the early twentieth century made trust reform a pivotal and decidedly durable political issue. Indeed, the trust question dominated political discourse in America from the 1880s until the start of the First World War.[34]

CHAPTER 3

Brandeis and the Origins
of the FTC

THE FORMAL REGULATION of business combinations in America dates from the passage of the Sherman Antitrust Act of 1890. The Sherman law in practice proved an unclear guide: its broad language raised problems of interpretation and left both business managers and government officials uncertain as to which commercial practices were being prohibited. During the first decade of the twentieth century, proposals to revise the Sherman Act appeared from every quarter. Neopopulists wanted a tough law to break up existing trusts and prevent additional ones from forming. Executives of center firms sought greater reassurance about the legality of their operations. Managers of peripheral firms wanted guarantees of immunity from prosecution for their own cartel-like activities. Although these groups disagreed about the specific provisions desirable in new legislation, there developed a consensus that a special federal regulatory commission might be helpful in interpreting and administering antitrust policy.

Theodore Roosevelt admired the commission form of government, and as president he encouraged the formation in 1903 of the United States Bureau of Corporations. The bureau's elite staff of economists and lawyers soon began to produce extremely useful studies of such center firms as Standard Oil, American Tobacco, and International Harvester. In general, the bureau performed in the same type of sunshine-commission role pioneered by Charles Francis Adams in Massachusetts. Many of the bureau's admirers became convinced that its scope should be broadened. An "interstate trade commission," they believed, might combine the bureau's investigative activities with powerful new regulatory functions based on the model of the Interstate Commerce Commission. As the ICC oversaw railroads, the new trade commission would supervise manufacturing, wholesaling, and retailing. When Roosevelt once more ran for the presidency in 1912, his Progressive Party platform called for just such an agency.

Some Democrats also favored an interstate trade commission. The influential Senator Francis Newlands of Nevada, for example, introduced a commission bill in 1911 and worked diligently but unsuccessfully for its passage. Other Democrats, suspicious of bureaucratic government and fearful that a commission might indirectly accord legitimacy to big business, looked askance at Newlands' idea. One of these doubting Democrats was Governor Woodrow Wilson of New Jersey.

In the presidential election of 1912, Wilson defeated Progressive Theodore Roosevelt and Republican incumbent William Howard Taft, who took a pro-commission position less enthusiastic than that of Roosevelt. During the election campaign, Wilson departed from his anti-commission stance and supported the creation of a sunshine agency, to be coupled with tough and explicit new antitrust laws. But once in office, Wilson found it hard to decide on the shape of his antitrust program. Not until 1914 did he launch a two-part legislative package: one part would clarify the ambiguities of the Sherman Act through a specific enumeration of forbidden practices; the other would create a new regulatory agency. Finally, late in 1914, the Federal Trade Commission emerged, as a hybrid of proposals from Roosevelt, Newlands, and certain of Wilson's own advisers.

No individual person played the role of "father" of the Federal Trade Commission, in the sense that Charles Francis Adams had fathered the Massachusetts Board of Railroad Commissioners. In truth, the FTC had many parents, but it captured the special attention of none. Troubled in infancy, awkward in adolescence, clumsy in adulthood, the agency never found a coherent mission for itself. Nor did any of the early FTC commissioners exhibit the vigor and intelligence that Adams had shown in Massachusetts. By common agreement of modern scholars, the FTC has been a singularly unsuccessful agency during most of the seventy-odd years since its creation. The primary reason behind this dolorous history has been identified as the persistent confusion and ambiguity of American public policy toward competition—the very problem that the FTC Act was intended to solve.

Insofar as the career of a single person illustrates both the problems that led to the FTC's creation and the reasons for its subsequent failure, that person is Louis D. Brandeis. The most influential critic of trusts during his generation, Brandeis served from 1912 until 1916 as Woodrow Wilson's chief economic adviser and was regarded as one of the architects of the FTC. Above all else, Brandeis exemplified the anti-bigness ethic without which there would have been no Sherman Act, no antitrust movement, and no Federal Trade Commission.

The Man and the Legend

As the "people's lawyer" of the Progressive Era, Brandeis embodied the popular revolt against the sudden domination of the nation's economic life by big business. His career as a practicing lawyer, which began in 1878 and ended with his appointment to the Supreme Court in 1916, coincided almost precisely with the principal phase of the rise of center firms, which occurred between about 1880 and 1920. Brandeis watched the business revolution as it developed, tried his best to understand it, and found it, on the whole, hostile to his own values of autonomous individualism. For that reason he fought it, and in his crusades against what he called the "curse of bigness" he was a formidable champion.

Several different forces in his background shaped Brandeis' individualistic values. Eight years before his birth in 1856, his Bohemian Jewish parents had fled Europe during the suppression of the democratic movements of 1848. Settling in Louisville, Kentucky, the family prospered in the grain-merchandising business but suffered setbacks during the depression of the 1870s. Louis Brandeis, an intellectually gifted child, was educated at the German and English Academy in Louisville and, later, when the depression in America drove the family temporarily back to Europe, at the Annen-Realschule in Dresden. He entered Harvard Law School in 1875, at the age of eighteen, and made a phenomenal record. Because he finished the standard course of study at Harvard before he reached twenty-one, a special ruling was required to allow him to graduate. A year later, in 1878, a fellow student wrote a letter to his mother describing the young Brandeis:

He graduated last year from Law School and is now taking a third year here—was the leader of his class and one of the most brilliant legal minds

they have ever had here—and is but little over twenty-one withal. Hails
from Louisville—is not a College graduate, but has spent many years in
Europe, has a rather foreign look, and is currently believed to have some
Jew blood in him, though you would not suppose it from his appearance—Tall, well-made, dark, beardless, and with the brightest eyes I
ever saw. Is supposed to know everything and to have it always in mind.
The Profs. listen to his opinions with the greatest deference, and it is
generally correct. There are traditions of his omniscience floating
through the School. One I heard yesterday—A man last year lost his
notebook of Agency lectures. He hunted long and found nothing. His
friends said—Go and ask Brandeis . . .—he knows everything—perhaps
he will know where your book is—He went and asked. Said Brandeis—
"Yes—go into the Auditor's room, and look on the west side of the room,
and on the sill of the second window, and you will find your book"—And
it was so.[1]

Thus the Brandeis literature began as hagiography, and it continued in that vein for a hundred years, until the 1980s.[2] In many respects it resembles the Lincoln literature, and indeed the two men
have often been compared: Kentucky origins, self-made success,
even physical resemblance—their craggy, quizzical features, their
disorderly hair, their deep-set bright eyes.

Substantial biographies began to accumulate long before Brandeis' death in 1941, and in the years afterward there came a flood
of writing, nearly all of it elaborating on the established legend.
Despite this mass of scholarship, a few mysteries lingered. Why,
for example, would a mild-mannered, privacy-loving commercial
lawyer, having made his fortune, abruptly turn in middle age into
a merciless muckraker? Or why, having never paid much attention
to religion or to his own ethnicity, would Brandeis in his middle
fifties suddenly embrace Zionism with such zeal that he became
the national leader of the movement? The answers to these questions came only when Brandeis' personal papers were made
widely available to scholars.[3] In 1971, thirty years after his death,
the first two volumes of his collected letters appeared, and by 1978
the remaining three volumes. For a number of scholars, these
papers were a treasure; their publication represented an event
that would illuminate the history of American Zionism, American
reform, and the character and career of Brandeis himself. It was
thought that the collected letters might force open the last unknown chambers of his life.[4]

What they in fact showed was that Brandeis had been much less a man of thought than of action. None of the letters conveyed the impression of a deep conceptual intelligence. In them there was little evidence of reflection, none of rumination. There was no Adams-like agonizing over one's proper role in life or relationship with God, no self-doubt on any score. Instead, the letters depicted a quick, confident, and often rigid mind preoccupied with some immediate practical task—a controlled, carefully managed life with no wasted motion, little humor, and no frivolity.[5]

Brandeis held himself aloof from other men. He encouraged awe and veneration, and he seemed impossible to know well. As Harold Laski once remarked, he was "not quite human in his contacts." Didactic and moralistic, he liked to instruct his wife, daughters, and others around him as to how they should live. For both his intimates and the outside world, he deliberately cultivated a particular image for himself, and he shaped his behavior in service to that image. As the editors of his letters put it, Brandeis "understood how to behave like a symbol." Today we see something of what that symbol represented. For Brandeis almost perfectly embodies some of the best and the worst elements in the American regulatory tradition. On the one hand, he epitomized the dogged militancy which has given that tradition its distinctive sense of righteousness and moral passion. On the other, Brandeis offered regulatory solutions grounded on a set of economic assumptions that were fundamentally wrong.[6]

After graduation from law school, Brandeis associated himself in practice with Samuel D. Warren, a classmate whose wealth and family connections provided a ready clientele as well as entry into Boston social circles. Brandeis himself, with all his brilliance and his new Harvard connections, was yet a young Jew from Louisville, and Boston was one of the most snobbish and ingrown of American cities. As a social outsider, he could afford no false steps. "I wish to become known as a practicing lawyer," he wrote Warren. "I wish to wait particularly for your letter giving the results of our examination of the prospects of a young law firm and more particularly your own prospects of securing business through your social and financial position." The firm of Warren and Brandeis enjoyed immediate success, in part because its first client was the paper-manufacturing company owned by the Warren family.[7]

Brandeis' continued prosperity, however, depended not on the Warren connection but on his own drive and ability. Both were of the highest order. At Harvard, where he compiled what is still the best record in the law school's history, he had written of his "desperate longing for more law" and of the "almost ridiculous pleasure which the discovery or invention of a legal theory gives me." He referred to the law as his "mistress," holding a grip on him that he could not break.[8] This passionate attachment served him well. In his career as a litigator, Brandeis became one of the most effective advocates the United States has ever produced. He had all the requisite talents: the persistent inquisitiveness, the quick study, the drive to win, the skepticism, the sympathetic style, the love of combat. He had two even more useful qualities. The first was a remarkable ability to convey a sense of the rightness of his client's cause. As one of his partners put it, "The prime source of his power was his intense belief in the truth of what he was saying. It carried conviction."[9]

The second quality was the very close attention he gave to the care of clients. "Cultivate the society of men—particularly men of affairs," Brandeis once advised a young associate in his firm. "A lawyer who does not know men is handicapped ... Every man that you know makes it to that extent easier to practice, to accomplish what you have in hand." Brandeis himself took great pains to know men. During his early years in Boston, he kept a small notebook in which he listed the names of everyone he met at social gatherings. Gradually he accumulated dozens of thick scrapbooks on all sorts of personal, legal, and political subjects. "Perhaps most important of all," he emphasized to his young associate, "is the impressing of clients and satisfying them. Your law may be perfect, your ability to apply it great and yet you cannot be a successful advisor unless your advice is followed; it will not be followed unless you can satisfy your clients."[10]

Brandeis' careful development of his lawyerly skills reflected a characteristically shrewd management of his own career. "Know thoroughly each fact," he remonstrated in a memorandum to himself on the practice of law. "Don't believe client witness. Examine documents. Reason; use imagination. Know bookkeeping—the universal language of business: know persons. Far more likely to impress clients by knowledge of facts than by knowledge of law. Know not only specific case, but whole subject. Can't otherwise know the facts. Know not only those facts which bear on direct controversy, but know all facts and law that surround." Brandeis' emphasis on facts became a minor legend in itself, an important part of the sociological jurisprudence he advocated later in his career. "It has been one of the rules of my life," he once told a newspaper reporter, "that no one shall ever trip me up on a question of fact." Brandeis advised the young associate in his firm that the person "who practices law—who aspires to the higher places of his profession—must keep his mind fresh. It must be alert and he must be capable of meeting emergencies—must be capable of the tour de force." No American lawyer has ever been more capable of the tour de force than was Brandeis himself.[11]

Brandeis' love for the advocacy system contrasted vividly with the opposite reaction of Charles Francis Adams, who still served as chairman of the Board of Railroad Commissioners when Brandeis began his law practice in Boston. Adams had abandoned the practice of law to concentrate his attention on the railroads. Year after year, he plodded through statistical tables and other documents, accumulating vast amounts of information. He wrote books, articles, and annual reports on different aspects of this one industry. Adams' single tour de force, "A Chapter of Erie," came early in his career, and his second thoughts as a regulator rebuked the recommendations implicit in his great article. Whereas Adams preferred to conceptualize about broad policies, Brandeis, as a practicing lawyer, focused on particular episodes. Whereas Adams tended to think in generalizations and to seek methods of accommodating divergent points of view to one general public interest, Brandeis thought in terms of immediate cases and controversies and sought victory for his client's interest at the expense of all others. (As one prominent member of the Boston bar wrote of Brandeis' intense competitiveness, "He fights to win, and fights up to the limit of his rights with a stern and even cruel exultation in the defeat of his adversary."[12]) As a busy attorney, Brandeis went rapidly from case to case, on a schedule set not by his own choice but by the dockets of courts and commissions. He became, as trial lawyers must, a quick expert on many different subjects: now railroads, now trusts, now conservation, now banking, now labor, now retailing. Of necessity, the expertise so rapidly acquired seldom ran very deep. Consequently, Brandeis never understood big business—the target of his crusades—so well as Adams understood railroads.

As an outsider and a Jew, Brandeis did not attract the largest clients available to Boston law firms. These were the major banks and insurance companies, the railroads headquartered in the city, and the new giant manufacturing firms arising from the reorganizations and mergers of the period. His typical clients were not center firms, but peripherals: small and medium-sized manufacturers of boots, shoes, and paper, along with prominent Jewish wholesalers and retailers such as the Hechts and the Filenes. Following his own advice, Brandeis came to know these clients intimately. He impressed them with his factual knowledge of their businesses, and they employed him as counselor and adviser on a wide range of legal and business problems. Ultimately, this work on their behalf made him a millionaire. In turn, Brandeis also became identified politically with their interests; and much in his later campaigns as the "people's lawyer"—particularly his approach to the antitrust question—can be traced back to the problems and interests of these clients.[13]

The most striking thing about Brandeis' triumphs as the people's lawyer was his almost extrasensory instinct for the winning ground. Here, time after time, he showed himself capable of the tour de force. He won his cases repeatedly, often against heavy odds, and the reputation for winning in turn became an essential element of the emerging Brandeis mystique. This talent for finding the winning ground, present in many great lawyers, in Brandeis reached extremely pronounced form, as several of his best known cases show. Three of these were *Muller v. Oregon* (1908), the Ballinger-Pinchot controversy (1910), and the Advance Rate Case before the Interstate Commerce Commission (1910). Together, these three episodes made him a celebrated national figure. In each, he deftly shifted the terms of the dispute away from his clients' weak points and onto novel ground. In all three situations, he caught the opposition by surprise, and in each he won the case.

The Winning Ground

In *Muller v. Oregon*, Brandeis defended the power of the state to enact a law limiting women's hours of work. The case represented a clash of two constitutional principles: on the one hand, freedom of contract, under which a worker and an employer could agree on any schedule of work, without limit; on the other, the right of a state to enact regulatory legislation for which it had a reasonable and not arbitrary basis. Three years earlier, in *Lochner v. New York* (1905), the Supreme Court had enunciated an extreme form of freedom of contract by overturning a statute that limited the working hours of New York bakers to ten per day. The controlling precedent, therefore, seemed squarely against the state of Oregon.[14]

In defense of the Oregon statute, Brandeis shifted the focus of argument away from the law of contract, on which basis he could not win. Instead, he took the radical step of arguing on the grounds of statistical, sociological, and medical information concerning the physical consequences of overwork. If he could persuade the Supreme Court to accept his novel forms of evidence, he might win. One part of his brief before the court (pages 1–24) explored the relevant legal precedents and argument. But a much larger part (pages 24–113, which became famous in legal circles as the "Brandeis brief") detailed the testimony of numerous experts on the effects of overwork. In all, Brandeis cited or quoted from over ninety reports from American and European factory inspectors, commissioners of hygiene, and other authorities.[15] Some of Brandeis' evidence in the *Muller* case strikes modern ears as a bit odd: "Long hours of labor are dangerous for women primarily because of their special physical organization." But the evidence showed clearly that the state had reasonable grounds on which to legislate. And from the time of *Muller* down to the present day, Brandeis' "sociological jurisprudence" has exercised a profound influence on the development of American law.[16]

In a second case, Brandeis found a different kind of winning ground: management of publicity to discredit a political leader. This was in the Ballinger-Pinchot affair, the most sensational controversy of the Progressive Era. The case kept Brandeis in the national spotlight for much of the year 1910, and it confirmed his growing reputation as a legal magician.

The Ballinger-Pinchot dispute grew out of a disagreement over natural resources policy among former lieutenants of Theodore Roosevelt after his departure from the White House in 1909. Eventually the controversy precipitated a split between Roosevelt and his chosen successor, William Howard Taft. It thereby contributed to the Republican schism of 1912 and the third-party candidacy of Roosevelt. The battle of Ballinger versus Pinchot proceeded on several levels at once: as a dispute between warring

Republican bureaucrats; as a harbinger of the Roosevelt-Taft split; and, because of Brandeis' genius for publicity, as a holy crusade of good against evil.[17]

The affair began when Louis Glavis, a young employee of the Department of the Interior, went to his supervisor, Secretary Richard A. Ballinger, with a report that certain mining claims involving the wealthy Guggenheim family might be illegal. Ballinger, who had once done some legal work for the Guggenheims, dismissed Glavis' charges as unfounded. Glavis then took his tale to Chief Forester Gifford Pinchot, a holdover from the previous Roosevelt Administration and a symbol of Roosevelt's widely admired conservation policies. Pinchot, never one to miss an opportunity to score against an opponent, now brought Glavis' charges to the attention of President Taft. This act moved the issue beyond the mining claims and toward the question of Secretary Ballinger's integrity.[18]

Taft responded by asking Ballinger for an explanation. The secretary went to see Taft at the president's summer home, taking along numerous documents bearing on the mining claims. Taft accepted Ballinger's explanation and in a long letter authorized him to dismiss Glavis for insubordination. Next Glavis, stung by his firing and egged on by officials within Pinchot's Forest Service, took his story to *Collier's Weekly*, a popular magazine that specialized in muckraking stories. *Collier's* editor Norman Hapgood, a friend and political ally of Brandeis, printed Glavis' article. (The cover of this issue depicted Secretary Ballinger in the middle of a large question mark with the caption, "Are the Guggenheims in Charge of the Department of the Interior?") An ensuing barrage of articles in newspapers and other magazines attacked Ballinger and focused public attention on the upcoming conservation hearings in Congress. Now facing possible action for libel, the publisher of *Collier's* hired Brandeis to defend the magazine. By this circuitous route, Brandeis appeared before the congressional committee as Glavis' attorney. Meanwhile, Pinchot heaped more fuel on the fire by ostentatiously challenging Taft and forcing the president to fire him from the post of chief forester.[19]

In his role as Glavis' lawyer, Brandeis in effect was opposing Secretary Ballinger, President Taft, and Attorney General George Wickersham, who had advised Taft on the firing of Glavis. Unfortunately for Brandeis, a close examination of the evidence and of

Ballinger's record as secretary yielded little ammunition for the Glavis-Pinchot-*Collier's* forces. The secretary was a capable public servant who would not be easy to discredit. But Brandeis found Glavis to be an articulate, appealing underdog who might excel on the witness stand, if only some focus could be provided for the contention that Ballinger was dishonest.[20]

The necessary focus materialized when Brandeis discovered that members of the opposition had made a colossal error. They had antedated an important document pertaining to Taft's investigation of Glavis' original charges and had concealed the existence of a second such document. Brandeis decided to play out this discovery in small increments and thereby maximize the suspense. By shrewd management, periodic leaks to the press, and relentless questioning of witnesses, he gradually shifted the focus of the hearings from conservation policy and the propriety of Ballinger's conduct of the mining investigation to the honesty and integrity not only of Ballinger but also of Attorney General Wickersham and even of President Taft. The revelations about the antedating, which had little to do with the original issues but were intensely embarrassing to the administration, now became a national scandal, reported and embellished day after day by delighted journalists. Brandeis' management of the case, coupled with Ballinger's clumsy efforts to defend the administration, ended in total vindication of Glavis and Pinchot. Glavis proved "an extraordinary witness," Brandeis observed with pleasure. "Have never seen his equal." Ballinger and Wickersham, on the other hand, "fell into every trap set."[21]

Sensing that the real jury was not a congressional committee but public opinion, Brandeis saw to it that the affair received wide publicity. He sent copies of his argument to numerous editors, provided summaries to reporters, and tried (unsuccessfully) to persuade the popular columnist Finley Peter Dunne to write a "Mr. Dooley" piece against Ballinger, Wickersham, and Taft. Brandeis also discussed with Pinchot how best to use the controversy to prevent President Taft's renomination. Meanwhile, Richard Ballinger, though innocent of the original accusations and officially exonerated by Congress, resigned from office more or less in disgrace. He lived out his life in bitterness, unable to change the image of corruption that clung to him and quickly entered the history textbooks. Louis Glavis, who started it all, fared little better. As the years passed he revealed himself as a mercurial, unreliable character, both in private life and in government service during the New Deal.[22]

The fairest verdict on the Ballinger-Pinchot controversy has been provided by the historian James Penick: "Ballinger had to be labeled a 'high-toned crook' or there would have been no contest. 'If they had brazenly admitted everything,' Brandeis said, 'and justified it on the ground that Ballinger was at least doing what he thought best, we should not have had a chance.' It was the lying that did it, he added." On the role of Brandeis, Penick goes on to say that the Boston lawyer "was too astute to fail to recognize the true basis for the vindication of Glavis' contention that Ballinger was a dishonest public servant; but he was too much the servant of an adversary system to find the truth it revealed very peculiar."[23]

In a third celebrated episode, Brandeis surpassed even his Ballinger-Pinchot performance. This was in the so-called Advance Rate Case before the Interstate Commerce Commission. The case began in 1910, when American railroads petitioned the ICC for an across-the-board increase in freight rates. The railroads alleged that their costs had risen rapidly because of much higher labor costs and inflationary pressures. Shipping interests hired Brandeis to oppose the railroads' petition, and he embraced their cause with great vigor. He identified them with the entrepreneurial firms he had long represented in Boston, some of which were significant shippers chronically involved in New England rate controversies. Also, Brandeis' father, a Louisville merchant, had dealt regularly with railroads, and Brandeis' brother Alfred was one of that city's major shippers of grain.

The national railroads, on the other hand, were sprawling interstate business giants. Several employed more than 100,000 persons, and the industry as a whole was widely regarded as unduly wealthy and powerful. If there were a "curse of bigness," American railroads were among the most cursed institutions in the world. Their request in 1910 for the rate increase was neither well timed nor well managed. Indeed, the very idea of a jointly requested across-the-board increase for all railroad corporations (the profitable along with the unprofitable) and for all items of cargo (money makers and money losers) seemed to reflect a political arrogance that had characterized the industry since the 1850s. Yet in retrospect it is clear that the railroads did need a rate increase.

Their costs were rising because of inflation and spiraling wages, and their roadbeds were deteriorating under pressures of extremely heavy traffic. The railroads' attorneys and financial officers presented a strong case before the ICC for a rate increase, buttressing their argument with page after page of persuasive statistical analysis.[24]

Brandeis' response, breathtaking in its boldness, took opposition lawyers completely by surprise. He readily conceded that the railroad companies needed much more money. But he insisted that the proper source was not higher rates for shippers, but lower internal operating costs for the companies themselves. In his brief before the ICC, Brandeis stated: "As an alternative to the railroads' practice of combining to increase rates we offer cooperation to reduce costs. Instead of a dangerous makeshift, we offer constructive policy—scientific management, under which as costs fall wages rise."[25]

As his most telling point, Brandeis impressed on the commissioners the "fact" that the railroads were operating inefficiently. The companies, he said, were ignoring "scientific management," a series of new techniques associated with Frederick Winslow Taylor, Harrington Emerson, and Frank Gilbreth (Gilbreth was later made famous in the book *Cheaper by the Dozen*, an affectionate reminiscence written by two of his children). Taylor and other "efficiency experts" enjoyed huge popularity during the Progressive Era. Their methods had already brought productivity gains to a number of manufacturing firms. When Brandeis called several of the experts to the witness stand, they made the most of this free publicity as an unpaid advertisement for their consulting services. And with their help Brandeis spun out, day by day, a tale of miracles, of almost certain efficiencies that would accrue from the railroads' conversion to the new system:

Scientific Management [said Brandeis] differs from that now generally practiced by the railroads, much as production by machinery differs from production by hand . . . Under scientific management nothing is left to chance. All is carefully prepared in advance. Every operation is to be performed according to a predetermined schedule under definite instructions, and the execution under this plan is inspected and supervised at every point. Errors are prevented instead of being corrected. The terrible waste of delays and accidents is avoided. Calculation is substituted for guess; demonstration for opinion. The high efficiency of the limited passenger trains is sought to be obtained in the ordinary operations of the business. The same preparedness is invoked for industry which secured to Prussia her victory over France and to Japan her victory over Russia.[26]

As if all these remarkable results were not enough in themselves, Brandeis promised one final miracle. With his uncanny sense for the winning ground and ear for the catchy idiom, Brandeis elicited from expert witness Harrington Emerson the opinion that, under scientific management, the nation's railroads could save "at least $1,000,000 a day." This million-dollars-a-day slogan was taken up and broadcast throughout the country by newspapers. Cited again and again during the rate hearings, it took on a life of its own. Ultimately it seemed to be made true by virtue of endless repetition. Once more, Brandeis won his case. The ICC refused to give the railroads an additional penny.[27]

In retrospect, what seems to have determined this peculiar outcome was the fact that, while the ICC and the interested electorate wanted a reliable transportation system and were persuaded that the railroads needed more money, they did not want to give the railroads a rate increase. Brandeis provided the only possible resolution of this dilemma by discovering the million dollars a day waiting to be harvested through scientific management. It was a master stroke. Although American railroad corporations included some of the most efficient organizations in the world at that time, they nevertheless could not possibly prove themselves unable to save that much money. Appealing to scientific management, an idea very much in the air in 1910 and 1911, Brandeis turned it against a despised industry and thereby rescued the ICC from an uncomfortable predicament.

Later on, railroad men and some disinterested analysts as well complained that Brandeis had simply dazzled the ICC and the public with promises of miraculous savings. Subsequent events in the railroad industry all but proved that scientific management had much less relevance for transportation and other service industries than it did for manufacturing. In fact, Brandeis himself gave little mention to scientific management during a second rate case he conducted for the ICC only a few years later, in 1914. By that time the efficiency craze had begun to wane and the railroads were in deep trouble.[28] And by the time of the war emergency of 1917–18, the railroads had fallen into such desperate financial straits that the federal government temporarily took over the entire industry. After a brief study, the government instituted by fiat very large across-the-board rate hikes of about the size of the combined increases the railroads themselves had requested in the years between 1910 and 1918. It would have been hard to devise a clearer demonstration of the insubstantiality of Brandeis' argument of 1910.[29]

The rabbit-from-hat character of all three of Brandeis' celebrated victories foreshadowed the kinds of arguments he would make later against big business. There too he often substituted slogans for careful analysis. In his rhetoric against the trusts he appealed, as always, to the best moral instincts of his various audiences. But at the same time he misled them, perhaps unintentionally, about the practicability of his remedies. Unlike Charles Francis Adams, Brandeis never made the transition from muckraker to administrator, at least before his appointment to the Supreme Court. At the crucial moment in 1914, when the Wilson Administration's antitrust program bore fruit in the Federal Trade Commission, Brandeis declined the seat Wilson offered him on the commission. More important, in the legislative maneuverings that preceded the FTC Act, Brandeis' sloganeering and his almost willful refusal to rethink the trust problem contributed to the institutionalization of a confused and contradictory regulatory program, one that stood almost no chance of working.

Brandeis Interprets the Evolution of the Trusts

Brandeis first became seriously interested in the trust question during the economic depression of the 1890s. A major influence on his thinking was Henry Demarest Lloyd's *Wealth Against Commonwealth*, a muckraking analysis of the Standard Oil Company. Brandeis' correspondence with a reviewer of Lloyd's book illustrates a characteristic focus on the small businessman rather than on the consumer and also a sophisticated understanding of methods for molding public opinion. "I cannot quite agree," Brandeis wrote, "that 'Wealth against Commonwealth' is the 'Uncle Tom's Cabin' of the industrial movement." While the book had great merit, Lloyd had not pitched the argument to a sufficiently broad audience. "The great trouble with the efforts against the trusts," Brandeis went on to say, is "that these efforts are not backed by the people. The American must be educated. The man who has consciously suffered from the trust is the individual competitor, and, in some instances, the producer. The public as a whole have perhaps suffered in many instances, but not suffered consciously. Our people still admire the Captains of the trusts." In his own muckraking, Brandeis never left any doubt about who was suffering or why the captains must not be admired.[30]

At about the same time he wrote this letter, Brandeis was preparing a series of lectures for a course on business law at the Massachusetts Institute of Technology. As a topic, he chose the trusts, and the unpublished text of his lectures offers an unusually precise measure of his understanding. "The term 'trust,'" he began, "is commonly used in a broad, and perhaps inaccurate, sense as including all kinds of combinations of concerns engaged in the same line of business." The combination might use territorial restriction as a method of limiting competition, or it might use some other means. Whatever the means, the end was clear: "Its general purpose is usually and mainly one of monopoly and the difference is merely the extent to which it is carried out."[31]

In the text of his lecture notes, Brandeis went on to describe four different varieties of trusts and to argue that, all together, these four had evolved sequentially. The first class, he wrote, "presents the cases of several competing manufacturers, producers or traders agreeing not to sell their product below certain prices." In this variety of horizontal combination, historically the first to appear in America, the agreements were informal: participants posted a deposit of money to be forfeited in case of violation, and a grievance committee adjudicated disagreements. Such a method of combination through contract was clearly in restraint of trade and therefore unenforceable at common law. Yet it appealed to Brandeis because it offered members "absolute freedom" in the management of their businesses in all areas except those covered by the agreement.[32]

The second class of trusts Brandeis identified "is presented by agreement creating some central body, created with the design of equalizing prices," and administered by "some neutral party, as trustee, committee or corporation." Brandeis noted that this form of trust often materialized as a "joint selling agency" in such industries as salt, lumber, and coal. (In modern terms, each of these was a peripheral industry with numerous individual competitors, low entry barriers, and no great economies of scale.[33])

"The third class of trade combinations," Brandeis continued, "is

the trust proper . . . all of the stockholders in a corporation trans-
fer all of their stock to certain individuals, generally three or more,
as trustees. These individuals then holding the stock, possess the
voting power of the stock, and have the absolute power to elect
any officers they please . . . These trustees then determine whether
the factory of one of these corporations shall be run or not; they
purchase the goods and sell the goods for all the corporations, and
as you have this unity of management, there is no possibility of a
breach of agreement. This was the original form of the Standard
Oil Trust and the Sugar Trust." And this was the kind of combination that Brandeis himself detested, because it interfered with the
autonomy of the small independent businessmen who were absorbed into the trust.[34]

From our own vantage point, looking back nearly a hundred
years after Brandeis' analysis, it is clear that this third type of
horizontal combination worked well only in center industries. To
be viable as a trust, a company must be located in an industry with
strong economies of scale. To the extent that a trust's primary aim
was to control prices by limiting output, it tended to distort allocative efficiency. On the other hand, because such organizations
concentrated their production in their most efficient plants, they
increased productive efficiency. Very often, too, a company's assumption of the trust form presaged vertical integration by the
same company, and this process brought additional economies.
For all of these reasons, the net effect over time of "trustification"
in any given industry might well be the reduction of prices and the
enhancement of consumer welfare. But in Brandeis' time, these
long-term economic effects were difficult to foresee. For Brandeis
himself, the economic effects mattered far less than the social and
political ones. He focused not on increases in consumer welfare
but on decreases in the autonomy of small producers.

The fourth class of combination that Brandeis analyzed was an
actual merger of many companies into "one huge corporation." In
this tightest form of combination, he observed, "all semblance of
individual activity is removed. This is the form of the Diamond
Match Company, of the present Sugar Trust, the Standard Oil and
other trusts." Brandeis noted, quite accurately, that the four-stage
evolution "has been historical, in the order mentioned, and you
will see how the law hastened this development."[35] What had
started out as loose federations based on mutual agreement soon

succumbed to self-interest, as one or another member of the federation (types one and two in Brandeis's taxonomy) broke the agreement out of personal economic hardship. Meanwhile, the other parties to the agreement had no legal recourse against the violators. So these combinations nearly always disintegrated. As Brandeis put it, "You see in all the cases I have referred to, the combinations were broken up by virtue of civil remedies, that is, by denying to the parties the ability to enforce legally their contracts, or to maintain their organization." In this way, American law actually promoted tight combination, and Brandeis found that fact singularly unfortunate.[36]

In the text of his lectures, he explained the law's role in this process. When loose agreements did break down, he wrote, the parties entered tighter combinations such as his categories three and four. And even category three, the trust proper, sometimes ran afoul of the limitations of what a corporation could do legally under its charter. The only remaining step was category four: the tight combination, achieved through merger or acquisition of formerly competing firms into one huge enterprise. In other words, the legal limitation on loose combinations promoted tighter combinations. Brandeis regarded this result as extremely objectionable.[37]

On the whole, Brandeis was very perceptive in his analysis of the trust movement. But he erred in one important particular because he failed to take into account the nature of different types of industries. The evolution of corporate organizations from stage one to stage four occurred only on a limited scale; and many combinations that made it to stages one and two never progressed any further. Brandeis did not see it this way. Indeed, it is much clearer now than it could have been at the time that the combination movement progressed not in one but in two separate and distinct patterns—a reflection of the fundamental differences between center and peripheral industries. Companies in center industries went through all four stages; those in peripheral industries moved through only the first two, then ran up against insuperable barriers if they tried to go farther. Among center firms, Standard Oil pioneered the movement with its trust of 1882. This was followed by the American Cotton Oil Trust in 1884, the National Linseed Oil Trust in 1885, and the Distillers and Cattle Feeders Trust ("Whiskey Trust") in 1887. The greatest wave of actual mergers came in the period 1897–1904, during which 4,227 American firms merged into 257 combinations. By 1904, some 318 trusts—most of which were center firms—were alleged to control two fifths of the nation's manufacturing assets.[38]

Companies in almost all manufacturing industries attempted this sort of four-stage horizontal combination. A large number of such attempts failed, however, despite very capable management and despite everything financiers and others could do to save them. These numerous failures are vitally important to our understanding of the historical and economic patterns of the combination movement. Fundamentally, the architects of failed trusts had tried to construct center firms in peripheral industries, and this proved impossible. All of the successful center firms—Standard Oil, Carnegie Steel, American Tobacco, United Shoe Machinery, National Biscuit—possessed major economies of scale. All of them had vertically integrated structures, with highly organized functional divisions. Most of these companies combined mass production with mass marketing. By contrast, the unsuccessful trusts—Standard Rope and Twine, United States Leather, United States Button, American Glue, American Cattle, National Novelty, National Wallpaper, National Starch, National Salt, National Cordage—could claim no major scale economies. Size in their case proved to be disadvantageous. The industries to which they belonged were peripherals, with low capital requirements and few other entry barriers. Only modest resources were required to enter these peripheral industries; in consequence, the new trusts were immediately vulnerable to competition from still newer entrants. Such competition quickly arose and did the older trusts in. The attempts of peripheral firms to merge into center configurations simply did not work.

Meanwhile, under a distinctly different second pattern of combination, other peripheral firms were forming loose horizontal associations. These types of combinations emerged when local, regional, or even national groups of businessmen entered into agreements in defense against their sudden collective overcapacity. The number of loose combinations—pools, trade associations, cartels—reached into the thousands, far exceeding the few hundred successfully merged center firms (some of which, of course, had begun their evolution into center firms as loose associations under this second pattern). These numerous cartels and pools fell into Brandeis' categories one and two: loose horizontal combinations of peripheral firms whose arrangements with each other were unenforceable but which, to the extent that they effectively limited production and kept prices high, damaged allocative efficiency and reduced consumer welfare.[39]

Brandeis himself correctly sensed that the failure of so many trusts must have an important meaning. And he deduced, again quite accurately, that if size alone brought efficiency, then all trusts should prosper. Here he approached the edge of a conceptual breakthrough. But at precisely this point in his thinking, a deep-seated antipathy toward bigness clouded his judgment. Instead of drawing the correct conclusion—that large size was an advantage to firms in some types of industries and a disadvantage to firms in other types—Brandeis too simply asserted that bigness in general was inefficient.

As he expressed his ideas in testimony before a House committee in 1911, "Most of the trusts that had the quality of size, but lacked the position of control of the industry, [and] lacked the ability to control prices—have either failed or have shown no marked success. The record of the unsuccessful trusts is doubtless in all your minds." Brandeis recounted several past failures, then brought his analysis down to the present period. "Consider other trusts now existing, the Print Papers Trust (the International Paper Co.); the Writing-Paper Trust (the American Writing Paper Co.); the Upper Leather Trust (the American Hide & Leather Co.); the Union Bag Trust; the Sole Leather Trust; those trusts and a great number of others which did not attain a monopoly and were therefore unable to fix prices have had but slight success as compared with their competitors." Brandeis had first-hand knowledge of some of his examples. His own clients in Boston included a number of paper companies and an even larger number of shoe manufacturers who had dealings with the leather trusts.[40]

What Brandeis did not understand, though, was that few of these industries had any important economy of scale, and few if any of the firms he mentioned were vertically integrated. Combinations in such industries were almost certain to fail, and bigness in their case proved disadvantageous because it sacrificed flexibility without achieving corresponding gains in productive efficiency. To this extent, Brandeis' analysis was correct. The pivotal point for him, however, was that these leather, paper, and other trusts had failed to secure control of their markets. His observation was accurate, but he confused cause with effect, and he made the same type of error in explaining why only some trusts prospered: "Now, take, in the second place, the trusts that have been markedly successful, like the Standard Oil Trust, the Shoe Machinery Trust, the Tobacco Trust. They have succeeded through their monopolistic positions." This statement is a tautology. "They dominated the trade and were able to fix the prices at which articles should be sold. To this monopolistic power, in the main, and not to efficiency in management, are their great profits to be ascribed."[41]

As another illustration, Brandeis offered in congressional testimony the evidence of two firms that seemed to him to be in the same industry, transportation. The first was the International Mercantile Marine, a steamship combine financed and sponsored by J. P. Morgan and Company. This steamship trust failed to earn a profit, despite the great resources and business expertise of the Morgan firm. In contrast, Brandeis cited the Pullman Palace Car Company, which enjoyed a monopoly of the sleeping cars so popular with railroad passengers. Pullman, said Brandeis, enjoyed "profits so large as to be deemed unconscionable." He attributed the difference in the two companies' experience to the varying degrees of control each had over its market. In the case of International Mercantile Marine, he said, even good management could not save a trust that failed to gain such control. With tight control, the Pullman Company prospered.[42]

Once more his observation was correct, but not because of the reason he cited. In fact, the Pullman Company operated not only in the transportation business but also in metalworking and machinery. The company had a large manufacturing component, with major economies of scale and long production runs. Pullman's manufacturing division more closely resembled International Harvester or Ford Motor than it did International Mercantile Marine. The manufacture of Pullman cars, in other words, was a center industry; the operation of merchant ships was a peripheral. Any company with one ship could go into business and compete with the Morgan transportation combine. But to compete with the large, vertically integrated Pullman Company would require an immense initial investment in a substantial factory, the assembly of a large group of skilled workers, and very careful management. Even with all these resources, success would come only if the new company could undersell Pullman, or if the market for sleeping cars exceeded the demand that Pullman could satisfy alone.[43]

Pullman, International Mercantile Marine, Standard Oil, and Brandeis' other examples aptly illustrated the two fundamentally different types of consolidation that together made up the trust movement. On the one hand, the trusts included several hundred tightly integrated center firms (most of which were integrated vertically as well as horizontally); on the other hand, tens of thousands of peripheral firms associated with each other in a few thousand loose horizontal combinations. As Brandeis' future antitrust campaigns showed, his inability (along with that of most of his contemporaries) to grasp the distinctions between center and peripheral firms and between vertical and horizontal integration fed his confusion concerning how and why big businesses developed. This in turn led him into serious misconceptions about which business practices would or would not help consumers, and about which types of organizations were or were not efficient.

Price Fixing, the Consumer, and the Petite Bourgeoisie

One of Brandeis' most characteristic campaigns was his energetic work on behalf of resale price maintenance (that is, price fixing or, in the euphemism of its proponents, "fair trade"). This controversy began in 1911, when the Supreme Court, in the patent-medicine case of *Dr. Miles Medical Co. v. John D. Park & Sons Co.*, ruled that price fixing was illegal, under both the common law and the Sherman Act. The Miles company was a manufacturer of a popular elixir which it distributed through a network of 400 wholesalers and 25,000 retailers. The company's contracts with each of these dealers required that its elixir not be sold for less than a price specified by the company. If a wholesaler or retailer would not sign such a contract, the Miles company declined to do business with it.[44]

John D. Park & Sons, a wholesale drug firm, refused to sign. Instead, Park procured the elixir from another wholesaler at cut prices for the purpose of reselling it to consumers at a price below the figure desired by the manufacturer. Dr. Miles thereupon sued Park. In deciding the case in favor of Park, the Supreme Court unshackled competition and opened a new era of price warfare among retailers. In the process of doing so, the court provoked, in opposition to its ruling, one of the longest, most relentless, and best organized business lobbying efforts in American history. Brandeis spearheaded this lobbying. He lent his name to the crusade to overturn the court's decision, wrote articles and delivered speeches attacking the new doctrine, and drafted a bill to exempt small wholesalers and retailers from the Sherman Act so that they could resume their practice of fixing retail prices at uniform levels nationwide.[45]

The Supreme Court did not stop with the Dr. Miles case, but tightened the screws against price fixing in still other decisions. In response, Brandeis grew more and more frustrated at the irony that the antitrust movement to which he himself had contributed so much appeared to be hitting the wrong targets. To the secretary of commerce he wrote, "The [court's] decision plays into the hands of the capitalistic undertaking the chain of stores of the great concern which, like the Standard Oil, can retail an article as well as manufacture [it]." "We are much in the situation of those who love peace so much that they are ready to fight for it," he wrote Senator Robert M. La Follette, adding that "There must be reasonable restrictions upon competition else we shall see competition destroyed."[46]

In other words, Brandeis saw this new series of decisions, taken by the Supreme Court under the Sherman Act, as promoting bigness. He believed the decisions would drive manufacturers of goods that no longer could be fair-traded into setting up their own outlets—that is, integrating forward into wholesale and retail trade. This would squeeze out hosts of small druggists and storekeepers. Brandeis explicitly argued that maximizing the number of retail shops would also maximize competition. As he said of one consumer product, the Gillette safety razor, which prior to the Supreme Court's decision could be sold at fixed prices: "Now, the fixing of that price has possibly prevented one retail dealer from selling the article a little lower than the other, but the fixing of that price has tended not to suppress but to develop competition, because it has made it possible in the distribution of those goods to go to an expense and to open up another sphere of merchandizing which would have been absolutely impossible without a fixed price. The whole world can be drawn into the field. Every dealer, every small stationer, every small druggist, every small hardware man, can be made a purveyor of that article ... and you have stimulated, through the fixed price, the little man as against the department store, and as against the large unit which may otherwise monopolize that trade." Brandeis' argument accorded perfectly with his goal of maximizing the number of retailers. But as a brief in favor of "competition," it made little sense, assuming that competition had anything to do with low prices.[47]

Having decided to fight hard for legalized price fixing, Brandeis now faced a difficult task. He must somehow draft, and then persuade Congress to enact, legislation that would exempt from all antitrust laws resale price fixing in small stores, but without also exempting price fixing in what Brandeis called "capitalistic" concerns. He planned his campaign carefully. In order to bring pressure on Congress, he proposed to his friend Norman Hapgood, who had moved from *Collier's* to become editor of *Harper's Weekly,* a series of promotional articles. "There probably ought to be three, not very long, articles," Brandeis suggested. The first would be entitled " 'Competition that Kills'; the second, 'Efficiency and the One-Price Article'; the third, in substance, 'How Europe deals with the one-price goods.' " Brandeis closely coordinated his writing efforts with the overall program of the American Fair Trade League, a lobbying group sponsored by small retailers and their many trade associations. The league distributed copies of Brandeis' "Competition that Kills" to all senators, congressmen, Supreme Court justices, state governors and legislators, and to hundreds of newspaper editors. Then the league sponsored the publication of an excerpted version of the piece in twenty national magazines.[48]

The text displayed Brandeis at his muckraking best. He brought every symbol and ideological appeal to bear, turned every conceivable argument to his advantage, and invested the whole with his distinctive moral passion. "The prohibition of price-maintenance," he wrote, "imposes upon the small and independent producers a serious handicap." He predicted that the fateful next step in business would be vertical integration. "Some avenue of escape must be sought by them; and it may be found in combination ... The process of exterminating the small independent retailer already hard pressed by capitalistic combinations—the mail-order houses, existing chains of stores, and the large department stores—would be greatly accelerated by such a movement. Already the displacement of the small independent businessman by the huge corporation with its myriad of employees, its absentee ownership, and its financier control, presents a grave danger to our democracy." Worst of all, the wound was self-inflicted: "It is not even in accord with the natural laws of business. It is largely the result of unwise, man-made, privilege-creating law, which has stimulated existing tendencies to inequality instead of discouraging them. Shall we, under the guise of protecting competition, further foster monopoly by creating immunity for the price-cutters?" So stirring was Brandeis' rhetoric that it is even now difficult to keep in mind what he was in fact proposing: that small retailers be exempted from the antitrust laws and permitted, in concert with each other, to fix the prices of consumer goods. This, of course, would remove any incentive for greater efficiency. The entire burden of Brandeis' crusade for "fair trade" contrasted directly with his slogan of saving "a million dollars a day" through scientific management in the Advance Rate Case. And that had occurred only one year before the court's decision in the Dr. Miles case.[49]

Brandeis continued his appeal for fair trade in testimony before the congressional committee that considered the price-fixing bill he had drafted. These hearings produced some of the closest questioning he ever encountered. Brandeis told the committee that he had written the *Harper's* articles to educate both Congress and the voters. "The moment you allow the cutting of prices you are inviting the great, powerful men to get control of the business," he warned. "One retail association after another, national, State, and local associations, have gone on record, demanding that this illegitimate competition be put to an end . . . Big business is not more efficient than little business. It is a mistake to suppose that the department stores can do business cheaper than the little dealer."[50] The only reason department stores could undersell their smaller competitors, Brandeis went on to say, was that they bought in bulk and availed themselves of quantity discounts. This practice, he told the committee, gave an unfair advantage to large retailers and therefore should be stopped. Here Congressman Alben Barkley of Kentucky, knowing that quantity discounts were as old as business itself, could not believe he had heard Brandeis correctly. But Brandeis remained adamant: he predicted that quantity discounts, being "fraught with very great evil," soon would be outlawed.[51]

In this statement Brandeis revealed the heart of his concern. He was willing to take the extreme step of forbidding the ancient and universal practice of charging less per unit for large quantities than for small ones, in order to maximize the absolute number of retailers. The injury they suffered was *ipso facto* a legitimate grievance, against which there ought to be a law: "It is because they are injured that they demand relief. It is because of their inability to maintain standard prices that they have been injured . . . My point is that if the practice did not hurt them they would not be here complaining and they would not have endeavored elsewhere [by means of state laws] to secure this right; they would not have been spending large sums of money throughout the country endeavoring to protect their rights. They are not dreaming or imagining, but they have learned from experience."[52]

These small retailers, because of their relatively low sales volume, relied on high profit margins to stay in business. And Brandeis' defense of their interests forced him into the position of also defending their high margins. This reasoning led him to hold an attitude toward consumers that bordered on contempt. Consumers naturally preferred low prices to high ones, but Brandeis saw them as "misled." Shoppers, he argued, were enticed into large department stores by cut rates on a few items. Once in the stores, they were persuaded "to buy other goods for more than they are worth." Furthermore, consumers "lose time in their search for cut-throat bargains." Brandeis' line of thinking thus led him into something approaching a posture of elitism. One particular exchange during the congressional hearings highlighted this drift in his thought:

Brandeis: The practice of cutting prices on articles of a known price tends to create the impression among the consumers that they have been getting something that has not been worth what they have been paying for it.

Congressman Decker [Democrat of Missouri, who avowed that he had been "raised on a farm"]: That is presuming that the people have not much sense.

Brandeis: Well, everybody has not as much sense as some people.

Congressman Decker: Some people have more sense than other people think they have.[53]

For Brandeis and his allies, to be simultaneously against bigness and for consumers was extremely difficult. From our perspective three generations after this price-fixing controversy, it is clear that a substantial part of the battle represented an attempt by Brandeis to use governmental power as a means of reinforcing the strength of small shopkeepers in their war against large, price-cutting retailers. To the extent that consumers voted with their pocketbooks for department stores and mail-order houses, the fight against these large retailers became a fight against consumers as well. In Brandeis' personal case, the justification for making such a fight lay in a powerful ideological aversion to bigness. For the small shopkeepers themselves, however, the issue involved stark self-interest. As Congressman Barkley wearily told Brandeis during the hearings, explaining once again why the committee was not going to endorse his bill, "I am constitutionally and inherently opposed to class legislation and legislation on behalf of special interests."[54]

Brandeis' lament about the decline of autonomous individualism aptly illustrated one of the poignant themes of modern culture in an age of big business. This theme was the conflict between the small producer's values, which had characterized nineteenth-century American culture, and the emerging consumerist values of a twentieth-century mass society. Brandeis' hostility to the new consumerism found vivid expression in his own behavior. Though himself a millionaire, he disliked most other wealthy persons, being profoundly disturbed by their ostentatious consumption. He was incredulous, for example, when he read newspaper reports in 1911 that Elbert H. Gary of U.S. Steel had presented his wife with a pearl necklace valued at $500,000: "Is it not just the same sort of thing which brought on the French Revolution?" Brandeis also loathed such modern devices as automobiles and telephones. He practically never went shopping, even for his own clothes; he simply reordered suits and other items that had served him well in the past.[55]

His anticonsumption sensibilities led him to a hatred of advertising and from that to a feeling of contempt for the manipulated consumer. Ironically, the premise that people could be made to believe things they would not otherwise believe was central to Brandeis' own career as publicist and muckraker; and it underlay his great promotional campaigns for causes ranging from antitrust to Zionism. In this respect he was a very modern man indeed, one of the early masters of the opinion maker's art. "All law is a dead letter without public opinion behind it," he wrote in 1890. "But law and public opinion interact—and they are both capable of being made. Most of the world is in more or less a hypnotic state—and it is comparatively easy to make people believe anything, particularly the right." They also could be made to believe the wrong, however, and in Brandeis' view that was what usually happened with advertising.[56]

The ad man's pitch had other undesirable results as well. Dependence on advertising revenues caused newspapers and magazines to be less "free" than they should be. National advertising, Brandeis further argued, undermined the relationship between consumers and local retailers.[57] By the 1920s, when he was an associate justice of the Supreme Court, his dislike had deepened into abhorrence. "The nationally advertised branded goods," he wrote in 1923, "make the retailer practically an automatic machine, instead of an expert to whom the consumer pays, in profits, compensation for expert services and trustworthiness . . . In a large part of the field there is no social justification for the national widespread market for very many of the trademarked articles." Brandeis urged that journalists "teach the public" such lessons as "to refuse to buy any nationally advertised brand & to look with suspicion upon every advertised article."[58]

The consumer himself Brandeis judged to be "servile, self-indulgent, indolent, ignorant." Even worse, the consumer had abrogated his role as a countervailing power against bigness. "Isn't there among your economists," he once inquired of Felix Frankfurter, "some one who could make clear to the country that the greatest social-economic troubles arise from the fact [that] the consumer has failed absolutely to perform his function? He lies not only supine, but paralyzed & deserves to suffer like others who take their lickings 'lying down'. He gets no worse than his just deserts. But the trouble is that the parallelogram of social forces is disrupted thereby. It destroys absolutely the balance of power."[59]

The consumer, then, was not Brandeis' ideal American, and Brandeis himself never represented the type of consumer advocate so prominent in later years. Again, the reason had less to do with economics than with personal values. Repelled by the flaunting materialism abroad in America, Brandeis angrily denounced conspicuous consumption. But in so doing he drifted imperceptibly into an attack on consumer preference, a principle that lies at the very core of a market economy. Consumers had in effect betrayed him; they had refused to follow his precepts against bigness; they had revealed their true nature by passively buying the endless stream of goods that flowed from the center economy. In that way, consumers had guaranteed the success and permanence of the center firms Brandeis so detested. And for such a mistake, he would never forgive them.

Politics, Economics, and Bigness

Early in his career, Brandeis decided that big business could become big only through illegitimate means. By his frequent references to the "curse of bigness," he meant that bigness itself was the mark of Cain, a sign of prior sinning. "I think that if the methods pursued in business are proper," he once told a Senate committee, "and businesses too are allowed to grow, as distinguished from forcibly combining a large number of businesses, there is no such likelihood of any one business acquiring a control as to be really dangerous."[60] Throughout his life Brandeis believed bigness to be unnatural: "If the Lord had intended things to be big, he would have made man bigger—in brains and character." He simply denied the possibility that size brought efficiency in any industry. "I am so firmly convinced that the large unit is not as efficient—I mean the very large unit—is not as efficient as the smaller unit, that I believe that if it were possible today to make the corporations act in accordance with what doubtless all of us would agree should be the rules of trade no huge corporation would be created, or if created, would be successful."[61]

This was fundamentally an *economic* argument. But in the absence of an adequate framework of economic theory, Brandeis, like many later reformers, had only his personal and political sensibilities to guide him. His intense predisposition in favor of small units led him to endorse loose, horizontal, productively inefficient, consumer-injuring associations for the suppression of competition. Conversely, Brandeis opposed horizontally tight, productively efficient, consumer-helping, vertically integrated center firms on the grounds that their giant size and central management destroyed individualism. Here his economic argument merged into a more complex political judgment. Whereas center firms helped the economy but threatened the decentralist American polity, loose combinations of peripheral firms injured the economy but tended to protect the polity.

For Brandeis, a proper choice between the alternatives was not difficult. "I have considered and do consider," he said, "that the proposition that mere bigness can not be an offense against society is false, because I believe that our society, which rests upon democracy, can not endure under such conditions."[62] This comment shows once more the dominance of political over economic considerations in his thinking. But however dominant the goal was in his own mind, the subsequent record in all major capitalist economies has made clear an evolutionary pattern that Brandeis had no way of predicting: in most industries, the consolidation movement did not work and *most industries therefore remained peripheral.* At the same time, consolidation by firms in center industries—that is, those industries having economies of scale and long production runs—may well have been inexorable. As a consequence, to tear apart these center firms, when natural economic forces held them together so powerfully, would likely have required nothing short of authoritarian action by the state. Such behavior by an autocratic government, of course, would have violated some of Brandeis' own most deeply-felt principles.

The general problems Brandeis grappled with in trying to cope with the trust movement typified the larger dilemmas of national regulatory policy. How, in an age of big business, could the government preserve American democratic values? What steps should it take to balance the rights of producers against the new imperatives of consumers? How could government control bigness without interfering with personal liberty, let alone with economic efficiency? These questions dominated national political discourse during the twenty years surrounding the turn of the century, until they came to a head during the Wilson-Roosevelt-Taft-Debs presidential campaign of 1912. The formal response in public policy culminated with passage of the Clayton Act and the Federal Trade Commission Act of 1914, after a classic legislative drama in which Louis D. Brandeis played a very curious part.

The Candidates and the Trust Issues, 1912

Brandeis took no serious role in presidential politics before 1910, when he squared off against the Taft Administration during the Ballinger-Pinchot controversy. Overall, his positions on national issues tended to follow traditional Democratic Party tenets of free trade, sound money, and minimal government. He distrusted alike the free-silver evangelism of William Jennings Bryan, the high-tariff protectionism of traditional Republicans, and the hints of big government and statism represented by Theodore Roosevelt. In the election of 1912, Brandeis' original choice for the presidency was his good friend Robert M. La Follette, but the candidacy of "Fighting Bob" collapsed, leaving Brandeis temporarily without a candidate.[63]

The decision of the Democratic national convention in the summer of 1912 revived his spirits. "I have never met or even seen Wilson," Brandeis wrote, "but all that I have heard of him and particularly his discussion of economic problems makes me believe that he possesses certain qualities indispensable to the solution of our problems." Brandeis sent the new candidate a congratulatory note, and Wilson responded by inviting him to a private meeting at Sea Girt, New Jersey, Wilson's summer home. At this fateful meeting, the two men—both fifty-six years old, both transplanted southerners, both infused with a moralistic approach to politics—found an immediate rapport. In a three-hour discussion they discovered strikingly similar views on economic issues.[64]

After the Sea Girt conference, which occurred just three months before Wilson's election as president, the informal position of influence that Brandeis had attained as the people's lawyer became institutionalized. As Wilson's biographer Arthur Link puts it, "Because Brandeis understood the problem thoroughly, because he was ready with a definite plan for the bridling of monopoly, he became the chief architect of the New Freedom." Perhaps this overstates the point, but certainly Brandeis did make major contributions to Wilson's economic platform. Even before he met Wilson, he had developed a program he called "the regulation of competition," in opposition to the platform of Theodore Roosevelt's Progressive Party, which Brandeis characterized as "regulated monopoly." As Brandeis wrote in a magazine article, "The issue is not ... Shall we have unrestricted competition or regulated monopoly? It is, Shall we have regulated competition or regulated monopoly? Regulation is essential to the preservation and development of competition, just as it is necessary to the preservation and best development of liberty." Brandeis' slogan about "the regulation of competition" had an appealing sound, and later in the campaign it seemed to help Wilson's cause significantly.[65]

Wilson himself, however, never seemed certain about exactly what it meant. As the campaign progressed and his debate with Roosevelt intensified, Wilson telegraphed an urgent request to Brandeis to "set forth as explicitly as possible the actual measures by which competition can be effectively regulated." Brandeis replied with a detailed outline that in turn became the heart of the initial antitrust program of Wilson's New Freedom. His suggestions took the form of an open letter that would appear over Wilson's signature:

The two parties differ fundamentally regarding the economic policy which the country should pursue. The Democratic Party insists that competition can be and should be maintained in every branch of private industry . . . The New [Progressive] Party, on the other hand, insists that private monopoly may be desirable in some branches of industry, or at all events, inevitable; and that existing trusts should not be dismembered or forcibly dislodged from those branches of industry which they have already acquired a monopoly, but should be made 'good' by regulation . . . This difference in the economic policy of the two parties is fundamental and irreconcilable. It is the difference between industrial liberty and industrial absolutism.

In the open letter, Brandeis went on to propose a series of measures designed to implement a Wilsonian antitrust program. First he advocated a strengthening of the Sherman Act by prohibition "of the specific methods or means by which the great trusts, utilizing their huge resources or particularly favored positions commonly crush rivals." Then he suggested an invigoration of the judicial process, so as to ensure that antitrust convictions were followed by reparations to the victims and also by genuine dissolutions. Indeed, the most significant difference between the programs of Roosevelt and Brandeis-Wilson lay in the latter's insistence that the government forcibly break apart the center firms formed over the last thirty years, whatever the resulting disruption to the national economy. Finally, Brandeis endorsed the creation of "a board or commission to aid in administering the Sherman law."[66]

This new commission would investigate big business in much the same manner as the existing Bureau of Corporations had been doing; but unlike the bureau, it would have a close relationship with the Department of Justice. It would advise Justice on antitrust proceedings and help to enforce compliance with the law "not only in the interests of the general public, but at the request and for the benefit of those particular individuals or concerns who have been injured or fear injury by infractions of the law by others." Advocating government intervention on behalf of the petite bourgeoisie, Brandeis' draft letter declared that "The inequality between the great corporations with huge resources and the small competitor and others is such that 'equality before the law' will no longer be secured merely by supplying adequate machinery for enforcing the law. To prevent oppression and injustice the Government must be prepared to lend its aid."[67]

Even before the two met, candidate Wilson's views had resembled those that Brandeis articulated for the campaign. Wilson spoke for what he himself called "the man on the make"—the small entrepreneur who was finding opportunity foreshortened by center firms' preemption of markets. But despite his decentralist political stance, Wilson never shared Brandeis' total aversion to industrial bigness. Some of Wilson's remarks during the campaign revealed his ambivalence: "I am for big business, and I am against the trusts"; "I, for one, don't care how big any business gets by efficiency, but I am jealous of any bigness that comes by monopoly." As Brandeis remarked years afterward, "In my opinion the real curse was bigness rather than monopoly. Mr. Wilson (and others wise politically) made the attack on lines of monopoly—because Americans hated monopoly and loved bigness."[68]

Brandeis and the New Freedom, 1913

After his landslide electoral victory in November 1912, Wilson's first priority was reduction of the protective tariff. The new president called a special session of Congress and broke precedent by personally delivering his message on the tariff to a joint meeting of the House and Senate. In the succeeding days, he conferred continuously with party leaders, cajoled reluctant senators with numerous personal letters and private interviews, and denounced the swarm of lobbyists who engulfed Capitol Hill in desperate efforts to save the protected status of their industries. The ensuing investigation of lobbying helped Wilson's cause greatly. In the end he won a downward revision of the tariff, knocking a dent into the protectionism that had been national policy since 1861.[69]

In this first great triumph of the New Freedom, Brandeis played no important role. To the chagrin of his friends and a number of other reformers, he had not been offered a place in Wilson's cabinet. The president had apparently yielded to a strange coalition of anti-Brandeis elements: the regular Democratic party in Massachusetts, which on occasions past had felt the sting of the people's lawyer; antisemitic activists among prominent Wilson supporters; and a surprising opposition from important members of the Jewish community who did not regard Brandeis as a "representative Jew."[70] Even so, Wilson continued to consult Brandeis on economic issues such as the currency-reform movement that led to the Federal Reserve Act of 1913. Here Brandeis' role took two forms: first, he advised the president on the degree to which private and public management could be mixed within the new Federal Reserve System; second, he once again took up his publicist's pen. The result was *Other People's Money and How the Bankers Use It*, the longest and most memorable piece of muckraking he ever did.[71]

First published in *Harper's Weekly* installments during the summer and fall of 1913, *Other People's Money* rehearsed all the themes of the Brandeisian diagnosis: the suppression of competition by trusts; the inefficiency of all consolidation; the scandals and excessive underwriting fees characteristic of the securities markets; the concentration of power in New York, at the expense of Boston and other regional centers; the sins of the House of Morgan and its offspring, such as U.S. Steel and the New Haven railroad system; and—above all—the curse of bigness. Brandeis' text drew heavily on a recent congressional investigation of the "Money Trust," chaired by Representative Arsene Pujo of Louisiana. The Pujo Committee hearings had produced daily headlines detailing the degree of banker control of the nation's money supply, securities markets, and corporate boards of directors. The hearings played a major role in the fight for the Federal Reserve, and for Brandeis they provided invaluable ammunition in his campaign against bigness. The titles of his *Harper's* articles suggest both their content and Brandeis' talent for expressing complex issues in catchy slogans: "Big Men and Little Business," "The Inefficiency of the Oligarchs," "The Endless Chain: Interlocking Directorates," "A Curse of Bigness." The book version went through numerous editions, and all together the muckraker's efforts aided their author as much as his cause. They cemented Brandeis' popular reputation as an expert on economic issues, whose influence then persisted far into the future. The phrase "other people's money," for example, appeared in President Franklin D. Roosevelt's message to Congress in 1933, when he requested new securities legislation.[72]

Other People's Money remains a model of the muckraking genre. Read three generations after its composition, it still has a power to incite anger against Morgan and other villains. But as economic analysis, the book wears less well. For one thing, Brandeis' emphasis on the role of investment bankers was ill timed. Their once-powerful influence had long been waning because of center firms' use of retained earnings as a means of financing growth. Then, too, his attack on interlocking directorates implicitly assigned far greater power to corporate boards of directors than they in fact possessed in 1913, or at any time since. Interlocking directorates often reflected the insensitivity and power of top corporate managers (who selected most board members themselves) more than it did the power of the bankers, lawyers, and outside businessmen who sat on the boards. Finally, and most important, *Other People's Money* represents the purest sustained example of the Brandeisian tendency to lump all modern industrial ills together and seek one common cause for them. That single cause, of course, was excessive size: "Bigness has been an important factor in the rise of the Money Trust: Big railroad systems, Big industrial trusts, big public service companies; and as instruments of these Big banks and Big trust companies."[73]

The Movement Toward the FTC, 1914

Brandeis' articles stirred public opinion to support the Federal Reserve Act, and their publication in book form as *Other People's Money* in 1914 also stimulated new interest in a broad regulatory effort directed at big business. But within this movement Brandeis' influence was a good deal more complex, and the story of his activities more convoluted than is usually understood.

The roots of the support for a federal trade commission may be found in the history of antitrust prosecution under the Sherman Act. This legislation went on the books in 1890, but for a time indifferent enforcement made it almost a dead letter. From 1890 to 1905, the Department of Justice brought only 24 suits, or an average of only 1.5 per year. But the number leaped to an average of 18 per year over the next decade—a period of conspicuous trust busting by Presidents Roosevelt, Taft, and Wilson.[74] This twelve-fold increase in the rate of prosecution meant that the targets of antitrust law now stood at much greater hazard than before. The surprising identity of these targets epitomized the dilemma Brandeis and his allies faced in attempting to strengthen the Sherman Act, for loose combinations of peripheral firms comprised by far the largest category of defendants. The suits broke down as follows: 72 were filed against loose combinations of peripherals, 32 against tight combinations (some of which were peripheral, some center), 12 each against labor unions and agricultural produce dealers, and 10 against miscellaneous others. Only a handful of cases were filed against prominent center firms.[75]

Thus, as unlikely as it seems, government antitrust action usually opposed not huge integrated firms, but loose associations of small companies—the very groups on whose behalf Brandeis spoke. The Department of Justice singled out these small companies not because of economic theory (which, incidentally, would have suggested these very targets), but because of the mechanics of prosecution. The department quite naturally gravitated toward cases it could win. The rudimentary methods of horizontal control employed by associations of small companies—local price fixing, market division, boycotting, and the like—were easy to detect and prosecute. Business managers in peripheral firms, therefore, had good cause for concern about antitrust enforcement.[76]

Still their counterparts in center firms also remained apprehensive. These companies represented enormous investments that might at any time be endangered by antitrust prosecution. In the *American Tobacco* and *Standard Oil* decisions of 1911, the Supreme Court had shifted the already ambiguous terms of the Sherman Act toward even greater uncertainty. In the *Standard Oil* case, the court in effect determined that only "unreasonable" restraints of trade were illegal under the Sherman Act, not all such restraints. This "rule of reason," as it came to be called, satisfied none of the parties most directly concerned in the antitrust debate. For Brandeis and his allies, already dismayed at the focus of prosecution on small firms and associations, the court's new rule of reason appeared to weaken the potential for future prosecution of giant trusts. For business managers, on the other hand, the enunciation of the rule of reason implied a slight retreat by the court, but also a new unpredictability as to which business practices were permissible and which not.[77]

More than anything else, executives of both peripheral and center firms wanted certainty: a bright line between legality and illegality. Many of them began to think that continuous administration of economic policy by a regulatory commission was preferable to what they saw as the spasmodic whims of individual judges. Detailed opinion surveys taken by the National Civic Federation and the United States Chamber of Commerce in 1911 and 1914 showed overwhelming support among all businessmen for a new regulatory commission. This enthusiasm derived not from a desire for more regulation, but rather from a sense that expert *administrative* regulation would be more stable and predictable than hit-or-miss antitrust litigation.[78]

During the campaign of 1912, Theodore Roosevelt's Progressive Party put forward the most highly developed conception of such a commission advanced by any of the three major parties:

We urge the establishment of a strong fundamental, administrative commission of high standing which shall maintain permanent, active supervision over industrial corporations . . . Such a commission must enforce the complete publicity of those corporate transactions which are of public interest; must attack unfair competition, false capitalization and special privilege and by continued trained watchfulness guard and keep open equally to all the highways of American commerce. Thus the business man will have certain knowledge of the law and will be able to conduct his business easily in conformity therewith.[79]

Brandeis' own conversion to support of the commission idea came late in the presidential campaign of 1912 and then primarily as a political response to the Progressives. Wilson's qualified endorsement of the idea, encased in the "regulation of competition" program outlined by Brandeis, did not reflect a coherent strategy or detailed program for such an agency. As noted earlier, by the time of Wilson's election in 1912, a national consensus had developed in favor of a commission; but Wilson, once inaugurated, did not begin his legislative effort on the issue until 1914. The historical evidence suggests that this delay derived from the need of Wilson's advisers for more time to think through the administration's policy. A second reason was that Wilson himself, a close student of congressional government, carefully paced and sequenced his overall legislative program so as not to dissipate his supporting coalition on Capitol Hill. Under this schedule, Wilson devoted the first year of his administration to the campaigns for tariff reduction and for the creation of the Federal Reserve System.

During the year's delay in dealing with antitrust, the economic and political situation changed. By 1914 the country was facing a serious economic recession, and Wilson had used up some of the good will new presidents enjoy during their early months in office. By the time antitrust reached the top of his agenda, he had fewer bargaining chips. Furthermore, the autumn of 1914 would bring off-year congressional elections. The Democrats, the country's minority party, would have to be careful or their supremacy in the House and Senate might quickly disappear. Wilson's currency legislation and especially his tariff revision of 1913 had offended a number of important industrial and commercial interests. If the administration went much further, it ran the risk of appearing to be engaged in a vendetta against business. Yet if Wilson did nothing about antitrust, he would surely alienate his reformist supporters. This situation was hazardous for a president elected with only 42 percent of the popular vote.

As might be expected in these circumstances, Wilson received a good deal of conflicting advice. Some cabinet members urged caution, others boldness. The president's business supporters warned about trying to do too much in the face of waning prosperity. Brandeis stood as firm as ever: "The President's policy of New Freedom involves necessarily the hostility of the great banking and financial interests; for they want industrial and financial absolutism, while we want industrial democracy. The conflict between us is irreconcilable." Accordingly, Brandeis recommended a program much like the one he had designed for Wilson during the 1912 campaign: strengthened antitrust laws that would enumerate illegal practices and an interstate trade commission with advisory and investigatory powers.[80]

Working on the assumption that some sort of commission must be formed, Brandeis strongly endorsed the creation of a type of sunshine agency. As its function, however, he had in mind not merely the accumulation of neutral facts but the tendentious use of selected facts to help peripheral firms, especially in their associational activities. "We should differentiate clearly," he wrote a member of Wilson's cabinet in 1913, "capitalistic industrial monopolies from those relations between competitors in industry which are really a regulation of competition." If this were not done, antitrust legislation would continue to hit the wrong targets. "Capitalistic monopolies have been fully investigated and we know how to deal with them. But we have no comprehensive detailed information concerning the character and effect of these trade agreements between competitors; and in the absence of such data we cannot deal with them intelligently. To obtain such information an investigation should be undertaken, and meanwhile those who supply the necessary data should be protected against criminal prosecution."[81]

Wilson, after assessing the state of the economy, the mood of the country, and the divergent advice he was receiving, decided to go forward with his antitrust program. Yet the text of his message to Congress of January 20, 1914 shows vividly his effort to harmonize conflicting pressures:

The antagonism between business and government is over . . . The Government and business men are ready to meet each other halfway in a common effort to square business methods with both public opinion and the law. The best informed men of the business world condemn the methods and processes and consequences of monopoly as we condemn them; and the instinctive judgement of the vast majority of business men everywhere goes with them. We shall now be their spokesmen.

In this same speech, Wilson went on to outline the details of his plan: a strengthening and clarification of the antitrust laws, a prohibition of interlocking directorates, and the creation of an interstate trade commission. The new commission would serve "as an indispensable instrument of information and publicity, as a clearing house for the facts by which both the public mind and the managers of great business undertakings should be gained, and as an instrumentality for doing justice to business" in those instances where the judicial process alone is inadequate. "The opinion of the country," said Wilson, "would instantly approve of such a commission."[82] Wilson's speech delighted Brandeis, who wrote his brother, "He has paved the way for about all I have asked for and some of the provisions specifically are what I got into his mind at my first interview. Confidentially I think he rather overdid the Era of good feeling."[83]

Writing the Legislation

A number of antitrust bills had been introduced since the *Standard Oil* and *American Tobacco* decisions of 1911. In addition, Congress had considered several interstate trade commission bills, including one submitted as early as 1908. Wilson's message of January 1914 opened the final stage in the movement for new laws. The administration pushed an antitrust bill sponsored by Representative Henry D. Clayton (Democrat of Alabama), chairman of the judiciary committee, and a trade commission bill offered by Representative James J. Covington (Democrat of Maryland), of the commerce committee. The curious progress of these two bills through the 1914 session of Congress—their repeated emendation, their intermittent support by Wilson—aptly illustrates the difficulty of balancing unclear economic policy with very clear political necessity.[84]

As originally written, the Clayton antitrust bill took exceptionally stringent form. It enumerated a long list of prohibited practices (such as price cutting, tying contracts, and interlocking directorates), along the same pattern that Brandeis had outlined for candidate Wilson in 1912. The harshest aspect of the original Clayton bill lay in the criminal sanctions it imposed. Section 11, for example, provided:

That whenever a corporation shall be guilty of the violation of any of the provisions of the antitrust laws, the offense shall be deemed to be also that of the individual directors, officers, and agents of such corporation authorizing, ordering, or doing any of such prohibited acts, and upon conviction thereof they shall be deemed guilty of a misdemeanor, and punished by a fine not exceeding $5,000, or imprisonment not exceeding one year, or by both said punishments in the discretion of the court.[85]

If the bill passed in this form, and if the Department of Justice enforced it vigorously, tens of thousands of American businessmen might go to jail.

In contrast to the severe criminal sanctions of the Clayton bill, the Covington trade commission bill contemplated not an enforcement agency but a sunshine commission very like Adams' Massachusetts tribunal of the 1870s. The commission would secure and publish information, conduct investigations as directed by Congress, and suggest methods of improving business practice and antitrust enforcement. Essentially the Covington bill pointed toward an expanded Bureau of Corporations. Since its founding in 1903, the bureau had compiled a superb series of reports on U.S. Steel, American Tobacco, and other giant center firms. These reports constituted the most important source of information used by

Brandeis and other publicists, who often quoted Commissioner of Corporations Herbert Knox Smith and his colleagues. Smith himself warmly endorsed the idea of a trade commission. Using language reminiscent of Adams' comments on regulation forty years before, Smith wrote in 1912 that the new commission must be "permanent, flexible, composed of trained experts, having available the accumulated knowledge of continuous service and investigation, capable of co-operation, of prevention as well as cure, and above all, furnishing effective publicity."[86]

Though it fell short of Brandeis' model of an information agency that would aid small business, Covington's design with emphasis on the sunshine function seemed to accord with Wilson's message to Congress of January 1914. In that speech, the president said that the new commission's powers should be limited; that the country "would not wish to see [the commission] empowered to make terms with monopoly or in any sort to assume control of business, as if the Government made itself responsible." (For Wilson, to "make terms with monopoly" referred to the kind of commission Roosevelt had proposed, which would have made big companies legitimate by failing to dissolve them.) During the subsequent legislative progress of both the Clayton antitrust bill and the Covington trade commission bill, however, Wilson's original intention became entangled in political problems. A good deal of confusion ensued, and the outcome did not bode well for the long-term success of the new commission.[87]

At first it appeared that all would go smoothly. Both the Clayton and the Covington bills passed the House of Representatives by large majorities in early June 1914, less than five months after Wilson's speech. Meanwhile, though, the president began to have second thoughts about the inconsistent approaches represented by the two pieces of the package: a strong antitrust bill and a weak commission bill. The two were supposed to be companion measures, but they had been developed in different House committees and they took divergent approaches to the delicate problem of business regulation in a time of deepening economic recession.

Business managers themselves were becoming disturbed—some almost panicky—at the criminal provisions of the Clayton bill. Many businessmen from peripheral firms objected vehemently because they engaged in the very practices enumerated in the bill. Like Brandeis and other administration spokesmen, they were running up against the central irony of antitrust enforcement. As the secretary of commerce put the issue in a letter to the White House, "Instead of striking at the things we mean to hit, it [the bill] does, as a matter of fact, seriously injure the small business men whom we are aiming to help." And as one small businessman from Mississippi expressed it,

I respectfully submit that while Big Business is the alleged aim of these drastic laws, they hurt small business far more than they do the larger and stronger concerns for they can bear burdens that we can not. They can exist on a margin of profits fatal to us ... We may not combine to save costs, may not agree to desist from trying to take away markets from each other, may not agree to hold our goods for prices fairly remunera-tive ... Really we are being governed to our undoing.[88]

The Clayton bill represented a very serious political hazard for the Wilson Administration.

The trade commission bill, on the other hand, had gained great popularity. Much milder in tone, it was also sufficiently general to be all things to all men. To business managers of both center and peripheral firms, it seemed a more appropriate measure, espe-cially in the context of a deteriorating national economy. At about the time the House passed these two bills, the U.S. Chamber of Commerce conducted a national referendum, polling a variety of businessmen on their views of the two bills' provisions, with the following results:

Provision	Favor	Oppose
For a Federal Trade Commission	522	124
Interlocking Directorate Prohibition	491	41
Holding Company Prohibition	432	75
Price Discrimination Prohibition	22	531
Exclusive Contract Prohibition	35	514

As the tally shows, most of these businessmen readily accepted the commission idea; they also endorsed structural rules such as those against interlocking directorates and holding companies. But they overwhelmingly opposed prohibitions against commonplace asso-ciational activities, especially in view of the criminal sanctions set forth in the Clayton bill. These prohibitions would hit peripheral firms with particular force. As one businessman explained to the House judiciary committee, "Certainly the majority of people doing business do not want to be looked upon as criminals because they mutually agree among their associates to protect themselves against what is known as cutting prices to a point below the cost of production. Not that they want exorbitant prices, yet they feel that they have the right to protect themselves to the extent of a reasonable price that will render them a fair profit on the capital invested."[89] Wilson and his allies now faced a clear choice: either do something about the harsh provisions of the Clayton bill or risk political disaster.

Brandeis' Abdication

Congress' consideration of the Clayton and Covington bills, during the spring and summer of 1914, was the climactic moment in the entire antitrust campaign. For Brandeis, it would seem to have been a unique opportunity to write into law and thereby institutionalize everything he had been fighting for. Nobody had more influence with President Wilson than did Brandeis, and this meant having direct access to the most capable manager of legislation to occupy the White House in many years. In these circumstances, one would expect to find the Boston lawyer working night and day with the congressional committees, shuttling back and forth between the White House and Capitol Hill, taking a major part in drafting and redrafting the bills until they were in exactly the right form. Surely Wilson himself would very much have liked to see Brandeis fill this role. But during these pivotal months, he instead continued to do lawyer's work, concentrating on an immediate task, which now happened to be an ICC rate case. What might have been Brandeis' greatest role in the making of national economic policy, then, was to be played by a stand-in.[90]

That stand-in turned out to be George Rublee, a wealthy lawyer and former member of the Progressive Party. As a friend of Brandeis and of *Harper's Weekly* editor Norman Hapgood, Rublee had assisted both men several times in the past. He had drafted Brandeis' brief, for example, in the Ballinger-Pinchot hearings. The first graduate of the Groton School (in a class of one), Rublee was something of a dilettante and self-styled aristocrat. He had spent several years abroad, during which he occupied himself in such pursuits as playing tennis with the king of Sweden. Rublee practiced law intermittently with a Wall Street firm, but he always seemed to be available for special assignments. Thus he responded enthusiastically when, in 1914, Brandeis asked him to come to Washington and help with antitrust legislation.[91]

A Roosevelt supporter in 1912, Rublee subscribed to the Progressive Party plank that called for a very strong interstate trade commission, quite unlike the sunshine agency favored by Wilson and Brandeis and contemplated by the provisions of the Covington bill. Accordingly, in his lobbying on behalf of Brandeis, Rublee tried somehow to work around the Covington bill. Initially he got nowhere. But when the negative national reaction to the harsh Clayton bill began to raise political problems for Wilson, Rublee saw his chance. Accurately sensing that the Clayton bill would be amended beyond recognition, Rublee conceived a strategy of accepting a milder Clayton bill but at the same time substituting a much stronger trade commission bill in place of the Covington measure. Rublee worked out his plan in cooperation with Representative Ray Stevens of New Hampshire, another ally of Brandeis. Norman Hapgood reported these developments to President Wilson:

Mr. Brandeis has been so tied up with his railroad work that he has given only general thought to the trust situation as it has developed in the bills now before Congress, and as it has been affected by recent decisions of the Supreme Court. The most important part of the really hard work done recently by the little group he represents has been carried on by Mr. George Rublee . . . Mr. Stevens has introduced the bill which was really drawn up by Mr. Rublee . . . The Stevens Bill declares unfair competition to be unlawful, and empowers the Commission, whenever it has reason to believe that a corporation is using any unfair method of competition, to hold a hearing, and if it is of opinion that the method of competition in question is unfair to restrain the use thereof by injunction.[92]

Rublee's new bill, introduced by Stevens, provided for a commission very similar to the one advocated during the campaign of 1912 by Theodore Roosevelt and the Progressive Party. In 1914, however, the Democratically controlled House committee that was considering commission legislation still preferred the existing Covington bill and quickly voted down the new Stevens-Rublee draft. Next Rublee sought support from members of Wilson's cabinet, but to no avail. At this point in the fight, as he later recalled, he would have given up had his wife not kept urging him on:

What we then decided was to go to the President and see if we could do anything with him . . . Stevens made an appointment with the President to see us. Just before that, although I didn't know what Brandeis would think about it, I went to him and told him that we were going to do this. I knew this wasn't his approach to the problem and I hadn't thought of him as going along with our plan—I was afraid he wouldn't go or would oppose it . . . I don't believe we should have succeeded if he hadn't gone along . . .

It was such a beautiful summer day that the meeting was outdoors in the garden on the south side of the White House. I remember that the President was beautifully dressed—white linen—and looked very well. After Stevens' introductory statement I made the main statement . . . I saw that it was making an impression on the President as I spoke and he listened very attentively and asked some questions. When I finished speaking, to my great surprise, Brandeis entered the fray with enthusiasm and backed me up strongly.[93]

As Rublee implies, Brandeis' support of the Stevens bill represented a dramatic turnabout from his longtime stance on the nature of a new trade commission. Wilson, however, hearing Brandeis's endorsement, decided to shift his own position as well and to go along with Rublee. Moving quickly now, the president asked the House committee to substitute the Stevens measure for the Covington sunshine bill, which the entire House had passed just five days previously. After several weeks of intense debate, resolved ultimately by Wilson's direct intervention, both the House and Senate passed the Stevens bill.[94]

The outcome was the Federal Trade Commission Act of 1914, which provided for a board of five members, no more than three of whom could come from the same political party. The commissioners were to be paid salaries of $10,000 each, a high figure for 1914, intended to give prestige to the new agency.[95] The core of the FTC's authority lay in three fundamental provisions Rublee had inserted into the bill: that "unfair methods of competition in commerce are hereby declared unlawful"; that the commission in effect had the power to determine which methods were unfair; and that it could order offenders "to cease and desist" from using such unfair methods. Altogether, the act envisioned a far more powerful and active agency than anything Brandeis had proposed.[96]

According to his own recollection, draftsman Rublee developed the ideas behind these key provisions after studying a number of existing judicial decisions and after poring over the texts of other proposed legislation. "There were a number of other bills besides the Clayton Bill in which monopolistic practices were defined,"

Rublee said afterward. "I had noticed that in most of these bills at the end of the list of forbidden practices there was a general clause prohibiting all other forms of unfair competition. The same general clause appeared at the end of lists of specific practices enjoined in various decrees of Federal Courts in cases arising under the Sherman Law . . . It therefore appeared that the phrase 'unfair competition' had a recognized meaning in the terminology of anti-trust law." Thus Rublee shaped his new bill in accordance with his own interpretation of these existing cases and legislative drafts. He intended that much of the new FTC's power would emanate from the "unfair methods" clause that he had gleaned from his study.[97]

As it turned out, Rublee had been woefully naive in thinking that the phrase "unfair methods of competition in commerce" meant something clear and coherent. He had little experience in drafting this kind of law, and the ambiguity of his key phrase became an Achilles heel, raising insuperable problems during the very first months of the commission's operation. Rublee may have carried the day in 1914, but in so doing he had set off a time bomb that would soon explode. In the first full-scale judicial review of the FTC's authority, which came in 1920, the Supreme Court held that "The words 'unfair methods of competition' are not defined by the statute and their exact meaning is in dispute. It is for the courts, not the Commission, ultimately to determine as matter of law, what they include." And until the court softened its ruling a bit, some fourteen years later, the commission was unable to exercise many important powers.[98]

Partly as a result of its ambiguous statute, the FTC got off to a rocky start. In no one's eyes did it represent a distinguished regulatory body. President Wilson tried to conduct a careful search for good appointees, but with the national economic outlook so uncertain, he worried about alienating business. When Wilson asked Brandeis to serve as a member, the Boston lawyer declined, perhaps sensing that the tasks before the commission were impossible. The president did appoint George Rublee, but the Senate, bowing to the opposition of a senator from Rublee's home state, refused to confirm him.[99]

Of the original five appointees, two were businessmen, one a career politician, one a lawyer-politician, and one (Rublee) a practicing lawyer. None had administrative talents of the first rank. By 1918, only three years after the commission's first meeting, not a single one of these first five members remained in office. The FTC itself, lacking strong leadership, drifted aimlessly from this task to that, making little impact. And on those few occasions when the commission did try to do something important, Congress or the Supreme Court intervened.[100] Almost nobody connected with the FTC could take much pride in its early accomplishments. Looking back several years later, Brandeis himself provided a harsh verdict on the performance of the first FTC commissioners. "It was," he said, "a stupid administration."[101]

The Confusion over the FTC's Functions

Besides weak appointments, many other reasons lay behind the commission's early failures. For one thing, the severe recession of 1914 placed Wilson and other Democrats in a difficult position. As leaders of the party committed to reform of the tariff, currency, and trusts, they now bore the stigma of having regulated prosperity out of the economy. Although nobody fully understood the connection between the business cycle and the program of the New Freedom, everyone understood that if Wilson were regarded as antibusiness during a period of economic downturn, then the Democratic party would suffer in the off-year elections of 1914. This was one reason why Congress balked at voting adequate appropriations for the new FTC.

Then too, the Great War in Europe erupted in August 1914, only a month before the passage of the Federal Trade Commission Act. The commission's first meeting, in 1915, came just a few weeks before the sinking of the *Lusitania*, an event that brought the first wave of war fever to the United States. Of course the war itself ultimately crowded trusts off the front pages; it ended for a time the national preoccupation with the dark side of big business. When the United States joined the conflict in 1917, the FTC was called upon to help in setting prices for essential commodities. By 1918, new and stronger appointees had begun to give more spirit to the commission's efforts. Yet, in a setting of war emergency, the FTC's investigations of business practices struck some critics as bureaucratic busywork—idle snooping that did nothing to facilitate economic mobilization.[102]

In the longer run, the FTC's erratic career derived from its

faulty enabling legislation and from a related absence of any coherent organizational strategy. "Unfair methods of competition"
had no self-evident meaning. "Cease and desist," despite its acerbic ring, turned out to be just another formula for procedural
delay. In the last analysis, Rublee's solution of 1914, so eagerly
grasped by both Brandeis and Wilson as a means of resolving the
dilemma raised by the Clayton bill, had been hollow at the core.
Thus the new commission could have succeeded only through
strong leadership, informed by an exceptionally clear sense of mission. This was the second vital element that the FTC lacked. Different members of the commission, like the different groups that
had supported its creation, put forward conflicting ideas about
how the agency should discharge its duties. Since definitions of the
mission itself were even more ambiguous and conflicting, the
chances for success never amounted to much.

The political consensus that had produced the Federal Trade
Commission clearly did not extend to its functions or procedures.
Instead, the idea of an administrative agency assigned to take care
of the trust question served as a type of panacea whose precise
content must not be specified too closely. If it were, the consensus
might vanish. This kind of problem typified regulatory legislation
in general; but it had its most serious consequences in the FTC
Act, which affected not just one industry but almost all of American business. Merely to review the list of groups which had favored the creation of a commission will suggest the breadth of the
problem.[103] Among political parties and business interests, (1) The
Progressive Party wanted a trade commission as a means of avoiding the dismemberment of center firms—by regulating and
thereby legitimizing them. (2) The Republican Party advocated a
commission less powerful than that contemplated by Roosevelt
and the Progressives, but stronger than the sunshine agency described in Wilson's message to Congress of January 1914. (3) The
Democratic Party—with the exception of Senator Newlands and a
few other legislators—came to the commission idea reluctantly,
first as a means of pacifying business sentiment during the campaign of 1912, later as an alternative to the stringency of the original Clayton bill. Even so, a number of powerful Democrats
remained suspicious of the idea, as the congressional debates of
1914 and the subsequent appropriations fights clearly show. (4)
Center firm executives supported a strong commission as an alter-

native to harsh new antitrust laws. (5) Peripheral firm managers anticipated that a trade commission would help them with several different problems, such as legitimizing their associational activities, helping them in the battle for retail price-fixing authority, and prohibiting the marketing divisions of center firms from underselling them in local competition. (6) Important forces within the federal bureaucracy supported the commission idea as an extension of administrative government. Commissioner of Corporations Herbert Knox Smith, as noted earlier, endorsed the FTC idea with great enthusiasm. And the respected ICC Commissioner Charles Prouty spoke for other high civil servants when he declared that "the regulation of trusts and monopolies is plainly an administrative rather than a judicial function."

A number of influential journalists and academic intellectuals wrote powerful arguments in favor of a trade commission. Herbert Croly in *The Promise of American Life* (1909), Walter Lippmann in *Drift and Mastery* (1914), and many other writers denounced the practice of regulating business by means of intermittent lawsuits and called instead for continuous surveillance by administrative commission. They were joined by numerous academic economists such as John Bates Clark and John Maurice Clark, who argued for a commission in their important book, *The Control of Trusts* (1914). The most thoroughgoing proposals came in Charles Van Hise's *Concentration and Control: A Solution of the Trust Problem in the United States* (1912). In arguing for a commission, Van Hise, president of the University of Wisconsin and a political ally of Senator La Follette, drew on a wide variety of sources, including the work of his economist colleague at Wisconsin, Richard T. Ely. With all of these commission advocates—whether political parties, business groups, bureaucrats, journalists, or intellectuals—in fact wanting different things, it seems unlikely that any single agency could have satisfied a majority of its supporters. Indeed, no group of supporters gained unalloyed pleasure from the agency that emerged.

Advance Advice

Business groups in particular—both center and peripheral—were acutely disappointed when the commission failed to provide greater certainty in drawing the line between legal and illegal practices. As is abundantly evident from the congressional hearings, large numbers of businessmen supported the idea of a new commission because they anticipated receiving what they called "advance advice." That is, they expected to be able to go to the agency routinely with inquiries about the permissibility of contemplated business moves such as pricing decisions, mergers, and certain types of contracts. The commission could then declare that, if the transaction were carried out exactly as proposed, the commission itself would not enjoin it or prosecute the company for unfair trade practices. On the other hand, if the commission advised that it would oppose the contemplated move as a violation of the antitrust laws, then the transaction could be revised or abandoned, without placing the inquiring businessmen in jeopardy of prosecution.

Although advance advice could not confer total immunity from future prosecution, it could provide administrative guidelines tailored much more precisely than any of those available in statutory and case law. For many business managers, this was the great virtue of administrative regulation. Where litigation was formal and governed by elaborate rules of procedure, advance advice would be less formal and relatively unburdened by red tape. Where litigation looked to past acts and toward punitive resolutions, advance advice looked to the future and sought to be preventive. Where litigation occurred spasmodically, advance advice went on continuously. Advance advice, in short, was just the kind of administrative process that Charles Francis Adams had envisioned in 1869.

Later on, in the twentieth century, agency after agency developed different forms of advance advice. The Internal Revenue Service came to issue innumerable "private letter rulings" in response to questions posed by taxpayers. The Securities and Exchange Commission sent out hundreds of "no-action letters" regarding a wide range of securities transactions contemplated by corporations. Ultimately the Federal Trade Commission itself developed a set of trade practice conferences and merger guidelines for the use of corporate executives. Over the years, these forms of advance advice evolved into a type of administrative art characteristic of mature and intelligent regulatory procedure. It may be no exaggeration to say that the idea of regulation itself has hinged on the workability of one or another form of advance advice. The aim, as Adams had pointed out, was to avoid tedious and self-defeating legal proceedings and to permit economic policy to take precedence over judicial process.

Even so, advance advice flew in the face of some central tenets of Anglo-American jurisprudence. Because it avoided adversarial procedure, it offended the judicial principle that decisions be based not on conjecture but on the formal record of evidence developed by the parties at issue in some definite case or controversy. (When courts themselves have received requests for advance advice in the form of "declaratory judgments," they have refused the requests in the absence of prior statutory authorization.) Then too, because advance advice was negotiational—that is, discussed between a government agency on the one hand and a citizen or corporation on the other—it ran counter to the prevailing model of adversarial advocacy. Under the adversarial system, truth was assumed to be reached best through a contest between citizen and government (or citizen and citizen), played out under elaborate rules of advocacy before a judge who stood above the fray. With advance advice, both the judge and the contest disappeared. Finally, unlike court decisions, advance advice had no precedential value. Advisory opinions by agencies were directed only to the inquiring party and did not constitute authoritative statements of law on which others could rely directly. In practice, however, the knowledge of criteria consistently applied by an agency in its advance advice on a given subject created guidelines on which large numbers of business executives could rely informally in making decisions in the future.

For all of these reasons, advance advice initially encountered only lukewarm endorsement from the legal profession as a whole. Insofar as regulatory agencies emerged into an institutional context already dominated by lawyers and judges, they naturally encountered spirited opposition to the grafting of administrative discretion onto the existing formalistic judicial structure. This was true even if the regulators themselves were lawyers, as a majority of them were. And because of the requirement that administrative rulings be subject to review by the courts, advance advice was certain to be circumscribed.[104]

As soon as the Federal Trade Commission was organized in 1915, businessmen deluged it with requests for advance advice. Because the five commissioners themselves disagreed on what to do about these requests, they called on several outside consultants. One of these, as might have been expected, was Brandeis. On the afternoon of April 30, 1915, he spent several hours talking with the commissioners, and the unpublished stenographic transcript of this discussion shows in vivid detail the collision between adversarial and negotiational approaches to regulation and between legal and administrative mind sets. In this conversation Brandeis may be seen as expressing not just his own views but some of the core principles of the Anglo-American legal tradition.[105]

The commissioners' first question was whether they should entertain applications for advance advice. Brandeis responded with an emphatic no. Determinations of legality, he declared, must come from courts and courts alone. If the commission gave advance advice, "the public would be tricked," and the commission itself "hoodwinked." Since determinations of legality had to be made on the basis of facts that "do not exist yet," the commissioners would have to regulate in the dark. On any controversial matter, said Brandeis, both sides of an issue had to be represented, but this would not be likely to occur under advance advice. Such advice was unnecessary anyway, he added—when businessmen were acting morally. Executives' consciences should be the best guide. As Brandeis told the commissioners (in what could not have been a very helpful comment, considering the problems they now faced), "Your conscience, if you are honest with yourself, would tell you, nineteen times out of twenty, whether you intend to restrain trade; and if you could say to yourself clearly, and honestly, that you did not intend a restraint of trade, you would not need to go to a lawyer at all." As for the commissioners' own role in policing business behavior, Brandeis reiterated his warning that they must refuse all requests for advance advice.[106]

But if the commissioners were not to give advance advice or to have the power to determine the meaning of "unfair methods of competition," then why had Brandeis supported Rublee's draft of the FTC Act? Certainly it was inconsistent to back Rublee and then afterward oppose FTC discretion regarding advance advice. It would seem, therefore, that Brandeis had not understood Rublee's draft, that he had not paid sufficiently close attention to it, or that at some point he had changed his mind. The last possibility seems unlikely, because he opposed the idea of advance advice not only in his 1915 conversation with the commissioners but earlier as well. In February 1914, four months before Rublee's presentation of the idea and Brandeis' support of it on the White House lawn, Brandeis had testified on this very topic before a House committee considering antitrust legislation. One congressman, noting the extreme difficulty of enumerating every unfair trade practice in a statute, asked Brandeis why Congress should not "give to the interstate trade commission discretionary power to determine what is fair trade between man and man." Brandeis responded: "I feel very clearly on this question that it would be extremely unwise to vest in the trade commission any such power . . . It seems to me that it would be very unwise, and might, instead of resulting as these gentlemen suppose in a just settlement, create very grave difficulties."[107] Whatever the reasons for Brandeis' inconsistency, the FTC in fact came into existence with a broad mandate to define "unfair methods of competition" but without power sufficiently explicit to survive judicial review. In its early regulatory activities, the FTC attempted halfheartedly to define unfair methods, but it also declined to give advance advice freely. This sort of timidity and tentativeness burdened the agency with the worst of both worlds.[108]

In retrospect, it seems likely that to have been successful as an organization the Federal Trade Commission had only two strategies to choose from. Under one strategy, it might have shaped itself as a super sunshine commission by building and expanding on the investigatory work begun by the Bureau of Corporations. Such a plan would have been easy to implement because the bureau, an excellent organization in its own right, was absorbed *in toto* into the new Federal Trade Commission. (The FTC's early operations, in fact, were conducted in the bureau's old offices.) This type of strategy might well have produced a steady accumulation of detailed and systematic bodies of information about corporations such as those later developed by the Securities and Exchange Commission.

As a second potentially successful strategy, the FTC might have issued advance advice freely, to all comers. It might have struck forth boldly with a series of bright-line definitions of unfair methods of competition and gone back to Congress for a clearer line of authority. This kind of strategy had recently been followed by the Interstate Commerce Commission, which had asked for and received from Congress repeated refinements of its original legislative mandate. Later on, in the 1930s, the Securities and Exchange Commission followed a similar strategy, mixing bold initiatives with advance advice and receiving further powers from Congress.[109]

Brandeis himself had wanted the Federal Trade Commission to function as a clearinghouse of information for the benefit of small business. He elaborated on this theme at length in his discussion with the commissioners in 1915. They were in a position, he said, to inform small businessmen about the prices and policies of their competitors. In maximizing the information available about competitors the FTC could preserve independence and prevent combination: "The real way to mend this terrible competition which is leading men to want to make these agreements is to play the game with the cards right up on the table." Brandeis told the commissioners about his own service to one industry (probably shoe manufacturing), when he placed information before a group of competitors who were engaged against each other in fierce mutual price cutting. In that instance, he related, he had required that each of the competitors submit to him monthly reports of their production, prices, and inventories, which he in turn gave to all participants. "Well," Brandeis told the commissioners, "they have done it, and for some years, and it healed the trouble in that particular business, and those people are just as independent as can be." Yet when the commissioners asked Brandeis whether they themselves might give favorable advance advice for such a purpose—as they in fact had been asked to do—Brandeis could only equivocate.[110]

He did urge the commissioners to perform similar types of service, particularly in helping associations of small businessmen. "There are several thousands of these associations in this country. I think it would be eminently proper for you to investigate what is being done . . . how far they regulate or undertake to regulate trade . . . how far they supply information, and how far they correct abuses, like abuses in regard to discounting, and dating, and different questions of that sort. Get all that information together, and present it, with the explanation and operation of these different associations." After the facts were gathered the commission might issue its own views of which practices were helpful, "but not in the way of giving men advice as to what they can do and what they can not do, because that is the business of the lawyers, and of the Department of Justice."[111]

Along with helping trade associations, the FTC was urged to

perform research and development functions on behalf of small business. Brandeis had made this kind of recommendation many times before, in magazine articles, congressional testimony, and suggestions to members of Wilson's cabinet. In effect, he sought to offset the power of center firms through government assistance to peripheral firms. "We shall erect a great bulwark against the trusts when we thus offer to the small business man what is procurable only by the great industrial concerns through their research laboratories and bureaus of information." Under this plan, the Federal Trade Commission would become a central fact-gathering bureau for all types of small business. It would develop and make available to them reliable sets of statistics showing standard operating ratios, typical costs and prices, and characteristic profit margins. As an overarching trade association, it would perform for peripheral firms the kind of informational and research functions only center firms were customarily able to afford.[112]

Throughout his discussion with the commissioners, Brandeis said practically nothing about the commission's role in antitrust proceedings. The text of the transcript outlines no direct FTC mission at all with respect to center firms. Under Brandeis' plan, center firms would be reached by FTC action only indirectly, through the building up of peripheral firms. His premise—a largely incorrect one except in wholesaling and retailing—was that center and peripheral firms competed directly with each other.[113]

Nor is there anything in Brandeis' many discussions of the Federal Trade Commission, in 1915 or earlier, to suggest that he conceived of it as a consumer-protection agency. Rather, he confined his attention to the small producer, wholesaler, and retailer. There was no sense of the clash between the price-fixing and other associational activities of small firms and the interest of the consumer. Indeed, Brandeis all but said that the FTC's constituency did not include the consumer and that its role did not involve the public interest. When one of the FTC commissioners asked him why he seemed to be implying that the concerns of the Interstate Commerce Commission were somehow more "public" than those of the FTC, Brandeis replied: "The Interstate Commerce Commission deals wholly with public business. The business of the railroads is all public business. There ought not to be a secret about a railroad. The railroad is a Government agency. Anybody who had anything to say about a Government agency could well say it in public. I think you [at the FTC] are dealing with interests that are private." Thus the public—whether as consumers or merely as citizens of the polity—had no important stake in business-to-business dealings.[114]

Brandeis and Regulation

In January 1916 President Wilson nominated Brandeis to a seat on the United States Supreme Court. That nomination, which came as a complete surprise to nearly everyone concerned, touched off a national furor. There had never been a Jewish member of the court, and Wilson's action occasioned both open and covert expressions of antisemitism. Additional opposition came from the Boston establishment, which had turned against Brandeis during the long controversy over the New Haven railroad. The most serious chorus of objection, however, came from legal organizations. Seven former presidents of the American Bar Association sent a joint protest to the Senate, urging that the appointment not be confirmed: "The undersigned feel under the painful duty to say to you that in their opinion, taking into view the reputation, character, and professional career of Mr. Louis D. Brandeis, he is not a fit person to be a member of the Supreme Court of the United States." The confirmation fight, which went on for five months, became one of the year's most newsworthy events. In the end the defense, bolstered by Wilson's ringing affirmation of Brandeis' merits, carried the day. The nomination clinched Wilson's own claim to progressive credentials, and the event itself became a cause célèbre in the history of American liberalism.[115]

Once on the bench, Brandeis surprised his critics with his impartiality, wisdom, and judicial depth. His tenure on the court lasted for twenty-three years, until he retired in 1939 at the age of eighty-two, and he made a truly great judge. It was almost as if, having spent his entire previous career hurrying from one case to another and spreading himself too thin, he now at last could take the time for the kind of reflection essential in thinking through his positions. This is not to say that those positions changed in any important ways. The central themes of his court career accorded well with the chief interests of his earlier life: a preoccupation with actual social conditions, an insistence on individual rights and autonomy, and—most important for his decisions on economic issues—a powerful commitment to judicial restraint.[116] Because of this emphasis on judicial restraint, it is difficult to separate law from economics in his judicial opinions. What is clear, though, is that he always retained a passionate feeling against the curse of bigness. And, despite his impartiality in most other matters, he also exercised a powerful preference for the interests of small producers, wholesalers, and retailers over those of consumers. Several of his best-known opinions demonstrate this preference vividly.[117]

Brandeis' long career touched on so many matters that his significance in the history of regulation, and in American history generally, is not easily summarized. Even so, several conclusions now seem warranted. For one, it is impossible to understand his career without recognizing that above all else Brandeis was a professional litigator, primarily committed to the business of advocacy. Of course that was hardly inappropriate, since the advocacy system is so basic to the American polity, and even to the national temper, as to be a defining characteristic. This has been true from the beginning of the American Republic. Lawyers such as Adams, Otis, Henry, Hamilton, Jefferson, and Madison led the revolution. The Declaration of Independence itself is a two-pronged legal document, combining a brief for the cause of liberty with a bill of particulars against George III. The dominance of lawyers in America was so often remarked by insightful observers (Crevecoeur, Tocqueville, Bryce) that, by the end of the nineteenth century, the observation had become a commonplace. From 1790 to the present, about two thirds of all U.S. senators have been lawyers and about one half the members of the House.[118]

Again, the history of regulation falls very much into the same legal pattern. A substantial majority of all federal commissioners have been lawyers by training. One scholar calculated that from the time of the founding of each commission to the year 1969, the number of lawyers as a percentage of all commissioners was as follows.[119]

Interstate Commerce Commission (founded in 1887)	75%
Federal Trade Commission (1914)	82
Federal Power Commission (1920)	58
Securities and Exchange Commission (1934)	70
Federal Communications Commission (1934)	54
National Labor Relations Board (1935)	54
Civil Aeronautics Board (1938)	66

Lawyers dominated the American polity before the rise of commission regulation and afterward as well. Institutional success for any given commission required policies and processes shaped so as not to interfere unduly with the interests of the organized bar or with the professional canons and prejudices of lawyers. This meant that the very serious problems raised by the agencies' relationships with the three existing branches of government must be worked out in a certain way. These problems included the issue of agencies' "independence" from the executive and the legislative branch and—most important—the issue of review by the judiciary of both the commissions' decisions and the limits of their administrative discretion. In such a context, the existing legal system found itself in conflict not only over aspects of administrative technique—such as advance advice and the general informality of the regulatory process—but also over substantial ideological issues. The very notion of a "public interest" implied not adversarial struggle but consensual decision making on behalf of the greatest good for the greatest number. In the regulatory process, lawyers' predilections often buried an agency's mission in a mass of procedural red tape. As Woodrow Wilson once put it, "I am almost afraid to appoint a lawyer on any of the commissions for they immediately tie it up into technicalities, and so limit its scope by reading limitations into its enabling act." Even Brandeis, whom Wilson embraced as an unlawyerlike lawyer on this point, still tended to insist on rigid adversarial and evidentiary procedures, as in his warnings to the FTC about advance advice.[120]

Brandeis himself, as one of the first American lawyers routinely to take his cases beyond the courtroom and into the mass media, cultivated and shaped public opinion as carefully as he might have done with a jury. Because he conceived his role to be that of champion, he sought out and embraced conflict. Whereas Charles Francis Adams characteristically studied the long-run results of any problems and tried to avoid or finesse immediate conflict, Brandeis went out of his way to find a good fight. Once the fight had started, Brandeis displayed a marvelous inventiveness, seeking novel routes to victory. This is what made him such a splendid advocate, and what gave such an air of anticipation—almost an expectation of surprise—to so many of his cases. As one senator said of Brandeis during the Supreme Court confirmation hearings, "He seems to like to do startling things and work under cover. He has disregarded or defied the proprieties . . . He is of the material that makes good advocates, reformers, and crusaders, but not good or safe judges." The senator was wrong only in the prediction that Brandeis would make a poor judge.[121]

In his crusade against bigness, Brandeis combined an intense moral passion with a compelling drive for victory, and the result gave his analysis an inflammatory tone more appropriate to the media to which he turned than to the courtroom from which he had come. "We are confronted in the twentieth century, as we were in the nineteenth century with an irreconcilable conflict," he wrote in 1911 in a newspaper article. "Our democracy could not endure half free and half slave. The essence of the trust is a combination of the capitalist, by the capitalist, for the capitalist."[122] His fervor led Brandeis, as it had led the antislavery abolitionists before him, to advocate root-and-branch solutions. "For their by-products shall you know the trusts," he declared. He insisted that the only way to eliminate the by-products was to eradicate the center firms altogether, to rip them out root and branch. Given his task, he had no choice but to argue that big business became big only through unfair methods. Positing bigness to be unnatural, he was forced to discover illegitimate means of its evolution. Only there would he find the winning ground.[123]

It is clear now that center firms did indeed threaten the atomistic commonwealth of Brandeis' imagination. It is equally clear, however, that these companies were not necessarily hostile to the values he saw as damaged through their "by-products." It might have reassured Brandeis to see into the future and to know that a very large number of industries (most, in fact) are peripherals, with only a slender chance of becoming big businesses.[124] It did reassure him in the 1930s to see securities legislation bring an end to frenzied finance and achieve new protection for investors. Brandeis' old age was gladdened too by the New Deal's Wagner Act (the National Labor Relations Act of 1935), which gave explicit federal protection for the right of workers to organize.

But as these events occurred, and as the center-peripheral split appeared in country after country, they constituted a step-by-step demolition of the Brandeis brief against bigness. They demonstrated that it was not bigness per se that had brought these abuses and that bigness raised no barrier to their abolition. In fact, for resolving some abuses, bigness held powerful advantages: it was far easier for the government to enforce legislation such as the Wagner Act against one huge corporation like General Motors or U.S. Steel than against thousands of small sweatshops. Only the mistaken idea that these by-products derived from one root cause made them part of the trust question at all. As the political scientist Louis Hartz once remarked, "We think of the trust as an economic creation of American history, and we fail to see that it was just as much a psychological creation of the American Progressive mind." Brandeis' thinking reflected this tendency of the period. In that sense as in others—his moralism, his fixation on the redemptive value of "facts"—he may be seen as a man of his time.[125]

This is not to say, however, that he stood in the forefront as an economic thinker. Some pioneering economic analysts of his time, in fact, became impatient with Brandeis' loose rhetoric. Charles R. Van Hise, for example, the author of the penetrating *Concentration and Control* (1914), often took issue with him. Though the two men were great mutual admirers, Brandeis' articles in *Collier's* during the campaign of 1912 offended Van Hise. "Mr. Brandeis's viewpoint," he protested to *Collier's* editor Hapgood, "appears to be that in general large organizations are not efficient." By way of evidence, Brandeis had quoted from Bureau of Corporations' investigation of size and efficiency, particularly in the steel industry. Yet, Van Hise wrote, "it is very clear from this investigation that large companies [in the steel industry] are more efficient than small companies."[126]

For Van Hise, a professor as well as an adviser to Senator La Follette, Brandeis's muckraking methods did not square with the scholar's commitment to the whole truth. "This brings me to another point," he continued in his letter to Hapgood, "which is a distrust of the method pursued by Mr. Brandeis in his articles. He lays down a general proposition and as evidence of the truthfulness of the proposition gives one or more illustrations of it. The scientific mind demands not one or two cases of the principle to be considered, but that all cases or at least a large number of them be taken into account." Brandeis had said in 1912 that "the real issue is regulate competition or regulate monopoly," and this had been the slogan on which Wilson had pitched his campaign. "The sweeping, plausible statement is made and not a scrap of evidence is brought forth in its support," Van Hise objected.[127]

Nor were academics the only contemporary observers to pene-

trate to the real essence of the business revolution. Several journalists also expressed remarkably prescient insights into the fundamental division between center and peripheral firms. In 1911, for
example, editor Carl Hovey of *Metropolitan Magazine* invited
Brandeis to write an article on national antitrust policy:

Suppose it were shown that in certain industries consolidation is necessary and favorable, while in others competition is equally necessary and
favorable, to the general good. And suppose the writer were then to
classify the industries (in a general way) which would be better left competitive, or restored to competition, and those which are natural giants,
if not monopolies, which it would render no service to the public to dis-
sect into their original parts. Then the writer might indicate a plan, a
rule of law, or of common sense, or of public opinion—or all combined,
by which the reorganization of industry should be gone about. And, after
this, might follow an ingenious forecast of the concrete results of putting
such a plan into effect.[128]

Of course, Brandeis never wrote any such article, because in so
doing he would have granted legitimacy to bigness. This he was
constitutionally incapable of doing, even in the limited way editor
Hovey had suggested.

Perhaps the shrewdest contemporary critic of Brandeis' anti-
bigness ethic was Walter Lippmann of the *New Republic*. Lippmann, who in 1916 stood forth as the most eloquent defender of
Brandeis' nomination to the Supreme Court, earlier derided the
nominee's crusade against bigness. More than thirty years younger
than Brandeis, Lippmann always understood that the significance
of the business revolution lay not in size alone but in organization
and administration. As Lippmann wrote in *Drift and Mastery*
(1914), "The real news about business is that it is being administered by men who are not profiteers. The managers are on salary,
divorced from ownership and from bargaining." They stood outside the old Smithian model, immune from petty haggling. "The
motive of profit is not their personal motive. That is an astounding
change." Lippmann went on to say that the Brandeisian preoccupation with bigness directed all discussion to a dead end. Quoting
Brandeis' remarks that even the best organizations depend on one
man, Lippmann wrote: "In this statement, you will find, I believe,
one of the essential reasons why a man of Mr. Brandeis's imagina-
tive power has turned against the modern trust. He does not believe that men can deal efficiently with the scale upon which the
modern business world is organized. He has said quite frankly, that

economic size is in itself a danger to democracy. This means, I take it, that American voters are not intelligent enough or powerful enough to dominate great industrial organizations."[129]

Lippmann concluded his critique by inquiring about the natural limits of industrial size, observing that "It is not very helpful to insist that size is a danger, unless you can specify what size." Brandeis had been asked this very question by senators during the antitrust hearings. "They pressed him to state approximately what percentage of an industry he considered an effective unit. He hesitated between ten per cent and forty percent, and could not commit himself. Obviously—for how could he know?" Adam Smith, said Lippmann, had thought the corporations of his own eighteenth century were doomed for the same reasons Brandeis was now adducing. "Say today that one unit of business is impossible, tomorrow you may be confronted with an undreamt success. Here if anywhere is a place where negative prophecy is futile."[130]

In the last analysis, Lippmann was right. Brandeis' fixation on bigness as the essence of the problem doomed to superficiality both his diagnosis and his prescription. It meant that in his own thinking he was led irresistibly away from the organizational issues, where the real revolution lay. (The largest organization in which he himself ever worked full time was the Supreme Court.) It meant that he must argue against vertical integration and other innovations that enhanced productive efficiency and consumer welfare. It meant conversely that he must favor cartels and other loose horizontal combinations that protected individual businessmen against absorption into tight mergers but that also raised prices and lowered output. It meant that he must promote retail price fixing as a means of protecting individual wholesalers and retailers, even though consumers again suffered. It meant, finally, that he must become in significant measure not the "people's lawyer" but the spokesman of retail druggists, small shoe manufacturers, and other members of the petite bourgeoisie. These groups, like so many others throughout American history, sought to use the power of government to reverse economic forces that were threatening to render them obsolete. In Brandeis they found a talented champion.

Yet Louis D. Brandeis endures as an American hero. In the minds of his countrymen he remains a properly revered symbol of individualism, integrity, self-reliance, and willingness to fight hard for cherished values. As we have seen, he also symbolizes one of the characteristic shortcomings of the American regulatory tradition: a disinclination to persist in hard economic analysis that may lead away from strong political preference. This shortcoming appears vividly in the subsequent tangles of twentieth-century antitrust policy, in the continuing institutional schizophrenia of the Federal Trade Commission, and in the frequent unwillingness of legislators to act on the unpopular principle that protection is usually anti-competitive and anticonsumerist, even when it is small business that is being protected.

CHAPTER 4

Antitrust, Regulation, and the FTC

WITH THE COMING of the Great War, and afterward the prosperity of the 1920s, the nation's preoccupation with the underside of business practice disappeared from view, to remain out of sight until the next emergence of general economic adversity. The antitrust crusade more or less expired, at least as a coherent movement. Meanwhile, the forward march of center firms continued without interruption. Many existing companies grew very large, and important new ones sprang up to dominate emerging industries. The automobile, electronics, and chemical industries spawned such giants as General Motors, RCA, and Dow. This maturation of the center economy was driven not so much by the outside choices of public policy as by the internal dynamics of changing technology and expanding markets. These same economic forces also acted powerfully to change some old peripheral firms like Du Pont (founded back in 1802) into new center-firm powerhouses. In all, the 1920s marked a watershed in American economic history, introducing unprecedented national prosperity and ushering in the first full-blown consumer economy.

Among peripheral firms, the continuing quest for legal approval of their horizontal associations now took a great leap forward. The remarkable record of intraindustry "cooperation" during the Great War—a performance viewed by many important administrators, politicians, and economists as enormously successful—set the stage for a resurgence of interest in finding methods for standardizing business practices among cooperating companies in the same lines of business. Prominent exponents of this ideology of voluntary collectivism included progressive busi-

ness executives such as Gerard Swope of General Electric, respected economists such as Rexford Tugwell of Columbia, and
leading politicians such as Herbert Hoover. Hoover in particular,
first from his post as secretary of commerce, then as president,
campaigned relentlessly in favor of industrial self-government in
the public interest. Never, though, did he advocate a syndicalist
solution, whereby government power would be used to legalize
the form and substance of those price-fixing and market-sharing
activities toward which horizontal business associations inevitably
tended. Indeed, for Hoover and many others during the 1920s, the
troubling line between legitimate standard setting for improved
trade practices, on the one hand, and criminal conspiracies to fix
prices, on the other, became more difficult than ever to draw. One
principal focus of both antitrust prosecutions and FTC regulatory
policy became the question of how to cope with this dilemma. Ultimately, rather than provoking a firm answer, the dilemma itself
remained unresolved, indeed became institutionalized in the New
Deal's National Industrial Recovery Act of 1933.[1]

The Pattern of Antitrust

By the beginning of the 1920s, at least one important dispute had
been settled: industrial bigness, in and of itself, could no longer be
considered unlawful, despite the opposing convictions of Brandeis
and other decentralizers. In the important *United States Steel* antitrust case of 1920, the Supreme Court laid down a forthright
rule: "The law does not make mere size an offense."[2] Yet, even
when the antibigness crusade had run its course and the popularity
of the antitrust movement was on the wane, antitrust retained
considerable vitality as a tool of national economic policy. Over
the next several decades, this distinctively American approach to
the question of business competition would undergo several trans-
formations. But never would the question itself or the antitrust
approach to it disappear from public view.

In the long run, American antitrust policy clearly served to en-
hance consumer welfare. It effectively contained horizontal price
fixing and market divisions by both center and peripheral firms,
thereby promoting allocative efficiency. At the same time, antitrust actions did not seriously interfere with vertical integration
and other organizational innovations. By prohibiting cartelization,

active antitrust enforcement actually encouraged these innovations, and to that extent it both promoted productive efficiency and contributed to a rapid rise of administrative science in the United States. (In Europe, by contrast, managerial innovations tended to lag for many years, in part because European governments continued to encourage old-style cartels.) America was on the road to ever bigger business, although such a result did not accord with the original intentions of Brandeis and many other antitrusters. The policy of antitrust may have been designed with other ends in mind, but it did, by a kind of perversely therapeutic effect, ultimately serve the consumer. The very existence of the antitrust laws also helped to legitimize big business in the eyes of the American people.

Perhaps the clearest evidence of the continuing pattern of antitrust activities during the years between the Sherman Act and the New Deal may be seen in the number of cases instituted by the Department of Justice:

Five-year period	Number of cases initiated
1890–1894	9
1895–1899	7
1900–1904	6
1905–1909	39
1910–1914	91
1915–1919	43
1920–1924	66
1925–1929	59
1930–1932 (3 years)	15

From these figures, it is obvious that the zealous prosecutions of the 1910–1914 period, which preceded passage of the Clayton and Federal Trade Commission Acts, abated a bit after 1914. It is also clear, however, that by the 1920s antitrust had become a permanent part of American political and economic life. Throughout the period covered in the table (and subsequently as well), the Justice Department not only instituted dozens of cases but also won most of them (about 80 percent).[3]

Other revealing statistics pertain to the identity of the defendants. In the years after 1920, just as during the trust-busting presidencies of Roosevelt, Taft, and Wilson, by far the majority of cases (about six out of seven) were brought not against center firms but against peripherals, often in horizontal combination.[4] As one leading scholar concludes, "a large proportion of the [Antitrust Division of the Justice] Department's cases—and an even larger proportion of the FTC's—are brought in industries not normally regarded as highly concentrated"—such industries as lumber, furniture, apparel, and wholesale and retail trade. As in the early years of antitrust, so too later on: prosecutions focused on horizontal associations of peripheral firms.[5]

For a brief moment during the 1920s, the Supreme Court did waver between approval and disapproval of close horizontal cooperation among businesses. The court's decision in the *Maple Flooring* case of 1925, for example, upheld the activities of an association of lumber-product dealers, even though these activities might serve as a mask for cooperative price fixing. The majority opinion, written by Justice Harlan F. Stone, sounded almost Brandeisian in its logic (and, indeed, Justice Brandeis enthusiastically joined with the majority):

It is the consensus of opinion of economists and of many of the most important agencies of Government that the public interest is served by the gathering and dissemination, in the widest possible manner, of information with respect to the production and distribution, costs and prices in actual sales, of market commodities, because the making available of such information tends to stabilize trade and industry, to produce fairer price levels and to avoid the waste which inevitably attends the unintelligent conduct of economic enterprises . . . Competition does not become less free merely because the conduct of commercial operations becomes less intelligent.[6]

Later, the permissive doctrine of *Maple Flooring* became more narrowly circumscribed. In the *Trenton Potteries* case of 1927, where associational price fixing appeared in a less subtle form than in *Maple Flooring*, the court came down hard against it. Afterward, as in the preceding decades, price fixing continued to represent an inherent violation of the antitrust laws.[7]

Meanwhile, "big cases" against leading center firms all but disappeared from the dockets. In retrospect the explanation of this phenomenon, and of the history of antitrust in general, seems fairly clear. For one thing, the resources of the federal Antitrust Division remained small (about 25 lawyers during the 1920s, compared to around 400 today). Second, these lawyers, like litigators everywhere, liked to win. From their viewpoint, it was much easier to secure convictions in cases involving local price-fixing arrangements among associations of peripheral companies than in cases against giant center firms, whose most visible offense was the now immune characteristic of enormous size.[8] Third, during the 1920s, the overall number of associational activities among peripheral firms rose steadily, in keeping with the cooperative business spirit of the time. The opportunities for organized horizontal price fixing and output limitation simply multiplied. Businessmen met together more regularly than ever, and the government—including even the chiefs of the Antitrust Division—encouraged associational activities as never before.[9]

The Associationist Movement

Much of the new interest in associationalism emerged from the American war experience of 1917–18. In that turbulent time, the War Industries Board and other mobilization agencies demonstrated that industrial coordination could yield enormous productive efficiencies. The leaders of wartime mobilization seemed to have achieved, within a solidly democratic and voluntary framework, just the kinds of economic coordination that critics had formerly identified only with state-directed foreign economies and autocratic political systems. The American war managers, without the assistance of a large state bureaucracy, had successfully directed a national effort toward a single objective: victory over the Central Powers. When that victory was achieved, many participants in the mobilization effort—businessmen and public administrators alike—became evangelists for what they saw as the new model for organizing the American economy. In place of cutthroat competition, they insisted on enlightened cooperation, which had helped to win the war. Where disorder reigned, they advocated planning, standardization, rationality. The most effective instrument, just as during the war years, would be not state dictation, but the use of private associations: voluntarism catalyzed by an encouraging, prodding, but never enforcing government.[10]

This vision of the associationists surely contained more than a tinge of selective memory as well as a large measure of wishful thinking. In fact, there had been a good deal of coercive state management during the Great War, just as in other wars. But this coercion had been effectively camouflaged behind the wall of democratic rhetoric put forward by President Wilson, War Industries Board chief Bernard Baruch, and Public Information director George Creel, among other national leaders. Even with due allowance for mythmaking, it remained true that, comparatively speaking, the management of economic mobilization in America had been unusually free of such normal accompaniments of war as the confiscation of private property. One reason was that the government delegated much of its authority to private trade associations. In addition, a number of "dollar-a-year-men" and other business executives were temporarily installed in government offices as war managers. Finally, the fact that the war ended so soon after American entry, and that no battles were fought on American soil, helped to minimize the need for coercive activities by government. For all of these reasons, the pleasant lessons of cooperation within and among industries had some foundation in the facts.[11]

From this experience in mobilization, one corollary naturally emerged: the United States would be well advised to abandon its existing antitrust policy in favor of something better and more enlightened. During the months following the Armistice, a great deal of business sentiment developed to support the immediate revision of existing antitrust regulation, including that "antiquated enactment," the Sherman law. This early postwar revisionist movement soon lost momentum. The immediate onset of peacetime inflation, followed by a severe economic recession, served to make the American public temporarily less hospitable toward new business associations. Also, revelations of wartime abuses on the part of certain trade associations acted to diminish the popular reputation of trade groups in general. Then, suddenly, following the election of 1920, President Harding's new attorney general, Harry Daugherty, confounded antitrust revisionists by inaugurating an aggressive new program aimed at prosecuting all associational activities that had even a faint potential for the fixing of prices or the limiting of production.[12]

With Daugherty's initiatives, the real battle began, and there ensued a protracted intragovernmental policy dispute between the attorney general and the very powerful secretary of commerce, Herbert Hoover. Hoover agreed with Daugherty that price fixing and output limitation should not be tolerated. But Hoover had a much broader vision of what cooperation could legally mean. In his view, the proper function of trade associations was not to manage industry-wide cartels, but to rationalize the conduct of business. Associations would collect statistics, standardize accounting practices, promote equitable labor relations, and help to smooth out the violent ups and downs of business cycles. These activities were entirely legitimate, so long as they did not drift into a cartel-style fixing of prices or a division of markets. And industrial self-policing achieved one final, transcendent virtue: when it worked properly, it minimized the need for external regulation by government bureaucracies. An internal self-policing, Hoover believed, would preserve American democratic values even in an era of industrial mass society. Most enlightened businessmen and politicians of the 1920s probably agreed with him. Franklin D. Roosevelt, for example, worked with Hoover to set up one important trade association—the American Construction Council—and Roosevelt served for seven years as its president.[13]

Hoover eventually won his fight with Daugherty, and subsequent attorneys general during the 1920s saw things Hoover's way. The secretary's extremely energetic programs favoring industrial cooperation now went ahead. But an inherent problem persisted: how, precisely, could business groups that were involved in legitimate associational activities be prevented from simultaneously engaging in illegitimate ones? Hoover himself thought he had the answer—benevolent supervision by government—and the experiences of business groups throughout the 1920s seemed to vindicate his position. Subsequent events, however, proved that Hoover had placed too much faith in industrial self-discipline. During times of great prosperity, like the 1920s, most businesses felt no need to fix prices or to divide markets. But after the crash of 1929, business groups could not maintain self-discipline as a higher priority than self-preservation; the collusive fixing of prices and dividing of markets became much more important than the vaguer policy of business statesmanship urged on them by Hoover. Under the pressures of national economic depression, Hoover's dream of a privately managed cooperative commonwealth simply collapsed. Yet the experience of the 1920s left behind certain important legacies for regulation.[14]

The FTC During the 1920s

As the prevailing ideology of the American government shifted toward greater acceptance of intraindustry cooperation, even at the risk of cartel-like behavior, the Federal Trade Commission seemed to have little choice but to follow the election returns. Not only was the commission weakened by internal feuding, as it had been from the beginning, but by the early 1920s even its external reputation had begun to go through a remarkable transformation. Briefly, its former supporters among progressive insurgents now turned into faultfinding critics, and erstwhile detractors among business groups gradually became ardent admirers. For the commission, some confusion about the identity of its real friends was inevitable.[15]

Yet this peculiar history also reflected the confusion about mission which had attended the FTC from its birth in 1914. Even in the early years, the commission proved an unlikely baby; it pleased nobody, at least consistently. At times, the FTC did seem to fulfill the expectations of some of its antitrust-oriented sponsors. For example, once the Great War ended, the commission completed a thorough investigation of the meatpacking industry. The packers had been a target of reformers for many years, not only because of the conditions in the slaughterhouses portrayed in Upton Sinclair's powerful novel, *The Jungle*, but also because meatpackers maintained an obvious but equally despised trust. When the FTC concluded its extensive investigation by announcing that the five largest packers were engaging in unlawful combinations and unfair trade practices, the commission also suggested structural changes in the industry, including public ownership of some parts of it. A violent response greeted this proposal. Legislators friendly to the meatpackers denounced the FTC, calling its recommendations socialistic. Other critics called for a new investigation, this time not *by* the FTC but *of* it. Although such an investigation never materialized, Congress withdrew the industry from FTC jurisdiction, placing it instead under the more sympathetic watchfulness of the Department of Agriculture. But already, damage to the FTC had been done.[16]

The commission was absorbing even heavier blows from the federal judiciary. The agency's pursuit of business complaints, after a moderately energetic beginning, ran up against a wall of resistance in 1920 when, in the *Gratz* case, the Supreme Court denied to the FTC the power to define "unfair methods of competition." This decision stripped the commission of one of its principal functions, and for the remainder of the 1920s the FTC could do little more than nurse its wounds and try to find a new function as a fact-finding agency. The Supreme Court struck at the commission here as well, by sharply limiting its efforts to extract information from reluctant corporations. Because of these limitations, the FTC had to work hard to conduct as many successful investigations during the 1920s as in fact it did. (Its outstanding single achievement during that decade was a rigorous investigation of public utilities, a notable effort that bore fruit during the New Deal in the Public Utility Holding Company Act of 1935.)[17]

The commission's most characteristic activity during the 1920s lay in assisting the efforts of business groups themselves, especially in helping them to rationalize their industries through associational activities. By the late 1920s, the chief mission of the FTC had become the sponsorship of "trade-practice conferences." These were formal meetings of large numbers of business executives from a single industry (most often a peripheral industry), where rules for the conduct of their business would be discussed, codified, and later promulgated. Most of these rules, of course, carried no force of law, but the fact of commission sponsorship would not escape the attention of judges in the event of subsequent litigation. In its involvement with trade-practice conferences, therefore, the FTC was dipping its toe into the pool of advance advice—but without exercising the authoritative powers, sounding the depth of involvement, or paying the attention to detail that the original business supporters of the FTC Act had hoped for. Again in these trade conferences, as in the earlier Hoover-Daugherty dispute, the old question of how to draw a sharp line between legitimate and illegitimate associational activities remained unresolved. Yet trade practice conferences did keep the FTC alive and active.[18]

The principal proponent of such conferences was FTC Chairman William E. Humphrey, one of the most colorful (if least effective) commissioners in the history of federal regulation. Appointed by President Coolidge in 1925, Humphrey had been a congressman and lumber lobbyist. After joining the commission, the garrulous and acerbic new chairman missed no opportunity to broadcast his own view that the FTC's job was not so much to police business practices as to assist executives in doing what they already wanted to do. An unrestrained partisan of Old Guard Republicanism, Humphrey often publicly berated his fellow commissioners. He also attacked progressive Democrats and Republicans in Congress and generally disrupted whatever atmosphere of calm deliberation might otherwise have settled over the FTC. On one occasion, for example, Humphrey received a letter of criticism from the progressive Gifford Pinchot, who had recently left office as governor of Pennsylvania. Humphrey replied with a letter of his own, which he released to the press: "My Dear Gifford: Your letter of unregurgitated filth received. For your own famished sake, and for the infinite relief of the country, have your keeper lead you to a thistle patch." This disdain for proprieties on the part of the FTC chairman, however entertaining, did not make easier the tasks before the commission. Equally troublesome, Humphrey often subjected the FTC's trade-practice clients (and the commission itself) to abrupt reversals of policy, which eventually threw the entire question of trade-practice conferences into utter confusion.[19]

Despite Humphrey's clowning, incompetence, and violent partisanship, President Hoover appointed him to a second six-year term, beginning in 1931. This act, perhaps more than any other single episode during the commission's first generation of existence, hammered home a message that already had been indicated by repeated actions on the part of Congress and the courts: the Federal Trade Commission was not to be taken seriously.[20]

Nothing less than the New Deal would be required to change that view and to breathe new life into federal regulatory authority. In 1933, Franklin D. Roosevelt proved equal to the challenge. In the early weeks of his administration, he fired William E. Humphrey from the Federal Trade Commission. As it turned out, Roosevelt lacked the legal authority to take such drastic action, but, by the time an appeal worked its way to the Supreme Court, Humphrey had died. His executor collected back pay for the Humphrey estate, and the court's ruling had important implications for the future independence of regulatory commissions. But Roosevelt had sent to the American people a new message about the seriousness of regulation.[21]

More important, the New Dealers went on to create several new federal regulatory agencies, ushering in the modern administrative state on a large scale. Roosevelt and his era came to represent the high tide of popular faith in the ability of expert commissioners to shape business practice in accordance with the public interest. The greatest apostle of that faith, oddly enough, turned out to be a protégé of Louis D. Brandeis: the lawyer-regulator, James M. Landis.

Charles Francis Adams

Young man about town, 1860

Age 20, Harvard senior picture, 1855. "No spark of enthusiasm was sought to be infused in me."

In the field with officers of his regiment
(Adams second from right), ca. 1864

The railroad commissioner, 1876.
Portrait by Francis Millett.
Adams thought it a "tremendous
likeness."

MR. CHARLES FRANCIS ADAMS MAKES HIMSELF
HEARD.

The railroad commissioner,
mid-1870s (newspaper cartoon)

The new president of the Union
Pacific Railroad, 1884.
Photograph by Marian Hooper
(Mrs. Henry) Adams

Watching the loading of cheeses
in Holland, 1898
(Adams at center, age 63)

The American aristocrat at the turn of the century

Louis D. Brandeis

Young lawyer in the 1890s

Louis and his brother
Alfred, 1890s

The urban reformer,
early 1900s

The national reformer,
1910–1915

The legal craftsman, ca. 1910

Taking his leisure in youth (at center in shelter),
middle age, and old age—but never without coat and tie

James M. Landis

Federal Trade commissioner, 1933

Securities and Exchange commissioner, 1934

The SEC, 1936. Left to right: George C. Mathews,
William O. Douglas, Chairman Landis, J. D. Ross, Robert E. Healy

The protégé affects FDR's cigarette holder, 1937

With Felix Frankfurter in Cambridge, en route to the law school,
late 1930s

Lecturing at Harvard,
late 1930s

At age 60,
just before writing
the Landis Report

Alfred E. Kahn

At Cornell reunion, 1977

Age 5, on a visit to
relatives in Poland,
1923

Assistant professor,
chairman, and entire
economics department,
Ripon College,
1945–1947

As Jack Point in
Yeomen of the Guard, ca. 1965

As Pvt. Willis in
Iolanthe, ca. 1964

Advising a Cornell undergraduate, mid-1960s

With President Carter, 1978

Signing of the Airline Deregulation Act of 1978. President Carter
is second from right, Representative Levitas to his right,
then Senator Cannon, Secretary of Transportation Adams, and Kahn

Landis and the Statecraft
of the SEC

IN THE HISTORY of regulation in America, few names loom larger than that of James M. Landis. An academic lawyer, Landis began his career in 1925 as clerk to Justice Brandeis. Later he served as a member of three federal commissions; and in between his assignments as a regulator, he spent several years as dean of the Harvard Law School. While still a young man, Landis emerged as the outstanding theoretician of American regulation. His book of 1938, *The Administrative Process*, provided the most thoughtful analysis of regulation by an experienced commissioner to appear since Charles Francis Adams' *Railroads: Their Origin and Problems* (1878). Landis' second extended examination, published in 1960 as the *Report on Regulatory Agencies to the President-Elect*, proved to be a landmark critique; it also laid the foundation for important changes in agency procedures, begun during the Kennedy Administration. In the history of American liberalism, Landis embodied the generational links from Brandeis, the old progressive, through Roosevelt and the New Deal, down to John F. Kennedy and the New Frontier. He served all three men.

Landis' greatest contribution to regulation came during the 1930s, in his design and administration of the Securities and Exchange Commission. The SEC, in the half-century since its creation in 1934, has often been cited as the most successful of all federal regulatory agencies. Of course, to arrive at a precise definition of bureaucratic success is difficult. But certainly among federal commissions the SEC has earned the best reputation. In 1940, Sam Rayburn called it "the strongest Commission in the Govern-

ment." In the late 1940s, an exhaustive study of the federal bureaucracy cited the SEC as "an outstanding example of the independent commission at its best."[1] A later study undertook to rank
the performance of federal commissions and held the SEC superior to all others.[2] In 1977, the Congressional Research Service of
the Library of Congress polled over one thousand members of the
regulatory bar in Washington, who "rated the SEC commissioners
most positively and the FMC [Federal Maritime Commission] and
FTC commissioners most negatively." Even Ronald Reagan's presidential transition team had a good word to say in its report of
December 1980: "In comparison with numerous oversized Washington bureaucracies, the SEC, with its 1981 requested budget of
$77.2 million, its 2,105 employees and its deserved reputation for
integrity and efficiency, appears to be a model government
agency."[3]

Best known for its supervision of "Wall Street," the SEC also
has jurisdiction over regional stock exchanges, over-the-counter
markets, corporate reporting activities, accounting practices, and
a number of specialized undertakings such as bankruptcies and
public-utility holding companies. Nearly all American business executives are familiar with the agency because of the reporting requirements it enforces. These include the public disclosure of
detailed information about their companies and—if the executives
are sufficiently high-ranking to be officers or directors—disclosure
of their own salaries and perquisites. If corporate managers do not
precisely quake at the mention of the SEC, they do have healthy
respect for it. And the SEC itself has seldom suffered from problems of credibility or been accused of capture by regulated interests.

There have been many reasons behind the SEC's success. Perhaps most important were the careful design of the enabling legislation of 1933 and 1934 and the extraordinarily talented
leadership the agency enjoyed during its formative years. In both
the design and the early administration, the most influential person was James Landis.

The Early Years

Landis' life was destined to be a tragic one, but most of his misfor-
tunes did not come until late in his career. Earlier, there was little

shadow on what seemed to be infinite promise. Like Felix Frankfurter, who was to be his Harvard Law School mentor, Landis did
not set foot on American soil until his early teens. Born in Tokyo in
1899, the son of Presbyterian missionaries, Landis grew up in an
intensely religious family. It was a learned family as well, the father a philologist, cartographer, and teacher in the missionary
school, the mother a native German who taught that language to
her five children. As a boy, Jim Landis loved the peace and harmony of the self-contained community and enjoyed playing with
the other missionary children. (In 1935, one of his former Japanese
neighbors wrote to a Wall Street lawyer who was having to deal
with Chairman Landis of the SEC: "I can recall him quite distinctly riding his bicycle in the Campus of Meiji Gakuin, a Mission
School in Tokyo, at the age of 'teens. He was a nice boy and we did
not expect him to grow up and become a man of trouble making.")[4]

Landis' parents combined their deep religious piety with a passion for constant hard work. Jim Landis, under the strict discipline
imposed by his father, thought it perfectly normal that he should
study Greek and Latin along with English and German. By the
time he left Japan for continued schooling in America, he was
reading Cicero and doing problems in solid geometry. Thirteen
years old at the time and on his own, he had little money and few
connections of any kind in his new country. But he proved to have
great intellectual gifts. A brilliant student, he led his class at each
of the schools he attended: Mercersburg Academy, Princeton University, and Harvard Law School.[5]

To support his education, young Landis worked at an assortment of jobs. He also took a leave from college during World War
I, to assist the British YMCA. Like his fellow Princetonian F. Scott
Fitzgerald, Landis tried to get into the ambulance corps, but he
did not know how to drive and was rejected. When he did at last
reach France, he witnessed such carnage at the third battle of
Ypres that his Christian faith seemed lost, along with what he
himself had thought to be a calling to the ministry. Even so,
Landis never lost the compulsion for commitment and hard work
that had been driven into him during his boyhood—a compulsion
that would bring him great accomplishment and a good deal of
grief as well.[6]

In all, Jim Landis seemed an appealing but still somewhat odd youth, alternately tough and soft, cynical and sentimental. One friend recalled him as "that slight, wiry, intense, idealistic and often cynical young man with piercing blue eyes, brilliant smile and frayed collar." Notorious as an expert cardplayer (poker and bridge), he also found time to write emotionally charged poetry, usually sonnets. Landis' most striking characteristic, however, was sheer mental power—an extraordinary reach and quickness of mind. While still an undergraduate, he placed an article in an important law journal; and as a student at Harvard Law School, his academic performance made him famous, as he almost equaled the record Brandeis had compiled forty-five years before. Landis' contemporary, David E. Lilienthal, said of him, "Of all the intense, brilliant, ambitious young men who made up my contingent at Harvard Law School in the twenties, the fierce, hawk-like Landis was easily at the top."[7]

Even at Harvard, however, Landis felt keenly the anomalies within him. Educated in the midst of privilege, rootless in a new country, he agonized over his own mixed reactions to American society as it existed in the 1920s. "I suppose I've bored you enough with this recital," he wrote a friend to whom he liked to pour out his feelings, "but do me the justice of believing, whether or not you agree with me, that my attitude [toward the American business system] is not the outcome of blind emotionalism and an inferiority complex against the powerful rich, but is based upon an attempted conception of some of the pressing problems in this industrial era, and primarily, that it is the almost white heat of idealism. I have so little to cling to in this life except these ideals and aims that have been and must be the motivating forces of all my endeavor." At Harvard, his passion found outlets in occasional articles for *The New Republic*, *The Survey*, and other liberal magazines.[8]

After encountering the formidable Felix Frankfurter, whom he met during his third year, Landis agreed to stay on at Harvard for a fourth year and pursue doctoral studies. Frankfurter's ability to discover and exploit first-class talent was already well-known, and he quickly agreed to direct Landis' program of research and writing. From the resulting collaboration came several pathbreaking law review articles and an important book, *The Business of the Supreme Court* (1928). In fact, the Landis-Frankfurter relationship satisfied two of Landis' strongest emotional requirements: his compulsion for work and his need for a mentor. As he chain-smoked his way into the night, as he drank cup after cup of black coffee, as he broke for a few hours' sleep on a cot in his law school office, Landis knew that Frankfurter respected this self-imposed regimen. Later Landis used himself at the same killing pace at the Securities and Exchange Commission in Washington. By that time, the personal costs were higher; he had married and become the father of two daughters, and his mania for work cost him heavily in neglected family relationships. Yet the habit formed during his year with Frankfurter persisted, and so did a continuous use of mentors who responded approvingly to Landis' devotion to work: Brandeis, Joseph P. Kennedy, Franklin D. Roosevelt. Because of a continuing need for this form of support, Landis' character never quite ripened—his persistent need for approval kept him vulnerable to personal tragedy. In particular, there was a perennial neglect of all matters concerned with his personal finances. Despite Brandeis' advice to him on the importance of financial security, Landis always seemed to be verging on destitution. "I just seem to have the habit of working in this fashion," he wrote after one period of nonstop research with Frankfurter, "extending myself to the utmost at the time and letting the future take care of itself."[9]

But the approval of his mentors, together with satisfaction in the work itself, seemed to provide sufficient reward. During the writing of the Supreme Court book with Frankfurter, he exulted in their collaboration: "F.F. is the whole thing. We live together in all the intimacy that close association breeds. He never tires and amuses himself as well as me by playing strictly with his mind. It's a marvelous gift. I satisfy myself with an idea; he's hungry for its expression in the ultimate finesse of words . . . I suppose I'm nearing more and more each day the brink of pure idolatry." Later a friend congratulated Landis on the "Felixity" of his style, and the identification with the brilliant mentor appeared almost complete.[10]

Next Frankfurter sent him to clerk for Justice Brandeis, and Landis enjoyed "one of the best years I ever spent in my life." Again he was struck by the quality of the mentor's mind, the pride and depth of Brandeis' legal craftmanship, his willingness to listen to Landis' views. "Again and again," the younger man wrote, "I can recall where he would hold up a majority opinion or a dissent, just because I disagreed." Brandeis also amazed Landis with un-usual work patterns of his own, for the justice employed no secre-tary or typist. He sent longhand drafts to the printer and revised directly from galley proofs, sending successive revisions back to the printer for resetting, often six or seven times. "In other words, he corrected them as you and I would correct something that came off the typewriter." In time, the admiration became mutual. When Landis, without ever having practiced law, was invited in 1925 to return to Harvard as an assistant professor, Brandeis gave his blessing. "I think it wiser for him not to wait," wrote the old justice. "He is so mature that he has less need than the ordinary teacher for a preliminary bout at the bar."[11]

At Harvard, Landis taught contracts and administrative law, occasionally relieved Frankfurter in the course on public utilities, and directed some of his own energy toward labor law, for which he wrote a casebook. But most important for his future as a regula-tor, he determined to strike out in a new direction. "I got the the-ory that we ought to do more with legislation than we were doing in law school . . . I felt that legislation itself was a source and should be regarded as a source of the law." Though formal courses in legislation later spread to other schools, in Landis' time they represented an intellectual departure away from the usual peda-gogical emphasis on appellate decisions. His pioneering in this field led Harvard to acknowledge the value of its young faculty member with an early positive decision on tenure and a new pro-fessorship of legislation. Landis was only twenty-eight years old. Dean Roscoe Pound, a bit taken aback by what he saw, called Landis' rise "meteoric, almost unheard of" in the academic pro-fession.[12]

Pound himself did not lack visibility. He was an intellectual and institutional founder of what became known as "sociological juris-prudence." This new legal methodology had been foreshadowed by Oliver Wendell Holmes's lectures of 1880 on the common law, highlighted by the Brandeis brief of 1908 on working hours for women, and institutionalized by the reform of the Harvard curric-ulum undertaken during Pound's deanship, which began in 1916. A powerful legal tool, sociological jurisprudence set experience, facts, and industrial conditions against the rigid formalism of an older jurisprudence that relied exclusively on legal precedent. Though Landis often disagreed with Pound over matters of policy, and though he had little respect for the "small men" who were turning sociological jurisprudence into a fetish, he devoted his own scholarly career to the service of this newer instrumentalist tradition.[13]

As the first professor of legislation at Harvard Law School, Landis started a seminar where he and his students explored a series of difficult issues: problems inherent in legislative draftsmanship; rivalries between courts and commissions during the critical stages of construing statutes and discerning legislative intent; and problems of shaping incentives for enforcement so that legislative policies would be followed once they had been determined. Among the scholarly results of Landis' first five years as a professor were numerous publications, the most important of which, "Statutes and the Sources of Law" (1934), quickly took its place as one of the standard essays of American legal scholarship.[14]

Already Landis' formal training and wide-ranging interests had launched him on an atypical legal career. In the future, his pursuit of these theoretical interests would lead without detour to a practical appreciation of the pitfalls in making and administering regulatory policy. Of the necessity for regulation—the base rock of his career—Landis, like Adams sixty years earlier, had no doubt whatever. In both their minds, the emergence of modern industrialism and the manifest inability of the traditional legal system to shape wise policy made it essential to chart a new path. In 1932 and early 1933, for example, Landis' seminar looked into state insurance legislation. This next led to a study of state "blue sky" statutes, those Progressive Era relics designed originally to protect investors against securities of dubious value (pieces of the blue sky). Once these laws had seemed to hold great promise in reforming unscrupulous investment practices. But the Great Crash of 1929 proved them inadequate to protect the securities industry or the public. All state laws, in fact, fell short of what was needed. And after the presidential election of 1932, federal securities legislation became inevitable. Early in 1933, President Roosevelt asked his old friend Felix Frankfurter for help in writing that new legislation, and Frankfurter in turn summoned Landis. Landis himself, though even now only thirty-three years old, could hardly have been better prepared or more enthusiastic about the job ahead of him.[15]

Stocks, Bonds, and Other People's Money

The securities industry is not easily categorized as either center or peripheral. It displays nothing like the huge economies of scale that characterize railroads and oil refining. Instead, it is more like insurance and commercial banking—industries based on paper transactions designed to facilitate the flow of investment capital into more tangible enterprises such as transportation and manufacturing. Parts of the securities industry do display tendencies toward vertical integration and other organizational patterns. On the whole, however, these traits are less important for understanding its real function than is another characteristic: like insurance and banking, securities trading lies at the heart of a vital but invisible paper infrastructure based on intangibles such as trust and perceived legitimacy. Although economic theory is helpful in understanding the internal structure of the industry, a more useful way to think about its overall role is in terms of the legitimacy it brings or does not bring to the larger corporate economy. For a similar reason, the regulation of securities is often best directed toward maximizing not just the efficiency of the industry, but also its legitimacy.

Fundamentally, of course, the securities industry in the United States developed because of a long unsatisfied need for investment capital. Businesses needed funds to start new enterprises, construct new plants, and replace old equipment. Governments needed capital as well, to build public works and to cover budget deficits. In order to raise the necessary money, governments and companies had several options: they could spend their own income from taxes or sales, or they could borrow from banks. Sometimes, however, they had to gain access to very large amounts of capital, preferably with long periods before the money had to be paid back. On such occasions, companies issued common stock and both companies and governments issued bonds. Stocks and bonds became available in an assortment of forms such as preferreds, convertibles, and debentures. All forms came to be called "securities," even though they might be anything but secure, and their initial sales for the purpose of raising investment capital came to be called the "primary market" for securities.[16]

A "secondary market" for stocks and bonds also arose. The liquidity of securities made them attractive as investments that need not tie up one's money for long periods, as did such other investments as real estate. In addition, bonds paid interest and stocks usually paid dividends, which made them even more attractive as items to buy and sell. This buying and selling formed a market different from the original issuance of the securities for the purpose of raising money. Secondary buying and selling was also one of the forces behind fluctuations in securities' value, a characteristic that made it possible for investors and speculators to realize large profits or losses on the secondary stock market. It was the intertwining of the primary and secondary markets—or, to put it another way, the mixture of investment and speculation—that created a need for the regulation of securities trading.

The organizational response to the historic need for investment capital (that is, the need for a primary market) was the investment banking industry. For the secondary market in securities trading, it was the stock exchanges. Because both types of institutions dealt in complex transactions, their functions acquired an air of mystery and, often, misunderstanding. Then too, because both used "other people's money" to conduct their affairs, they each became vivid in American folklore—curiously so, represented as they were at both ends of an unusual scale of rectitude. At one end stood the mighty investment banking houses: J. P. Morgan; Kuhn, Loeb; Kidder, Peabody; Brown Brothers Harriman; Lee, Higginson. These names, more than those in any other type of financial enterprise, evoked a popular image of solid respectability, of hushed rooms paneled in dark wood and carpeted with oriental rugs: an aura of gentlemen's clubs where a man's word was his bond. More than other businesses, investment banking was associated with dignity, integrity, judgment. Though it was also tied up with the Social Register, it despised publicity and shunned celebrity.

At the other end of the scale emerged the pirates of American finance, from the early rogues Fisk, Drew, and Gould immortalized by Charles Francis Adams to later legends such as "Bet a Million" Gates and "Diamond Jim" Brady. And in between these extremes stood a number of important figures who seemed to make alternate and confusing appearances at both ends of the spectrum, now as prudent investor, now as unscrupulous manipulator: E. H. Harriman, Bernard Baruch, Joseph P. Kennedy, Richard Whitney—names mixing honor with deception in ways emblematic of the industry's mixture of investment with speculation. Offstage, with no significant role other than as incidental beneficiaries or victims, have stood a befuddled chorus of common people, alternately fascinated and horrified with the doings of the major players. These common folk have managed to hold the conflicting intuitions that the tale of the stock ticker lay beyond the control of mortal man, but also that the whole process represented a conspiracy engineered by the men of Wall Street.

As early as 1792, American finance centered on "the Street," where the antecedent of the modern New York Stock Exchange (formally organized in 1817) emerged as a place in which the new securities of the United States Government could be bought and sold. New York was the nation's political capital at the time when Secretary of the Treasury Alexander Hamilton arranged for the funding of the debt of the American Revolution. Hamilton's financial sleight-of-hand simultaneously created a new money supply and tied the interests of wealthy bondholders to the fate of the new republic. Although the capital city was moved south from New York, Wall Street continued its financial dominance, spurred by the rise of the Port of New York to primacy on the American continent. This ascent in turn owed much to the development of the Erie Canal, whose own financing came from the New York Stock Exchange. What really brought Wall Street into its own, however, as the location of modern capital markets on a truly large scale, was the need to finance the American railroad industry.[17]

As the momentum rose in the market for railroad securities—beginning in the 1850s—trading on the New York Stock Exchange grew by one sharp leap after another. For the next sixty years, well into the twentieth century, railroad stocks and bonds dominated securities markets. In fact, not until the 1890s did any real market for industrial securities begin to emerge, eventually to challenge railroads for market leadership. The Dow system for measuring daily industrial and railroad averages (later the Dow-Jones) began to be used in 1897, just when the merger wave that led to so many giant center firms first began. Even so, at the turn of the century the securities industry did not yet involve masses of participants. In 1900, investment remained the business of the wealthy few.[18]

In American folklore, though, the place of Wall Street was already established, a solid foundation having been laid by Adams' uncomplimentary but unforgettable portraits of Fisk, Drew, and other shady figures. Even more important was the close identification of the Street with the onset of economic depressions. Nearly every downturn in the business cycle—such as those occurring in 1873 and 1893—seemed to be preceded by a break (downward spiral of prices) on the New York Stock Exchange. Often in such breaks the "bears" of Wall Street (those traders who sold short, anticipating and by their actions sometimes accelerating a downward spiral) profited hugely. This association between speculation and the fate of the American economy created a new category of national villains. For the fledgling science of economics, it also raised a problem of establishing with more precision the exact connection between the up-and-down prices on the New York Stock Exchange and the macroeconomic fluctuations of the economy. Even today this connection is not completely understood.

In the early years of the twentieth century, participation in stock trading became more widespread, as Americans entered the market in greater numbers. In 1899, the year of James Landis' birth, about half a million persons owned stocks. By 1930, when he was a Harvard law professor, the 1899 figure had multiplied by a factor of twenty. Some ten million Americans now held stocks—in part because of the new fashion in financing securities by which common citizens as well as experienced speculators would buy and sell "on the margin." (Margin trading required purchasers to put up only a small percentage of the total price of a security, say 10 percent; the remainder could be borrowed from brokers or banks.) During the 1929 Crash, of course, most securities began a precipitous decline in value, as the market dropped to its record low in 1932. This decline, coupled with the new mass ownership of stocks, created a popular thrust toward regulation, in the form of political demands for action by the federal government. So serious were the effects of the Crash on stock trading that the record 1929 volume of transactions on the New York Stock Exchange was not again reached until 1963.[19]

When Landis went to Washington in 1933, the New York Stock Exchange represented the largest and best known example of a genre that included regional exchanges in about two dozen other cities, including Boston, Pittsburgh, Cincinnati, and Salt Lake City. Some of these exchanges specialized in mineral issues (the San Francisco Mining Exchange) or in wheat, corn, and other agricultural commodities (the Chicago Board of Trade, which was the center for an immense international grain market). All exchanges functioned as secondary marketplaces where traders met to buy and sell, but had little to do directly with providing investment capital to corporations. Instead, the shares of corporations were traded on the secondary market as items with value intrinsic to themselves. In fact, the exchanges themselves were institutional hybrids: part private gambling dens, part legitimate public marketplaces, and part symbols of the rise and fall of national prosperity. In the economic sense, the exchanges had some characteristics of monopoly, since membership (the number of seats that admitted traders to the floor of the exchanges) was limited. On the other hand, seats themselves were readily bought and sold, and their prices reflected the shifting fortunes of the exchanges.[20]

When the exchanges were working as they should, their governing structures functioned much like specialized regulatory agencies. They made and enforced rules of trading on their members, which had the effect of regulating the buying and selling of securities. These rules, together with the exchanges' powers of enforcement through fines, suspensions, and expulsions, were upheld as legal in a long series of court decisions. The exchanges also imposed requirements on the companies whose securities were listed (made available for trading) with them. Usually such requirements related to the disclosure of information about each company and, for new companies, a good recent record of profit.[21] Becoming "listed on the New York Stock Exchange" (and later the American Stock Exchange as well) was an important rite of passage for American center firms and also for many peripherals. In this way, validation of new companies could be considered a legitimate function of the major national exchanges. One result of all these mixed functions of exchanges was a general increase in their importance, as they evolved from small private clubs into major markets and quasi-regulatory agencies. Not surprisingly, their relationship to state and national governments also changed in the process.[22] The way in which exchanges were being run raised questions about the legitimacy of public-private interpenetration, the delegation of political power to private groups, and the economic impacts of this power on affected interests. These were the issues that James Landis and the Securities and Exchange Commission confronted as they sought to regulate the exchanges, particularly the New York Stock Exchange.

As a final complicating matter, the securities industry by 1930 had become involved in two different problematical activities: the banking industry and the over-the-counter markets in securities. With the banks, the principal problem concerned the lack of separation between commercial banking and investment banking. Both of these quite different activities could be carried on within a single corporation. This meant, in effect, that bankers could use their depositors' money for any desired purpose and invest along the entire scale from gilt-edged bonds to wildcat stock issues. Thus regulation of the securities industry was intimately tied to regulation of the banking system, as Brandeis made explicit in the title of his popular book of 1914, *Other People's Money and How the Bankers Use It.*

The other complicating circumstance grew from the emergence of a totally unregulated over-the-counter securities market as a separate forum for buying and selling.[23] This "market" was really a diffuse group of thousands of independent brokers and dealers scattered in cities across the country. All securities not listed on the exchanges were traded over the counter, which meant those of all small and medium-sized companies and of some very large ones as well. In addition, most new corporate bond issues and all government securities were traded over the counter. Thus the over-the-counter market, though unregulated, was extremely important. Its dollar volume and total number of transactions exceeded those completed on the stock exchanges. Accordingly, the opportunity for chicanery on the part of the scattered brokers and dealers who handled over-the-counter transactions was almost unlimited. Ethical standards were not necessarily high among security salesmen. Even if they had been, no system of sanctions existed for disciplining wrongdoers, nor even any system of gathering reliable information about stock and bond prices. Purchasers dealt with over-the-counter brokers and dealers at their own peril.[24]

Whereas all corporations today must submit elaborate reports to various government agencies and to their own stockholders, such was not the case prior to 1933. Equally important, there was no requirement that corporate reporting be certified by independent public accountants. Some companies issued no reports or information of any kind. It was the established policy of the Singer Sewing Machine Company, for example, never to issue annual reports and to give such information as it chose to make public orally at stockholders' meetings. The Royal Baking Powder Company published no reports during the first quarter of the twentieth century.[25] Whether or not such information was actually useful to the average investor, its absence undermined the legitimacy of the securities industry and raised troubling questions about the capitalist system itself. Yet corporate managers persistently regarded their companies' affairs as private and privileged. Henry O. Havemeyer, the head of the gigantic American Sugar Refining Company, indicated as much when he testified in 1899 before the *ad hoc* Industrial Commission, set up by Congress to report on social and economic conditions. Havemeyer was questioned by Thomas Phillips, a member of the commission:

Phillips: You think, then, that when a corporation is chartered by the State, offers stock to the public, and is one in which the public is interested, that the public has no right to know what its earning power is or to subject them to any inspection whatever, that the people may not buy stock blindly?

Havemeyer: Yes; that is my theory. Let the buyer beware; that covers the whole business. You cannot wet-nurse people from the time they are born until the day they die. They have got to wade in and get stuck and that is the way men are educated and cultivated.[26]

Havemeyer and other managers did not want people to know what their companies were doing because they feared that valuable secrets might be revealed to competitors. A second reason was that, unlike railroads, which very early were required to report data to state governments, most industrial corporations originated as family firms. The disclosure of the company's business would amount to an unseemly parading of the family's finances. The resulting public ignorance of the affairs of great corporations led indirectly to reliance on the business judgment of the great investment banking houses. The public, including professional investors working for commercial banks and insurance companies, depended as much on the judgment and reputation of J. P. Morgan and other underwriters as on their own knowledge of the companies whose securities were being marketed. This was why Morgan and other investment bankers commanded such high fees for their services.[27]

As corporations became more important, powerful pressures for greater disclosure began to build. In the early part of the twentieth century, the most effective individual crusader for openness was Louis D. Brandeis. The Boston attorney's own uncanny ability to analyze financial statements, together with his experience with the New York banks and the New Haven railroad debacle, made him a powerful advocate of mandatory disclosure. It galled Brandeis that neither the companies nor the investment bankers would communicate more fully with the public. When, for example, he himself wrote to J. P. Morgan about his own research into the affairs of the New Haven, explicitly warning Morgan that the railroad's financial structure was about to collapse, Morgan did not even acknowledge Brandeis' letter. But Brandeis did have an enormous influence on other critics outside the corporations, including, later on, his law clerk James Landis.[28]

Along with dedicated individuals such as Brandeis, three private-interest groups worked for greater disclosure. There were the stock exchanges, the Investment Bankers' Association, and the accounting profession. The rules of the exchanges required that listed corporations submit for the record a substantial amount of information. Enforcement of these rules was uneven, however, and the lack of standardization in accounting practices remained a barrier to useful comparative analysis across companies. The Investment Bankers' Association, which included a large number of over-the-counter dealers, made some preliminary attempts at enforcement of tougher disclosure rules, but this effort had little effect in the years before the New Deal. The group with the strongest stake in raising disclosure standards was the accounting profession. Prior to the Progressive Era, American financial accounting (as opposed to internal cost accounting) had been regarded by Europeans as backward and inefficient, hardly advanced beyond simple bookkeeping. With the passage of the income tax law of 1913 and the excess profits tax of 1917, the profession was given an indirect boost by the federal government. In addition, the Federal Trade Commission and the Federal Reserve Board worked closely with the American Institute of Accountants to publish, in 1917, the book *Uniform Accounting*, which proved to be a breakthrough with respect to balance-sheet audits and the specification of essential elements in meaningful financial disclosure. Even so, the influence of accountants remained small before

the New Deal, and their recommendations were often modified to
fit the wishes of corporate management. The concept of the outside "independent auditor" had not yet come of age in the United
States.[29]

When, during the New Deal's Hundred Days, James Landis and
his colleagues arrived in Washington to write new laws for the
regulation of the securities industry, they confronted a very complex situation. Here was an industry that seemed hopelessly divided among warring groups of practitioners: investment bankers
on the one hand and speculators on the other; the exchanges, dominated by the New York Stock Exchange, of which all the smaller
regional exchanges traditionally were jealous; an over-the-counter
market, with its diffuse hordes of brokers and dealers held together
only by telephone lines and a loose set of unenforceable rules. And
everywhere in the securities industry, there prevailed a tradition
of nondisclosure and nonstandard accounting practice. Despite
such obstacles, Landis and his cohorts had some powerful *ad hoc*
allies. These included the most progressive elements among brokers and dealers within the stock exchanges and a larger number of
professional accountants, who found good reasons to cooperate
with the government. Already accountants had benefited more
from government regulations than from any source of support
among business groups.

   From Landis' own perspective, however, the most important
advantage the government would enjoy in the coming fight for
new legislation was the depressed psychological state of the securities industry itself, now combined in 1933 with a dreadful economic situation in the country at large. For always, in the best or
worst of times, the securities industry remained a hostage to psychology, to the feelings and intuitions of buyers and sellers. When
investors or speculators had no faith in the soundness of the securities industry or in the future of the national economy, they
bought few stocks and bonds. As transactions became scarce, brokers and dealers had no business, and the industry simply withered
away. This nightmare had already become a reality, and the reality threatened to persist indefinitely. By 1933, therefore, there was
obvious need to restore buyers' confidence. Everyone in the securities industry knew, by March 1933, when Roosevelt took office, that something must be done.

As always, the climate for action had to be ripened by that most powerful tool of all, public opinion. By 1933 the Great Depression had worked to translate the abysmal performance of Wall Street into a series of national clichés: the ruined speculators jumping out of windows; the lost fortunes and reputations of Samuel Insull, Ivar Krueger, and other icons; and, above all, the remarkable statistics. These numbers announced the greatest disaster in the history of American finance, and with it an economic catastrophe for the country.[30]

	1929	1932
Volume of sales on New York Stock Exchange	1.125 billion shares	.425 billion shares
Dow-Jones Industrial Average	381 (September)	41 (January)
New corporate issues of securities	$8.0 billion	$0.325 billion ($0.161 billion in 1933)
Brokers' loans for stock market purchases	$4.1 billion	$0.43 billion
Unemployment (national, all workers)	3.2%	23.6% (24.9% in 1933)

The Legislation

The American public gasped at the figures, then called for new laws. In all, five major pieces of New Deal legislation shaped the regulation of the securities industry.

1. *The Securities Act of 1933.* This legislation became the keystone; it mandated the disclosure of detailed information pertaining to the issuers of new corporate securities. All such securities had to be registered with the Federal Trade Commission (which was assigned the regulatory tasks until the new Securities and Exchange Commission was created in 1934). The detailed financial information in the registration statement required certification by an independent accountant.

2. *The Securities Exchange Act of 1934.* This law ordered similar disclosure of information about companies with *existing* securities through regulation of the New York Stock Exchange and other exchanges. The 1934 act created the Securities and Exchange Commission and empowered it to change the rules of the exchanges, prohibit stock manipulation and other practices, and formulate a

range of additional regulations as necessary. Throughout the text of the act, the phrase "in the public interest and for the protection of investors" occurred dozens of times, providing a rough guide to the intent of the legislation. This act also empowered the Federal Reserve Board to set minimum margin requirements for the purchase of stock on credit. Such margins had been as low as 10 percent in the 1920s; afterward they ranged from 40 percent to 90 percent.

3. *The Public Utility Holding Company Act of 1935.* Under this law, public-utility holding companies were required to register with the SEC. The agency in turn would oversee breakups and dissolutions of some companies and simplification of others' multilayered corporate structures. The SEC would also help plan the physical integration of utilities so as to maximize engineering efficiency and minimize the exploitation of operating units for the profiteering of holding companies.

4. *The Maloney Act of 1938.* Named for its sponsor, Senator Frank Maloney of Connecticut, this legislation brought the over-the-counter market under the close supervision of the SEC. The commission was given authority to oversee and change the rules of the private associations that the industry was encouraged to set up in order to administer the new regulations.

5. *The Glass-Steagall Banking Act of 1933.* Also named for its sponsors, this vital piece of New Deal legislation did not apply specifically to the securities industry, but it did have a powerful effect. The new law forced a separation of investment banking from commercial banking and thereby ended the opportunity for banks to use demand deposits (checking accounts) for the purpose of underwriting or speculation. Equally important, the act created the Federal Deposit Insurance Corporation to insure small accounts and rebuild confidence in the banks.

These important pieces of legislation marked the high tide of congressional activity aimed at Wall Street during the period 1933–1938. Yet the writing of new laws continued into the next decade as well, with the Investment Company Act and the Trust Indenture Act, which completed the SEC's legislative mandate for thoroughgoing regulation of the securities industry. Because so much time elapsed between the passage of the first and last of these laws, the circumstances of passage differed dramatically from one law to another. For example, the Glass-Steagall Act and the Securities Act sailed through during Roosevelt's first Hundred Days. They occasioned little open debate or challenge, despite their extraordinary significance and despite the decades of controversy that preceded their enactment. The Maloney Act of 1938 also raised little excitement, being sponsored jointly by the SEC and the investment banking industry. Two of the laws, on the other hand—the Securities Exchange Act of 1934 and the Public Utility Holding Company Act of 1935—were among the most harshly contested pieces of legislation in the twentieth century. Each act emerged only after months of bitter pulling and hauling. Because of the very different contexts of the enactment of the five laws, it is possible to measure with unusual precision the practical and political problems faced by Landis and his colleagues as they undertook to draft the successive pieces of legislation.

Landis himself, responding to Frankfurter's summons, arrived in Washington in April 1933. The early drafts of the Securities Act had run into problems, and Landis thought his role was going to be like that of a theater "doctor," called in to fix an ailing play before it opened on Broadway. But Roosevelt had set many others to work on the same problem, and—typical of the New Deal—a fair amount of confusion reigned over who was supposed to do what and for how long. Landis, for example, had come south to Washington on a Friday train from Cambridge, expecting to be released after a weekend of work. He ended by staying four years.[31]

In addition to Landis, the team assembled by Frankfurter included two other former students, Thomas Corcoran and Benjamin Cohen. These three Frankfurter protégés—all young, articulate, and good copy for newspapermen—became known as the "Happy Hot Dogs." By the end of 1933, each of them, along with their mentor, had become a national celebrity and a symbol of the New Deal. Even in the beginning, for the particular task at hand, the three comprised a formidable team. Both Corcoran and Cohen had practiced in Wall Street law firms, there acquiring intimate familiarity with the securities industry. Cohen had already made a small fortune trading in stocks. The group combined a sophisticated appreciation of the intricate nature of the industry (the special competence of Corcoran and even more of Cohen) with an extraordinary understanding of the virtues and defects of particular tools of administration (the distinctive strength of Landis). Eventually they worked together not only in writing the Securities

Act of 1933 but also the Securities Exchange Act of 1934 and the Public Utility Holding Company Act of 1935.[32]

Throughout this process of statute making, Landis persistently emphasized the necessity of using all the incentives potentially inherent in the industry to give every person involved—executive, accountant, broker, banker—a stake in helping to enforce the law. He had been thinking systematically about such problems for many years. Early in his professorship at Harvard, Landis had become fascinated by the obvious gap between legislation and administration that characterized modern American government. Studying the lack of connection, he tried to puzzle out the resulting paradox—so common in regulation—between admirable intentions of legislation and perverse results of administration. He thought he had found the key to a solution. As Landis wrote in 1931, two years before he went to Washington, "The concern of the lawyer with the statute rarely begins earlier than its enactment; the interest of the legislator usually ends at just that point." What was needed, then, was a way of institutionalizing the linkages between ends and means, between legislation and administration:

Not even a catalogue of the devices for enforcement is to be found, far less a knowledge of the fields in which they have been employed. The legislator must pick his weapons blindly from an armory of whose content he is unaware. The devices are numerous and their uses various. The criminal penalty, the civil penalty, the resort to the injunctive side of equity, the tripling of damage claims, the informer's share, the penalizing force of pure publicity, the license as a condition of pursuing certain conduct, the confiscation of offending property—these are the samples of the thousand and one devices that the ingenuity of many legislatures has produced. Their effectiveness to control one field and their ineffectiveness to control others, remains yet to be explored.[33]

Now, in 1933, thanks to the summons from Frankfurter and Roosevelt, Landis enjoyed the chance for exploration.

In writing the initial securities law, Landis began his quest for the proper regulatory devices by focusing on the production and uses of information. The Securities Act of 1933 became the quintessential sunshine law. As Roosevelt's message to Congress requesting the legislation put it, "This proposal adds to the ancient rule of caveat emptor, the further doctrine 'let the seller also beware.' It puts the burden of telling the whole truth on the seller. It should give impetus to honest dealing in securities and thereby bring back public confidence." With a tip of his hat to Brandeis, Roosevelt went on to say, "What we seek is a return to a clear understanding of the ancient truth that those who manage banks, corporations, and other agencies handling or using other people's money are trustees acting for others." Sam Rayburn, the floor manager of the legislation, added, "This bill is not so much a response to the frauds of criminals as it is to the reticence of financiers." For the drafting team, two questions became paramount: what information should the law require, and how could they make certain that the information provided was accurate and forthcoming on time?[34]

The answer to the first question emerged in a list of items carefully compiled by Ben Cohen. In his list, Cohen enumerated thirty-two categories of information that must be disclosed in the registration statements of corporations issuing new securities. These disclosure requirements—revolutionary for 1933—included detailed balance sheets, profit and loss statements, salaries and perquisites of the company's officers and directors, commissions paid to the underwriters, names and addresses of the lawyers who passed on the legality of the issue, and numerous other items of information seldom revealed by corporations.[35] Overall, the bill called for a detailed and intricate body of data, matching the complex aims of the regulators. As Rayburn said at the time, "In the 20 years that I have been a member of Congress, this is the most technical matter with which I have ever been called upon to deal." Rayburn's own sure-handed management of the legislation in the House proved an immense benefit to Landis, Corcoran, and Cohen, as they struggled to write an intelligible bill, free of loopholes.[36]

Next Landis himself took charge of the question of how to make certain that the information actually would be reported. Here three particular provisions of the Securities Act bore the mark of his creative drafting. The first had to do with the subpoena power exercised by the regulatory agency. In administrative hearings before commissions, the usual practice was to request persons giving testimony to appear at a certain time and place. If they did not appear, the commission would issue a subpoena. If they still failed to appear, the commission would go to court and show cause why the court should issue an order to enforce the subpoena. This la-

borious procedure often took so long that the desired testimony
became worthless. In the meantime, the recalcitrant witness had
lost nothing, so enforcement proved ineffective. Confronted with
the difficulty of obtaining timely information from the securities
industry—so traditionally close-mouthed but equally accustomed
to measuring time in seconds on the stock ticker—Landis hit on
what he called "the simple device of making non-compliance with
a legitimate subpoena a penal offense." This new provision put the
burden of proof—that is, of showing cause why the appearance
was or wasn't necessary—not on the commission but on the individual, who now risked jail if he ignored the subpoena. Enforcement rested on the imminent loss of personal freedom, an
unattractive cost to the individual working in the securities industry.[37]

A second procedural device Landis inserted into the act was the
"cooling-off period." This interval—thirty days in the original bill,
twenty in the final draft—specified the time between a corporation's submission of a registration statement and prospectus to the
commission and the time when the securities described by these
documents could first be offered for sale to the public. Landis reasoned that the feverish atmosphere surrounding large new stock
issues did not encourage wise investment decisions; that in fact
such high pressure worked to the advantage of unscrupulous promoters and of those company insiders who knew in advance when
an issue was about to go on the market. He concluded that a waiting period would solve these problems. At the same time, the
cooling-off period would give regulators an opportunity to scruti-
nize the registration statement and prospectus, verifying accuracy
and completeness. Yet the delay must remain limited. Knowing
that the proper timing of stock issues was vital to their success,
Landis proposed twenty days as a way of forcing prompt action
not only from business but also from regulators. Delay could not
continue, for if the regulators found nothing wrong with the documents, or if they simply did not get around to checking them, the
registration would automatically become effective at the end of
the twenty days. The cooling-off period functioned in the manner
of the traditional injunction at weddings: speak now or forever
hold your peace.[38]

Still another Landis invention was the "stop order." If, during
the cooling-off period, the regulators discovered something amiss
in the documents, they could issue an order suspending the pro-

spective issue until this discrepancy was resolved. Superficially the stop order resembled the "cease and desist" provision written into the Federal Trade Commission Act. Now, however, the impact proved different because of the unusual atmosphere of securities trading. Whereas cease and desist represented only a first step in a series of procedures that might take months to complete, the stop order had an instantaneous effect in preventing all further sales of securities. It was likely to shatter investor confidence and strike a mortal blow to the issue affected, without regard for the results of later hearings or appellate review.[39]

By thinking carefully about the nature of the industry and by drawing on his professional knowledge of the arsenal of sanctions available to Congress, Landis had planted valuable tools of enforcement within the basic securities law. Unlike so many other draftsmen of regulatory legislation, he recognized the importance of matching the sanctions to the problems. Through the stop order, the cooling-off period, and the change in burden of proof for subpoena processes, Landis paved the way for smoother enforcement of the law. And in so easing its enforcement, he also made unnecessary the large government bureaucracy that otherwise might have been needed to achieve the goals of the legislation.[40]

Given the haste with which Landis and his colleagues were forced to work, and considering the flawed draftsmanship of other Hundred Days legislation such as the National Industrial Recovery Act, it seems remarkable that they were able to do such a meticulous job with the Securities Act of 1933. As one congressman said during the brief floor debate, "I have never read a bill that appeared to be more carefully drawn, with reference to all its features and technicalities, than this bill." Drafting the bill had not been an easy task, and during the long nights of tiresome rewriting the high-strung Landis often quarreled with his colleagues. Completion brought peace, however, and after the House had passed the bill, Cohen gleefully reported to Landis: "There was virtually no dissent. The debate was rather dry and much of it off the point, but the votes were there. When it was over, Rayburn remarked he did not know whether the bill passed so readily because it was so damned good or so damned incomprehensible." Rayburn himself could not have been more delighted with either these results or with the young draftsmen. "I cannot close this letter," he wrote to Frankfurter, "without telling you what I think of the character and great ability of Mr. Landis. I have not known a man for the same length of time for whom I have a higher personal regard and for whose character and ability I have more unstinted admiration. In fact I think he would rank high in any brain trust that may be formed." As a practicing regulator, Landis had make his first important contribution.[41]

President Roosevelt signed the Securities Act on May 27, 1933, less than three months after his inauguration. The act was to be administered by the Federal Trade Commission, and Roosevelt appointed Landis to the FTC, with the understanding that he would focus his energies on its new Securities Division. A second new appointee, George Mathews, a La Follette Republican from Wisconsin, had special expertise in accounting and several years' experience in state regulation of utility securities. He and Landis would enjoy a productive four-year collaboration, first in the FTC, then the SEC.

Landis' and Mathews' first task as federal trade commissioners in 1933 was the onerous but important job of designing a series of registration forms for corporations to use in reporting new security issues.[42] Once the completed registration statements started to arrive, the commission began the painstaking process of examining each one for accuracy, sending many back to companies for additional information, and then approving the statements when they were finally in satisfactory form. For fifteen months, the FTC exercised responsibility for securities regulation (after that time, the new Securities and Exchange Commission took full charge). The FTC's *Annual Report* for 1934 acknowledged this special burden. It commented on the very heavy initial workload, noted the necessity for overtime work by its investigators, and then briefly summarized the proportions of the task:

From July 7, 1933, the first date on which the filing of registration statements was permitted under the act, to September 1, 1934, inclusive, 1,095 statements, together with prospectuses in the form proposed to be used in the sale of securities covered by them, were filed with the Commission . . . On September 1, 1934, 794 statements had become effective, 154 had been withdrawn by registrants with the consent of the Commission, and refusal or stop orders preventing or suspending effectiveness had been issued in 49 cases. Ninety-eight statements had not become effective, either being under examination by the division or having been delayed by the registrants . . . The 794 statements which had become effective involved security issues in the amount of $1,164,135,599.58 . . .

Registration statements were available for public inspection at the Commission's offices, and from October 11, 1933, to September 1, 1934, a total of 3,305 personal examinations were made of statements on file with the Commission. In addition, 52,681 photostatic pages of registration statement material were furnished to the public at nominal charges . . . Up to September 1, 1934, there had been informally docketed in the securities division of the Commission 382 complaints of violations of the act, which were investigated either by the division staff in Washington or by field agents. Approximately 638 inquiries and complaints were disposed of upon a finding that the Commission had no jurisdiction, mainly because the transactions involved occurred prior to passage of the act.

The entire commission, and especially Landis, took pleasure in noting that during this first fifteen months, "no ruling or finding by the Commission in any securities case was ever appealed to the courts." A sound beginning had been made; in particular, the unusual absence of judicial review—that bane of regulators everywhere—augured well for the commissioners' future administration of the Securities Act.[43]

For the commissioners themselves, the experience so far had been a heady one. "Within a few months," Landis reported to Frankfurter, "I have had a larger share in the handling of government than I ever had after years in the handling of the Harvard Law School." Landis worked inordinately long hours, driving his staff to a prompt disposition of cases, meeting with brokers and accountants, conferring with Rayburn about new legislation, and making periodic trips to the White House to plan strategy. "Again," he confided to Frankfurter, "take the fact that in these few months I have seen more of [Roosevelt], talked more genuinely with him, than in all the years at Harvard, contrasting my associations with the President of the University."[44] These discussions with Roosevelt concerned mainly the unfinished business of securities regulation. Wall Street continued its efforts to soften certain provisions of the Securities Act, and as yet unresolved were two additional hard questions: how to reform the stock exchanges and how to shape an effective regulatory system for the over-the-counter market. New legislation would be required, and the next step occurred in 1934.

The circumstances surrounding the Securities Exchange Act of 1934 proved less pleasant than those that had given birth to the Securities Act and Glass-Steagall Act in 1933. The crisis atmo-

sphere of the first hundred days no longer prevailed. The "Roosevelt boom" of the spring and summer of 1933—during which the
Dow-Jones industrial average rose dramatically—had come and
gone, and no further gains had been recorded. In general, the financial community, after a brief honeymoon with the New Deal,
began to turn away from Roosevelt, although another year would
pass before Wall Street's fanatical hatred of "that man" reached
full pitch. The signs of the new times were clear, however, when
the drafting team went back to work early in 1934.[45]

This time, trouble quickly emerged. "The Stock Exchange Bill is
receiving a terrific beating," Landis wrote. "All the corporate
wealth of this country has gone into the attack and carried it all
the way up to the White House." The scrupulous concern of the
draftsmen served to make the job harder. Their determination to
avoid mistakes meant repeated consultations with financiers, brokers, accountants, and many others. Because Landis and his colleagues personally disliked most of the Wall Streeters, the
draftsmen derived little pleasure from these sessions. "My office
for the last three weeks," Landis wrote to Frankfurter, "has been a
general reception room for brokers, bankers and the like who
come in and tell me their trouble. I listen honestly and conscien-
tiously, and always reaffirm my confidence that both Congress and
the President will see to it that a good and fair Stock Exchange Bill
will eventually be written. It is easy, though, to lose one's perspective in this whole turmoil, either to be too easy or too hard."
Landis, an obsessive worker even in the calmest of times, now
threw himself without stint into the drafting of this new legislation. "I rarely get home these days until midnight," he wrote
Frankfurter, "and I find that that does not even enable me to keep
up with the demands of the job." Some nights he did not get home
at all, but instead slept in a cot in his office, as he had done during
his bachelor years at Harvard. (Frankfurter wrote in response to
Landis' letter, "I am troubled, really troubled, by your statement
. . . you can't drive your mind as though it were a brewery horse."
Landis' wife, invited to a party and asked to bring her husband,
replied, "What husband?")[46]

Yet the drafting of the stock-exchange bill had to go forward,
fatigue or not. Behind most of the difficulties with this particular
bill lay an even larger matter of policy. On the one hand, there
were no fewer than thirty-four securities exchanges in the United

States, large and small, general and specialized. On the other hand, the New York Stock Exchange was by far the most important, and it presented certain unique problems. For example, Landis and others wished to segregate some of the functions performed by members of the New York exchange and prohibit the same person from performing more than one or two of these functions. This separation of functions would eliminate existing conflicts of interest, long a source of controversy in securities trading, in which brokers and floor traders could buy and sell for both their customers and their own personal accounts. There were other conflicts of interest as well. Traditionally, specialists who dealt in the securities of only a few companies also participated in "bear pools" designed to drive down the price of these very securities and thus to create the opportunity for a quick killing. Perhaps more often than anything else, leaders of the exchange had been known to alter the rules for their own protection and enrichment at the expense of newcomers and outsiders.[47]

To solve these problems, Landis and his colleagues had to write a bill with the New York Stock Exchange specifically in mind. Such a bill would inevitably contain provisions injurious to the smaller regional exchanges, where the division of labor remained quite different and where the mixture of functions was not only desirable but actually essential to economic survival. In the case of these regional exchanges, Landis and the other draftsmen—far from wishing to do any harm—wanted to strengthen them and ally them with the regulators, in order to bring the powerful New York Stock Exchange to heel. In the end, the New York versus regional problem could be worked out only by inserting specific terms of compromise into the act and by postponing a final decision about appropriate separation of function. This settlement permitted the draftsmen and the House and Senate conferees to agree at last on a bill satisfactory to them and to the president. The final Securities Exchange Act of 1934, though not quite so strong as some reformers would have liked, still represented a very rigorous piece of legislation. It effectively embodied each of the three principal goals that Landis and his colleagues had in mind.[48]

One goal was to establish federal jurisdiction over the margins required by brokers in making loans to buyers of stocks. In the flush days of the late twenties, with margins down around 10 percent, it had been possible for an investor to purchase stock valued at $1000 by putting up only $100 of his own money. He could then use the stock itself as collateral for a loan on the $900 balance. This $900 would be furnished by a broker, who in turn would borrow the money from a bank. In the opinion of many New Dealers, this unfettered trading on thin margins represented a primary cause of the stock market crash and the depression that followed. These observers reasoned that the borrowing process in effect mortgaged the assets of the banks—and therefore the nation's money supply—to the unpredictable gyrations of the stock market. So, when the market began its dive in 1929, brokers were forced to call in additional collateral to cover the diminished value of their customers' stocks. When stock prices continued to fall, investors, brokers, and banks toppled like so many dominoes. Because brokers' loans were enormous—they totaled several billion dollars—the effects of the stock market crash rumbled through the economy like a giant earthquake. The money supply contracted, causing hundreds of bank failures throughout the nation, and this in turn bankrupted thousands of individual depositors.[49]

The Securities Exchange Act of 1934 met this margin-trading question not by specifying a rigid numerical prescription of required percentages but rather by assigning this task to the discretion of the Federal Reserve Board, which already exercised overall responsibility for controlling the nation's money supply. In subsequent years, the board set various margin requirements at times as high as 90 percent and never lower than 40 percent. This action, prescribed in principle by the Securities Exchange Act, largely eliminated margin trading as a controversial issue and as a macroeconomic problem connected to national prosperity or depression.

A second major goal of the 1934 legislation was to impose federal discipline on the specific practices that speculators used to drive prices up or down at will. Here the Securities Exchange Act took direct aim at those time-honored devices employed by a long list of famous financial rogues, stretching from Jim Fisk in the 1860s to "Sell 'Em Ben" Smith in the 1920s. Section 9 of the act, entitled "Prohibition against Manipulation of Securities Prices," outlawed a series of questionable trading tactics involving "any such put, call, straddle, option or privilege." (These practices were not made illegal per se, but were proscribed only in certain circumstances.) In addition, the rules of the several exchanges now

were placed for the first time under the surveillance of federal regulators, who were empowered to alter rules as they saw fit. No
longer would an exchange be able to operate as an autonomous
private club; to the unrepentant leadership, especially of the New
York Stock Exchange, this supervision seemed the most presump-
tuous and offensive part of the entire act.[50]

A third goal of the legislation was to extend the rigorous disclosure provisions of the earlier Securities Act to other corporations,
by requiring detailed annual financial reports from all companies
whose securities were listed on a national exchange. The act of
1933 had applied only to issuers of new securities; that of 1934 applied to issuers of existing securities. Thus the unprecedented sunshine requirements of 1933 would now spread across wide areas,
to reach almost all corporations of any importance, excluding only
those with no new securities or whose existing securities were not
traded on any exchange.[51]

A New Securities Agency

Opposition to the 1934 legislation was led by the old guard of the
New York Stock Exchange, in particular the aristocratic and high-
handed exchange president, Richard Whitney. In general, Whitney and other opponents of the new laws tried to keep implementation out of the hands of the Federal Trade Commission. Landis,
George Mathews, and others at the FTC had proved too hard on
the securities industry for Whitney's taste. He and his fellow Wall
Streeters lobbied for the creation of a new and, they hoped, tamer
agency. Other powerful participants in the debate, including Virginia's venerable Senator Carter Glass, supported Whitney's idea,
but for reasons of their own. In the end, Sam Rayburn and his
allies in Congress directed a compromise between these factions
and added provisions Rayburn himself regarded as even more important. Consequently, the act of 1934, in addition to its novel
substantive provisions, created the Securities and Exchange Commission and charged it with the administration of *both* the 1934
act and the Securities Act of 1933.[52]

At first, Landis vigorously opposed the creation of a new
agency, but he soon found reason to change his mind. Franklin D.
Roosevelt, ever creative in matters like this, deftly moved Landis
and Mathews out of the old FTC and into the new SEC. In addi-

tion, Roosevelt further underlined the importance and power of the fledgling agency by naming as other commissioners two experienced legal prosecutors who had already inflicted deep scars on the men of the Street. These were Robert T. Healy, who, as general counsel of the FTC from 1928 to 1934, directed a vast study of public utilities; and Ferdinand Pecora, chief counsel for the Senate's well-publicized investigation of Wall Street, which ran from 1932 to 1934.[53]

Individually, each of these four men—Landis, Mathews, Healy, and Pecora—represented an exceptionally strong appointment. As a group, they provided a vivid contrast to the five original Federal Trade Commissioners of 1915, of whom George Rublee had been the best qualified. The SEC quartet left observers with no doubt that the new agency was going to be a very demanding tribunal indeed. Most outsiders expected that the chairmanship (chosen by vote of the five members) would go to Landis; Pecora, the celebrated architect of an extremely successful Senate investigation, was also known to want it. In the end, Roosevelt determined the choice. He stunned everyone by naming as the fifth member of the SEC Joseph P. Kennedy, and he dropped powerful hints that he wanted Kennedy to be chairman. Forty-six years old at the time and already very rich, Kennedy had been a bank president, the manager of an investment banking house, and even a film tycoon. He was also a veteran Wall Street speculator who, only a year before his appointment, had been involved in just the kind of pool operation that the Securities Exchange Act was designed to eliminate. Although the idea of his appointment originated with Roosevelt's braintruster Raymond Moley, many important New Dealers were aghast. While they knew that Kennedy had contributed generously to Roosevelt's 1932 campaign, they also felt that some more appropriate place could be found for him than that of fox in the chicken coop.[54]

Had Landis not already established an intimate relationship with Roosevelt, he too might have been troubled by the Kennedy appointment. But Landis was a realist and quite willing to give Kennedy a chance, both on Roosevelt's recommendation and because he knew Kennedy to be a capable administrator with connections in the Street that Landis himself could not claim. Later, in long retrospect, Landis came to believe that the special nature of the task in 1934 actually made the choice of Kennedy an inspired decision. For Kennedy, like the president himself, always remained an inveterate optimist whose upbeat temperament promoted confidence. With new investment at a standstill and the financial community now furious at the New Deal, Kennedy was exactly the kind of person who could help break the "strike of capital" that obstructed national recovery. The Securities Act of 1933, with all its disclosure provisions and penalties for misrepresentation, had done nothing to prime the pump of renewed investment. Many financiers began to blame the continuing drought on the New Deal in general and on the Securities Act in particular. Objecting even more vigorously to the Securities Exchange Act, some of them predicted that Roosevelt's apparent vendetta against Wall Street would soon turn the American economy into a wasteland. Roosevelt knew that something had to be done, and in his mind the Kennedy appointment was not so much a sop to enemies in the Street as a clear signal that the American president wanted action in the securities markets. Everyone agreed that Kennedy knew how to make things happen.[55]

Once in office, Kennedy set to work immediately in his effort to reassure investors and underwriters. Speaking both their language and that of the New Dealers, he endeavored to build bridges between them. As Kennedy said late in 1934, during a nationwide radio broadcast,

We have two major objectives in our work. One is the advancement of protection of decent business; and the other—even more important—is spiritual, and I do not hesitate to employ that word in connection with finance. We are seeking to re-create, rebuild, restore confidence . . . we do not have to compel virtue; we seek to prevent vice. Our whole formula is to bar wrongdoers from operating under the aegis of those who feel a sense of ethical responsibility.[56]

In Kennedy's view, an emphasis on ethical behavior would restore confidence, and renewed public confidence in turn would break the psychological barrier that prevented new investment. He admitted that national economic prospects seemed bleak, but he refused to sound a discouraging note. "This much I do know and make bold to state: The confidence of the investor has been so completely shaken that, regardless of blame or justification, it required an agency such as our Commission to help regain this lost confidence; to restore the shattered prestige of the business." Finally, Kennedy emphasized, "There is no right or left in the processes of the Securities and Exchange Commission. All we are trying to do is to go forward."[57]

Yet energetic as he was, and as hard as he and Landis and the other commissioners worked, they could not avoid delegating considerable power to the specialists on the SEC staff. Here the commissioners were very fortunate. In part because the Great Depression had dried up other sources of employment, the SEC was able to attract to its staff a large numbr of first-rate lawyers, accountants, and statisticians. As Landis recalled years later, after having worked in several other public agencies, the early SEC represented a genuinely elite bureaucracy, with "very able people in there, and extremely hard working." As soon as the Securities Exchange Act took effect in 1934, a tremendous workload fell on the commission, as nearly three dozen exchanges and several thousand corporations had to be registered on short notice. "I know in the last two weeks, prior to the deadline date," Landis said, "we had a gang of about thirty guys working on it, and I had cots set up in the building . . . Some of them worked around the clock in order to meet that deadline, which they did. But that was the kind of aura and atmosphere under which people worked. There was no question about hours or anything of that nature. There was a tremendous enthusiasm to see that these pieces of legislation would work, and would work to the benefit of the financial community as well as everybody else." Somehow the commissioners were able to communicate their own enthusiasm throughout the organization, and the SEC quickly became known as one of the most dedicated agencies in Washington. The first *Annual Report* of the SEC captured well the spirit of the organization: "The Commission reports with appreciation the very effective service of personnel of all ranks. More than 72,000 hours of overtime were given by the personnel and the morale has been such that the additional work was given freely by the employees in the interest of the work." For the period covered by the *Report* (less than a full year), the unpaid overtime work averaged out to more than two and a half weeks per employee.[58]

Again, the picture contrasts vividly with the early months of the Federal Trade Commission, during which time the members—unsure of their strategy and divided on matters of basic policy—found it convenient to go on an extended train tour of the American West. During this trip they held leisurely hearings, tried to get acquainted with business leaders in various cities, and in general did nothing of real importance. The Securities Exchange Commission from the moment of its birth conveyed an impression of serious intent. It demonstrated every strength that the FTC before it had lacked. The SEC began with meticulously drafted statutes, designed for careful administration. It was led by talented men, who included not only Kennedy and Landis but the almost equally formidable commissioners Mathews, Healy, and Pecora. It attracted an exceptionally able staff, which by the end of the first year numbered nearly 700 persons. Perhaps most important, everyone seemed willing to work long hours, and in part unpaid, in order to fulfill the SEC's mission.

Private Incentives and SEC Strategy

One powerful force behind the unusual efforts of the SEC was the agency's evolving strategy. In part, this strategy had been delineated by the original statutes, which mandated thoroughgoing disclosure of information by corporations, forbade numerous specific abuses in securities trading, and gave the SEC broad powers over the governance of exchanges and of the securities industry in general. As the statute drafters knew, an equally important part of the strategy could not be set down in words; it would have to come from the commission's practice in administering the enabling legislation. Though the acts were detailed and specific on many topics, the SEC retained wide discretion concerning what additional rules it would make, what further legislation it might propose, and what overall approach the commission would choose in carrying out its mandate.

Although the basic legislation had been placed safely on the statute books, many of the structural problems of the securities industry remained to be solved. The industry itself was still in a state of disorder. It dealt with the securities of thousands of corporations, listed on a multitude of separate exchanges, together with an unknown but much larger number of unlisted corporations whose securities were traded nationwide in the unregulated over-the-counter market. In addition, securities trading still wallowed in the trough of bad fortunes, close to its historic nadir, with practically no important new issues offered for sale. The men acknowledged as leaders of the industry had already suffered great humiliation at the hands of a merciless market. Now they stood, in effect, both indicted and convicted by Congress, waiting angrily but unrepentantly for sentencing by a group of determined but unseasoned SEC commissioners. All of this helped to make the psychology of the investor, a phenomenon that could be an invaluable tool if the commission could determine how best to use it, ready for propulsion toward the public good.

For the SEC commissioners, then, the basic strategic choices had to be governed not by what they might like to do to the oligarchs who ran the New York Stock Exchange. Instead, wise choices must flow from the obvious need for economic recovery and, beyond that, from the equally obvious longer-term need to make the marketing and trading of securities safe and legitimate for the American public. The possible courses of action leading to this goal did not include a mindless destruction of the existing institutional practices. However satisfying that might be, it could hardly serve the larger and more transcendent purposes of recovery for the national economy and legitimacy for the securities industry.

Still another fundamental strategic choice confronted the SEC. Should it pursue its mandate exclusively with its own staff? Or by working through the existing institutional framework of the industry? Either method entailed serious risks. If the commission decided to do the job entirely with its own forces, those forces would have to be enormous. The policing of corporate financial reporting alone would require thousands of auditors and accountants, each under some form of supervision. Then too, if the commission decided to administer the stock exchanges itself, this would necessitate an organization with several new SEC divisions, including large components in Washington and in every city that boasted a securities exchange. On top of all this, an effective engagement of the over-the-counter question would have to be initiated by a formidable SEC effort to bring together brokers, dealers, and over-the-counter firms into some alliance of contending parties that the commission could hope to regulate. This strategy of direct control had obvious drawbacks, including a decided unlikelihood of getting from Congress the funds to carry it out.

As it happened, the SEC decided to work through existing private structures and, where necessary, to create new ones. Landis believed such a course to be more in keeping with legal precedents and American traditions than was the alternative path of direct and coercive action by an army of government regulators. Furthermore, as an expert in shaping legal sanctions, Landis remained confident that the commission could hammer out, step by step, a complete regulatory scheme that would minimize any danger of the SEC's becoming a captive of special-interest groups. Commission strategy would be presented to accountants, bankers, and brokers as an attractive plan for "self-regulation." The heart of the regulatory system would be a careful shaping and bending of the incentive structures, so that each of the major players would voluntarily carry out SEC policies. The industry's role in self-regulation would apply to the means only.

This strategy derived primarily from Landis' early appreciation of the necessity of manipulating the incentives implicit in the industry, so as to give those involved a self-interest in obeying and strengthening the law. He had recognized the complexity of the situation from the very first, as he struggled during the Hundred Days to write a coherent Securities Act. That first piece of legislation had represented only the beginning. As Landis wrote in 1933, in his letter asking Dean Pound for a leave of absence, "An Act of this character, which strikes deep into corporation law and its practices, and deals with so many complex situations, calls for considerable administrative organization. We have been working desperately to create the type of administrative organization which will be adequate to administer the Act." And a little later, to Frankfurter: "The kind of things I want to do with this Commission take time and effort. As you see you cannot build an instrument of this nature in a few months, and if I want to keep my hand on this job, I will have to stay." Another letter to Sam Rayburn, written later as Landis and his colleagues worked out the SEC's strategy, commented: "The wheels of Government move slow in setting up a new organization, and I sometimes get very impatient with the amount of 'red tape' out of which we seem constantly trying to extricate ourselves. But though we move slowly, I think we are building upon pretty sure foundation. Our first official promulgation of rules were indeed somewhat gentle; but a little gentleness at this stage seems to me wise statesmanship. I think by proceeding along lines of this nature you will get both the exchanges and the industry keen about the Act rather than opposed to it." Never, though, did Landis even consider abandoning the government's own initiative, as some New Dealers in other agencies (such as the National Recovery Administration) often did. "To me it is somewhat amazing," he commented to Frankfurter, "how our younger men are falling for this idea of partnership with industry without any recognition of the significance of keeping an independent judgment together with an independent leeway of action." Clearly, Landis consciously weighed the costs and benefits of the SEC's chosen strategy at every step along the way.[59]

Yet the strategy itself did not win easy acceptance, even within the commission. In general, Landis received enthusiastic support from his old FTC colleague, George Mathews, and from Chairman Kennedy, whose political instinct coincided with Landis's carefully reasoned analysis. Landis was often supported with less enthusiasm by Commissioner Robert Healy, a Vermont Republican with stern ideas about punishing sinners; and more reluctantly by Ferdinand Pecora, who recoiled from the idea of securing the cooperation of the men of Wall Street, whom he had so righteously pilloried when they testified before the Senate committee. (Pecora proved to be ill fitted to the role of SEC commissioner; after six months, he resigned to accept an appointment to the Supreme Court of the State of New York. As Pecora's successor, Roosevelt named J. D. Ross of Seattle, a utility expert and veteran of the public power movement; Ross was expected to take a major role in the administration of the Public Utility Holding Company Act of 1935.)[60]

For himself, Landis aimed to get the industry back on the road to legitimacy. As he described the SEC's efforts in an article written for the 1934 *Yearbook of the Encyclopedia Britannica:* "In all its efforts the Commission has sought and obtained the cooperation not only of the exchanges but also of brokerage houses, investment bankers, and corporation executives, who in turn recognize that their efforts to improve financial practices are now buttressed by the strong arm of the government." Even with the touch of wishful thinking in this portrait, there still was no mistaking the SEC's intention to turn private incentives to its own ends.[61]

Enlisting the Accountants

When Congress passed the Securities Act of 1933, with its severe sanctions against misrepresentation of "material fact" by the lawyers, corporate officers, and others involved in preparing registration statements, these persons protested vigorously against the risks they now seemed required to accept. Among the professionals enumerated by the act were those public accountants who prepared the required financial disclosure statements. Like most other groups, accountants did not react kindly to the 1933 sanctions. An editorial in the *Journal of Accountancy* declared: "Hardly any one is courageous enough to be even remotely associated with the flotation of securities when the act holds over the head of everyone penalties which are staggering." The accounting profession, having suffered historic indignities at the hands of corporate management, now felt itself threatened from the other side as well, by an impractical government that seemed to be motivated (as the journal editorial went on to say) by "the ambitions of pious theory."[62]

The putative theorists, of course, were Landis and his fellow draftsmen, whose academic backgrounds offered easy targets. For Landis, the more serious problem was less to defend himself than to cut through such hostility, so that he might enlist these skeptical professionals in his own strategy for building effective regulation through existing mechanisms. His solution was to go directly to the source of the problem—the accountants—and to make them understand his strategy by explaining it as clearly as he could. Even though this course would involve him in numerous face-to-face encounters with those who were attacking him, Landis saw no alternative. Accordingly, beginning in 1933 and continuing throughout his tenure in Washington, he sought out opportunities to meet with and speak before professional groups, including those that seemed antagonistic to his ideas.[63]

Speaking, for example, before the New York State Society of CPAs, Landis bluntly told the accountants, "We need you as you need us," and indeed the overlap of interests was large.[64] Because their profession had labored for years to escape the tight grip in which corporate management held it, most accountants ardently wanted to exercise, in fact, more of that "independence" they claimed to be essential to good accounting practice. Corporate managers, lacking respect for such independence, often tried to dictate to the auditors, encouraging them to shade the truth or even to misrepresent that state of a company's financial health. Since the managers' own positions, at least in the eyes of corporate

directors and stockholders, depended on the success of the company as measured by financial statements, they felt a temptation
to manipulate the accounting figures, especially during a period of
economic depression. And since the practice of accounting was art
as much as science, ample room existed for wide variation in the
reporting of such important accounts as depreciation and asset
valuation.

When the leaders of the profession realized that a unique opportunity to gain respect lay at hand, their hostility to regulation
abruptly ceased. Quickly, the American Institute of Accountants
formed a Special Committee on Cooperation with the Securities
and Exchange Commission, and this group became a permanent
liaison. Now the *Journal of Accountancy* praised Landis and his
colleagues for their conciliatory approach: "The present is the
most important epoch in the history of accountancy."[65] One
writer, citing Landis' wisdom and effectiveness, informed the profession that the new legislation was a godsend: "No longer must
the public accountant single handed strive against the prejudiced
desire of the officers of clients for what he believes to be fair and
correct presentation of facts in the financial statements." And a
leading scholar of the profession noted that with the SEC's policy,
"the control function of accounts takes on a new and quite different form. Instead of being merely a tool of control by business enterprise they become a tool for the control of business enterprise
itself." The skeptics had turned into boosters of the SEC.[66]

Landis showed no particular affection for accountants, and he
sometimes seemed impatient with what he regarded as their habitual spinelessness. Even with some reservations, however, it struck
him as far preferable to use their existing expertise and to make
their professional institutions the vehicle of change, rather than
attempting to force results with direct government action. For direct action would require new resources that Congress was unlikely to authorize and that the SEC would have trouble putting to
good use. Thus, despite his intense interest in reform and his personal dislike of many accountants, Landis continued to promote a
cooperative approach. Specifically, he cultivated opportunities for
consultation with the leaders of the accounting profession; and
when he became SEC chairman, after Kennedy's departure in
1935, he encouraged his colleagues and subordinates to do the
same.[67]

Eventually, within the SEC, Landis and his colleagues created a special subdivision and put at its head a Chief Accountant. Immediately, this new officer became the most important individual regulator of auditing practice in the United States. He was charged with leading a professional drive toward more rigorous audits, more serious sanctions against violators, and more uniform accounting standards—ones that would permit the comparability of companies so desirable for both investors and regulators. In 1937, the SEC's Chief Accountant began issuing "Accounting Series Releases" to inform the profession about acceptable methods and procedures. Over the next forty-five years, the SEC issued nearly three hundred of these "ASRs" and they became basic guidelines for the practice of accounting. In addition, the SEC tried to encourage the profession's self-regulatory efforts and to promote the standardization of accounting practices within particular industries. It delegated much of its power to the accountants' own professional associations, but kept up constant communication to stimulate effective action by these groups.[68]

"In a real sense," wrote one student of accounting regulation, "the Commission's examiners have become accountants' accountants or auditors of audited statements." Another reported that the commission in one month had set standards for the profession "which years of futile committee work within the professional societies have not been able to produce or begin to produce." Over the retrospective of half a century, it is clear that the rigor of SEC accounting regulation has tended to vary with the identity of the Chief Accountant and of the commissioners. But it is equally clear that, measured by what existed prior to the New Deal, and comparatively against systems in other countries, the SEC's strategy of using accountants to serve its own ends has been successful.[69]

The most dramatic evidence of the nature of the strategy has been a sharp increase in the number of professional accountants in America. The first stimulus came from the Securities Act, which required that financial statements be attested by "an independent public or certified accountant." Later acts multiplied the number of required statements, and the result was a huge new demand for accounting services. Compared to other professions, accounting grew very rapidly during and after the New Deal. It increased by 271 percent between 1930 and 1970, compared with 73 percent for physicians and 71 percent for lawyers. Small wonder that accountants cooperated enthusiastically with the SEC.[70]

Taming the Stock Exchanges

In establishing control over the New York and regional stock exchanges, the SEC followed the same strategy that had worked so well with the accounting profession. Again, Landis carefully spelled out the commission's strategy to all members of the industry who would listen, as he delivered his message in person at one meeting after another. The following excerpts from some of his many talks help to explain why his candid approach to regulation proved both refreshing and effective.

June 19, 1935, in an address before the New York Stock Exchange Institute:

Self-government is, of course, the desirable thing. Everyone will admit that the less regulation there is, the better it will be, provided the objectives are always kept clear; and the better the self-government, the less need there is for regulation.

October 10, 1935, in another speech to the New York Stock Exchange Institute, again showing the carrot and stick:

It has always been my thesis that self-government is the most desirable form of government, and whether it be self-government by the exchange or self-government by any other institution, the thesis still holds. I profoundly trust that this experiment will prove successful. [If it is not, the Commission will step up its activities, including referral of wrongdoers to the district attorney for criminal action.] So far we have moved quite a bit in that field. At the present time there are, I should think, some 140 individuals under indictment.

February 27, 1937, in a speech to the Swarthmore Club of Philadelphia, a major address in which Landis gave the fullest possible explanation of the SEC's strategy:

Regulation built along these lines welded together existing self-regulation and direct control by government. In so doing, it followed lines of institutional development, buttressing existing powers by the force of government, rather than absorbing all authority and power to itself. In so doing, it made the loyalty of the institution to the broad objectives of government a condition of its continued existence, thus building from within as well as imposing from without.[71]

Landis' plea for institutional support from the exchanges served to make the specter of government regulation far less threatening. During the early years the SEC persuaded the exchanges to adopt a series of new regulations worked out after extended negotiations. These rules originated with the SEC, but they were promulgated by the exchanges as their own and applied to such trading practices as the conditions of short selling and the limitations on specialists' trading on their own personal accounts. (Specialists, operating on the exchange floor, bought and sold the securities of only a few companies and attempted to stabilize the prices of these securities; if they also traded on their own accounts—without limits—they were in a position to reap large profits.)[72]

For the first three years, the regulatory system seemed to work well enough. Under the authority of the Securities Exchange Act, the SEC shut down nine exchanges, registered twenty-two more as "national securities exchanges," and exempted six as of insufficient consequence. Of the national institutions, the most important by far was the New York Stock Exchange, which handled more than 60 percent of all shares traded on the exchanges and more than 80 percent measured by dollar volume. Its leaders had fought hard in 1934 against the enactment of any legislation that would reduce their power. Under the existing system, the exchange was led by a president—who traditionally continued to do business for himself without regard for his official duties—and ruled by a Governing Committee, a subgroup of which (called the Law Committee) actually fashioned most exchange policies.[73]

At the SEC's creation, the incumbent president was the imperious Richard Whitney, a bond dealer with close family and business ties to J. P. Morgan and Company. Whitney, like Franklin D. Roosevelt, had graduated from Groton and Harvard, and he symbolized the aristocratic tone of the exchange oligarchy. During the crash of 1929, he had even become something of a folk hero when, backed by millions from Morgan and other bankers, he stepped forward in a dramatic bid to halt the frenzied selling. His famous order for 10,000 shares of U.S. Steel at a per-share price higher than the going figure, followed by similar bids laid down for other stocks, produced headlines announcing "Richard Whitney Halts Stock Panic." Later, as exchange president from 1930 to 1935 and as a member of the Governing Committee and Law Committee for even longer, Whitney sounded the most powerful voice in the important decisions of the organization. Naturally, Whitney remained adamantly opposed to government intervention. (In 1933, he told Senate staff investigators, "You gentlemen are making a great mistake. The Exchange is a perfect institution.") He represented a continual problem for the SEC. Landis, for his part, found Whitney's haughty manner alternately amusing and annoying. Once when Whitney came to Washington for a conference, Landis took perverse delight in treating him to a 45-cent lunch from the dingy FTC cafeteria, carried on a tray back to Landis' office. What could not be laughed away, however, was Whitney's lax enforcement of the new rules. Despite the SEC's efforts, he continued to run the exchange in the old way, and soon it became obvious that a nasty showdown between Whitney and the commission was inevitable.[74]

Yet this showdown was delayed for several years by the encouraging performance of the stock market, which seemed to be signaling the broad recovery so important to the exchanges and the New Deal. The Dow-Jones industrial average, which had dropped catastrophically from a high of 381 in September 1929 to a low of 41 in January 1932, seemed in 1933 to be climbing steadily back to good health. In the ten months between Roosevelt's inauguration and the end of 1933, the industrial average had doubled, going from 50 to 100. After a slow year in 1934, the Dow resumed its encouraging rise, reaching in March 1937 a new high of 194. But from that crest, the average now dropped 17 points in eight weeks, recovered briefly, then began its worst plunge since 1931. By the end of March 1938, after a high of 194 just a year before, the Dow stood at only 99.[75]

This slide, an aspect of the economic recession evidently brought on by the threat of a new war in Europe, by Roosevelt's ill-advised spending cuts, and by various other factors such as the General Motors sit-down strike, precipitated the collision between the SEC and the Governing Committee of the New York Stock Exchange. Just as had been the case in 1929–1932, it seemed only too clear in 1938 that short-selling insiders had made numerous killings in the falling market and that by so doing they had helped to push the market down still farther. Confronted with this situation, and furious at Whitney and other exchange leaders for their lack of cooperation, the SEC now moved decisively, as if to reflect a changed attitude under its own new leadership.

In the midst of the long market slide, James Landis had left the commission to take up new duties as dean of Harvard Law School.[76] His successor as chairman was William O. Douglas, who when appointed had been about to leave the agency himself to become dean of Yale Law School. Douglas had come to Washington from the Yale faculty in 1934, at the invitation of Kennedy and Landis, to direct the SEC's study of corporate reorganizations and protective committees. An expert on finance and a personal favorite of Roosevelt (with whom he played poker), Douglas became an SEC commissioner in 1936. On occasion he quarreled a bit with Landis, and before long it seemed clear that Douglas was less patient than his predecessor with the procrastinations of the New York Stock Exchange. When he took over as chairman in September 1937, Douglas was just under thirty-nine years of age. He projected the public image of a blunt, tough-talking westerner who amused himself by climbing mountains and taking long hikes over rough terrain. He was fully prepared, even eager, to bring the SEC's gun from behind the door and turn it on the likes of Richard Whitney. At the same time, Douglas was no statist, and he had no wish to take over control of the New York Stock Exchange. Despite his threats to that effect, Douglas believed in the fundamental SEC strategy of manipulating private incentives to serve public ends. He wanted to work with exchange members to develop some new, SEC-supervised form of private governance which could survive any crisis.[77]

Now his obvious first step was to look for allies within the exchange. Whitney had left its presidency in 1935, but he still controlled several votes on the Governing Committee. On the other hand, the new president, Charles Gay, recognized that time had finally run out. Even more important, other dissident elements within the exchange, led by Paul Shields and E. A. Pierce, were determined to leave behind the Whitney era and all that it symbolized. Much to Douglas' delight and astonishment, Pierce and Shields appeared one day at the door of his office at the SEC, where Pierce inquired of him, "How would you like to regulate the New York Stock Exchange?" The dissidents, it turned out, had long felt that Whitney and his friends served the exchange badly, especially the interests of commission brokers, who made their money through purchases and sales for customers. Instead, Whitney appeared to favor the pure floor traders, whose practical function was closer to out-and-out gambling. Thus the brokers and the regulators shared a single cause.[78]

With the SEC's cooperation, Pierce, Shields, and their allies engineered an internal coup that all but eliminated Whitney's influence. As the new masters of the exchange, the reform group then pushed through a series of tough new rules, including additional disclosure requirements for all exchange members. These reports, quite unexpectedly, began to turn up widespread irregularities in the affairs of Richard Whitney and Company. The ensuing inquiry led to shocking revelations. For years Whitney had been using his clients' securities (including some in the portfolio of the exchange's gratuity fund, designed to benefit the families of deceased members) as collateral for his own loans, which he needed to cover huge losses from his personal speculations. Between December 1937 and March 1938, Whitney had borrowed more than $27 million in 111 separate loans, in addition to more than $3 million that he owed his brother George and other Morgan partners. Now the judicial process worked swiftly, and within a few weeks of his exposure, Whitney was convicted of embezzlement and sentenced to Sing Sing Prison, where he remained for three years.[79]

Roosevelt, when Douglas told him of the scandal that was about to break, could hardly believe his ears. "Not Dick Whitney!" he exclaimed, repeating over and over that it simply could not be true. Douglas himself recognized the episode as a stroke of incredible good luck: "The Stock Exchange was delivered into my hands." The disgrace of Whitney, coming on top of the steep decline in stock prices, swept away further resistance to reorganization. After a long period of negotiation, the New York Stock Exchange cleaned its house. As Douglas wished, it shifted to a more democratic form of governance, which included a full-time, salaried president. To this office the exchange named William McChesney Martin, a reform-minded thirty-one-year-old broker, who had been secretary of the ad hoc committee to reorganize the exchange. (Years later, Martin became chairman of the board of governors of the Federal Reserve System.) The new president led a complete overhaul of the rules and regulations of the exchange, accomplished directly under the eyes of Douglas and the SEC. Far from the action, in his Harvard deanship, Landis noted this outcome with a feeling of satisfaction. He took equal pleasure in the way Douglas was completing the work Landis himself had begun four years earlier with the over-the-counter market.[80]

Enveloping the Over-the-Counter Market

As Landis had planned, the last major element of the SEC's institution building came in 1938, with the passage of important
amendments to the Securities Exchange Act. This new legislation,
sponsored jointly by the commission and the leaders of the over-
the-counter market, provided a mechanism for the industry to police itself, with the close cooperation of the SEC. Under the terms
of the legislation, the industry formed a new institution, the National Association of Securities Dealers, Inc., and made it a remarkably rigorous regulatory agency.[81]

As in other aspects of securities regulation, here again one of
the SEC's levers in forcing action was the psychology of buyers. In
the aftermath of 1929, hundreds of over-the-counter firms, together with thousands of individual brokers and dealers, sustained
losses not only of prestige but also of business. Most of the investing
public simply stopped buying stocks and bonds. No buyers meant
no business. As hard as this sales drought proved for the organized exchanges to weather, it hit over-the-counter brokers and
dealers even harder because they specialized in new issues, few of
which were now forthcoming. For another thing, the over-the-
counter market was largely informal and unorganized. Its competitive position vis à vis the exchanges, therefore, actually worsened
after 1929, as what little business remained went elsewhere.

Unlike the exchanges, the over-the-counter system had no central market but was tied together mostly by telephone wires.
Transactions occurred only spasmodically, in response to demand.
The system did not produce ticker-tape price quotations, and the
potential for abuse was very high, since the prospective buyer did
not know the true going price for a given over-the-counter security. In this situation, brokers and dealers could misrepresent
prices, charge excessive commissions, and collude with other investment advisers to make fictitious sales.[82]

To their credit, the majority of over-the-counter brokers and
dealers were legitimate businessmen who for many years had been
trying to bring better discipline to their industry. Much like the
beleaguered accountants, however, they made little progress because of the lack of effective government support. In 1933, however, a new opportunity appeared to them in the form of the
National Industrial Recovery Act, and the industry eagerly seized
this opening. Under the aegis of the National Recovery Adminis-

tration, the Investment Bankers' Association wrote into its "Code of Fair Competition" a series of stricter rules for the conduct of the over-the-counter business. The code mandated many of the same disclosure requirements set forth in the Securities Act of 1933. It established new rules for the offering of securities and laid down procedures for the supervision of sales practices. Most important of all, it set up an Investment Bankers Code Committee charged with administering the new rules. The code, drafted by an elite group of investment bankers, seemed especially well designed to meet the needs of the over-the-counter market. The *New York Times* called it "one of the most stringent regulatory documents under the NRA," a judgment that reflected Wall Street opinion. Thus, as early as September 1934, as the SEC itself was just getting under way, the Investment Bankers Code Committee was already doing business. Its rules were in place, and 2800 cooperating firms displayed the NRA's blue eagle in their windows.[83]

James Landis, from his vantage point within the SEC, watched this activity with a great deal of interest. From all he could learn, it appeared that the over-the-counter segment of the securities industry was moving more rapidly to put its house in order than the intransigent New York Stock Exchange. Still, under the securities legislation of 1933 and 1934, the SEC retained some authority to make its own rules for the conduct of over-the-counter business, and in the fall of 1934 Landis and his colleagues directed the SEC's general counsel to begin drafting a set of such rules.[84]

In the meantime, the Investment Bankers Code Committee continued to make some progress, even under serious handicaps. First, the investment-banking industry did not include all of the over-the-counter market, so the NRA code provided only a rudimentary start toward a fully functioning regulatory system. Then too, the position of the over-the-counter industry was not being strengthened by the SEC's policy of helping the organized exchanges to provide better self-regulation. As the prestige of the exchanges began to recover, the over-the-counter dealers feared an increasing loss of business. Finally, if all this weren't bad enough, in May 1935 the Supreme Court ruled the NRA unconstitutional and thereby pulled the rug from under the Investment Bankers Code Committee.[85]

As if they had anticipated this decision, the SEC in April 1935 acted to take a more determined stance. Three days before the

Supreme Court's historic announcement, Landis wrote to the NRA indicating the SEC's willingness to administer the code. Then, as soon as the court's decision was announced, the SEC asked the Investment Bankers Code Committee to work out, jointly with the SEC, a permanent regulatory structure for the industry. Soon the code committee reconstituted itself as the Investment Bankers Conference Committee and began intensive discussions with the SEC. As usual, Landis gave a clear picture of the strategy, in one of his many speeches to businessmen: "Just as the disciplinary committees of the exchanges have been invaluable to us in our effort to supervise the activities on the exchanges, similar machinery would seem to be of value for the over-the-counter market. Under a self-imposed discipline it is frequently possible to lift standards . . . more than through legislation and regulation."[86]

Months of close consultation followed, as the SEC and the Investment Bankers Conference Committee drafted and redrafted legislation to implement their goals. The commission aimed at a functional duplication of the SEC-supervised structure now in effect for the organized exchanges. The over-the-counter brokers and dealers hoped simply to gain respectability and parity with their competitors within the exchanges. Early in 1938, Senator Frank Maloney introduced the bill. (Maloney, a Democrat from Connecticut, was a friend of Douglas, who by then had succeeded Landis as SEC chairman.) The bill provided that the industry could set up, under SEC supervision, an association or group of associations open to any applicant engaged in over-the-counter transactions. This private agency could then fine, suspend, or expel those members whom it found in violation of the rules jointly worked out with the SEC. The Maloney Act specifically exempted the association from the antitrust laws, since collective behavior of the type contemplated might be in restraint of trade.[87]

For its part, the industry responded by creating the National Association of Securities Dealers. The NASD had a central governing council and fourteen regional offices, a structure much like the SEC's own. At once, the association moved to regulate maximum fees for brokers' commissions, setting an informal upper limit of 5 percent. It began to investigate violations of the rules, both on its own motion and on referrals from the SEC. By law, NASD membership remained open to all comers, and the governance of the association seemed unusually democratic. No broker or dealer was required to join. Abstainers, however, quickly found themselves at a competitive disadvantage because nonmembers missed out on wholesale rates and commissions available only to members. They were reduced to the status of a retail customer for securities. In addition, since all major underwriters joined the NASD, and since its rules kept nonmembers out of underwriting groups, any broker-dealer with underwriting ambitions had to belong.[88] In the design of the NASD, like other institutions that grew indirectly from the National Industrial Recovery Act, elements of cartelization clearly appear: in the standard 5 percent pricing arrangement and in the exclusive membership provisions. Normally in the course of American government, the sponsorship of any sort of cartel has represented unwise public policy, since cartels tend to diminish allocative efficiency. For the over-the-counter industry in the context of economic depression, however, a dose of cartelism in the form of the NASD seemed inescapable. For SEC planners, it represented the only possible means of organizing an industry that had to be organized before it could be regulated.

The NASD itself took on hybrid form: part regulatory agency, part trade association. The investment bankers and over-the-counter dealers retained the existing Investment Bankers Association as their primary industry group. The NASD, by contrast, assumed the functions and structure of a regulatory agency. At the SEC's insistence, it began to develop its own professional staff, which eventually included several hundred examiners and investigators. Over its first forty-odd years, the NASD has freely imposed its sanctions against wrongdoers. Between 1939 and 1960, it expelled 237 firms and suspended, censured, or fined several hundred others. These rigorous activities continued into the next generation as well. In the single year of 1974, for example, the NASD expelled or suspended 152 firms and 394 individuals.[89] Over the years, the SEC maintained a close relationship with the NASD. The commission seldom overruled an NASD disciplinary action; when such a reversal did occur, it came more often on grounds of excessive harshness than of leniency. The evidence seems conclusive that the NASD, closely supervised by the SEC, did an excellent job in bringing order and discipline to the over-the-counter market, a setting that once harbored some of the sleaziest characters in all of American business.[90]

The Virtues of Participatory Regulation

From the viewpoint of Landis and his SEC colleagues, the system of participation in regulation by accountants, stock exchange members, and over-the-counter dealers helped to accomplish several goals simultaneously. First, it sharply reduced the kind of "government encroachment" often bewailed by industry groups. Active involvement by an industry—when involvement worked efficiently—could serve to turn such complaints into affirmation. When these groups were themselves closely involved in shaping and enforcing the regulations under which they did business, their sense of voluntary participation and commitment to the rules had to be strengthened. Then, too, such a system compelled the industry to think about the need for change. It provided a permanent structure of governance that, in turn, institutionalized the means for achieving effective reforms. Again, this made the industry active rather than reactive—more eager to initiate improvements rather than merely to respond to ideas coming from outsiders. Finally, and in the case of the SEC certainly most important, active industry participation provided a means of imposing quick and severe sanctions for violations. Under the American system of government, when a public agency employs police power (or some other form of organized pressure by the state), it assumes the burden of ensuring legal due process. Enforcement agencies must follow tedious standard procedures, designed more to protect the rights of the accused than for swift corrective action. Beyond the process itself, there looms always the specter of judicial review, with its added potential for endless appellate procedures.

Landis, because of his academic research into such matters even before the New Deal, was especially sensitive to these and other pitfalls. In particular, he searched for methods of administration to minimize the red tape that inevitably accompanied legal due process. So, wherever possible, he wrote self-enforcing provisions into the basic securities acts; later he encouraged the involvement of accountants, exchange officials, and over-the-counter brokers and dealers, all of whom helped to shape the detailed SEC regulations. In the larger sense, of course, industry participation provided no panacea for the many ills of business-government relations, either in the securities industry or elsewhere. Chicanery, apathy, and self-aggrandizement still made an appearance. The acts of Con-

gress, and their administration by the commission, could not resolve every problem. As a former SEC Chief Accountant once put
it, meaningful industry participation required the "hanging of
scalps." If no scalps were hung, then the regulatory structure had
no credibility. Indeed, if any one thing has defeated privately administered regulation even in professions such as law and medi-
cine, let alone in business associations such as the stock exchanges,
that failing has been a disinclination to hang scalps. In general,
however, the results of the SEC's institution building seemed fully
to justify Landis' reasoning. The National Association of Securities
Dealers, for example, imposed quick, rigorous sanctions that
would have been impossible for the SEC alone to duplicate.[91]

A more general barrier to effective reform was the simple refusal of an industry to participate. The SEC itself encountered this
kind of stonewalling in 1935, when Congress passed the Public
Utility Holding Company Act. That act produced a violent reaction among utility executives. After suffering defeat in Congress,
they moved on to the courts, taking with them the heaviest legal
artillery they could hire. Athough the SEC offered to negotiate,
the utilities did not accept the invitation. By 1937 they had instituted 58 lawsuits against the SEC and had enlisted in their cause
such leaders of the American bar as John W. Davis, John Foster
Dulles, and Dean Acheson. In defense, Landis and Douglas—no
mean lawyers themselves—planned a careful counterassault,
which ultimately routed the utilities. This campaign consumed
more than a decade, however, and only in the late 1940s did the
1935 mandate become fully implemented.[92]

The SEC's entire campaign during the 1930s showed that successful internal regulation by industries would be extraordinarily
difficult to achieve. Landis himself sometimes wondered how the
SEC managed it with so much success. In 1937, as he entered his
final year as a member of the commission, he took the occasion of a
speech to reflect in some depth on the SEC's strategy. His hosts
had asked him to select the topic he himself would most like to
discuss:

Broadly speaking, the problems of legislation and of administration divide themselves into two phases. The first relates to the determination of
what policies to pursue; the second, to the discovery of how to make the
chosen policies effective. Political discussion commonly centers about
the first. The choice of policy is attended by all the excitement of conflict

among varying philosophies and among diverse group pressures. Yet this phase is transitory . . . The administrative phase, on the other hand, is enduring in character. It requires a continuing effort of indefinite duration . . . Yet, by a kind of perverse irony, this second phase all too often receives only casual attention.

These words Landis chose to summarize the role of the commission and of himself. On other occasions he noted how "law has been carefully built upon law" and compared the SEC's work to "that of constructing a complex machine."[93]

Yet to make the machine run smoothly required the active participation not only of regulators themselves but also of managers working in the securities industry. Landis had little personal affinity for businessmen, and his early experience in Washington seemed to confirm this prejudice. "Of one thing I am sure," he wrote Felix Frankfurter late in 1933, "my name will be 'mud' with our playmates in the street—and that includes both Wall and State. But how truly despicable some of their tactics are. I really thought that they were essentially decent though somewhat misguided people, but I have my doubts now." In response Frankfurter urged him to "demobilize your fighting mood" and think objectively, "as though you were still a professor." But when Landis followed this advice, he encountered charges of having sold out to Wall Street. The liberal *New Republic* kept up a tattoo of criticism, urging the SEC to abandon its cooperative attitude and attack the industry frontally. Powerful elements within the SEC staff pressed similar recommendations. Landis held firm, however, overcoming both these pressures and his own personal feelings, and worked hand in hand with business executives during his four years in Washington. His behavior at the SEC forms an instructive contrast to that of many other militant regulators. For example, Landis' mentor, Louis Brandeis, had found it impossible to transcend his own aversion to the "curse of bigness" and his dislike of wealthy businessmen. So his ideas about regulation seldom allowed for the type of business-government relationship that lay at the heart of Landis' strategic design for the SEC.[94]

The Personal Tragedy of James Landis

Shortly after his departure from the SEC in 1937 to become dean of Harvard Law School, Landis delivered the prestigious Storrs

Lectures on Jurisprudence at Yale. As his topic he chose "The Administrative Process," and later the lectures were published in a 160-page book of the same title. This eloquent book represents the apogee of faith in the practical uses of regulation to achieve just ends; it is a landmark in the history of that idea. Later I shall discuss the arguments of *The Administrative Process* in more detail. For now, it will suffice to relate its tone of celebration to the author's own ebullient mood at the time of its writing.

Not yet forty years of age, Landis had already accomplished more than most men can do in a lifetime. As a brilliant student at Princeton University and Harvard Law School, clerk to Justice Brandeis, author of several standard legal treatises, and a full professor at Harvard before he was thirty, Landis was used to being acknowledged by those who knew him as one of the brightest people in his generation. Only a year after his arrival in Washington, he had been made the subject of a *Fortune* article entitled "The Legend of Landis."[95] At the SEC, he presided over the New Deal's single most successful regulatory agency, the plans for which he had helped to draft. Because of his extraordinary talents and his friendship with President Roosevelt, many observers considered him one of the strongest possible candidates for an eventual seat on the Supreme Court. Then, as *The Administrative Process* was being written, Landis became dean of Harvard Law School, the most conspicuous position in American legal education. He had good reason to feel on top of the world.

That pinnacle, however, proved to be a turning point. Life after the New Deal was destined to take Landis mostly downhill. As dean at Harvard, he did introduce several significant changes, but after two or three years his heart just was not in the job. The long period of constant excitement in Washington had bred in Landis a distaste for the quieter life of an academic. So he eagerly accepted a series of special tasks Roosevelt asked of him in the late thirties and during World War II. First, as a special judicial examiner he heard the deportation case of Harry Bridges, following attacks on that labor leader's alleged communist connections. Then, after Pearl Harbor, he managed the Office of Civilian Defense, and during the latter years of the war he lived abroad as economic minister to the Middle East. In all these assignments he did very well, but none of them engendered the kind of excitement he had known at the SEC. Meanwhile, some of Landis' closest friends—

even Felix Frankfurter—began to drift away. Worse still, his family life started to disintegrate.[96]

Earlier, during his time as a professor, Landis had tended to neglect both his family and his personal finances. He demonstrated a fanatical zeal for work, both at Harvard and in the frenzied early years of the SEC, but at great cost to family relationships and to his own health. Now, in his middle forties, Landis began to drink heavily; he found it impossible to sustain the round-the-clock work routines characteristic of his twenties and thirties. In 1946, with his marriage in ruins and his alcoholism a serious problem, he resigned the Harvard deanship, from which he had already taken unconscionably long leaves of absence. Nor were questions about his personal conduct confined to heavy drinking. Persistent rumors that he was having an affair with his Harvard secretary, who had accompanied him to Washington during the war, were confirmed. After Landis' divorce (on grounds of desertion), the two were married.[97]

In 1946 President Harry Truman asked Landis to become chairman of the Civil Aeronautics Board, and he accepted, with a sense of relief. His old friend Thomas Corcoran had first suggested the appointment to Truman's advisers; it offered a way of salvaging Landis' stale career by providing an acceptable exit from the embarrassing situation at Harvard. Truman himself regarded it as a "ten strike" that so distinguished a regulator could be induced to join the CAB. The period was a turbulent one in aviation history, when the airline industry was struggling to become an important part of the national transportation network.[98]

Landis once more threw himself into his role as administrator, trying perhaps to compensate for the troubles in his personal life. But the obstacles were formidable: the established airlines, in a precarious position themselves, recoiled at Landis' policies of opening up the industry to new entrants and promoting expensive new safety requirements. The more support Landis received from airline pilots and other labor groups, the less he got from the established carriers. He also became involved in running personal feuds with officials of the other federal agencies that shared in the making of overall airline policy.[99] Many of these problems, of course, were common to regulatory administration. Unlike his experience in the SEC, however, Landis found at the CAB few resources and little support. The CAB itself had no coherent strategy, and his efforts to give it one encountered repeated objections from many sides, including the White House. As the terminal date of his appointment approached (he was filling the unexpired term of a member who had resigned), his enemies stepped up the pressure on President Truman to get rid of him. Landis, who had naively taken it for granted that he would be given a new term, was astounded when Truman called him to the White House and told him that he would not be renominated. Even a storm of protest from notable liberals in Congress and elsewhere failed to move Truman. So Landis, with no savings, no firm prospects, and a heavy burden of alimony payments, found himself out of a job.[100]

Again his old SEC friends stepped in. Corcoran appealed to Joseph Kennedy to find something, and soon Landis received an offer of a vaguely defined post with "Kennedy Enterprises," which he accepted. Over the next several years, his duties included legal work for Kennedy's far-flung business interests, and an assortment of somewhat demeaning tasks for the Kennedy children: planning the itinerary for Eunice's and Jean's trip to the Middle East, helping Bobby write the minority report for the Army-McCarthy hearings, doing research for *Profiles in Courage*. In addition, Landis opened his own law offices, in both Washington and New York. Now, in his fifties, he began for the first time in his life to earn enough money to live well. But he remained careless in managing his financial affairs.[101]

When John F. Kennedy opened his campaign for the presidency during the late 1950s, Landis worked full time for him. Right after Kennedy's victory in November 1960, the president-elect asked Landis to prepare a report on the status of the federal regulatory agencies, which, Kennedy correctly believed, needed renewed attention. Landis, sixty-one years of age, was still beset with physical and emotional problems, though his mind remained as acute as ever. He launched one of his crash programs of research and writing, and in less than six weeks he produced the document Kennedy had requested. Eighty-seven printed pages in length, the "Landis Report" became another landmark of regulatory analysis. It was a merciless dissection of the commissions' failures, informed not only by the author's years of study and experience but also by a bitter sense of the historical betrayal of the regulatory ideal. Whereas Landis' book of 1938, *The Administrative Process*, had heralded the high tide of administrative achievement under the

New Deal, his *Report to the President-Elect* of 1960 represented a stunning turnaround. Now Landis denounced years of regulatory neglect under Truman and Eisenhower, and lamented the growing decrepitude of the commissions.[102]

Landis' powerful arguments for regulatory reform found a receptive ear at the White House. During the early months of Kennedy's New Frontier, the president appointed some aggressive new regulators to the commissions and, together with his allies in Congress, began to plan a thoroughgoing overhaul of the agencies. Landis, in his new assignment as special assistant to the president, was expected to take a major hand in this overhaul. In the midst of all the excitement over the new policies, however, two separate scandals broke over Landis' head. The first occurred when he was named as corespondent in the divorce suit brought by the husband of his young secretary, to whom Landis had foolishly written some love sonnets. It never became clear how much beyond literature the relationship had developed, and the suit against Landis was withdrawn four months later. Meanwhile, he quietly submitted his resignation, which Kennedy accepted.[103]

A second scandal, much more serious, emerged when it was discovered that Landis had not filed federal personal income tax returns between 1955 and 1960. He had put aside most of the money, filled out most of the forms, but failed to send them in. The ensuing investigation brought acute embarrassment to the Kennedy Administration, compounded by the fact of Landis' long association with Joe Kennedy. Now Landis' prominence, his background as a brilliant lawyer, and his relationship with the Kennedy family all combined to make the process of indictment and prosecution for tax evasion more harshly pursued by federal authorities than it otherwise might have been. After these two scandals broke, Landis again began drinking heavily; he also suffered from insomnia and severe depression. His lawyers wanted him to plead not guilty by reason of incompetency, and a case could have been made on the expert testimony of psychiatrists. It seemed simple to chart Landis' history of procrastination and neglect of his financial affairs. One psychiatrist consulted by the lawyers, diagnosing the patient as a deeply self-destructive individual, described Landis' condition as "a long standing personality disturbance in a man of high intelligence and moral conviction," a disturbance sufficiently severe to impair "his capacity to conform to the income tax laws."

No better defense would be required to protect a fallen man.[104]

But Landis, despite his lawyers' advice, refused to plead incompetency. Not only would such a tactic further embarrass President Kennedy, he felt; it might also endanger Landis' own program for regulatory reform. In deciding instead to admit his guilt, Landis and his lawyers believed that the worst penalty would be a stiff fine and a suspended sentence. Relying on the mercy of the court, Landis said at his hearing, "I would like to express regret, indeed repentance, for the folly that led me to put off filing of those returns. At no time did I intend to deprive the government of any revenue." Unfortunately, he and his lawyers had miscalculated. The judge decided to make Landis a public example. "You have formed a habit [alcoholism] you found difficult to control," he told Landis, adding that persons of the judge's own Irish heritage "often have had such difficulties," as if to make the defendant feel that he was in good company. The judge then sentenced Landis to thirty days in prison, followed by one year on probation. Not an unduly harsh punishment, perhaps, but certainly an unusually heavy one in a tax case like this, especially when most of the tax money owed had already been paid and where the psychological problems of the defendant were so obvious. The sentence, said the judge, would "give you an opportunity to reflect and straighten yourself out."[105]

"Ex-Harvard Law Dean Jailed," read the newspaper headlines. "What a tragedy," a friend wrote of Landis to Felix Frankfurter, adding that Landis' was "the most wasted life of our time." But this was not the end of his tragedy. In July 1964 the New York Supreme Court suspended him from the practice of law for one year. Although not a permanent disbarment, such a punishment seemed painfully close to a denial of Landis' profession and of all it meant to him. The personal effect on this legal craftsman, eminent legal scholar, and dean can only be imagined.[106]

During that same month, on a hot and humid day, Landis left his Manhattan office after a morning of work and went home to swim in his backyard pool. A little later, two neighborhood teenagers who had a standing invitation to use the pool arrived to find him floating face down, dead. Speculation hinted at suicide, but the evidence was inconclusive. The coroner ruled accidental drowning, probably caused by a heart attack that came upon Landis as he was swimming.[107]

His body was cremated and his ashes scattered over the garden, near the pool in which he had died. The Internal Revenue Service, with claims still outstanding for the tax penalties, continued to press for an additional settlement against his estate. Finally, the government ended its case against Landis by seizing and reselling his house, together with its pool and garden.

CHAPTER 6

Ascent, Decline, and Rebirth:
The New Deal and Beyond

PRIOR TO 1930, only two important federal regulatory agencies existed: the Interstate Commerce Commission and the Federal Trade Commission. An early version of the Federal Power Commission had been created in 1920, but this agency accomplished little before it was reorganized in 1930. By the end of the 1930s, a bewildering maze of new government organizations had sprung up as if by magic. Four new federal commissions were born, surpassing the total number that had appeared in all the years before 1933. These were the Securities and Exchange Commission, the Federal Communications Commission, the National Labor Relations Board, and the Civil Aeronautics Authority. Almost as significant, all existing agencies were given new responsibilities or additional industries to regulate or both. The Federal Power Commission received broad new authority from both the Federal Power Act of 1935 and the Natural Gas Act of 1938. The Federal Trade Commission assumed major new responsibilities under the Robinson-Patman Act of 1936, and the Interstate Commerce Commission was charged, under the Motor Carrier Act of 1935, with regulation of the very important and growing interstate trucking industry.

This explosion of regulatory legislation during the 1930s reflected something besides the economic crisis of that decade. It also represented a widespread popular conviction that the free market was hopelessly flawed. The same premises that underlay the Keynesian revolution in macroeconomics during the 1930s— that government should take a hand, that expert public servants were more likely than business executives to choose the wise course—also applied to microeconomic regulation. During that decade such regulation tended toward government-sponsored protection from industrial overcapacity. This was most vivid in the National Recovery Administration, which sought to keep prices up by limiting the output of industrial products. In place of vigorous price competition, the NRA sponsored the same kind of industrial cooperation that had worked wonders for American mobilization in 1917 and 1918. Such policies reflected a judgment that the depression had come about because too many business managers had responded to the original economic downturn by cutting prices and wages, thereby forcing competitors to do the same thing, until the entire economy was swept into a downward spiral.

If the remedy of cooperation required a suspension of the antitrust laws, then so be it. The country was in a *de*flationary crisis, and some means must be found to keep prices from falling further. Under the NRA's plan, each industry would be governed by a "code of fair competition," and the system as a whole would amount to industrial self-government. Thus the frenzy of NRA-sponsored code writing in 1933 and 1934, for hundreds of industries large and small. And thus the publicity of the Blue Eagle and the slogan "We Do Our Part." In substance, the codes called for the restriction of output in order to push up prices, and for the standardization of work practices and product quality.

Despite all its hoopla, the NRA did not work well. The clash between labor and management, consumers and producers, large companies and small ones, all made it a disillusioning experience. Even if the Supreme Court had not ruled the NRA unconstitutional in 1935, Congress would probably have allowed it to die. Yet the experiment had provided an important psychological boost, and it did give the appearance of action. In the large sense its failure derived both from its inherent logical contradictions and from the overall failure of the macroeconomy to recover. Had prosperity somehow returned in 1934 and 1935, the NRA doubtless would have received much of the credit. But the measures in and of themselves, for good or ill, had too little impact to be held responsible for either the success or the failure of the national economy.[1]

Vestiges of NRA-type thinking did survive, of course, in such areas as the regulation of trucking and airlines, and in such public-private arrangements as the National Association of Securities Dealers, administered jointly by the SEC and the over-the-counter industry. In all these cases, the essential tradeoff lay between the pressing need to regulate the industry and the danger of allowing regulation to facilitate protectionism. In later years, as scholars looked back on the 1930s, some argued that insofar as the regulation of particular industries actually did become protectionist, then perhaps the entire New Deal might best be understood as a gigantic drive for protection by business executives and other beneficiaries of the Roosevelt policies. This was a penetrating and wonderfully appropriate question to raise about the New Deal: had the Roosevelt Administration, against all its antibusiness image, somehow assisted business in capturing the government?

The answer was that in a few cases the system did evolve into a condition of capture (symbiosis might be a better metaphor), but that in most it did not. For every pattern like that in aviation and trucking, the New Deal also took some different regulatory gambits. There was, for example, the prohibition of child labor and, in the late 1930s, the strengthening of antitrust. There was the Public Utility Holding Company Act of 1935, which along with the Tennessee Valley Authority and the Bonneville Power Administration was anathema to the utility industry and to most business managers in general. There was the securities legislation of 1933 and 1934, which at last tamed Wall Street. And behind all these programs of microeconomic regulation stood not a particular ideology, not *a* New Deal philosophy, but several competing ones.

The single overarching idea that tied the competing philosophies together was the conviction shared by a majority of New Dealers that economic regulation by expert commissions would bring just results. The clearest individual expression of this conviction came from James Landis, in his book of 1938, *The Administrative Process.* Landis' arguments, which received an enthusiastic welcome from legal scholars and political leaders, mark the high tide of American confidence both in the idea of regulation and in the benefits derived from it in practice. The book therefore merits a close examination, not only in its historical context but also because it remains today the most forceful argument ever written in favor of regulation.

Landis' Theory of Administrative Regulation

Landis took up the case for regulation at the place where Charles Francis Adams had left off roughly seventy years earlier. The line of reasoning from Adams' comment in 1869 about "a new phase of representative government" could hardly have been more direct. As Landis argued, "In terms of political theory, the administrative process springs from the inadequacy of a simple tripartite form of government to deal with modern problems." The problems of industrialization seemed so urgent and complex that they threatened to overwhelm all three existing branches of national government. At the same time, the prevailing forces of democratic power in the United States made certain that these problems could not be ignored, that they somehow must be addressed. This simultaneous rise of industrialism and of democracy ensured that the role of government must in fact increase. Since the existing branches were no longer sufficient to the task, the rise of an administrative branch became inescapable.[2]

By framing his argument in this step-by-step fashion, Landis undertook to establish legitimate bloodlines for the new form of regulatory government. Overall, the design of *The Administrative Process* was calculated both to explain the rise of this phenomenon and to justify its "quasi-legislative, quasi-executive, quasi-judicial" functions. Landis took aim at those lawyers and political scientists whose writings sought to deny regulation its legitimacy:

That literature abounds with fulmination. It treats the administrative process as if it were an antonym of that supposedly immemorial and sacred right of every Englishman, the legal palladium of "the rule of law." The process is denounced by worthy lawyers and others heralding the death knell of ancient liberties and privileges. Only a year ago a distinguished group of scholars, reporting to the President of the United States—in language hardly indicative of academic restraint—described the independent administrative agencies of the federal government as constituting "a headless 'fourth branch' of the Government, a haphazard deposit of irresponsible agencies and uncoordinated powers," whose institution did "violence to the basic theory of the American Constitution that there should be three major branches of the Government and only three." Such apotheosizing obscures rather than clarifies thought. Despite this chorus of abuse and tirade, the growth of the administrative process shows little sign of being halted.[3]

Throughout his book, Landis rested a substantial part of his argument on the expertise of regulators. Given the technical nature of their tasks, he said, the need for specialization and expertise should be self-evident. But, at the same time, certain other traditions of government service in the United States militated strongly against expertise, elitism, and long tenure in office. By and large, these traditions were legacies from Jacksonian Democracy, which conceived of civil servants as interchangeable parts, forever shifting about to make room for deserving political workers. In Landis' mind, this egalitarian "spoils" tradition represented an obstacle that the administrative process must overcome. Expertise, he wrote, obviously thinking of his own service with the SEC, "springs only from that continuity of interest, that ability and desire to devote fifty-two weeks a year, year after year, to a particular problem.[4]

Yet expertise in regulation also tended toward a government by elites, which was a clear step away from the Jacksonian tradition. Landis took that step without hesitation. Like Adams before him, Landis accepted the departure from an egalitarian management of regulation as axiomatic, even inevitable. From that point Landis went on to argue that the increasing need for expertise and efficiency meant an eventual proliferation of agencies. Here, too, he had no reservations:

The most superficial criticism which can be directed toward the development of the administrative process is that which bases its objections merely upon numerical growth. A consequence of an expanding interest of government in various phases of the industrial scene must be the creation of more administrative agencies if the demand for expertness is to be met ... Efficiency in the processes of governmental regulation is best served by the creation of more rather than less agencies. And it is efficiency that is the desperate need.[5]

In meeting this need for efficiency, the installation of specialized experts also made it possible for an agency to offer direction and advice *in advance of regulatory action.* Thus advance advice— that very form of administrative government which Landis' mentor Brandeis had earlier rejected—Landis himself now embraced, with confidence and enthusiasm. Drawing on his own experience in two different commissions, he explained that the denial of advance advice had hamstrung the FTC but that an ingenious use of it had liberated the SEC. Specifically, Landis showed how advance advice had been foreign and contrary to "a very precise tradition which governed the Federal Trade Commission"; and how this tradition had handicapped the administration of the Securities Act during the brief period of the FTC's jurisdiction over the act. Once the more specialized SEC appeared, however, it was in a position to develop advance advice through a finely calibrated series of agency pronouncements:

The most authoritative device is the Commission regulation. Another, on a slightly lower level, is the Commission opinion. A third is an opinion by the General Counsel of the Commission. The Commission can repudiate this opinion without getting into the embarrassing position of having openly to repudiate itself. A fourth, an informal opinion of the General Counsel ... is commonly employed as a means of responding to enquiries. It receives no publicity nor is it normally the subject of discussion by the Commission as a whole or by any of its individual members.[6]

Here the point was that the SEC, unlike the FTC before it, boldly took the initiative and developed a series of special regulatory devices to meet particular types of administrative problems. During the years following the publication of Landis' book, the SEC issued thousands of informal advance opinions through devices ranging from those enumerated by Landis to SEC no-action letters, which were issued by the commission in response to specific questions submitted in advance by business managers and their lawyers.[7]

Landis met and attempted to rebut every point in the critics' case against regulation. As he saw it, the chief weapon in their arsenal was a constitutional argument that regulatory agencies violated principles of checks and balances. In rebuttal, Landis noted that each branch of government actually retained effective checks against abuses of power: the executive branch checked regulation through the appointment process, the legislature through enabling acts and control of appropriations, and the judiciary through review of agency decisions. Landis particularly emphasized the judiciary's role, and in so doing he lambasted the courts' habitual hostility toward the growth of administrative discretion. He wrote his book, in fact, during the popular crisis brought on by the Supreme Court's invalidation as unconstitutional of much New Deal legislation. So it is not surprising that he chose to defend the rise of administrative law by explicitly attacking the courts:

The power of judicial review under our traditions of government lies with the courts because of a deep belief that the heritage they hold makes them experts in the synthesis of design. Such difficulties as have arisen have come because the courts cast aside that role to assume themselves experts in matters of industrial health, utility engineering, railroad management, even bread baking. The rise of the administrative process represented the hope that policies to shape such fields could most adequately be developed by men bred to the facts. That hope is still dominant, but its possession bears no threat to our ideal of the "supremacy of law." Instead, it lifts it to new heights where the great judge, like the conductor of a many tongued symphony, from what would otherwise be discord, makes known through the voice of many instruments the vision that has been given him of man's destiny upon this earth.[8]

Once the justification of administrative practice had been completed, Landis ended his book by invoking an Adams-like choir of harmonized professional voices, all singing in praise of the public interest.

The Climate of Regulation from the 1930s to the 1950s

The powerful argument made in *The Administrative Process* must be understood not only in terms of its compelling internal consistency, but also for its relevance in the context of its time. Part of that context derived from the author's own exuberant personal mood in 1937 and 1938. Then, too, Landis' thinking about regulation during those two years clearly reflected the practical lessons of his own recent life as a working regulator. Thus, although he seemed to be writing about broad problems in *The Administrative Process*, Landis actually focused on a narrow range of regulatory experience. His book was dominated by specific references to the Securities and Exchange Commission, and most of his discussion selectively demonstrated the achievements of that very successful agency. From a narrow and atypical range of personal experience, Landis drew broad and sometimes reckless conclusions about the whole field of regulation. In most respects—as is now clear—the evidence did not warrant his conclusions, not even evidence drawn from the New Deal's most enthusiastic endorsements of regulation.

Elsewhere, always in the background of Landis' analysis, lay the intense contemporary controversy over the basic questions of administrative government. As the New Deal spawned one new agency after another, the growing delegation of administrative discretion by Congress attracted more and more criticism. At the same time, those questions raised by the principle of delegation— the constitutional legitimacy of bestowing broad powers on administrative bodies, the discretionary latitude assumed by these bodies, the propriety of judicial review of their administrative decisions—all of this and more came under scrutiny by appellate courts and by the academy. Initially, court attention resulted in the invalidation of such New Deal legislation as the National Industrial Recovery Act and the Agricultural Adjustment Act, on grounds of unlawful delegation. Later, President Roosevelt's attempt to pack the Supreme Court—an attempt which Landis, among only a handful of important lawyers, strongly endorsed—produced a larger controversy, as it brought the country to the brink of constitutional crisis. Among university scholars, the principle of administrative discretion drew especially heavy fire from lawyers and political scientists, who denounced the practice of combining tripartite governmental functions within single agencies. Landis, in the content and tone of his book, demonstrated that he, like Brandeis earlier, was a man of his time, passionately engaged in these intellectual and political struggles.

What showed how quickly times could change, however, was the clearly mediocre performance of federal regulatory commissions during the 1940s and 1950s. Even the SEC itself, after its glory days during the New Deal, went through a period of quiet. The exigencies of World War II relegated securities law to a low national priority, and the commission relocated its offices from Washington to Philadelphia in order to make space for more important mobilization agencies. The SEC did not return to the capital until 1948. During both the Truman and Eisenhower administrations, the appointment of undistinguished commissioners tended to dim the luster of all federal regulatory agencies; and not until the Kennedy Administration did the SEC, or any similar commission, begin to recover its old distinction.[9]

In a broader sense, as economic prosperity returned with a rush during the 1940s and 1950s, economic regulation simply became less important as a national problem. The practice of regulation during those years naturally fell into less capable hands. This decline in the quality of commissions brought with it, in turn, a new wave of negative criticism: heated attacks not only on regulatory practice but even on the theories underlying regulation. In the minds of many critics, the multiplication of regulatory agencies, together with other programs of assistance to special-interest groups, served chiefly to multiply the opportunities for "capture" by regulated interests. As always, skeptics questioned just how independent any regulatory machinery could be—or, indeed, how independent any form of government regulation properly should be. For one thing, executive appointment of expert, nonpartisan commissioners removed them from popular control through the normal elective process, and this represented a departure from the nation's democratic traditions. For another, genuine independence might be unsustainable against the wills of powerful presidents or governors, who might wish to interfere with scientific evaluation or even defeat every hope of independence by appointing political cronies and hacks to regulatory commissions. Even more likely, considering what usually went on inside the lobbies of legislatures, regulated corporations might easily direct their potent economic influence toward regulators—might, in fact, capture them.[10]

The threat of capture represented only one of many potential sins and shortcomings ascribed to regulation by its opponents. Although their critical attack did not reach its peak until the 1960s, it had started to build momentum much earlier. During 1937, for example, the year in which Landis began to write his lectures on the administrative process, the president's Committee on Administrative Management issued a general negative verdict on the regulatory system Landis was preparing to celebrate. Instead of offering praise, the committee recommended a drastic overhaul of regulation, including the merger of most existing agencies into regular government departments. This suggestion, like many others put forward by the committee, eventually ran aground on the shoals of disagreement between Congress and the president; but the very fact that Roosevelt himself would push for a retreat from independent agencies, even though his own administration had sponsored the creation of so many, stands as a revealing measure of the controversy and uncertainty surrounding the whole subject.

Still more critiques followed in regular progression, almost like the beat of a drum. In 1941, the attorney general's Committee on Administrative Procedure made its own report, which also strongly criticized prevailing regulatory practice. Responding to these and other pressures, Congress in 1946 passed the important Administrative Procedure Act, which laid down strict requirements for fair hearings to be offered all affected parties—a protection against arbitrary judgments by regulators and other government officials alike. In 1949, the first Hoover Commission issued its report on governmental operations, which included a long and critical section on regulation. In 1955, a second Hoover Commission task force again suggested a thorough reorganization of most regulatory agencies. Finally, in 1956 the American Bar Association presented its own modifications of the second Hoover Commission's recommendations.[11]

During these same years, criticism from the academy rose in an uninterrupted crescendo. Scholars took careful note of the across-the-board decline in the overall quality of commissions. In particular, they charged that the Civil Aeronautics Board and the Federal Communications Commission—two agencies born during the New Deal—appeared to be following policies that equated the public interest with the desires of the most powerful elements in the airline and communication industries. By the 1950s, respected scholars such as Samuel P. Huntington and Louis L. Jaffe, both of Harvard, had begun to analyze the ties between regulator and regulated, and to probe the internal contradictions in regulatory theory itself. In 1955, Marver H. Bernstein of Princeton published a devastating book that synthesized all the diverse objections to regulation that had been gathering force since the New Deal. Then in 1960, James Landis himself, in his report on regulatory agencies to President-elect Kennedy, catalogued the breakdown of the system he had celebrated only twenty-two years earlier.[12]

The Landis report put the indictment of regulation into general terms. Whereas efficiency had been the goal of the 1930s reforms, Landis claimed that by 1960 delay had become the hallmark of federal regulation. At the Civil Aeronautics Board, which Landis had once chaired, the average docketed case was now taking thirty-two months to settle, and 166 current cases had been pending for more than three years. At the Federal Trade Commission, 309 cease-and-desist orders were currently pending, of which 118 were more than a year old and 30 more than three years. At the Federal Power Commission, which, Landis declared, "without question represents the outstanding example in the federal government of the breakdown of the administrative process," it would require some thirteen years to clear up those natural-gas rate cases already pending in 1960. "With the contemplated 6500 cases that would be filed during that 13 year period it could not become current until 2043 A.D. even if its staff were tripled." Landis went on to say that in many agencies the absence of an overall regulatory policy made each case sui generis. The commissions, by refusing to formulate active strategies, had drifted instead into passive, court-like methods of operation.[13]

Weak appointments to the agencies had made things even worse. The quality of personnel had deteriorated under lax appointment policies of the postwar presidents, in sharp contrast to the outstanding talent that marked Washington during the exciting 1930s. "The fires that then fed a passion for public service have burned low," Landis observed. To solve this personnel problem, he proposed stronger powers for agency chairmen and higher salaries and longer tenure for all commissioners. "A ten-year term is not too much to suggest." Most important, Landis proposed thorough reorganization of nearly all the agencies, including a centralization of power in the chairmen and a stronger institutional tie between these chairmen and the president.[14]

On the agencies themselves, the effect of the report was a shock. Indeed, the mere fact that the White House was paying such close attention, after years of neglect, encouraged the commissions to reform themselves. Congress responded with generous appropriations, convinced by Landis' argument that the agencies had long been starved of resources. President Kennedy underscored his own commitment to change by appointing new first-rate commissioners—such men as William Cary, whom Kennedy named to the SEC, Newton Minow, who chaired the FCC, and Joseph Swidler, who took over at the FPC. Landis himself became special assistant to the president, charged with overseeing the reorganization plans outlined in his report. In addition, the Kennedy Administration sponsored new laws in Congress designed to implement the plans. The result of all this activity was to reinvigorate the federal regulatory process and, for a season, to draw the public's attention to the seriousness of long-neglected problems. The agency reorganizations achieved perhaps one-half of what Landis and Kennedy wanted, and this derived more from decisive administrative action by the new chairmen than through congressional action. Congress, as it had done so often with other reorganization bills, balked at giving additional discretionary authority to the executive, as Landis' recommendations would have required.[15]

The attention of Congress and the president soon turned to other pressing matters, such as civil rights, tax policy, and foreign affairs. Regulatory reform, a major issue during the first year of the Kennedy Administration, did not again become a focus of national policy until the severe economic problems of the early 1970s brought it once more to center stage. By that time, the play of regulation would come to be dominated by an entirely new set of dramatis personae: professional economists preoccupied with the free market, who set out to upstage the older generation of legally trained regulators.[16] One of the first targets of these economists would be the protectionist regulation set up under the New Deal.

CHAPTER 7

Kahn and the Economist's Hour

I N *Nixon Agonistes*, his bestseller of 1970, the journalist Garry Wills argued that "America is distinguished by a 'market' mode of thought in all its public (and even private) life." Wills went on to identify four market systems, each with its reigning prophet: the economic market system (Adam Smith), the political (Woodrow Wilson), the moral (Ralph Waldo Emerson), and the intellectual (John Stuart Mill). These four systems, Wills wrote, combined to yield up the strange and anomalous figure of Richard M. Nixon.[1]

Nixon Agonistes now seems both profound and half-baked. More important, however, the book's popular success signaled an unmistakable restoration of "the market" to intellectual respectability. For the principles that Wills made acceptable to a popular audience also found an enthusiastic if less boisterous welcome in the halls of academe. There a group of innovative scholars had spent the preceding years sending a similar message to students and colleagues. In economics the "Chicago school" of free-market theorists gradually gained reinforcements from a corps of young monetarists who became impatient with the policy activism favored by Keynesians. The Chicago school exerted only moderate influence before 1970, although occasionally a member might score a popular hit, as Milton Friedman did with *Capitalism and Freedom* (1962). By and large, however, the Chicago economists hardly entered the consciousness of most Americans, who took in what they knew about economics from the witty John Kenneth Galbraith. Even in 1970, few people realized that time and circumstance were now on the side of the Chicagoans. But over the next dozen years, the Chicago school came to exercise great influence on public policy in America and on regulatory policy in particular. During this brief period, three Chicagoans (Milton Friedman, Theodore W. Schultz, and George J. Stigler) were awarded Nobel Prizes in Economic Science.

In 1970, when *Nixon Agonistes* was published, *The Economics of Regulation* by Alfred E. Kahn also reached print. Kahn taught at Cornell, and he had been a liberal Democrat since the New Deal. In no sense did he belong to the Chicago school. Yet much in his book appealed to Friedman, Schultz, Stigler, and other Chicagoans: in particular, the arguments that regulation and competition are often at odds; that government officials often misunderstand the economic consequences of their decisions; and that market incentives are usually preferable to command and control regulations.[2]

At the time his book appeared, Kahn was not well known beyond the Cornell campus, where he served as dean of arts and sciences and as professor of economics. A few years later, he was a national celebrity. His success rested on the power and timeliness of his ideas, combined with a magnetic personality, which won him a series of political appointments. The first appointment came in 1974, when Kahn was named chairman of the New York Public Service Commission—at the time the most important state regulatory post in the country (and the highest paid, state or federal). In 1977 and 1978, he presided over the Civil Aeronautics Board, which then carried through the first major deregulation of an entire American industry. From 1978 until 1980, he chaired the president's Council on Wage and Price Stability and became known to the public as "the nation's chief inflation fighter." He was a media favorite, a fixture on the evening news.

A good deal of Kahn's newsworthiness derived from the simple fact that he was great copy. He loved Gilbert and Sullivan, enjoyed singing in amateur productions of *Iolanthe* and *Yeomen of the Guard,* and could quote hilarious lyrics from obscure operettas. In his best form Kahn was the model of a modern media general. When as chief inflation fighter he broached the possibility of "a deep, deep depression" and suffered the inevitable White House reprimand, he proffered a substitute word: "banana." That witticism prompted a second deluge of coverage. *Newsweek* called him "Alfred 'Bananas' Kahn," while a second magazine ran "The Sayings of Chairman Kahn." Even this did not end the game;

apprised of protests from banana interests, Kahn took fresh refuge in a new term, "kumquat."[3]

Later, when a Polish cardinal became Pope John Paul II, thus igniting a round of Polish jokes, Kahn—with his mind on the aberrant forecasts of his colleagues—solemnly declared that the new Pope had conquered Rome by telling economist jokes. For Kahn, one-liners became a trademark, even though he resisted the media's attempts "to make me a character," a "Walking Mouth." Profiled in the magazine *People* (surely one of few regulators ever selected for the honor), he complained afterward, "All life is a concatenation of ephemeralities." And during his tenure at the Civil Aeronautics Board, Kahn astonished Frank Borman and other Eastern Airlines executives, who were trying to educate him about the merits of different aircraft, by admitting that "I really don't know one plane from the other. To me they are all marginal costs with wings." Words seemed never to fail him.[4]

Yet to Kahn the principle of marginal costs—a fundamental tool of regulatory economics—represented no ephemerality and certainly no laughing matter. Unlike many other commissioners who shared his humanist values, he attached great importance to this favorite economic idea. He argued that in its neglect of marginal costs, more than at any other point, regulation had gone wrong. Once in office, Kahn determined to oversee improvements in regulatory practice by personally supervising the application of marginal-cost pricing.

Sound regulatory policy, he never tired of explaining, requires that buyers pay the marginal cost of all the goods and services they receive. If five units of an item cost $40 to produce and six units cost $60, then the marginal cost of the item is not $8 or $10 but $20. If the sixth unit is priced at $10 (that is, at average cost), consumers will purchase too many units—often not just one too many, but several—and since consumers have only a certain amount of money to spend, they will be able to buy too few units of other items, relative to what they would do under allocative efficiency. When goods and services are not priced according to marginal costs, therefore, consumers will automatically bring about a misallocation of society's resources. In order to prevent this unhappy result, Kahn believed, the prices of all goods and services should be set "at the margin"—that is, they should be pegged to the cost of producing one more unit at a particular time.

But Kahn went further than this. He argued that marginal-cost pricing in regulated industries should also include the social cost of minimizing such "externalities" as air and water pollution. For an item such as electricity, pricing below marginal social cost would have not only the usual result of encouraging excessive consumption; it would also lead to the additional construction of expensive, polluting power plants, all the while driving the electric company toward bankruptcy. Remarkable as it now seems, this process was already underway in the state of New York in 1974, when Kahn became chairman of its Public Service Commission.

Kahn worked to persuade both producers and consumers of electricity that only some drastic change in the pricing system could avert disaster. Eventually he succeeded in getting marginal-cost principles partially incorporated into standard rate designs, so that they were factored into price levels. The resulting prices took the form of time-of-day differentials, designed in particular to discourage the careless use of air conditioning, which requires large amounts of electricity. Marginal-cost pricing nearly always raised difficult problems of implementation; but even so, in the case of New York, some of the practical changes were dramatic, as the difference between off-peak and peak hours now reflected the social cost of each type of use. In one of Kahn's "proudest accomplishments," for example, the New York Public Service Commission made summer air conditioning extremely expensive to consumers. As Kahn explained it,

In Long Island, if you are a large residential user of electricity, you used to pay roughly five cents a kilowatt-hour, a damn high price no matter when you consumed it. Now you pay 3½ cents on a normal summer day per kilowatt-hour . . . and 2½ cents at night; and on summer days, when the temperature gets above 82 degrees, you pay 30 cents per kilowatt-hour. Now, that represents a much closer reflection to the comparative economic costs of your being supplied. Notice, this is a ratio of 12 to 1, as between night and a hot summer day, a much closer approximation to the respective marginal costs of supply. Think what that does to people's conservation habits. Think what it does to encourage the development of a technology that will enable you to use your electricity at night.[5]

The new pricing schedule discouraged careless use, checked the growth of demand, and diminished the need for new construction to serve the peak load.

Kahn liked to illustrate the point by comparing electric utilities to retail stores. To him, charging a flat rate for electricity regardless of the time of consumption seemed "like charging a flat price per pound for all items in a grocery or department store. What would happen if everything that came out of the cow—steak, hamburger, suet, bones, and hide—were priced at average cost per pound?" His answer, of course, was that everyone would buy steak and no one would want suet or bones. A basic principle emerged: "The only economic function of price is to influence behavior—to elicit supply and to regulate demand." No Chicago economist could have said it more clearly.[6]

A Scholar's Odyssey

That Alfred Kahn should become the nation's best known evangelist for marginal-cost principles—a set of ideas seldom associated with Kahn's liberal noneconomist friends—may seem ironic. Yet an explanation can be found in the long intellectual journey that marked his life. Kahn was born in Paterson, New Jersey, in 1917, the son of a Russian Jewish immigrant who worked in a silk mill. Young Alfred (or Fred, as he was called) soon proved to be an intellectual prodigy. At the age of fifteen he completed high school in New York City. At eighteen he graduated *summa cum laude* and first in his class from New York University, and before he turned twenty took a master's degree at NYU. He pursued further graduate work at the University of Missouri, then moved on to Yale for his doctorate.

During the same years, he also worked at a series of research jobs in Washington, for the Brookings Institution, the Department of Commerce, and the Antitrust Division of the Justice Department. Early in his career, Kahn began to acquire firsthand experience with the kind of policy-oriented social science research that was linking universities, foundations, and public bureaucracies into an integrated network with real power. For the next thirty years, he would continue to shuttle among the bases within this system. He worked with the War Production Board, the Federal Trade Commission, the staff of the Council of Economic Advisers, and as a member of the three-person Economic Advisory Council of American Telephone and Telegraph. And, whenever he needed to, Kahn returned to a stable anchorage: Cornell University and the life of a teacher and publishing scholar. He and his wife lived in Ithaca, near the campus, and found it a wholesome place in which to raise their three children.[7]

Between 1940 and 1974, when he took his seat as chairman of the New York Public Service Commission, Kahn wrote two books and coauthored two others. All four proved to be major works. In addition, he managed to publish some two dozen articles and comments, most of them in the *American Economic Review*, the leading journal of the discipline. Nearly all of this writing reflected, in one way or another, the influence of his two principal advisers, Myron Watkins and Joseph Schumpeter. It also evidenced deep intellectual debts to the pioneering institutional economists, Thorstein Veblen and John Maurice Clark.

Kahn had begun graduate study in the 1930s, the last decade during which many of the leading economists in the United States were still avowed institutionalists. The giants in this distinctively American tradition—Richard T. Ely and John R. Commons of Wisconsin, Wesley Clair Mitchell and John Maurice Clark of Columbia, Schumpeter of Harvard—characteristically looked less to a deductive theory of prices and markets than to the social influence of economic institutions. Taking a cue from Veblen, they studied the sociological and anthropological aspects of such institutions as the leisure class, the business cycle, the capitalist legal system, the labor union, the business corporation, and the regulatory agency. This last "institution" proved especially important, and many institutional economists interested themselves in regulation. John R. Commons, Balthasar H. Meyer, and Rexford G. Tugwell, for example, actually helped to write regulatory legislation; they and many others also served as members of regulatory bodies.

In the late 1930s, when Kahn was coming of age as an economist, the institutionalist approach was moving steadily out of fashion, in the face of a revolution in macroeconomics—that subdiscipline devoted to the study of national economies. Of course, the Great Depression helped to stimulate this change by encouraging the new line of such work, including the masterpiece of macroeconomics, John Maynard Keynes's *General Theory of Employment, Interest, and Money* (1936). Within a decade, institutionalism had lost its eminence. Within three decades, Keynesian macroeconomics held the fort, overshadowing all other subdisciplines. Kahn stood as witness to the change.

In the meantime, classical microeconomics had slowly begun to recover from an earlier slump of its own. Common topics of that subdiscipline included the theories of prices and markets pioneered by Adam Smith, John Stuart Mill, and Alfred Marshall. These giants of an earlier era had long dominated the field of economics. Over the first half of the twentieth century, however, the classical approach suffered three severe blows. The first came from institutionalism. Veblen, among others, savagely attacked Adam Smith's proposition that an invisible hand moved the free market automatically to serve the public interest, with no need for government intervention. The institutionalists asserted that here classicism was simplistic and merely deductive; it sacrificed both common sense and empirical observation to an alleged theoretical rigor that on close inspection turned out to be chimerical. As a case in point, argued the institutionalists, Smith and Mill offered no help for the human costs of industrialization. More than anything else, classicism's implicit assumption that whatever is, is right angered the institutionalists, who pointed to the Great Depression as a confirmation of their views. Clearly, the invisible hand—if there was one—had guided the world of the 1930s to disaster.

As if the institutionalist attack were not bad enough, classicism, like institutionalism itself, now began to suffer from Keynesian macroeconomics. For thirty years after the depression, many of the best advanced students were attracted to the new Keynesian theories. The remarkable performance of national economies offered a series of practical experiments for the benefit of those scholars and planners who thought in terms of aggregates. National economies were growing very rapidly, and only the "new economics" of Keynes seemed to offer clear explanations. Keynesian economists in many countries became the honored prophets of society.

At the start of the 1970s, however, the period of miracle growth abruptly ended, as a variety of powerful forces struck almost simultaneously: rising inflation, the first "oil shock," and intensified competition from Japan and other advanced industrial nations. Suddenly, in America, the old topics of classical microeconomics began to reassert their original value, as unfamiliar concerns about scarcity, overregulation, and the functioning of different types of markets again emerged to become the most serious problems for policy. In a short time, classical and "neoclassical" approaches (as the redeveloping philosophy came to be called) took center stage. And with the revival of the classical framework came a resurgence of interest in marginal-cost pricing, already a favorite idea of Alfred Kahn's.

In fact, almost the entire intellectual history of twentieth-century economics played a part in Kahn's professional career. He entered graduate school during the late 1930s, at the ebb tide of institutionalism but before the flood of Keynesianism. Kahn understood microeconomics, yet felt a greater fascination with the macroeconomic side of his discipline. Even so, he emerged from his training as a disciple of neither school but as a broadly informed empiricist, equipped with an eclectic mixture of research tools, special interests, and what Keynes liked to call "propensities."

One propensity, inherited from his institutionalist forebears, committed Kahn to dissatisfaction with the status quo. In his first published article, an attack on American patent law appearing in the *American Economic Review* in 1940, the young scholar showed his reformism by protesting that the law unduly rewarded holders of patent pools, such as General Electric and other giant companies. Their "great research laboratories are only incidentally technological centers. From the business standpoint they are patent factories: they manufacture the raw material of monopoly." With its echoes of Veblen, this article was unmistakably the credo of an institutionalist. At the same time, it also bore the marks of a youthful impetuosity and a habit, which its author never outgrew, of saying more than he should—of issuing torrents of words, in part on extraneous subjects.[8]

Kahn's first book, *Great Britain in the World Economy* (1946), reflected broad research, careful thought, and the author's persistent effort to superimpose a theoretical framework onto an empirically dominated philosophy of institutionalism. The book seemed at once technical, historical, and theoretical. Well-written and bursting with energy, it was innovative chiefly in its eclecticism.[9] Like several of Kahn's subsequent publications, it also expressed his deep interest in development economics and in macroeconomics generally. In fact, except for the critical essay on patent laws, all of his work during the 1940s was directed at macroeconomic or international themes. Kahn himself moved from assorted government jobs in wartime Washington to a two-year stint teaching at

Ripon College in Wisconsin and later, in 1947, to an assistant professorship at Cornell, where he would remain. Many times, even after he became established as a scholar, he considered going to law school. He thought that a law degree, added to his training in economics, would increase his understanding of (and opportunity to influence) the making of public policy. As it turned out, he gained ample understanding and influence even without formal legal training.[10]

In the early 1950s, Kahn's interests began to shift toward regulation and marginal-cost pricing. The evidence appears in a second book and several articles on antitrust. Within the profession of economics, antitrust forms part of a larger field called industrial organization, which tends to combine some of the old policy concerns of the institutionalists with a more rigorous and theoretical analysis of market structures. The topic is microeconomic and heavily freighted with the ideological overtones that surround every discussion of the role of big business in a democratic society. If the central value implicit in classical microtheory was allocative and productive efficiency, the central value of antitrust—at least as the practical basis for enforcement of antitrust laws—seemed broader and fuzzier. For Kahn this new concern posed a dilemma he could not easily resolve. As a liberal Democrat writing in a time of national prosperity, he now found himself preoccupied less with the improvement of efficiency than with the promotion of social justice. In particular, he believed that national policy should not be misled by what he regarded as misdirected paeans to the American business system, such as David E. Lilienthal's popular book, *Big Business—A New Era* (1953) and John Kenneth Galbraith's *American Capitalism: The Concept of Countervailing Power* (1952).[11] Typical of the time in which they were written, both books derided antitrust controls as ineffective in promoting efficiency and, even worse, as harmful to American businesses threatened by international competition. Other analysts from both the political right and the left also argued for overhaul of the antitrust laws.[12]

Uncharacteristically, Kahn responded by defending the status quo. He insisted that the antitrust laws worked well and should not be altered. In a book he wrote with his colleague Joel Dirlam and in articles for the *Harvard Law Review*, the *Journal of Political Economy, Fortune,* and other periodicals, Kahn outlined a thorough justification of the antitrust system. His argument took as its text not the deductive theories of microeconomics but the actual practice of antitrust control represented by leading judicial decisions.[13]

His book entitled *Fair Competition: The Law and Economics of Antitrust Policy* (1954) provides the most complete analysis of the problem. Here the burden of the argument, in particular its insistence that economics offers a poor guide to practice, departed from the approach Kahn would take in his later scholarly work and in his practice as a regulator. This episode turned out to be the intellectual crossroads of his life. In the pages of *Fair Competition* may be seen a struggle between the sentimental feelings of the liberal activist and the reasoned arguments of the analytical economist. In this case, for one of the few times in Kahn's professional life, sentiment routed reason.

The argument began on sufficiently sound footing. "One cannot simply equate the 'public interest' in a democracy with the 'consumer interest,' defining the latter as the interest of all citizens 'in getting more and better goods for consumption at ever lower prices.' " But from this solid platform Kahn and Dirlam stepped off into a quagmire. They asserted that even though the Sherman law promoted active government intervention in business decisions, "it represented, paradoxically, a departure from laissez faire in the ultimate interests of laissez faire." Through the device of "preserving the competitive regulator it [antitrust] would in the end minimize coercion."[14] Although the authors had a point here, they failed to recognize the connection between ends and means. Employing coercion as a means of minimizing coercion did not make sense. Whatever else antitrust prosecutions may have signified, they certainly were not undertaken "in the ultimate interests of laissez faire." Kahn and Dirlam also appear to have misunderstood the actual effects of antitrust policy. They too easily assumed that center firms must be the usual targets of prosecutors, ignoring the much greater impact antitrust actions had on loose horizontal combinations of peripheral firms—an impact that indirectly but powerfully promoted the rise of that very bigness in business which they themselves opposed.

Kahn and Dirlam worked themselves into a logical dilemma very much like the one experienced by Louis Brandeis forty years before. Their argument has a number of Brandeisian overtones: a marked preference for small size, an assumption that consumers could be helplessly manipulated, and an abhorrence of advertising. As the authors describe what they see:

In our society the individual's consumption pattern and the businessman's costs are surely not determined by truly untrammeled choices or truly free bargaining. Instead it is the business culture which imposes more or less invariable standards of the "good life" on consumers and fixes interest rates, wages, and other costs of doing business. And constantly disrupting the consumer's tranquillity are the advertising agencies . . . A large portion of our "highest per capita income in the world" consists in expenditures that are necessary to offset the horrible consequences of our unplanned, ugly, dirty, crime-ridden cities, and to keep up with the ubiquitous ad-man.[15]

Like Brandeis, Kahn and Dirlam moved from a disaffection with some of the aesthetic horrors of modern life to a rejection of the consumer values that seemed to underlie those horrors.

In a remarkable abnegation of their own profession, the authors went on to argue that because economists could never achieve unanimity, economics itself "does not offer clear-cut objective criteria for antitrust superior to those which have long prevailed" (that is, the legal criteria developed in judicial decisions). Certainly Kahn and Dirlam were correct to point out that economists, like other students of public affairs, did disagree about criteria for effective antitrust policy. But their argument for the irrelevance of economics on the grounds of economists' disagreements seems comparable to insisting that medical research has nothing to do with the care of patients so long as researchers continue to dispute over forms of treatment.[16]

Reading Kahn's book now, a generation after its completion, one reaches the conclusion that its analysis is largely confused and lacking in rigor. As a reviewer noted, the book falls between two chairs because "it mixes, in unspecified proportions, vague moral values and unsystematic economics."[17] To Kahn and Dirlam this kind of attack was especially painful, since they knew that in many respects they had written a courageous book. They had taken on all comers regardless of discipline, reputation, or popularity: falling between chairs sometimes cannot be avoided when scholars work at the borders of several disciplines.[18] It is now clear, however, that the real problem was not the lack of a disciplinary fit, but that the book exposed a significant division in Kahn's thinking about the problem of antitrust policy. That division, we have seen, originated in the mixed legacy of his graduate training; it grew more pronounced in the clash between his personal values and his increasing analytical powers.

In the years after publication of this book, Kahn's confidence in the rigors of deductive and theoretical research in neoclassical economics began to overcome his strong personal objections to the choices made by American consumers. Twenty-five years after the appearance of *Fair Competition*, he wrote a letter to the editor of a college newspaper, chiding the young journalist in language that Kahn himself would have done well to heed a quarter century earlier:

You tended in your article to mix together your own tastes and values (most of which I share) with objective analysis; it is important to try to keep these two separate. For example, it is popular to define some kinds of consumption as wasteful and undesirable and others as necessary. But one of the values that we hold important in our society is the substantial freedom of each consumer to choose what to consume within the constraints of income. We let the individual decide how many children to have, how many cars, how much food. We let the individual decide how hard to work and on what to work jointly with any willing employer. We let people save and invest, work for wages or take entrepreneurial risk. We leave definition of want and waste to the market.[19]

These lessons came hard for Kahn. But he learned them well and then proceeded to teach them to others.

Toward Marginalism and a Masterwork

Alfred Kahn's transformation took place gradually over the 1950s and 1960s. In part, this change reflects important shifts in the basic economics of those industries that captured his attention; in part, change was in the man, as he grew older and developed new interests in fields dependent on neoclassical methods. His public declaration of this transition came in 1970, with the appearance of his *Economics of Regulation*, one of the most important books ever written on the subject. Here Kahn managed brilliantly to fuse the economics of institutionalism and classicism. That achievement, in its turn, led to a new phase of his career: in 1974, he entered public office as a regulator.

By the middle 1950s, shortly after the publication of his book on antitrust, Kahn had begun to interest himself in the related area of regulation, particularly of the oil and gas industries. Again the evidence may be found in a book, which he wrote with another co-author and published in 1959 as *Integration and Competition in the Petroleum Industry*. Spinoffs from Kahn's research included articles on the control of crude oil production, an examination of the oil depletion allowance, and—most important for his future interests—a critical analysis of the Federal Power Commission and its role in the regulation of natural gas. Here he faced one of the most controversial and convoluted subjects in the entire history of regulation in America. The stakes at issue in oil and gas regulation were very high; by the late 1950s, the issues had developed such complexity that institutionalist economic methods could no longer be used to study them adequately. One reason for this is that oil and gas are joint products. They occur together in nature and the drilling for one often results in production of the other, without regard to what the driller intended. If one or both are to be subjected to utility-like price regulation, then joint production costs must be allocated between the two; this problem alone requires a mixture of economic and accounting theory that moves beyond the reach of institutional analysis. Indeed, any systematic thinking about the price issue requires a sophisticated application of neoclassical price theory, including the concepts of cross-elasticities, substitution, and marginalism.

Yet as a scholar steeped in institutionalist methods, Kahn enjoyed certain advantages. In the real world, neither oil nor gas was priced solely through the interaction of supply and demand. Instead, the prices of both were influenced by regulation. Oil was "prorationed" to market demand by the policies of state and federal agencies. It also was subject to a series of laws designed to help certain parts of the industry: schemes ranging from depletion allowances and other tax advantages to oil import quotas. By itself, natural gas also was regulated; it came under the purview of the Federal Power Commission, which engaged in a constant struggle to rationalize its pricing. Just at the time Kahn became interested in the subject, the FPC seemed to be failing in this job. As James Landis, in his *Report to the President-Elect* of 1960, reminded his readers, the FPC "represents the outstanding example in the federal government of the breakdown of the administrative process." The point was not lost on one reader at least.[20]

Kahn knew that if he were going to do serious work on the regulation of oil and gas, he must master every relevant tool of economic analysis. To be sure, some of these tools belonged to institutional economics. But even more essential, he must learn to use better the methods of neoclassical microeconomics. His research into the pricing mechanisms of oil and gas had to be based on the theory of price. At this point in his career, Kahn began the final stage of his intellectual odyssey.

He now became directly involved in the difficult problem of pricing natural gas. In testimony before the Federal Power Commission during the early 1960s, he introduced a set of ideas that later became institutionalized as the "two-tier pricing system." Under FPC regulation, "old" gas, drawn from fields already discovered and producing, would be priced more cheaply than "new" gas, from fields brought into production more recently. Although at the time this seemed to Kahn a worthwhile idea (since it would prevent big companies from reaping unearned benefits from rising gas prices), in fact the two-tier arrangement raised a host of problems. Not only was the idea itself grounded in mistaken economic theory, but once in operation it also proved impossible for regulators to administer. Kahn later expressed his regret that, in attempting to impose discipline on large gas companies, he had "bequeathed to the nation an impractical system." In overestimating the actual degree of concentration in the natural gas industry, he had set in motion a policy that inadvertently penalized small companies along with large ones. Intellectually, it amounted to the same type of mistake made fifty years before by Brandeis, and indeed the same kind made only six years earlier by Kahn himself in his book on antitrust policy.[21]

But Kahn was learning fast now. He continued to study the natural gas issue, as he immersed himself in the vast multidisciplinary literature of regulation and started intensive work on his new book. As he later recalled, "My sense of the economics of all this [pricing of natural gas] didn't really get straight until I wrote my *Economics of Regulation*." By 1967, Kahn had begun to chart the course of his masterwork and to present his early conclusions in several exploratory papers, each one delivered first at one of the many conferences on regulatory reform being held at this time. In 1970, the first volume of his great book appeared in print (volume two followed in 1971). *The Economics of Regulation: Principles and Institutions* soon took its place as the leading textbook in the field of regulation. Measured by its impact on practitioners—both business executives and commissioners—it remains the most influential work written on the subject. Reviewers praised Kahn's "enormous job of scholarship," his "mature, confident and witty humanism," his "wholesome discipline and restraint." The book examined every aspect of economic regulation, from utilities and airlines to railroads and trucks; from externalities and the theory of second-best to the economics and politics of valuation and pricing.[22]

The triumph lies in Kahn's ability to join two subdisciplines of economics in what had long been regarded as an impossible synthesis. His intention is clear: "Together, the two volumes are an attempt to join neoclassical theory with 'institutional economics.' The latter is aimless if it is not informed by theory. And a normative theory of public policy is not of much use if it cannot be related to the selection of the best set of social arrangements for achieving those norms. Therefore, each volume [one subtitled *Principles*, the other, *Institutions*] is written with continuous reference to the other."[23] Fusing neoclassicism with institutionalism meant fusing economics with law, with history, with political science. It also meant analyzing the experience of public ownership in America and bringing together a colossal mass of heterogeneous material, much of it laden with misinformation and tainted with controversy. The two volumes totaled almost 600 large pages, with more than 1300 footnotes. Dozens of these footnotes were little articles in themselves: discussions of the legal, political, and economic literature of regulation and extended analyses of judicial decisions. Kahn brought all this off in a virtuoso performance, and thus made his escape from life's "concatenation of ephemeralities."

Most of *Principles* is devoted to an exposition of marginal-cost pricing. This approach was still unusual, but it foreshadowed Kahn's priorities when he later served as a regulator. Now, he wrote, "The economist who asks a politician 'Won't you let me advise you on your legislative program?' deserves another question in response: 'What do you *know*?' And only the economist who can answer 'Well, I can tell you that if you pass a law that says such-and-such, these are the things that will probably happen,' or 'If you do nothing about such-and-such, this is what will probably happen,' deserves to have his offer taken seriously." The message seems clear: in the arena of practical regulation, Kahn knew with a rare certainty that the economist's hour lay at hand.[24]

He could hardly have timed his book better. The two volumes appeared in 1970 and 1971, the early years of a period destined to be plagued by a set of economic problems newly christened as "stagflation." The marvelous postwar era of rapid growth had suddenly ended. Now, for utilities as for other industries, the future called for reduced markets. This prospect clashed with the prevailing business strategies of many utilities, especially electric companies. These companies had anticipated—based on steady growth of demand and increasing economies of scale in their new plants—that they would continue to build large projects and would need ever-growing amounts of capital. In terms of net capital investment, electric power was America's largest industry and also its most capital-intensive, requiring the greatest amount of investment to produce a given dollar of revenue. With the total invested capital measured in hundreds of billions of dollars, utilities faced a continuous obligation to pay their heavy burden of debt. For a generation after World War II, this problem did not seem serious. So long as sales increased and fuel remained inexpensive, so long as inflation remained moderate and interest rates on borrowed capital stayed low, so long as construction costs held steady and technological innovation continued—under these conditions the task of utility management was simple: to promote a steady growth of demand and to build the generating capacity to meet it.

By the time Kahn's *Economics of Regulation* reached the public, every element underlying this task had begun to disappear. National economic growth, which had averaged more than 4 percent a year for thirty years, dropped to 2.6 percent in 1969 and then further, to a negative .3 percent for 1970. (The average for the 1970s stood at 2.87 percent, nearly a third lower than the rate for the preceding three decades.) And the national inflation rate, which had averaged 2.5 percent a year in the 1950s and 1960s, climbed to 5.3 percent in 1971 and averaged 6.7 percent for the decade of the 1970s. These national trends meant that the economics of the utility business was about to be turned upside down.[25]

Stagflation represented bad news for utilities, and three additional developments made things even worse. First, the environmental movement: again the watershed year was 1970, when the celebration of Earth Day ushered in the creation of a new federal Environmental Protection Agency. The sudden popularity of environmental concerns hit utilities hard. Power plants pollute the environment in almost every conceivable way—indirectly through the strip mining of the coal they burn, directly through smokestack emissions, thermal pollution of cooling water, and leakage of radioactive materials. To prevent pollution, even to control its sources, soon becomes extremely costly. A utility must pay for nuclear-waste facilities, scrubbers for high-sulfur coal, and towering stacks (some more than 1000 feet high), and all are expensive. A national consensus, however, required that environmental quality be improved, and it formed just when economic growth began slowing and when inflation and interest rates began rising.

A second problem emerged from the sudden slowing of technological progress in the design and fabrication of generating equipment. For almost a century after the construction of Thomas Edison's first electric power plant, technological progress brought steady gains in productivity. Engineers and utility managers had come to take such gains for granted, thinking they would continue indefinitely. Beginning in the 1960s, however, a technological plateau was reached in the industry, as yearly gains came to an unexpected halt, particularly in those large-scale electric generating plants on which most power companies relied. Between 1967 and 1976, utility executives discovered that the most technologically advanced plants, which used steam at very high temperatures to turn gigantic turbines, went out of service almost three times as often as smaller-scale plants. Bigger came to mean not necessarily better, only less reliable.[26]

Then late in 1973 the price of imported crude oil shot up to four times the summer 1973 figure. Utilities were stunned, especially those located in the northeastern United States—where the companies had earlier converted to oil as a fuel less polluting than coal—and where Alfred Kahn was about to become a key regulator.[27] With the shock of the new oil pricing, the last comfortable assumption of regulatory commissioners and utility managers disappeared, along with every shred of confidence in low interest rates, low inflation, high economic growth, and constantly improving technology.

The impact of these multiple revolutions transformed the entire economic picture. The overall effect on power companies can be gauged by the rapid rise in their combined requests for new rate increases.[28]

Quarter ending	Cases filed nationally during quarter	Total increases requested
3/31/70	12	$89 million
3/31/72	22	$171 million
3/31/74	45	$638 million

Because of accelerating inflation, utilities that based their rates on historical costs, as most did, had difficulty in meeting current expenses. Even when a regulatory agency did grant the requested rate increase in full, the time lag between petition and decision guaranteed that the companies would keep running faster and faster in pursuit of outdated targets. By 1974, the length of procedural delays averaged eleven months; and when inflation approached double digits, "regulatory lag" soon became a serious problem. All this set the stage for a warm reception of Kahn's work, which addressed itself directly to the revolutions in the underlying economics of utilities and of regulation in general.[29]

Ratemaking versus Stagflation

Kahn knew about the utilities' mushrooming revenue requirements, but he was even more concerned about the structure of their rates. Here, as he wrote in *Economics of Regulation,* Kahn could point to an area in which the professional economist might make a distinctive contribution, by starting from a foundation of marginal-cost pricing. The existing rate structures contained an implicit assumption that the costs of production would always be declining, as indeed they had done until the late 1960s. During those happier years, utility companies had experimented with declining-block rates, under which the price of a kilowatt-hour would be reduced with every increase in the total consumed, much like volume discounts for large purchases in retail stores.

A pioneer in this field, the publicly owned Tennessee Valley Authority, introduced as early as 1933 its radical declining-block rate structure:[30]

First 50 kwh per mo.	3.00 cents per kwh
Next 150 kwh	2.00 cents per kwh
Next 200 kwh	1.00 cents per kwh
Next 1000 kwh	0.40 cents per kwh

The central mission of the TVA was to encourage the widest possible usage of electricity, thereby improving the standard of living in the depressed Tennessee Valley region. This 3¢-2¢-1¢ rate schedule, based on a commercial jingle of the period that touted 3-2-1 Shoe Polish, directly promoted the goal. Fully electrified homes, each charged at an average rate of about 0.7¢ per kilowatt-hour, represented TVA's objective, at a time when the national average stood at 5.5¢. The agency took an enormous gamble: that, by slashing prices, it could multiply consumption and, further, that such increased consumption would permit savings based on scale economies in generation, which in turn would justify the price cuts already made. Only a government body could afford to take such a bold step, and the gamble did pay off. In one district located in Mississippi, as rates dropped from 7.40¢ to 1.58¢, usage more than tripled. By 1937, three years after the start of the experiment, the price of electricity in the entire TVA region stood at less than half the national average, and usage was about 60 percent greater.[31]

These results proved revolutionary. News of the TVA experiment stimulated thinking all over the world, especially the thinking of economists on the responses of utility customers to strong price signals. Kahn himself, while still a graduate student, became enamored of the experiment. One of his boyhood idols had been Senator George W. Norris, the "father of the TVA." And as Kahn remarked years later, "TVA did what regulatory commissions could not require private companies to do: set low rates and see what happened to demand and cost."[32]

Before fixing their rates, TVA's planners had made two important assumptions. First, all of the agency's generating capacity, including new production from hydroelectric dams under construction, would actually be sold. Only if this power was sold would the lower rates cover TVA's costs; that is, the "marginal cost curve" could tend downward only if usage tended upward. (Henry Ford had demonstrated the same principle years earlier, by making Model T's at less and less cost and then continuously cutting the selling price of each manufactured unit.) Second, TVA assumed that the annual "load factor" for its system would soon reach 50 percent. Load factor, a vitally important statistic for every utility, expresses average usage by all customers during any given period as a percentage of their usage during the heaviest period of the year (or, simply, as a percentage of the utility's capacity). For electric companies today, the peak-load period often comes in midsummer, when residential consumers use their air conditioners. Thus, if the average load on a company's system is 75,000 kilowatts and the peak load 150,000, then load factor is 50 percent. Eventually TVA achieved such success that its load factor reached 70 percent, an extremely high figure among electric utilities.[33]

Such numbers are watched closely by all power companies because of the peculiar economics of the industry. Electricity, unlike most other goods and services, cannot be stored efficiently. It must be generated, transmitted, and consumed—in almost the same instant. This means that the companies must have enough generating capacity to meet not only the usual demands of their customers (average load) but also the highest demands (peak load). Since the companies are often required by law to serve all customers, whatever their demands, utility managers and regulatory commissioners have tended to assume that they themselves have little discretion in raising or lowering either the supply of electricity or the demand for it. Instead, company managers planned for the future by forecasting the total demand their customers would impose, then scheduling the construction of new generating plants to meet the pace of added demand. So the task of managing an electric utility largely amounted to planning and financing new construction. Managers gave little thought to measures that might affect consumer demand, except to promote ever greater consumption. This, in turn, had the effect of promoting more and more construction of new plants.

Utility managers acted in this way for several reasons. First, they felt the normal urge of business executives to encourage the consumption of whatever they sell. Second, and less obvious, they could factor the full cost of capital expenditures into their company's rate base and thus augment the potential revenues requested from the regulatory agency.[34] Finally, they could take advantage of the rapid rate of innovation in the technology of electric generation, particularly innovation within extremely large plants. Scale economies in this industry always seemed impressive;

in the post–World War II period, however, they looked to be unbelievably advantageous. Kahn pointed this out in one of his early papers on the subject. He said that the annual productivity increases in electric utilities averaged an astonishingly high 5.5 percent over the first half of the twentieth century. This figure dwarfed the 1.7 percent for the American economy as a whole during the same period. (At 5.5 percent per year, productivity will double every thirteen years. At 1.7 percent, it will double only every forty-one years.) The technology of electric power generation, therefore, was far outstripping innovation elsewhere in the economy—even *before* the construction of the gigantic and extremely efficient power plants that characterized the postwar period.[35]

The results of these innovations and scale economies could be read in a steady decline of the consumer's real costs. As Kahn later said, the real price of energy (not electricity alone) had dropped by 43 percent between 1951 and 1971, a period in which consumer prices as a whole rose by 56 percent.[36] Electricity seemed uniquely to be a bigger bargain every year. But then, at the close of the 1960s, this felicitous situation abruptly changed, and the real costs moved steadily higher during the 1970s and early 1980s. Inflation, stagnation, the environmental movement, rising interest rates, technological stasis, and the skyrocketing cost of fuel struck the industry simultaneously. Utilities' marginal-cost curves, which had shifted downward since the first Edison stations had opened nearly a century before, now moved ominously upward. Construction of new plants became almost prohibitively expensive. This meant that, for the first time in the industry's history, electricity coming from new plants would cost more than equivalent amounts from existing sources. Thus the declining-block rate structures in effect throughout the United States now gave exactly the wrong signals to consumers. Utility advertising campaigns, moreover, continued to urge greater consumption, which would inevitably lead to greater peak loads and increased demand for the construction of new power plants. The cycle seemed insane.

Into this setting, Kahn launched his *Economics of Regulation* in 1970 and then his own career as a regulator in 1974, when he became chairman of the New York Public Service Commission. For him the complex situation proved exhilarating rather than depressing; he knew that he had answers to the questions that baffled utility managers and other commissioners. In the last academic paper he published before taking his seat in Albany, Kahn returned to the theme of the economist's role in making policy. Clearly, Kahn felt very sure of himself, as he pointed to the place where answers would be found: "Applied microeconomics is the exciting new frontier of public policy."[37]

The New York Public Service Commission

Together with California and Wisconsin, New York for many years was acknowledged as a leader of regulatory practice. This had been the case since the early part of the twentieth century, when the movement to regulate electric and gas utilities began to spread throughout the country. Later on, a bewildering variety of other industries fell under state commissions, and in many states the same agency exercised jurisdiction over these industries as well as over electric and gas utilities. The New York commission in 1974 regulated more than forty, including telephones, buses, water supply systems, docks and wharves, and warehouses. The degree of authority actually exercised, of course, varied widely according to the industry, both in New York and elsewhere. It also varied according to the vigor and resources of the state commissions.[38]

In many other states, regulatory commissions served as dumping grounds for political hacks and cronies of the governor. So long as regulation remained unimportant—which it did, relatively speaking, during the years of steady economic growth and declining costs for utility services—membership on the commissions did not receive much public attention. Even during the boom years of increasing prosperity, however, a commissionership in one of the three leading states, and especially a chairmanship, offered a prestigious and desirable post for a talented candidate.[39]

Most state commissions had three members, but the numbers in 1974 ranged from one in Oregon to seven in Massachusetts and South Carolina. The typical term of office was six years, with staggered appointments designed to minimize the disruption from turnover and to provide some insulation from partisan politics. Governors appointed the commissioners in three-fourths of the states, voters elected them in one-fourth. Some states specified that consumer interests must be explicitly represented among the commissioners, and about half of these state agencies, like most federal commissions, by law had to have minority party representation.[40]

The state and federal commissions were filled with lawyers, who together accounted for more than 80 percent of the total membership of some federal commissions and at no agency less than 50 percent. Their representation on state commissions was very large as well, and their domination of important regulatory jobs is a phenomenon full of significance for the study of the values reflected in the commissions' policies. In particular, lawyers and legal patterns of thought must be seen to underlie a tendency of the commissions to emphasize procedural due process rather than economic efficiency. Alfred Kahn is only one of many economists who have made this point in criticizing regulatory performance.[41]

As bureaucratic institutions, the state commissions varied greatly in size and complexity. Some were only slightly larger in 1974 than Charles Francis Adams' Massachusetts agency had been in 1874. New Mexico's commission had only 17 staff members. The Massachusetts commission, on the other hand, had grown to a total of about 120 full-time employees.[42] The New York Public Service Commission was second in size only to California's. As chairman, Kahn headed an agency of some 650 persons, with an annual budget in 1974 exceeding $12 million. Kahn received the highest salary of any regulator in the United States—about $51,000—and in addition enjoyed a chauffeur-driven limousine and many other benefits. A listing of his professional staff, together with their individual specialties, provides us with a useful index to the nature of the agency at the time Kahn took charge. Notice the dominance of engineers, accountants, and lawyers, and the minor role played by professional economists.[43]

Professional staff		Division of labor	
Inspectors and investigators	103	Chairman's office	17
Engineers	57	Energy division	231
Auditors	54	Acctg. and utility finance	97
Accountants	28	Communications division	92
Attorneys	21	Ofc of administration	79
Administrative staff	14	Ofc of general counsel	46
Rate analysts	13	Ofc of environmental planning	41
		Water division	34
Hearing examiners (admin. law judges, mostly lawyers)	13	Ofc of hearing examiners	20
Economists	8	Ofc of economic research	12

Even though its economic expertise far surpassed that of regulatory agencies in most states, the New York commission did not emphasize economic analysis in its work. For Kahn this situation posed a dilemma. He could not inaugurate major new hirings because the commission's budget was practically frozen. This left two alternatives. He could attempt to overhaul the present staff, letting go some of the inspectors, investigators, engineers, accountants, and lawyers, and hiring trained economists in their places. Or he could try to convince his existing staff members that economics must be relevant to their own jobs, even though many of them had been doing their work for years without any formal training in the discipline. Neither choice seemed to provide an easy road to popularity. Even so, the prospect of retooling his commission staff appeared to Kahn entirely feasible as he looked outward at the condition of the utility industry in 1974.

The Commission's Strategy

The combined impact on New York's electric utilities of inflation, higher fuel costs, technological stasis, and other forces may be gauged in the history of rates charged by the Consolidated Edison Company, the state's largest utility. Con Edison served Greater New York City, and there residential customers saw the average monthly electric bill double quickly during the early 1970s.[44]

1965	$ 9.68
1970	10.65
1974	22.08

In 1974, even with these higher rates, Con Edison still found itself in the worst financial shape in its history. So it naturally expected to request from the Public Service Commission still another large increase in rates during 1975.

Kahn anticipated this situation and came into office with a clear idea of what he should do. As a fundamental strategy, he planned to reform rate structures so as to make them reflect true costs. Of course he wanted to do this not for Con Edison only, or even for electric utilities alone, but also for gas and telephone rates. As an economist, he knew that such free services as telephone directory assistance were in fact not free at all. They were subsidized by other charges that subscribers who never dialed Information paid as part of their bills. Kahn believed that each consumer should pay for services actually received and for no others. Yet his studies had convinced Kahn that such subsidies were being paid on a large scale. He found the rate structures of nearly all the state's utilities to be shot through with unfair distortions, resulting in general abuse: some consumers were subsidizing others, and nearly all customers were receiving signals to buy when they should be warned to conserve. Kahn accepted the chairmanship with a conviction that only decisive action by the commission could correct these signals and encourage conservation. If the commission acted quickly, moreover, it might help slow or even reverse New York electric utilities' ominous drift toward bankruptcy. Kahn's strategy was to make electric rates coincide with the companies' accelerating current costs, and not with obsolete, mythical patterns predicated on a continuing decline in costs.

Now the question became not what to do but rather how to do it. How could Kahn convince his fellow commissioners, his 650-member staff, the utilities themselves, and eight or ten different classes of consumers that the old practices of the companies and the commission were inappropriate to current reality? Generally in the American regulatory system, commissions act as collegial bodies, led by chairmen who have little more power than do each of their colleagues. Chairmen possess almost no executive authority; they cannot compel anyone (except a member of their personal staffs) to do anything. Such use of force did not suit Kahn's style in any situation. His strength was persuasion, not dictation. For twenty-seven years he had been one of Cornell's best teachers, as his classes filled with students eager to hear his famous lectures. He excelled in small seminars as well, helped by an engaging manner, wit, and conviction. These same qualities would work for him in the commission setting, as Kahn the master teacher determined to win over a new group of students: the commission staff.

To begin, he did almost no hiring or firing but instead worked with a few carefully chosen pupils, then a few more, spreading his message in widening circles. Even those who disagreed with a marginal-cost philosophy had to respect Kahn's learning, and nearly all staff members appreciated his informal manner. A visitor from the *New York Times* found him padding around the office in his socks. Kahn spent little time behind his desk, wrote this

Times reporter, preferring instead "the informality of a bentwood rocking chair and a pair of couches that fill a corner of the office." The chairman "is an educator at heart who believes that he can convince any rational person of the rightness of his position."[45] Small wonder that the press felt an interest in this new kind of bureaucrat. Yet Kahn was not merely putting on a show for reporters. Such informal behavior was his pattern throughout three years on the Public Service Commission. He talked endlessly with his staff about the principles of marginal-cost pricing. He delighted in teaching them at every opportunity: over lunch, in meetings, even at the daily swims he initiated. Immersed in the water, visible only from the neck up, Kahn lectured on the technicalities of cross-substitution, elasticities of demand, and marginalism. For a professor in his late fifties, he seemed amazingly youthful and vigorous and, above all, sincere.[46]

Kahn's friendly manner proved especially important in his effort to convert the commission's rate engineers. Because of the technological history of electric utilities—improved technology as a basis for the steady growth of scale economies and declining rates—engineers became much enamored of the usual system of volume discounts for businesses and declining-block rates for home consumers. In the engineers' view, large users of electricity deserved to pay less per unit consumed. On other hand, the engineers also felt close to panic over the current situation, which they clearly saw as an unprecedented crisis.[47] They defined this crisis as one of "revenue erosion" for the companies: costs were accelerating faster than revenues, and this produced a conflict between the volume-discount rate structures and the upward movement of marginal-cost curves. Here Kahn's marginalist approach provided his engineers with a convenient solution to the problem of revenue erosion. For a time, the engineers remained skeptical about marginalism because so much was left to guesswork. Kahn told them that marginalism was indeed difficult to implement, that it was full of subjective judgments. His candor seemed appealing yet, given their training, the engineers naturally preferred precise solutions over rough approximations. To meet their objections, Kahn again and again asked them, "Do you want to be precisely wrong or approximately right?" Ultimately he won them over.[48]

When approached by people from outside the commission, Kahn took a conciliatory position. He insisted that all parties forget their anger of the moment and take a longer view. Much as Charles Francis Adams had done a century earlier, Kahn emphasized the unity of interests between companies and customers. Also like Adams he used the *Annual Reports* of the commission to set forth his strategy in explicit terms. The commission's aim, he wrote in his first report, was to set policy not in a series of dramatic and episodic rate cases, but in a continuum—to relate the past to the present and the future. In the 1950s and '60s, Kahn wrote, rate cases were rare, problems not serious. Both producers and consumers benefited from the declining-block rate structure. The world of the 1970s was very different. Inflation, tight money, and high interest rates had brought from the utilities an endless stream of requests for rate increases, and the response by consumers had been equally reflexive. "All too often," Kahn wrote, "the proponents [of] 'consumerism' interpret their responsibility as one loudly opposing any and all rate increases." This too was understandable. But because of strong pressure from consumers, "it should not be surprising that regulators in 1974 generally squeezed utility profits harder than may be in the consumer's long-term interest." Kahn expressed his determination to regulate with an even hand, favoring neither producers nor consumers.[49]

Generic Rate Hearings

The regulatory process in the United States has been desultory in character. State and federal commissions, somewhat like courts, have seldom initiated action on their own, but instead have responded to petitions or complaints. As a consequence of this reactive role, they find it difficult to change policies quickly, especially when such changes are opposed by powerful interest groups. These groups are often ready to prevent loss of advantage by falling back on litigation calculated to delay any change.

Kahn knew that, in New York, he could not allow for these normal delays, despite the high level of controversy that surrounded his ideas. The commission must move quickly, rather than wait for utility companies to initiate proceedings, especially since nothing could be expected of the companies except additional requests for rate increases. The major problem, Kahn believed, lay not with rate levels (the total amount of revenue needed by the utilities) but rather with rate structures (the mix of charges to different classes of customers spread over different blocks of electric power). These structures could not be altered by the usual process of increase after increase.[50]

Confronted with the dilemma, Kahn found his answer in the device of holding not individual rate cases but a "generic hearing" instead. His hearing would amount to an intensive study of the rate question, conducted outside the heated atmosphere typical of the usual rate case. Not one company but all companies would be involved, and testimony would include evidence from environmental experts and other specialists interested in the proceedings. Best of all from Kahn's viewpoint, he himself might be able to shape the procedures and influence the outcome far more than in the usual commission hearing. In short, he viewed the generic hearing as a novel opportunity to educate all parties on the benefits to them of marginal-cost pricing. Confidently relying on his own ability to convince doubters, Kahn foresaw enormous gains and very little risk.[51]

Yet he sought to reduce the risks still further by cultivating a set of useful allies, among them the Environmental Defense Fund. For several years this organization had been intervening in regulatory proceedings throughout the United States, at first from an almost purely adversarial position. Like many other environmental groups, it tended to oppose almost all projects, especially the construction of new power plants. As time wore on, some staff members of the Fund, in particular a young lawyer named Edward Berlin, began to search for ways in which the organization could make a more positive contribution.

This quest led Berlin to the device of marginal-cost pricing for electricity. But whereas Kahn's motivation in advocating marginalist principles was to hold down the need for rate increases, and to achieve allocative efficiency in the economic sense, that of Berlin and his colleagues emphasized the use of a new price system as the means of slowing new construction of generating plants. The traditional declining-block rate structure had encouraged greater use of electricity and more new construction. But now, if utility customers could be persuaded through price signals to reduce their consumption (or to shift consumption to off-peak hours), then existing plants could better serve their needs. New construction could be delayed, perhaps defeated altogether, and the environment would be protected. This general line of thinking led the

Environmental Defense Fund to adopt a spirited advocacy of marginal-cost pricing. Kahn already knew Berlin and others in the Fund through a consulting firm of economists with which Kahn himself had been affiliated. Berlin and the consulting firm had participated in a pioneering marginal-cost case in Wisconsin.[52] Based on that experience, the Fund quickly accepted Kahn's invitation and petitioned the New York Public Service Commission to hold generic hearings. In this way, the initiative for the new hearings seemed to derive from a broader base of interest than if it came from Kahn alone.

Still, assistance from the Fund could prove a mixed blessing. If the new chairman seemed to align himself with an interested party in a rate hearing, he would be courting serious trouble—and doubly so because of Kahn's prior connection with the consulting firm, which was also expected to take part. Kahn met this difficulty by broadening his support even more. He asked the chief executive officers of New York state's seven major utilities to come to his office in Albany for a conference. Gathering them all in one room, he explained his devotion to marginalist principles, listened to their views, and went on to persuade them to petition as a group for the generic rate hearing. They agreed to his choice, and Kahn had scored a great coup. Now the most important utility companies were joining with a leading environmental group to ask the commission to do what the chairman had wished in the first place.[53]

The various companies had different reasons for joining in this petition. Several had already become interested in marginalist principles themselves as possible alternatives to declining-block structures. Others regarded a generic hearing as a harmless academic exercise, and they wanted to appear cooperative. And a few others of the seven saw the hearing as a welcome opportunity to delay more serious actions by the commission. In all, the year 1974 was a very bad one for utilities, not only financially but also because the first oil crises of the 1970s had tarnished the already poor image of oil companies and electric utilities. Everywhere consumers were angry, and companies hoped that a generic hearing might last long enough for passions to cool. They knew that the normal rate case in New York lasted no more than eleven months from the calling of the first witness to the final order of the commission. But it seemed possible that a generic hearing could go on indefinitely.

Kahn assumed office in the summer of 1974; his generic rate hearing began in January 1975 and ran in intermittent session for more than eighteen months. The entire written record comprised some 5000 pages of testimony and cross-examination. In all, twenty-two parties submitted briefs, many of them extremely detailed. Among numerous witnesses called to the stand were a score of experts on the theory of marginal-cost pricing, including some who thought it impractical. Kahn opened the proceedings by warning all interested parties that this hearing was not to be an exercise conducted solely for lawyers. In language again reminiscent of Adams' approach a century earlier, the chairman told the participants, "I may call for innovations in our procedures . . . I hope we can proceed as cooperative seekers of the truth, rather than as adversaries seeking an advantage over one another."[54]

So the hearing went. The chairman himself presided, and most of the sessions resembled academic seminars more than formal rate hearings. Kahn insisted on organizing groups of witnesses into panels, then lining up each panel face to face with a similar lineup of attorneys, who sat side by side at another table. The lawyers took turns asking questions. Kahn encouraged interruptions, especially his own, after the witnesses had given their presentations. As might have been expected, some of the lawyers objected to these unusual procedures. Counsel for one group of industries filed a formal motion asking that Kahn be disqualified from the hearings because of his "preconceived notions regarding the appropriate elements of rate design" and for having "departed from his quasi-judicial role as a regulator." The chairman, his challengers argued, had "indulged in extensive cross-examination" and made "extensive extrajudicial comments on the record." In other words, Kahn had failed to behave like a judge at a courtroom trial.[55]

In response to this motion, Kahn presented a statement addressed to the whole commission:

I have adjured all parties to look upon at least the theoretical phase of the proceedings as an intellectual exercise, to treat it in the nature of a running seminar, in which our purpose was essentially to explore certain academic ideas. That is the spirit in which I have behaved whenever I have presided. I have never pretended to play the role of a passive receiver of evidence . . . I intervened freely—attempting, however, not to interrupt the train of a lawyer's cross-examination—to make certain that I understood what a witness was saying and what he was not saying, to

test his ideas, to offer hypotheses of my own in order to get his reaction
... I propounded problems—questions of whose answers I was myself
uncertain; and when the witness was uncertain about the answer I asked
him, and all the others, to think about it. No witness, of whatever point
of view, was ever denied an opportunity to express his opinion, as fully as
he wished.[56]

As expected, the commission ruled against the motion to disqualify
Kahn. Certainly, he did not feel at all defensive about his behavior. He could not have been happier about the way the hearings
went, especially since publicity remained favorable throughout. In
a remarkable parallel development, Edward Berlin of the Environmental Defense Fund was appointed to the commission a few
months after the hearings began. Berlin excused himself from further participation and took no official role in the hearings. Kahn,
on the other hand, not only continued to preside but also evange-
lized about the proceedings in many speeches to outside groups.
During one address to a meeting of investment analysts, he con-
fessed, "I am having the time of my life running that seminar."[57]

The generic hearing did not convince all parties about the benefits of marginal-cost rate structures. But it convinced many. The
final lineup for and against can be summarized.[58]

Strongly affirmative	*Affirmative but less strongly so*
Long Island Lighting Company	Consolidated Edison Company
Environmental Defense Fund	Central Hudson Company (utility)
Federal Energy Administration	New York State Electric and Gas Co.
City of New York	Orange and Rockland Co. (utility)
Chemung County Neighborhood	Public Service Commission Staff
Legal Services	State Consumer Protection Board

Strongly opposed
Airco (large industrial user of electricity)
General Services Administration (federal agency)
Industrial Power Consumers Conference
Multiple Intervenors (industrial customers' group)
Niagara-Mohawk (large utility)
Rockland County Industrial Energy Users Association

Although Kahn had obviously not won all the parties to his side, he
had achieved the next best thing: he had divided the potential opponents. What might have been a united front of utilities standing
against his proposals had been split into three distinct groups. At

this point, the only adamant opposition to marginal principles came from large industrial and commercial users of electricity, who feared paying higher rates under time-of-day pricing schemes. Otherwise, Kahn had begun to teach his lessons to an admiring and sometimes enthusiastic group of listeners. Even so, his work had only started.

Installing New Rate Structures

The hearing on marginal-cost principles opened the way to actions on several fronts at once. Choosing their arenas carefully, Kahn and his fellow commissioners moved to put their ideas into effect as quickly as they could, for at least one large electric utility. This utility would be a model for their demonstration. All other power companies, the commission ordered, must prepare and submit plans for implementing similar rates. The model chosen for electric rate reform, and the first major utility to file under the new plan, was the Long Island Lighting Company (LILCO). As indicated in the list above, LILCO strongly supported Kahn's marginalist position. The company knew it needed help; it had a poor load factor, a heavy burden of debt, and a rapidly growing demand for its electricity during the summer months. With both company and commission anxious to institute marginal-cost-based rates, no obstacle appeared to stand in the way of a quick reform of the declining-block structure.[59]

While he recognized these advantages, Kahn remained cautious. A single mistake in implementing the plan would give support to his opponents among the large industrial users. As he mulled over this problem in one of many brainstorming sessions with his staff, Kahn came up with the idea of giving a financial guarantee to all customer classes, large industrial users included: a solid reassurance that, *as a class*, no group would pay more under the new system than they had under the old. In this way, businesses would not have to subsidize householders or vice versa. All necessary adjustments would be confined to shifts within (and not between) customer classes.[60]

While the lawyers and rate engineers on the commission staff regarded the chairman's proposal as a stroke of political genius, the economists protested that such a guarantee would require a

significant departure from pure marginalist principles. But Kahn
knew that the commission needed good will to nurture its mandate; it must take care not to create additional enemies. A guarantee of no increase for any class of customer meant that no solid
phalanx of opposition to the commission would develop, and "rate
reform" would not be used as a political vehicle to soak business.
Of course, some of the industrial users would pay more under the
new system, but at the same time others would pay less; the winners and losers could not be expected to combine in a common
cause against marginalism. With these anticipations, Kahn decided to move ahead, and his staff economists reluctantly agreed.[61]

The chairman presented the new commission plan to about
forty industrialists at another meeting in his Albany office. This
time many members of the group arrived in an angry mood. Several were already on record as having demanded Kahn's impeach-
ment. As assistant to the chairman recalls the scene:

Fred's handling of that meeting was simply a delight to watch . . . Some-
body asked whether or not there could be other values than efficiency
taken into account in setting prices, like fairness. Fred said something to
the effect that we've got to set prices some way, and that setting them in
accordance with cost seems the most logical way to do it. If you want to
argue for something else you're going to lose. He said that—he, simply
with fist in hand, said [to the business customers] that—"you're going to
lose." Then he posited the question, "Why?" and answered, "because if
prices are set in some fashion other than on the basis of cost, then it's the
political process which will set prices and the political process asks who
will gain and who will lose. And let's see who's going to gain? Schools
will gain, hospitals will gain, the small business user will gain, and the
residential customer will gain. And who will lose? You are going to lose
. . . it's not the little guy but the industrialists that they are going to sock
it to . . . you ought to stand up and cheer this proposal, because it is the
only thing that will save you."[62]

Kahn's mixture of logic with unsettling prediction drove his points
home, one after another. Most of the industrialists caved in.

The new LILCO rates represented a compromise between pure
marginalist principles and political reality. As a model, this structure proved practical and enlightened. Marginalist thinking was
reflected powerfully in time-of-day pricing differentials that
penalized summer peak users and rewarded off-peak consumers.
Here the chronic marginalist problem of precise measurement

(which came down to a problem of installing meters that would record usage by time of day) seemed to be solved by applying the new rates at first only to LILCO's 750 largest consumers, all of them business firms. These customers could afford the cost of new meters, which ranged from $400 to $4000. Within a few years, time-of-day rates had been applied to many other customers, and the price spread between peak and off-peak had reached a ratio of twelve to one (30¢ per kilowatt-hour on a hot summer day versus 2½¢ on a winter night). Kahn's marginalist approach had been vindicated by evidence drawn from real experience.[63]

The LILCO case proved to be a landmark in the history of regulation in the United States. For the first time, after an exhaustive generic hearing followed by a brief rate case involving a single company, marginal-cost principles had been put into operation on a large scale. Chairman Kahn deserved the credit. Working assiduously over a two-year period, he artfully shaped a political consensus among unusual bedfellows: environmentalists, electric utilities, consumer groups, business firms, and residential customers. At the same time, he neutralized all significant opposition to his own strategy. Much like James Landis at the SEC, Kahn deliberately modified his thinking in order to get the policy exactly right. But then he moved on with equal care to the issue of implementation. Thinking perceptively about the nature of the opposition both inside and outside the commission, Kahn isolated the interest of every opponent in turn. One by one, he enlisted each of them in his cause, winning now by force of intellect, now by charm and cajolery, now by political compromise. It was nothing less than a tour de force of regulatory strategy.

Still, a strategy for electric utilities represented only one part of Kahn's program. Even in the midst of the generic rate hearing, the commission found time to deal with the perennial problems of Consolidated Edison, as they ordered the elimination of declining-block rate structures for that company's millions of residential customers in New York City. Simultaneously, Kahn and his colleagues demanded that all electric utilities in the state prove that their declining-block rates were cost-justified. The commission next forbade the inclusion of gas and electric charges in rental payments for new apartments. Kahn's reasoning here was that, when tenants paid lump-sum rents that included utility bills, they would have no incentive to conserve. Given the psychology of landlord-tenant relations, some renters actually delighted in wasting energy at their landlords' expense. Under the new rules, tenants would pay utility bills separately from rents. Finally, at Kahn's behest, the commission instructed several utilities to submit their practices to systematic review, done under contract by management-consulting firms. Here the purpose was to offset the effects of the cost-plus philosophy that still permeated companies under traditional rate regulation. If rates were to be based on costs, it was important for both the utilities and the commission to understand as fully as possible the nature and extent of costs. Since the companies seemed unable to explain their costs adequately and the commission lacked the necessary staff, both needed help. Again, Kahn's strategy resembled Landis' with the SEC: where Landis used accountants to gather essential data, Kahn used consulting companies. The approach opened the way for a broader application of Kahn's regulatory philosophy.[64]

New York Telephone

For many New Yorkers, the most vivid illustration of Kahn's approach to regulation came from his two highly publicized battles over telephone rates. In one, he fought against the New York Telephone Company, trying to alter its rate structure. The other battle pitted him against consumer groups, on the issue of charges for directory assistance.

Throughout most of his career, Kahn displayed as much interest in telecommunications as in any other area of regulation. He served on the economic advisory board of American Telephone and Telegraph, where he learned that the company made a policy of bundling its charges. That is, the Bell System, partly in keeping with its slogan "The System Is the Solution," did not like to publish cost data on individual parts of its business: long distance, local telephone service, Bell Labs, Western Electric, Yellow Pages advertising, and equipment rentals. Instead, Bell preferred to price its services as a "bundle," without direct reference to their individual costs. This practice offered the company wide discretion in deciding which segments of the business would subsidize other segments. Bundling provided a valuable management tool because it permitted Bell executives to raise or lower long-distance and local-service rates as market opportunities or political pressures required. For example, Bell often held down basic monthly charges to residential users—a politically popular thing to do—while subsidizing the resulting revenue shortfalls with excessive long-distance fees. Bundling did not, however, always work to the advantage of masses of consumers. Kahn had reason to believe that New York Telephone was using the practice to subsidize its business customers at the expense of residential users, specifically by undercharging for business switchboard services.

To remedy the many abuses associated with bundling, Kahn decided to take direct action. Accordingly, when he and his commission colleagues approved a telephone rate increase in 1975, they also ordered the company to prepare detailed, unbundled cost and distribution studies before its next application. When that application, which included a $393 million rate hike, did come in 1976, no such studies were included. The commission rejected the application outright, without even taking up the merits of New York Telephone's case. The company had been forewarned, said Kahn, that it must produce the cost data. "But they didn't give that to us. Why? Because the tradition that this was management's prerogative is very strong and . . . they have never done good cost studies. They want to be free to set their rates the way they want. It just goes to show how sloppy rate-making has been in the past—totally permissive to the companies. We just aren't going to permit that any more."[65]

Though critical of management's abuses, Kahn did not speak as a special-interest consumer advocate determined to punish companies and reduce prices without any reference to costs. He insisted that consumers pay their share, especially for directory assistance, rather than receiving it free from New York Telephone. As an economist, he knew that nothing was free. Directory assistance, in fact, could not readily be automated, and the obligation to give information tied up hundreds of operators. The service was costing New York Telephone about $100 million a year, and the company simply passed along those charges to the consumer, indiscriminately across its entire list of subscribers. Acting on the fundamental principle that every individual must pay for what he receives, Kahn insisted that "free" directory assistance had to stop.[66]

Consumers responded about as he had expected: they were loud, hostile, and abusive. Kahn did not waver. New York Telephone and the commission together worked out a compromise formula under which each caller who dialed Information would be charged 10¢. All customers, however, would begin each month with three free calls. If these calls were not used, the company agreed to credit each nonuser with a 30¢ rebate. While the amounts may seem tiny, the results proved that the issue was not trivial. Within the first two months under the new system, the volume of directory-assistance calls in New York declined by more than 40 percent. Eighty-five percent of residential customers and 70 percent of the business consumers received the full 30¢ per month rebate. Total saving to the company (and the consumer) amounted to an impressive $25 million per year.[67]

Even so, Kahn was not satisfied. He wished to push the company and the commission further, toward a complete marginal-cost pricing system. Under Kahn's plan, which took advantage of the sophisticated computer systems already installed at New York Telephone, callers would pay more during peak phoning periods, less during off-peak. They would also pay for distance—more for calls stretching across five miles than across only one. The new minimum charge for intrastate toll calls would entitle a caller to talk for two minutes, not three. For all telephones—residence and business—conversations of long duration would be more expensive than brief chats. Kahn's system was full of innovations. Like the directory-assistance proposal, this new plan did not win universal acclaim. One official of the American Telephone Consumers Council denounced it as "the beginning of the end of the consumers' right to rap in New York State ... Telephone users will be running up charges like a taxi meter." Not even Kahn could have put it better. Should a twenty-mile taxi trip cost the same as one of two blocks? Again he showed no inclination to retreat: "It is our intention (and the Company's) eventually to go to a full-blown 'Message-Minute-Mile' pricing system, according to which charges per call would vary according to the marginal costs of merely setting up a call, of minutes of additional conversation time, and of distance." The chairman's voice sounded the same, on or off the telephone.[68]

After almost three years of favorable media attention in Albany, Kahn enjoyed a national reputation as an innovative regulator. During the same three-year period, old regulatory issues had surfaced in a new way—to become a national preoccupation. This happened primarily because of the oil crisis of 1973–74, the rise of inflation, and the deep economic recession of 1974–75. These events focused attention on the cost of almost all goods and services, and consequently on the price the nation was paying for its regulatory goals. Regulation suddenly assumed a political importance it had not attained since the Progressive Era. During the presidential campaign of 1976, candidates Gerald Ford and Jimmy Carter both fixed on regulatory reform as a central concern for the next administration. When Carter won the election, it was a forgone conclusion that many new faces would appear in federal regulatory agencies.

For himself, Kahn would have preferred to serve on the Federal Communications Commission, where he might have continued his crusade for marginalist principles in telecommunication pricing. Carter had other ideas: he wanted Kahn for the Civil Aeronautics Board, where some momentum for deregulation seemed to be underway but in danger of failing. Kahn first refused Carter's offer of appointment, pleading ignorance of the airline industry. But after a second invitation, which included specific assurances of the president's full backing, he accepted the job. His years on the New York Public Service Commission had provided ample recommendation for Kahn's new federal office. But now he had to learn his way in yet another complicated industry.[69]

The Airline Industry

The American air age began in 1903, with the Wright brothers' flight at Kitty Hawk. But it was Charles A. Lindbergh's solo trip across the Atlantic in 1927 that first made Americans aware of the possibilities in commercial aviation.[70] Airline companies, which had transported only 6,000 passengers in the entire year before Lindbergh's flight, carried 48,000 in 1928, 162,000 in 1929, and 383,000 in 1930. Not even the Great Depression halted the growth of the fledgling industry. By 1938, the year in which Congress created the Civil Aeronautics Authority (later Board), passenger traffic surpassed one million. Then it reached almost four million in 1941, when World War II temporarily set back further growth by giving priority to military demands.[71] Equally, though, the war reinforced the glamour of flying and helped to make the federal government more aware of both its potentials and its risks. As in the earlier history of the railroads, airline accidents were often spectacular, and deaths became commonplace. Safety regulation thus presented an obvious arena for government action.[72]

Commercial aviation, however, was a very different kind of industry from railroading. The business was relatively cheap and easy to enter; all anyone needed was an airplane, a few pilots, and a ticket office. So airlines could not be considered natural monopolies in the fashion of early railroads or of gas and electric utilities. In theory, dozens or even hundreds of companies could compete for passengers and freight. This ease of entry played a large role in the history of airline regulation. It forced the Civil Aeronautics Board into the dilemma of either maintaining an orderly industry with a small number of participants or allowing market forces to shake out a multitude of competitors, with only the fittest eventually surviving. By the 1930s, some competitors of the fly-by-night variety had already given that term its literal meaning. In an industry posing grave threats to the passenger's life and limb, the job of regulation seemed difficult and messy.[73]

Nor was the market for airlines so simple a thing as, say, the market for lightbulbs. Airline companies sold something like a trip—really the promise of a guaranteed seat of a certain class, on a scheduled flight between "city-pairs." Each pair of cities represented a separate market, with customers in each, and the airline market became segmented in several different ways. Some companies specialized within single states (Texas International, Air Florida); some in regions (Ozark, Piedmont, Pacific Southwest); some in hub-and-spoke networks serving national markets (American, United, Delta). Others catered to charter traffic, leasing individual airplanes to travel groups by the trip or month. Of course, none of these details made the airline industry easy to understand, much less regulate. By the time Alfred Kahn came to the Civil Aeronautics Board, most of the significant markets were served by ten major scheduled airlines. Together, these ten flew to about 430 cities with more than 90,000 possible city-pairs, of which about 58,000 actually received sheduled service.[74]

In another way, the airlines were characterized by unusual volatility. Because air travel is expensive and because a large percentage of potential passengers are vacationers—and thus subject to changes of mind about the trip when money is short—the airline business has always had violent ups and downs. It remains among the most cyclical of industries. The historical fluctuations in the prices of airline securities on the New York Stock Exchange illustrate this characteristic: in the early 1960s, the average price of a share of airline common stock stood at about $5. The subsequent national economic boom, however, quickly drove prices up by a factor of nine—to an average of $47 a share in 1966. By the recession year of 1970, the price had dropped back down to $13.[75]

Nonetheless, the salient trend of the industry from the 1930s to 1977 was its enormous growth. Every indicator displayed the same message.[76]

Year	Persons employed	Number of aircraft	Seats per aircraft	Revenues ($thousand)	Revenue (passenger-miles)
1938	13,274	311	14.2	$57,997	0.533 mil.
1958	152,510	1,899	57.0	2,243,964	31,499 mil.
1977	310,674	2,420	148.1	19,212,228	187,681 mil.

The Civil Aeronautics Board

By 1977, when Kahn became chairman of the CAB, the airline industry was still growing. But it had also developed a number of chronic problems, chief among them a depressed load factor. For all flights by all major airlines in 1977, the composite load factor stood at only 55.5 percent, which meant that on average each plane was flying a little more than half full. Critics of airline regulation contended that this unsatisfactory performance could be traced directly to the policies of the CAB. To explain how this had happened, they cited the unusual circumstances in which the board had been created.[77]

The first important attempts to bring order to the industry began during the 1920s, under the stimulus of Secretary of Commerce Herbert Hoover. Safety rules were legislated in 1926, and Congress began to appropriate federal subsidies to airlines for the carrying of mail. By 1933, the postmaster general's administration of these subsidies had led to a concentration of the industry in a handful of important firms. For reasons of its own convenience, the Post Office placed nearly all of its twenty airmail contracts with three holding companies, and these three became the ancestors of today's Big Four airlines: United, American, Eastern, and

TWA. Because of this concentration, and more particularly because of the apparent evasion of competitive bidding requirements, the Senate conducted an extensive investigation which turned up such a mass of damning evidence that President Roosevelt canceled all airmail contracts. Roosevelt said that the Army Air Corps, not commercial airlines, would now carry the mail. This too proved unworkable, and in 1934 a new round of bidding began. Again the three holding companies walked off with most of the lucrative routes. Meanwhile, competition for shorter routes became very keen, and a consensus in Congress began to develop that the industry needed a comprehensive system of regulation for the management of all passenger-fare levels, airmail subsidies, and route structures. In 1934, the first New Deal bills for economic regulation of airlines were introduced, and in 1938 Congress passed the Civil Aeronautics Act.[78]

The principles expressed in the act of 1938 closely resembled those embodied in the Act to Regulate Commerce of 1887 and the Motor Carrier Act of 1935, legislation that had begun the economic regulation of railroads and trucking. In fact, had the Interstate Commerce Commission itself not been overburdened with these other two industries, Congress might well have vested the ICC with airline regulation as well. One congressman complained that the government was taking a big chance in starting a new agency. "Once you establish a commission . . . you have the devil's own time passing any act abolishing it."[79]

A brief report on the new legislation, issued by the Senate Committee on Commerce, explained that the bill provided for "the usual system of economic regulation," according to "the recognized and accepted principles of the regulation of public utilities, as applied to other forms of transportation." This language suggested that the committee regarded airlines, like railroads or electric utilities, as a natural-monopoly industry. Thus a mistaken economic assumption seems to have formed the foundation of the bill. The Senate report went on to say that "competition among air carriers is being carried to an extreme."[80] In this judgment the House report agreed. Instead of being awarded on the basis of ability to serve, said the House, airline routes went to the lowest bidder for air-mail contracts. As a result, "the air carriers, in their desire to secure the right to carry the mail over a new route, have made absurdly low bids, indeed, have virtually evinced a willingness to pay for the privilege of carrying the mail over a particular route." In addition, the House committee was told by the president of the Air Transport Association (the industry's trade group) that $120 million of private investment funds had been poured into the existing system, and that half of that sum had simply been lost. "He further testified," said the committee report, "that unless legislation is enacted which would give the carriers reasonable assurance of the permanency of their operation and would protect them from cutthroat competition, a number of the air lines would soon be in serious financial trouble." Prospects for the industry seemed bleak.[81]

Clearly, in passing the Civil Aeronautics Act, Congress intended to bring stability to airlines. What is not clear is whether the legislature intended to cartelize the industry. Yet this did happen. During the forty years between passage of the act of 1938 and the appointment of Kahn to the CAB chairmanship, the overall effect of board policies tended to freeze the industry more or less in its configuration of 1938. One policy, for example, forbade price competition. Instead the CAB ordinarily required that all carriers flying a certain route charge the same rates for the same class of customer. This rule conformed to a basic principle of public-utility regulation, and, however odd the policy appeared later on, it flowed logically from the concerns expressed by Congress in 1938. A second policy had to do with the CAB's stance toward the entry of new companies into the business. Charged by Congress with the duty of ascertaining whether or not "the public interest, convenience, and necessity" mandated that new carriers should receive a certificate to operate, the board often ruled simply that no applicant met these tests. In fact, over the entire history of the CAB, no new trunkline carrier had been permitted to join the sixteen that existed in 1938. And those sixteen, later reduced to ten by a series of mergers, still dominated the industry in the 1970s. All these companies participated in the immense growth shown in the table above. All developed into large companies under the protective wing of the CAB. None wanted deregulation.[82]

What the airlines did want was new routes. And since the CAB declined to permit either rate competition or new entry, its regulatory activities came to focus on the question of which airlines would receive new routes. At the same time, the board exercised responsibility for the development of sound route structures for all companies. This meant that profitable long hauls must be mixed with less lucrative short hauls, and that only a few companies— sometimes just one—should be allowed to fly any particular route: that is, a monopoly in some city-pair markets would be necessary to compensate the airline for other, unprofitable routes it was required to fly elsewhere.

To maintain this complex balancing act, the board was ultimately drawn into the adjudication of trivial decisions at the lowest levels of airline management. The CAB came to function more and more along the lines of a court, and its members began to think of themselves as judges, not as proponents of economic efficiency.[83] James Landis treated this problem in his 1960 report to Kennedy, citing inordinate delays as a characteristic of the CAB's proceedings. Landis went on to denounce the agency's failure to do "forward planning of the type necessary to promote our air commerce to its desired level of efficiency" and added that the Board's regulatory efforts were frustrated by a courtroom-style routine that prevented sensible resolution of issues.[84] The board's usual pattern of lengthy cross-examination, Landis concluded, was "a wasteful manner of establishing many of the basic facts." In making awards, the board "selects a route pattern for reasons that it frequently cannot even articulate." In contrast to the SEC of Landis' own design, the CAB simply had no strategy.[85]

The particular questions the board took upon itself to decide tended to preclude the development of an overall strategy. What difference did it make to public policy whether the third or fourth carrier selected to serve a particular city-pair was Eastern, Delta, or American? On what basis should such a decision be made? There was none, other than giving some desirable route to a carrier as compensation for an undesirable one. In such circumstances of arbitrariness the CAB, in writing its decisions, could rationalize its own cartel-like policies only through arbitrary lines of reasoning. Given the emphasis on procedure so characteristic of American administrative law, together with the wide substantive discretion usually enjoyed by regulatory agencies, almost any line of reasoning was likely to be upheld by appellate courts, provided only that the CAB's procedures had been according to form. This meant that the CAB could do almost anything it wanted so long as it went through the proper motions. By contrast, should it actually articulate its practice of cartelization, or openly acknowledge its implicit compensatory policies, then substantive challenges might arise and threaten the board's very foundation.[86]

Still another difficulty grew from mismatch between the CAB's courtlike atmosphere and the issue of *"ex parte* considerations." Whereas conventional judges must not consort with plaintiffs and defendants, regulatory commissioners sometimes had to make nonlegal types of decisions, especially on economic matters. If CAB members could not converse with airline executives, how would they learn about the industry? One of Kahn's colleagues on the CAB, himself a former judge, put the dilemma this way: "In some respects, we are held to the same rigid standards that a court is held, with regard to making decisions, and yet, we are determining policy in which all sorts of inputs should be received before you can make very much of a quality decision, and where I can obtain that it is a bit of a problem without some contact with the industry."[87] Over the years, several board members had resigned, citing frustration caused by the mixed roles they were expected to play. Yet, in this awkward situation, legal experience proved invaluable. If the primary role of the CAB was to be not the framing of a regulatory strategy but rather the assurance of a fair hearing and complete record, then legal procedures seemed natural as the stock in trade of the board. And lawyers did dominate its membership: of the thirty-four members who served between 1938 and the mid-1970s, twenty-four were trained in law. The second-place profession, engineering, accounted for only four.[88]

The Ferment of Reform at the CAB

When Alfred Kahn came to the CAB in 1977, change was in the air. Academic studies had long since established beyond much doubt that an airline cartel existed in America, as a result of CAB policies. These studies argued convincingly that, by restricting economic competition, the board encouraged greater competition in frills: fancier in-flight food and drink, more movies, additional attendants—all minor forms of service to the customer. Much more important, the board's policies also induced the airlines to schedule too many flights. This happened because, once a carrier had been "certificated" by the board to fly between a pair of cities, it was left free to fly as many trips along that route as it wished. Since airline managers held as an article of faith that travelers gravitated to the company with the most departures at the most convenient times, competing airlines scheduled more and more flights. With the number of customers constant, they were forced to fly emptier airplanes. As a result, the industry drifted into its woeful load factor of 55.5 percent. For several years the CAB had responded to this situation by imposing an implicit route moratorium. That is, in addition to forbidding rate competition and denying all applications for entry into the industry, the board also refused to grant any new routes to the existing carriers. The route moratorium had loosened up a bit just before Kahn's arrival in Washington, but the practice of restricting new routes lingered as evidence of the board's single-minded opposition to competition.[89]

By the mid-1970s, several major airlines were in serious financial trouble. Much as in the electric utility industry, a series of converging problems—the skyrocketing price of fuel, the economic recession, and an expensive inventory of wide-body aircraft (Boeing 747s, Lockheed L-1011s, Douglas DC-10s)—had caught the airlines in a trap of rising costs and declining revenues. The CAB's inflexibility prevented rapid adjustment by the companies themselves. It was not that the board had caused all these problems, but rather that its opposition to any real competition made it impossible for the industry to adjust through normal market mechanisms.[90]

Public indictments of the CAB began to grow. In 1975, a subcommittee chaired by Senator Edward M. Kennedy subjected the industry and the board to searching scrutiny. The stage manager of the Kennedy hearings was Stephen Breyer, then a professor at Harvard Law School and later a federal circuit judge. A specialist in regulation and a man of vivid imagination and agile mind, Breyer wanted to demonstrate in a public arena that the CAB form of regulation did violence not only to the principles of competition but even to the administrative process it seemed designed to serve. Senator Kennedy, to whom Breyer fed dozens of "zinger" questions for a lineup of witnesses from the board and the industry, responded with a virtuoso performance. It was Kennedy's finest hour as a legislator, and his participation guaranteed the hearings wide publicity.[91] The clincher in the case against the CAB proved to be the example of airlines that operated intrastate routes beyond board jurisdiction. Two companies in particular, Southwest Airlines in Texas and Pacific Southwest in California, had developed successful business strategies that combined extremely low fares with high load factors. Breyer and Kennedy demonstrated startling differences between the fares customers paid in 1974 in city-pair markets regulated by the CAB and those in Texas and California, where price competition was permitted.[92]

City–pair	Miles	Fare	No. of passengers
Los Angeles–San Francisco	338	$18.75	7,483,419
Chicago–Minneapolis (CAB)	339	$38.89	1,424,621
New York–Pittsburgh (CAB)	335	$37.96	975,344
Houston–San Antonio	191	$13.89	490,000
Boston–New York (CAB)	191	$24.07	2,493,882
Reno–San Francisco (CAB)	192	$25.93	312,811

The Texas and California airlines achieved these remarkable results by offering numerous flights at cut rates. They started with the assumption that the market for air travel was much bigger than the trunklines or the CAB imagined—that the barrier to increased traffic was simply the high price of an airline ticket. They eliminated first-class accommodations and crowded as many additional seats into the cabins as possible without seriously interfering with passengers' comfort. As the Kennedy subcommittee pointed out, Pacific Southwest Airlines "puts 158 seats in a Boeing 727-200 jet aircraft and fills approximately 60 percent of these seats on average. American Airlines puts 121 seats in the same plane and flies it on average 55 percent full. Thus, when flying PSA, 95 passengers must share the cost of flying the airplane, while, on an American plane, 66 passengers must share the same cost." Obviously, the price of a ticket could be cut dramatically, and the price cut in turn would bring in new categories of customers. Explaining the phenomenon to the Kennedy subcommittee, an official from the Texas Aeronautics Commission testified: "These [passengers] are people who are coming to the airline instead of going to the bus . . . you kind of wait for them to tie the chicken coop on top of the airplane."[93]

The remarkable results of the cut-rate fares in Texas and California had been available to any interested observer long before Kennedy's 1975 hearings. Kahn, in fact, included an analysis of the Pacific Southwest story in the second volume of his *Economics of*

Regulation, published in 1971. He viewed the case histories as "the closest thing to a 'controlled experiment' in public policy," and especially appreciated the marginal-cost aspects of the experiment. As Kahn knew, the cost of flying a plane between a pair of cities was more or less fixed, no matter how many passengers made the trip. Obviously the airline could not give away tickets, but it could cut rates on a trial-and-error basis—charging less, for example, for off-peak travel. In a situation of depressed load factor and industry distress, the point of marginalism was to furnish a rationale for any sort of radical price cut. Once fares went down, new travelers would be induced to fly in such numbers that the airlines might soon reach an advantageous load factor.[94]

In all, the Texas and California experiences provided powerful ammunition to the Kennedy subcommittee and to other proponents of deregulation as well. A General Accounting Office study estimated that actual fares in national airline markets exceeded hypothetical fares derived by methods similar to those in Texas and California by 22 to 52 percent. Passengers traveling under the hypothetical rates would have saved between $1.4 billion and $1.8 billion annually during the years 1969–1974. The GAO study added that the lowered fares would have persuaded so many new travelers to fly that the total saving would have been more than $2 billion a year.[95]

By the time of Kahn's arrival in Washington, a broad and strikingly mixed coalition had already begun to lobby for deregulation. One group included a number of strange bedfellows: the National Association of Manufacturers, Common Cause, Sears Roebuck, the American Association of Retired Persons, the Aviation Consumer Action Project, the National Taxpayers Union, the Cooperative League of the U.S.A., the American Conservative Union, and the Public Interest Economics Group. "There is some amount of culture shock," conceded one member of this unusual alliance, "but we do all agree on this issue." A writer in *Fortune* called the deregulation advocates "an odd coalition of academic economists, Naderite consumerists, liberal Democrats, and conservative Republicans." Diverse as this group seems, they were already gathering momentum and political power.[96]

Shortly after Kahn's appointment, the Carter Administration held a "reform gala" at the White House to underscore its commitment to deregulation. Kahn took a prominent part. Holding forth later on to a *New York Times* reporter, he explained why the movement united so many disparate interests:

First of all, I guess it has been this experience of the last 10 years of disappointment with the notion that you solve your problems by passing a law and then going away. The second I suspect has been the sheer proliferation of regulations. I mean, we get new regulatory agencies every year, and it does grow kind of astronomically. A third has been a kind of pendulum effect . . . So you have these real conservatives who have always said, "We don't want the Government messing in here," joining with the liberals of the Ralph Nader kind who say, "Well, where competition could work, you should leave it to competition."[97]

Of course, not everyone wanted airline deregulation. The opponents still held the upper hand, even though two years had passed since the Kennedy hearings. Kahn realized that a crucial part of his job would be to convert skeptical majorities in several constituencies, including Congress and even the CAB itself. The final measure of his success would come from what he could do within his agency and from his attempts to break the logjam on Capitol Hill, where deregulation bills had been stalled for months. During the Kennedy hearings, the airline industry had presented a solid phalanx against deregulation. Without exception, top executives had testified in favor of continued regulation, many of them in vehement tones. Now, two years later, some tiny fissures in the proregulation front had begun to appear, in the representatives of Hughes Airwest and Frontier Airlines; and mighty United Airlines was showing signs of wavering. But a proregulation majority controlled the industry.

Ironies abounded. Delta, the most profitable of all airlines and by common agreement one of the nation's best-managed corporations, liked to profess from its Atlanta headquarters a free-enterprise, antiunion philosophy. Yet, in Washington, Delta remained the most vocal proponent of regulation. Its outspoken chairman denounced the deregulation movement as a wolf in sheep's clothing. Under the banner of "free enterprise" and "less government regulation," he said, the movement actually promised more regulation and perhaps eventual nationalization."[98] Industry trade papers offered equally conspiratorial theories. One journal outlined its answer to the "most mystifying question" of "why air transport regulation, eminently successful by any yardstick, has been singled out for sustained attack." A two-stage plan, said the paper, had been hatched in the executive branch. First, deregulation would get the independent CAB out of the picture. The way would then be clear for manipulation by operatives from the White House and Department of Transportation. Yet in point of fact, the Department of Transportation stood on the side of the airlines. Secretary Brock Adams was an energetic advocate of regulation, and later on he became a problem for Kahn when the two men battled for influence over national transportation policy.[99]

During Kahn's early months as CAB chairman, his most difficult tasks lay within the board itself and with Congress. In the House, the chief obstacle to Kahn's program was Democratic Representative Elliott Levitas of Atlanta, who held a key committee post. (Journalists, mindful of Levitas' services to his Delta Airlines constituents, referred to him as a "Deltacrat.") Other congressmen also responded to the intense proregulation stance of the airline industry.[100] As things happened, the most solid support of continued tight regulation came not from airlines but from labor unions; and the unions put even heavier pressure on their representatives to shield them from deregulation. Airline employees, assisted by ·the cost-plus thinking and protectionist policies of the CAB, had come to receive exceptionally high pay. In 1976, trunkline workers—including all categories from baggage handlers to pilots—earned an average wage of $19,000, which put them at the very top of all employee groups in the United States. Not surprisingly, then, the industry's labor force, led by the Air Line Pilots' Association and including the unions of flight engineers, transport workers, machinists, and aerospace workers, conducted an active campaign against deregulation. Their well-publicized power in Washington presented Kahn with a problem unlike any he had encountered at the New York Public Service Commission.[101]

The Early Strategy

At first Kahn felt overwhelmed by the complex task of moving the airlines toward deregulation while at the same time lobbying Congress for new legislation.[102] But, as in New York, he quickly learned his way. One of the first things he did was to lay down the law to the CAB about the language it used in orders and correspondence. Over the years, the agency had involved itself in so many petty details, so many arbitrary decisions, that it seemed unable to write convincing explanations and opinions. As Kahn read through the files, he became incredulous, then furious, with what seemed to be intentional obfuscation. Aware that he might be risking the success of his chairmanship, he nevertheless decided to launch a campaign for clarity. The opening gun was a memorandum to the CAB staff:

One of my peculiarities, which I must beg you to indulge if I am to retain my sanity (possibly at the expense of yours!) is an abhorrence of the artificial and hyper-legal language that is sometimes known as bureaucratese or gobbledygook . . .

May I ask you, please, to try very hard to write Board orders and, even more so, drafts of letters for my signature, in straightforward, quasi-conversational, humane prose—as though you are talking to or communicating with real people. I once asked a young lawyer who wanted us to say "we deem it inappropriate" to try that kind of language out on his children—and if they did not drive him out of the room with their derisive laughter, to disown them.[103]

Bureaucrats who doubted the new chairman's seriousness found their drafts repeatedly bounced back for revision. Letters were rewritten four and five times, as drafts with Kahn's corrections came back to writers with instructions to revise. Board employees said that the experience of writing for Kahn was like preparing a college term paper.[104]

His critics questioned whether the expenditure of all this energy was the best way for an agency head to be spending his time. Kahn, however, remained adamant: "If you can't explain what you are doing to people in simple English, you are probably doing something wrong." Part of the problem came from lawyers' domination of the regulatory process. "One cannot hope over night to wipe out the effects of three years of law school, or decades of non-lawyers trying badly to imitate lawyers (some of whom, by the way, write extremely well)." But, he emphasized, the point was not one of style alone. "I really have certain very profound not only esthetic but philosophical objections to people in Government hiding behind a cloud of pompous verbiage which creates a gulf between them and the people." Reporters enjoyed hearing such messages from the head of a bureaucracy, and the crusade for clarity received wide coverage.[105]

Kahn's second target in the early days of his chairmanship was the CAB's crushing workload. Almost eighteen years after the

Landis report, with its criticism of the agency's backlog, Kahn determined to learn why the workload remained such a persistent problem. He found that the CAB, by insisting on courtroom routine, frittered away time on "cumbersome procedures required to assure due process to all affected parties." Substantively, moreover, the board was adjudicating not only the important decisions that compelled due process, but a mass of trivia as well.[106] Here what Kahn said about the "picayune decisions" that the CAB had to make concerning airlines applied with equal accuracy to the ICC's regulation of trucking and to the Federal Power Commission's oversight of the natural gas industry:

May a freight forwarder receive commissions from a cargo carrier? To how many travel agents may a tour operator give free passage to inspect an all-inclusive tour? And must those agents then visit and inspect every one of the accommodations in the package? May an air taxi acquire a 50-seat plane? May a supplemental carrier carry horses from Florida to somewhere in the Northeast? Should we let a scheduled carrier pick up stranded charter customers and carry them on seats that would otherwise be empty at charter rates? May an air taxi operate a single round-trip passenger charter flight between two points in substitution for a supplemental? Should we take review of an order by our Bureau of Enforcement dismissing this or that complaint, even though no party has appealed the dismissal? May a carrier introduce a special fare for skiers that refunds the cost of their ticket if there is no snow? May the employees of two financially affiliated airlines wear similar-looking uniforms? . . . Is it any wonder that I ask myself every day: is this action necessary? Is this what my mother raised me to do?[107]

Despite the disarming final question, Kahn was teaching a much larger lesson: "the inexorable tendency for regulation in the competitive market to spread." What he said applied to economic regulation in general:

Control price, and the result will be artificial stimulus to entry. Control entry as well, and the result will be an artificial stimulus to compete by offering larger commissions to travel agents, advertising, scheduling, free meals, and bigger seats. The response of the complete regulator, then, is to limit advertising, control scheduling and travel agents' commissions, specify the size of the sandwiches and seats and the charge for inflight movies. Each time the dyke [sic] springs a leak, plug it with one of your fingers; just as a dynamic industry will perpetually find ways of opening new holes in the dyke, so an ingenious regulator will never run out of regulatory fingers.[108]

The master teacher knew how to hold an audience. It remained for him to make the CAB practice what he preached.

The New CAB

The Civil Aeronautics Board had been in ferment for some two years before Kahn arrived, ever since the Kennedy hearings of 1975. Kahn was the agency's fourth chairman in four years. His immediate predecessor, John Robson, had spoken out in favor of competitive new rate structures and more liberal entry policies. But beyond Robson's rhetorical "one-man reform crusade" (as a trade paper called it), he had not been an effective chairman. He was unpopular with much of the CAB staff; a number of legislators disliked him; and many airline executives despised him. Two highly regarded industry chiefs, Frank Borman of Eastern and Robert Six of Continental, were quoted as saying that Robson was perhaps the worst chairman in CAB history.[109]

This situation benefited Kahn. Not only did he step into the shoes of an unpopular Republican chairman, but as a Democrat he entered office with a board majority on his team. President Carter strengthened Kahn's hand by naming as a Republican member another deregulation-minded economist, Elizabeth E. Bailey, a young veteran of research at Bell Labs. As board colleagues, Bailey and Kahn sometimes disagreed on noneconomic matters, such as smoking by airline passengers. (Bailey took a tough antismoking approach, whereas Kahn favored local option on the grounds that the airlines themselves should respond to customers' preferences.) But on the important questions of regulatory policy, such as freer entry and competitive fares, the two thought alike.[110]

With the backing of his two Democratic colleagues plus Bailey, Kahn took quick steps to reorganize the board. Whereas in New York he had not had this option, in Washington he saw no alternative. He was convinced that the excessive influence of lawyers and the absence of first-rate economists made it impossible for the agency to respond to the economic crisis besetting the industry.[111] In size the CAB was only a little larger than the New York Public Service Commission. Its staff of some 800 was divided between 438 professional, technical, and research personnel, of whom about 120 were lawyers or persons "trained in law," and a remainder of nonprofessionals. The organization included nine staff offices and six line bureaus, each with the power to act:

Enforcement, Economics, Accounts and Statistics, International Affairs, Operating Rights, and Administrative Law Judges. The board's headquarters, located on Connecticut Avenue in Washington, conveniently housed the entire organization.[112] Under Kahn's reorganization plan, the board would retain three of the existing six bureaus (Accounts and Statistics, International Affairs, and Administrative Law Judges) and abolish the others. In their stead, two new bureaus would be formed and reinforced with specialists in economics: Pricing and Domestic Aviation, and Consumer Protection.[113]

More important than any of these was another Kahn brainchild, an Office of Economic Analysis. In asking for additional personnel to staff this unit, Kahn wrote to the chairman of the Civil Service Commission, "I find it simply incredible that the Board has had no genuine Bureau of Economics: the Bureau that until recently had this title was actually concerned only with fares and tariffs and was and is run entirely by lawyers." Kahn elaborated in a letter to a former student who was also a prominent economist. "The reason I set up an Office of Economic Analysis is that I wanted to have objective economists watching carefully what we are doing and how it works out, prepared to identify problems, rather than simply to shut our eyes and rely on faith." Kahn added that "liberals like me" had been too prone in the past to rely on government to solve all problems. Now, he wrote, "I do not want . . . to fall into the opposite error of simply substituting the cliche 'leave it to the market' to take the place of using my own eyes."[114]

Kahn's next step was to bring in a cadre of young bureau chiefs devoted to deregulating the airlines. To head the Office of Economic Analysis, he appointed Darius Gaskins, a well-trained economist with prior experience at the Federal Trade Commission. As general counsel, he hired Philip Bakes, who, as Stephen Breyer's deputy, had played an important role in the Kennedy hearings. And as chief of the Bureau of Pricing and Domestic Aviation, Kahn brought in Michael E. Levine, who twelve years earlier had written for the *Yale Law Journal* the pioneering article on the experience of Pacific Southwest Airlines. Entitled "Is Regulation Necessary?" Levine's article had anticipated with uncanny accuracy the national developments of the succeeding decade.[115]

These appointments of deregulation partisans left no question of Kahn's resolve to make things happen at the CAB. As one of the new appointees himself put it, "All the bomb throwers are here and in place. You have to judge this agency starting from this point forward; now there are no excuses." A new Civil Aeronautics Board had been born.[116]

At least at one level, the mission for Kahn and his new CAB seemed clear: to create a competitive airline industry in place of the forty-year-old noncompetitive model, so largely defined by public-utility regulation. To do this, the CAB must first melt a frozen rate structure and then encourage competition between airline companies on the basis of price. Routes also had to be made genuinely competitive, so that carriers could choose to serve or not serve particular city-pairs. Finally, new entry into the industry must be invited from all qualified applicants. Each of these tasks for the CAB flowed from a single source: the study of economic reasoning to which Kahn had devoted his professional life.

What remained less clear was the exact method by which he should proceed. Difficult questions of implementation constantly nagged at Kahn, much as they had plagued James Landis and his SEC colleagues during the New Deal. But whereas Landis had devised a successful strategy to impose a regulatory regime on an industry accustomed to laissez faire, Kahn had to do just the opposite. He was about to impose competition as a replacement for overregulation. But where should he begin, and at what pace could he move? Should deregulation come gradually, so as to minimize trauma, or in one "big bang," so as to reach his target quickly? Should Kahn focus his attention on Congress and try to get the existing statutes changed? Or, since the present laws seemed to permit a good deal of tinkering, might it not be better to work within the CAB itself? These questions seemed quite enough to confound any new chairman. Kahn had little time for reflection, however, because the immediate question pressed: should his first move come on rates, routes, or entry? All three must be liberalized—economic theory was clear on that—but in what order?

His pragmatic answer grew out of what happened. The issue of rates drilled the first hole in the aging dike, and reform, if not revolution, had begun. Shortly before Kahn came to Washington in 1977, Texas International Airlines had proposed an off-peak "Peanuts" fare for some of its city-pairs within Texas. The company also flew routes outside the state, and for that reason it was subject to CAB jurisdiction in all of its operations. The Peanuts fare was designed to compete with the low-cost rates already being offered by Southwest Airlines, the intrastate carrier that had played a starring role in the Kennedy hearings. A few weeks after Texas International's Peanuts application, American Airlines proposed a "Super Saver" coach fare between New York and the west coast, with discounts ranging from 35 to 40 percent, depending on the day of travel. In the last weeks of the Robson chairmanship, the CAB launched an investigation of both these proposals. Then, in a significant reversal of policy, the board agreed to let the proposed rates become effective, pending the outcome of the full investigation.[117]

Now, with Kahn on the scene, the dike burst. As the CAB's *Annual Report* declared, in the kind of understatement typical of such documents, "Thereafter, discounts became more widespread as competing carriers either matched these [Super Saver] proposals or initiated promotional fares of their own. Before long, other reduced fares—'Simple Saver,' 'Super Coach,' 'Super-APEX,' and 'Budget'—proliferated across the Nation and the North Atlantic." Once it became apparent that load factors were indeed climbing rapidly—just as theory had predicted—discount fever swept through the industry. By the summer of 1978, one year after Kahn's arrival, about half of all coach-class revenue-passenger-miles in the United States were being flown at discount rates, with effects especially evident during summer vacation months.[118]

Month	Percentage of total fares subject to discount	Month	Percentage of total fares subject to discount
October 1977	25.9%	April 1978	35.7%
November	24.6	May	36.8
December	31.8	June	41.0
January 1978	31.5	July	56.9
February	32.0	August	56.0
March	35.3	September	48.0

Load factor for the trunklines exhibited its largest jump in history, climbing from 55.5 percent for the year ending in September 1977 to 60.7 percent for the year ending in September 1978. This gain was extremely significant. It meant that on average nearly 10 percent more passengers were flying on each plane, but at practically no additional expense to the companies. Even with the discount fares, therefore, the positive impact on airline earnings proved to be dramatic. Operating profits nearly doubled for the trunklines as a whole, climbing from $490 million for the year ending in September 1977 to $905 million for that ending in September 1978.[119] From Kahn's viewpoint, of course, this was the best possible outcome. Even so, what had happened was not quite as simple as the numbers alone seemed to suggest, and some troubling questions persisted. How long would the airlines' prosperity continue? Would load factors continue to climb? And what was the effect on the quality of service in ever more crowded airplanes?[120]

For the fifteen months between Kahn's arrival in Washington and the reporting of these September 1978 figures, several things stand out. One is his determination to make the experiment go forward. "Historically," Kahn said in one speech, "the Board has insisted on second-guessing decisions by individual carriers to offer price reductions." That role, he made clear, had ended. Now carriers could not only reduce prices on their own, but in applying for rate increases they could use projected rather than historical costs as a basis for their application. This represented a major departure from traditional regulatory practice, and for Kahn it repeated one of the changes he had earlier pushed through at the New York Public Service Commission. In a time of inflation, the use of projected rather than historical costs was not merely a more realistic policy; it was also a device calculated to reduce the number of new applications for rate increases, thus cutting the CAB's workload. The board's endorsement of this point, by a vote of 5–0, had major implications for all American industries subject to rate-of-return regulation.[121]

A second concern is evident in Kahn's speeches and in letters to his friends. He became fascinated with the new system of rates proposed by the airlines, in part because they did not evolve in the way that economic theory had predicted. Instead of across-the-board cuts for all passengers, the companies rushed to offer a bewildering variety of special fares on particular days of the week, available to passengers on a first-come-first-served basis. "I realize that all this makes for a messy fare structure," Kahn wrote. "Before coming to the Board, I confess, I regarded all these variations as an abomination." Yet to him they now represented a decided improvement over the traditional "rigid, non-competitive, uniformly high fare level." What still worried him, at least theoretically speaking, was that the crowded condition of the airplanes might create a new type of discriminatory situation. As he put it to an economist friend, "As load factors rise, I don't quite see how the market process will work to satisfy the demands of people who are willing to pay fares equivalent to the cost of providing service at, say, an average 55% load factor, yet are getting service at 75% or 80%, with the difference this implies in the availability of reservations up to flight time." Here Kahn's institutionalist background helped a bit. "I come from a tradition in which it was considered important to recognize that competition is rarely perfect, and typically works extremely imperfectly."[122]

There were also some signs that basic fares might come down, along with the special rates. Competition might not be working perfectly, but certainly it was working well. If the board had prohibited discriminatory price cutting in the form of special fares (and discrimination indeed violated the rules of classical public-utility regulation), there would have been no breakthrough at all. As Kahn wrote to a law professor who had objected to this discrimination, "Observe the fact that the Super Savers are now available between all major cities of the country; observe the Chickenfeed fare, which is available to anyone who calls in time, regardless of race, creed, previous condition of servitude, or length of hair; and observe, finally, and most satisfactory, the beginnings of competition in the basic fares themselves."[123]

Everything considered, Kahn was having a wonderful time, just as he did in New York. When Barry Goldwater wrote him to complain about the reduced quality of life aboard crowded airplanes, Kahn replied that some discomfort was inevitable. "When a cartel-like regime begins to break up, it breaks up grudgingly, selectively, sloppily . . . When you have further doubts about the efficiency of a free market system, please do not hesitate to convey them to me. I also warmly recommend some earlier speeches and writings of one Senator Barry Goldwater." In response to a similar letter from one of his own best friends, who had complained about the experience of flying to Denver seated next to what the friend called a "hippy," Kahn wrote that the experience need not be unpleasant for everyone: "Since I have not received any complaints from the hippy, I assume the distaste was not reciprocated."[124]

Even in the midst of the revolution in rate competition, Kahn and his fellow board members still had to confront the question of how to open up entry into the airline industry by new competitors. Within the CAB, debates broke out over the best way to coordinate these two basic parts of the overall strategy for making the industry competitive. As it turned out, the rapid pace of rate competition forced an acceleration of new entry. As Kahn put it, coordinating rates and entry was "like equalizing the two sides of a mustache: one can do it much more rapidly by cutting down on the longer side than by extending the shorter one!" His answer sounds easier, though, than events made the change seem at the time.[125]

Liberalization of entry, which was only one side of the mustache, included within itself two different possibilities. On the one hand, existing carriers could apply for new routes, and some 600 such applications were pending before the board, many of them dating back several years. As noted before, this backlog reflected the agency's inability during the pre-Kahn era to deal adequately with its assigned responsibilities. Some of the 600 were "totally insincere," said Kahn; others were "actively sought for and prosecuted." But all had to be dealt with, and the prospect of taking them up piecemeal, through the laborious hearings typical of CAB procedure, did not seem pleasant.[126]

On the other hand, a second form of entry could also occur, through a new company's application for admission to the club. Although the CAB had admitted no new trunk carriers in its forty-year history, it had certificated scores of new regional airlines. Once the board began to encourage rate competition, both would-be new entrants and enterprising executives of existing regional airlines started making big plans. Working feverishly, they calculated how they might cut prevailing rates, steal some of the business from trunk carriers, and create new classes of passengers, on the Texas and California models. This frenetic activity within the industry presented the board with some vexing problems, but also with an unusual opportunity to showcase its new policy of competition. "I am reasonably persuaded," said Kahn, "that if we are to make genuine progress toward effective competition, we have to institute some system of automatic, discretionary entry into markets." Only in this way would airline executives be forced to think like other business managers—to plan which services their companies should provide and which should be left for competitors; and to determine how fare mixtures and route structures might be rationalized, so as to forestall every competitive challenge. Here Kahn's goal led him to inaugurate a policy of granting permissive and nonexclusive entry to airlines applying for new city-pair markets. "If two carriers are applying for a particular route, the traffic on which, it appears, is large enough to justify only one, I suggest that we should carefully be considering *permitting both* but *requiring neither.*" Kahn's idea represented a double reversal of traditional CAB practice. But it would discourage airlines from making preemptive bids for particular markets in order to prevent others from gaining a toehold.[127]

An opportunity to implement these principles came in the form of two dramatic cases involving underused airports in Chicago and Oakland. In the Chicago case, two different applicants asked the CAB for permission to fly routes between Midway Airport and several cities in the Middle West. Midway, situated in the heart of Chicago, was much more convenient for local travelers than was the giant O'Hare Airport located on the city's outskirts. But the major carriers did not like to fly out of Midway because they wanted to build additional traffic through connecting flights with their own scheduled services to other cities, services for which O'Hare provided the center of their hub-and-spoke systems. Since the new applicants had no such networks, they saw an opportunity to create a market niche for themselves in flights between Midway and several medium-sized midwestern cities. Both airlines quoted rates to the CAB 50 percent below those of existing carriers. As soon as these new entrants filed, the carriers already licensed to serve Chicago announced that they would reduce fares in line with the prospective new competition. This step raised the question of whether either of the two applicants could survive in a war with incumbent airlines.[128]

Because of the precedent that any CAB decision would set, the issue of survival held significance beyond the case at hand. As Kahn described it later, "Several civic parties urged us to protect one or both of the innovators by giving them for a year or two the exclusive right to service Midway Airport; some of them originally proposed that we also prohibit incumbent carriers even from matching the low fares at O'Hare. The innovators, they argued, needed and deserved a period of exclusive right to exploit their new idea." If the innovators did not get this protection, the incumbents might drive them out of business, then "drift back to O'Hare" in order to maximize connecting reservations. For Kahn, the Midway affair also illustrated his objections to gradual deregulation on a case-by-case basis. "Despite our use of extraordinarily expedited procedures, these applications had been pending for almost two years," during which the incumbents, who already operated over the routes at issue, had the advantage.[129]

Confronted with this situation, said Kahn, "We grasped the opportunity to make our first major grant of universal authority to all applicants, in the belief that this would ensure the fullest and most rapid possible exploitation of the market." In sorting out winners and losers, "the competitive market would do a better job than we." But in order to give the new entrants some breathing room, the board went beyond the case at hand, which involved six city-pairs, and extended multiple permissive authority to include seventeen additional markets. This was designed to prevent the incumbents from blanketing all routes and thereby preempting the potential business of the new companies. "The idea was to open up so many [opportunities that] the incumbents would simply run out of blankets." The new companies embraced this idea, even though during the case they had insisted that they needed temporary exclusive authority. One executive commented, "It's going to be harder for [the incumbents] to grab us in a bigger fishbowl." Added Kahn: "Precisely as we intended."[130]

The Oakland case was conducted along the same lines as Midway, with expedited procedures, multiple permissive entry, and no special protection for innovators. If some companies failed, then so be it. As the CAB's 65-page proposal for Oakland concluded, "We cannot agree to define healthy competition as that state where the fortunes of the competitors fluctuate but no competitor ever goes to the wall." This manifesto expressed a fundamental difference between the policies of the Kahn board and those of the old CAB. Whereas traditionally the CAB had looked on the prospect of an airline bankruptcy with horror, Kahn regarded bankruptcy as a normal result of competitive business pressures: "In healthy competition, producers who are inefficient or make bad decisons may fail, but efficient and well-managed producers can operate profitably." The CAB's achievement in Oakland, together with similar ones at Midway and elsewhere, made 1978 the year in which, as the agency's *Annual Report* put it, "the CAB route program entered its most active phase in the history of the Board." In the process, Kahn had given up all faith in the merits of gradual deregulation. He had shifted instead to deregulation at a breakneck pace, and the board's policy of proceeding on several fronts simultaneously seemed to be working beyond anyone's wildest expectation. The airlines were enjoying their most prosperous business in many years. And the CAB, said the *Annual Report,* in an explosion of polysyllables but with full accuracy, had "introduced unprecedented substantive and procedural innovations."[131]

Due Process and Competition

These gains did not come easily. The CAB had cut its procedural decision-making time in half, Kahn wrote a close friend, but there had been "blood on the floor." Overall, the chairman reported, the board's efforts to cut red tape "have come under attack from much of the practicing bar." In no case, however, had the CAB abandoned its traditional hearings process, and the repeated suggestions to the contrary always angered Kahn.[132]

Looking back now, it seems clear that the experience of the CAB in 1977 and 1978 provides an exceptionally vivid example of change along one of the main currents in American regulatory history: tradeoffs between economic efficiency and procedural due process. From the very beginning, as the Massachusetts experience of Charles Francis Adams demonstrated, all attempts to regulate economic behavior toward the goal of greater efficiency encountered obstacles based on traditional values of American life, liberty, and property—protection of which was guaranteed under the Bill of Rights and the Fourteenth Amendment. In the 1870s, Adams had sidestepped this difficult question by refusing to assert regulatory powers that would have interfered with the constitutional rights of persons and thus have drawn his commission into court. The Massachusetts Board of Railroad Commissioners emphasized publicity and shunned coercion. In that way it remained out of court, its powers ironically maximized through its own policy of restraint. But the tradeoffs between economic efficiency and due process continued long after Adams' time. In some ways, the entire history of responsible regulation is encapsulated in the ongoing effort to strike a proper balance between the two.

For Louis D. Brandeis, in contrast to Adams, the keys to regulatory definition making and standard setting did not emerge as a result of informal commission rulings, but rather from court decisions and procedures. For him, the essence of regulatory routine could be found in established legal rules of evidence, testimony, and cross-examination. The adversarial theory—two strong advocates arguing for their versions of truth before impartial judges and juries—lay at the heart of the Anglo-American conception of liberty, an ideal that Brandeis would not willingly undercut. Brandeis admonished the first members of the Federal Trade Commission not to give advance advice to business managers, but to rely instead on established judicial procedures as the best method for setting the limits of competition. This devotion to cherished principles symbolized not only Brandeis' stand but also the collective view of the American bar toward regulation itself.

In the early years of administrative regulation, American courts took a stern stance toward the upstart commissions. Partly from jealous guardianship of power, partly from unfamiliarity with administrative needs, judges often limited regulatory discretion so severely that the commissions had to return to the legislatures again and again for grants of clarifying powers. By the time of the New Deal, however, the discretion of administrative agencies had begun to spread beyond previous boundaries, as the powers of commissions and boards multiplied. James Landis celebrated this phenomenon in *The Administrative Process*, which caught the tenor of the times. Unlike Brandeis, Landis embraced advance advice and made it the normal routine of the SEC. By the end of World War II, then, the advocates of wide regulatory discretion and minimal judicial review were in command. For a brief moment the "conservative" opponents of this discretion—usually found in bench and bar—seemed to have lost the fight.

At just this point in American legal history, the old establishment staged a counterattack, the traditional viewpoint having been strengthened by two recent developments. One was a wave of national conservatism, a common aftermath of wars. The second brought to the foreground a reinforcing battalion of "liberal" lawyers who were growing uncomfortable with government threats to civil liberties. Conscious of the rise of totalitarianism in the 1930s and of its persistence in eastern Europe during the 1940s, civil libertarians now joined with the old opponents of commission power to oppose broad governmental discretion. The result was an effective political coalition that pushed the Administrative Procedure Act of 1946 through Congress.[133]

That act proved to be a milestone in the history of American administrative government. Over the next generation, not only regulatory decision making but nearly all administrative action came under the new rules of notice, reasonableness, and opportunity for all affected parties to give evidence and testimony. Later, in the mid-1960s, still another judicial revolution moved regulatory practice even farther down the track of procedural safeguards. This was the revolution in "standing," which brought new participants and issues into regulatory proceedings. Now matters of environmental impact, affirmative action, and rights of other affected parties added new layers of procedural requirements to the already sizable burden of the regulatory process.[134] In all of this, of course, the influence of lawyers on regulation—always extremely powerful—reached its historical zenith. Lawyers seemed indispensable, and the corporation or agency that tried to do its business without expert legal advice was simply being foolish.

Alfred Kahn viewed this situation with displeasure when he undertook to reform the regulatory scene. In New York, his chief response took the practical shape of the generic rate hearing. At the CAB, Kahn launched a frontal assault on what he regarded as the flagrant and broad-gauged abuse of due process, by public and private sectors alike. "It seems to this layman," he said, "that 'due process' is defined in an asymmetrical fashion: it seems inherently to give protection to the parties who benefit from delay, and to be injurious to the parties—typically the public at large—who are *adversely* affected by delay . . . In short, the requirements of *legal* due process, interposing the heavy hand of government between an idea and its application in the market, are directly antithetical to competition."[135]

Kahn favored decision making in the open; thus he championed the sunshine laws enacted by Congress in the late 1970s. But he knew that the basic problem transcended the issue of openness. Rather it had to do, as he wrote the chairman of the House Subcommittee on Aviation, with "being placed in the position of having to tell a businessman to wait two years until we bureaucrats have shuffled enough papers to permit us to reach a decision which probably shouldn't be any of our concern in the first place."[136] Kahn's best opportunity for a full expression of his thoughts on due process came when the American Bar Association invited him to speak to its members in New York. As a title for the session, planners had selected "Regulatory Reform at the Civil Aeronautics Board—With or Without Legislation—With or Without Due Process." Their provocative gesture gave Kahn the opening he had been waiting for. His speech, despite its manifest passion, represented his mature thoughts on the issue, framed after a career of careful writing about regulation and after more than four years' experience as chairman of two important regulatory agencies.

Ever the showman, Kahn began his address by quoting, in Scots dialect, four stanzas from Robert Burns's satiric poem, "To a Mouse." Such a "wee, sleekit, cowrin, tim'rous beastie" had devised "the inhospitable, smart-alecky title." Having captured the attention of the assembled lawyers, Kahn moved on to an analysis of their motives. Referring to route and entry procedures, "where we encounter by far the most complaints from some members of the aviation bar," he said that he and his colleagues had tried to substitute innovative methods for the "Perry Masonisms that characterize the typical CAB proceeding." The bar, deprived of long and "lucrative" procedures, had protested. And the lawyers' real objections, Kahn suggested, were not procedural but substantive; they did not wish to see so much new entry into the industry. "Indeed, I cannot help feeling that some among you, determined to resist our present policies with all the weapons at your command, have seized upon procedural arguments because you really can't refute our new policies substantively—just as in the past some of you used laws designed to protect the environment or to encourage energy conservation as devices to shield your clients from competition."[137]

Kahn continued his address, blistering the captive audience with the heat of his powerful attack:

Are we, in removing the restraints that for 40 years have kept people out of the airline industry, in proposing to open up markets to all fit applicants, and relieving incumbents of burdensome restrictions on their operating rights, are we running afoul of the Fifth Amendment's injunction against depriving persons of "life, liberty or property without due process of law"? . . . Are we in so doing depriving the incumbent carriers of property, with or without due process? I find no justification in either the Constitution or the Federal Aviation Act for the assumption that the certificates of public convenience and necessity that we issue under the Act for providing air service over particular routes need be exclusive, or that the Board is under the slightest constitutional obligation to safeguard their value, as protected property under the Fifth Amendment. I have been told by people who have been at the CAB a long time . . . that in the past the Board would often choose among competing applicants for the right to operate a particular route in secret sessions, held in a closed room from which all staff were rigidly excluded; that somehow out of that process emerged a name attached to the route in question; that the Chairman—or perhaps his assistant—would then pick up the telephone and call the General Counsel and tell him who the lucky winner was, and nothing more; that then a lawyer on the General Counsel's staff, amply supplied with blank legal tablets and a generous selection of cliches—some, like "beyond-area benefits," "route strengthening" or "subsidy need reduction," tried and true, others the desperate product of a feverish imagination—would construct a work of fiction that would then be published as the Board's opinion. Need I add that any resemblance between it and the Board's actual reasons for its decision would be purely coincidental? And then the courts solemnly reviewed these opinions, accepting the fiction that they truly explained the Board's decision, to determine whether the proffered reasons were supported by substantial evidence of record.

Well, we have come to grips with the institutional decision. The Sunshine law has helped force us to do so, but I would like to take some small credit too . . . I am particularly proud, for example, of our decision in the Midway case—not mainly because it is well written, although I think it is, but because it lays out, step by painful step, the actual agonizing process we went through in deciding to certificate all applicants, and to protect nobody from anybody . . . I believe that one substantive regulatory principle on which we can all agree is the principle of minimizing coercion: that when the government presumes to interfere with peoples' freedom of action, it should bear a heavy burden of proof that the restriction is genuinely necessary . . . The dispensation of favors to a selected few is a political act, not a judicial one . . . None of this exempts a regulatory commission from the requirement to be scrupulously fair. But due process in the fashioning of economic *policy* is not the same as due process in a criminal trial, and the attempt to hedge it about with the same kinds of procedural restrictions perpetrates all sorts of unfairnesses, in the name of due process.[138]

The discomfort among the audience can only be imagined, though many listeners must have admired Kahn's candor.

The CAB's Constituencies

Like Adams and Landis before him, Kahn considered it vitally important that his policies be made clear to his various constituencies. He spent an enormous amount of time making speeches, writing letters, and cultivating the press. In fact, one of his greatest strengths—perhaps his greatest—was as communicator and educator. Seldom did he mince words or try to sweet-talk hostile interest groups. Convinced of the correctness of his cause, Kahn attempted to explain his position, point out the inconsistencies of opposing arguments, and persuade through reasoned argument. As a teacher, he never retired.

More than any other group, the airline labor unions learned Kahn's lessons the hard way. Quite accurately sensing that wages would decline if the industry suddenly became competitive, the unions did not want to surrender the cartel-like protection afforded them by the old CAB. Kahn, despite the prolabor sympathies characteristic of his background as a liberal Democrat, met their objections head on. He conceded that regulation did raise the compensation received by labor, and not just airline labor. The reason for this, Kahn believed, could be found in the cost-plus character of traditional regulation, which induced companies to pass along input costs to their customers and which discouraged them from effective searches for cost reduction. Regulators, for their part, permitted such a policy because they wanted to keep peace within the industry and because they themselves were accustomed to cost-plus ways of thinking.[139]

After voicing his lack of sympathy with this view, Kahn was deluged with hostile mail from labor. He proved more than ready to answer his critics. In his typically open and didactic manner, he responded to one pilot who had protested against Kahn's statements about excessive pay:

You argue in rebuttal that being a pilot requires a high degree of skill, long training, and great responsibility and entails arduous working conditions. That is absolutely correct. From these facts, you conclude that the present high wages and short hours are justified. I disagree. The sort of value-of-service pricing you suggest is not the way that wages are set in the competitive sectors of our economy. Wages, like the prices of other goods and services, are determined on the basis of supply and demand. The long training and skill required to be a successful pilot will always limit the supply, and thus justify wages markedly higher than average in our economy—but not necessarily as much higher as today.[140]

Again, Kahn told a protesting executive of the Air Line Pilots Association that he was "badly misinformed" about what the CAB was trying to do. After denying that he himself was antilabor, Kahn insisted: "If I'm anti-anything, I'm anti-excessive government interference ... And I am *particularly* against government being used to protect powerful business interests by giving them special grants of monopoly privilege." His dander up, Kahn added that he resented "the cheap argument you repeat about my having tenure at Cornell ... I don't *need* tenure at Cornell." But the central lesson was, "Lower prices induced by more competition mean *more* jobs, not fewer: don't you forget that when you say it is you who speak for labor, and not I."[141]

Nor did Kahn limit his candor to distant correspondents or lone dissenters. Informed that Pan American World Airways had flouted the CAB's advice on discount tickets, he said, "I'm inclined to tell Pan Am to go to hell." When Jimmy Carter reversed the CAB's recommendation about an international route award, Kahn openly criticized the president. "There have been three major international decisions, and he has overturned me on all three." Expressing himself as thoroughly disappointed, Kahn told reporters that Carter "is the President and has the right to make a judgment, and I have a right to disagree with it, which I do." The chairman said later, on a television program, that Carter's decision "casts a shadow on the integrity of the [CAB] process."[142] Even so, throughout his tenure at the CAB, Kahn's relationship with the president remained warm and close. Kahn usually communicated with the White House on only a few kinds of issues, such as international aviation, where the president possessed much broader regulatory authority than over domestic policies. A related issue concerned the attempts of Secretary of Transportation Brock Adams to move into the domain of both the CAB and the State Department (which led American negotiations on international airline matters). Kahn vigorously repulsed Adams' foray.[143]

A third area of communication between Kahn and the White House concerned the appointment of new board members. In 1978, the terms of his two Democratic colleagues ended, and Kahn was concerned about suitable replacements. Not only his party majority but also his policies were at stake. "Above everything else," he wrote to Hamilton Jordan, "what I need on the Board is professionalism. Every step on the path to regulatory reform is politically charged. The *only* way we can persevere is if each Board appointee has a firm, independent professional background and qualifications, and is in a postion to make strong, intellectually-grounded professional judgments." So Kahn took an active hand, proposing specific names for President Carter's consideration. "I know you already recognize that my job in months and years ahead will be impossible if you do not actively involve me in this process."[144] A little later in 1978, Kahn sketched for the White House the general situation:

Remember we have a nervous Congress; our decisions are subject to Court review; and the airlines and the financial community are constantly demanding assurances that we are not a bunch of wild-eyed ideologues, and that we know what we are doing . . . [We have adopted] genuinely novel procedural and substantive policies. That process can work well only if each Member participates actively . . . What kind of people do I need, specifically? I need people with special skills in making highly technical public economic policy—with training and/or experience in the law, economics, regulation. I don't need politicians. Maybe I can stand one—two, absolutely not.[145]

In the end, Carter's appointments met with Kahn's approval. The president was on his side, in part because of the chairman's careful attention to White House relations.

Lobbying the Congress

Senators and representatives provided yet another set of constituents about whom Kahn must worry. In fact, because legislation to deregulate the industry was pending on Capitol Hill throughout his chairmanship, he spent more time dealing with Congress than with any other group except for the board itself.[146] The road to legislative change wound tortuously around the special interests opposing deregulation. The coalition of industry and labor spokesmen alone seemed an almost unbeatable opposition, even without their allies in the Department of Transportation and among remaining dissidents in the CAB. A related problem seemed the sheer weight of history. Over time, Congress had enacted an enor-

mous amount of regulatory legislation, beginning with the Act to
Regulate Commerce of 1887. And in the ninety years since that
beginning, the trend had all been one way: toward more of the
same. Congress had never taken anything like the giant step backward that Kahn and his allies were now urging. Even the word
"deregulation" had entered the national vocabulary only recently,
and so far there was little besides bombast to stand behind it. Numerous deregulation bills had been introduced; but, as a trade
paper reported late in 1977, "after three years of elephantine rhetoric," the lack of action made deregulation look like a mouse.
Powerful presidential support would have helped, but Jimmy
Carter was preoccupied with his energy legislation.[147]

Already Kahn had achieved spectacular success within the
CAB, with his policies of rate competition, open entry, and new
route authority. The industry responded with lower fares, higher
earnings, and service initiatives. Yet this very success seemed to be
giving ammunition to Kahn's opponents, who argued that the
CAB's turnabout made new legislation unnecessary.[148] For Kahn
himself, no argument could have sounded more ironic. The real
fight, he knew, had just begun. For one thing, the board's innovative procedures must still meet the test of judicial review. The
challengers who had appealed the CAB's Midway and Oakland
decisions might well win because they had "40 years of CAB precedent to back them up." Not only that, but the appointment of different board members could quickly reverse the progress already
made. Therefore Congress must act. A well-designed deregulation
bill, Kahn concluded, will "secure these advances against a change
of agency policy, and it will surely avoid a lot of difficult litigation
challenging the legality of the reforms we have already introduced."[149]

Many members of Congress balked at deregulation because of
their uncertainty about future airline service to small cities once
deregulation was on the statute books. These legislators were
acutely sensitive to their constituents' wishes for big-time airline
service, a concern augmented by their own dependence on frequent jet flights for quick trips to and from home. Hundreds of legislators, particularly those from rural districts, were loath to
tamper with the existing system. As noted earlier, the CAB's
forty-year pattern of dealing with local service had been to maintain a balancing act among routes with heavy and light traffic.

Confronted with this issue, and with the fears on Capitol Hill, Kahn took the same line of attack that had served him so well in the past. He acknowledged the reality of the problem, laid out a theory for its solution, and then sought by reasoned analysis to change the minds of skeptics. In addition to his many appearances before subcommittees of both houses, he talked with scores of legislators and their staff assistants, called them repeatedly on the telephone, and wrote one letter after another in response to specific queries. Even under the existing system, Kahn told one senator, the airlines were flying more than they had to under the terms of their certificates. "There is absolutely no reason to doubt that the same would be true under the automatic entry provisions." Fares would drop, traffic would grow, and the frequency of service might actually increase. "Is this prediction merely hypothetical, merely based on deductive reasoning? I submit it is not. It is based on the lessons of economic history; this is how a competitive market operates, and you can see proof of it everywhere about you."[150]

The chairman's own congressman, representing the Cornell district in New York, wrote him to protest the CAB's decision permitting Allegheny Airlines (later U.S. Air) to reduce its service to Ithaca. Kahn replied that eventually Ithaca and similarly sized cities would receive better service from small commuter airlines than the CAB could ever force Allegheny to offer. True, the market adjustment would take some time, and gaps would occur during which there might be no service at all. But Kahn saw no alternative, given the overall goal of making the industry competitive: "Telling carriers they must compete and cannot look to the government for protection is totally inconsistent with telling them also that they must provide unremunerative services at their own expense."[151] The chairman lobbied endlessly on this point, and he tried to enlist the help of local airlines themselves. "In almost every conversation I have had with Congressmen," he said in a speech to the Commuter Airlines Association, "I have encountered a tendency to deprecate the value of service by small aircraft. They and their constituents seem to think it is somehow demeaning to lose service by large jets once or twice a day, and receive instead service by the obviously more suitable and efficient smaller commuter aircraft, even when that means service four and five times a day—this in the face of all the objective evidence that travelers respond positively to such substitutions. I think you have a major public relations job here."[152]

Kahn himself, of course, excelled at public relations. He turned every contact with members of Congress into an opportunity for further lobbying. In one letter he sent to every member of the Senate, he noted that the CAB unanimously supported the deregulation bill, enclosed two pages summarizing key issues, attached fifteen pages of relevant testimony, and closed with an offer of further help: "I would like to extend to you an offer of my services and those of my staff to answer whatever questions you may have about the need for the legislation or any of its provisions. In particular, I know you are probably concerned about the provision of air service to the smaller communities within your state . . . If you would like information about that or any other aspect of the bill, please don't hesitate to call on me."[153]

Kahn was an effective lobbyist in part because he received such a good press. Congressmen liked to talk with him; he was interesting and considerate of their problems, and the media were making him into a national celebrity. He granted interviews freely and spent a good deal of time talking to reporters. Kahn understood their needs and prejudices, and played directly to both. He made a point of self-deprecation, but seldom failed to give each interviewer something new, some small exclusive. As a result, he received extremely wide coverage, nearly all of it favorable. Detailed feature articles about him appeared in the *New York Times*, the *Wall Street Journal*, the *Washington Post*, *Fortune*, *Forbes*, *Barron's*, *National Journal*, and many others. He was written up regularly in such trade publications as *Airline Reports*, *Aviation Daily*, and *Travel Weekly*. He appealed to even broader audiences, in writeups for *People* magazine and on television programs such as the "MacNeil-Lehrer Report" and William F. Buckley's "Firing Line." He was always a hit. After being told that the MacNeil-Lehrer producers had received a record number of requests for transcripts of his appearance, Kahn wrote a friend, "Maybe I should throw up my present job and do what I really would love to do—play musical comedy on whatever stage will accept me."[154] But in fact he stood on the right stage already. When a student who had taken his courses at Cornell thirty years before wrote him about his new celebrity, Kahn replied that he "was awfully pleased to hear your recollections of me as a teacher.

In a way, I feel that I am still in that profession—but giving my lectures from a slightly different platform."[155]

The Act of 1978

In October 1978, Congress finally passed the Airline Deregulation Act. It formalized all the principles Kahn had been enforcing administratively. Now, at last, the future of these principles seemed secure against adverse judicial challenge. Kahn's only regret, he said later, was that the passage of the act denied him the opportunity of defending the CAB's policies at the Supreme Court, where he would have "presented the ultimate Brandeis brief." The new legislation made the setting of fares competitive, gave the carriers almost unlimited route authority, and opened up the airline business to free entry by new companies. In a gesture calculated to emphasize that the act meant business, Congress added a provision calling for the disappearance of the Civil Aeronautics Board after a suitable transition period, defined by the act to expire in 1985.[156]

For all these changes, it is unrealistic to credit Kahn alone. Many hands helped, and some had been toiling long before Kahn came to Washington. The Kennedy hearings of 1975, planned and executed by Stephen Breyer, certainly began the groundswell of support for deregulation. The subsequent joint efforts of Naderites, conservative Republicans, and liberal Democrats amounted to a rare spectacle of cooperation by diverse allies. And the persistent lesson of experience—the examples of success without tight regulation in California and Texas—provided the necessary demonstration without which deregulation perhaps never would have arrived.

Kahn's primary contributions lay in two areas. First, by setting an example through powerful administrative action, he made it impossible for the opposition to paint a horrible picture of a deregulated future. During his sixteen months at the CAB, the airlines enjoyed the most prosperous economic times in their recent history. Their load factors climbed rapidly, their profits doubled, and they could no longer keep claiming that deregulation meant disaster. One by one, the airlines began to soften their stance. Led by United, the largest of the carriers, a few major companies broke ranks and went over to Kahn's side. Seeing deregulation as likely to come despite their campaigns against it, these defecting airlines decided on a policy of trying to shape the specific package enacted by Congress.

Second, having neutralized the opponents, Kahn moved to consolidate the supporters and mobilize them in favor of new legislation. He did this by a masterly orchestration of diverse forces. Like a gifted conductor managing an intricate composition, he brought every player, every instrument, into the piece at the appropriate time. He made sure that the movements of the symphony did not get out of proper sequence, as they were forever threatening to do. Kahn managed the media, the Congress, the White House, and most important of all the CAB itself, giving each its individual cues, its required up- or downbeat. Exploiting the momentum that had been building since the early 1970s, he said all the right words, called in all the right clichés.[157]

When the act finally passed, the magazine *Aviation Week and Space Technology* editorialized that Kahn had shaken the CAB out of its torpor. In an outburst of mixed metaphors, the magazine praised his tenure at the head of a board that had been "manned largely by political lame ducks and operated by a swollen, legalistic bureaucracy, was still flying through a DC-3 environment that regulated the airlines down to a minimal survival diet and denied the ingredients vital for healthy growth. Surgery always is drastic, and Mr. Kahn's actions induced a certain post-operative shock. But he effectively removed the palsied hand of the CAB from the airlines' growth throttle."[158]

On the day the deregulation act was signed, Kahn wrote several members of Congress to thank them for their support. To one senator he said, "I can't begin to tell you how happy I am that [the Act] has been passed or how confident I am that with it we can create a truly competitive airline industry that is genuinely responsive to the needs of consumers and better, too, for airlines and their employees." He added a handwritten postscript. "This is the last letter I will sign as Chairman of the CAB. As you may have read, the President has persuaded me to try to help him with the problem of inflation. I will try to apply in that job the same philosophy I've tried to apply to air transport." President Carter informed the CAB staff that Kahn was leaving with extreme reluctance and that he himself was taking the chairman away only because even more important tasks beckoned. "You at the Board,"

Carter wrote, "have presented my Administration with one of its great success stories."[159]

A number of his friends expressed surprise when Kahn accepted the anti-inflation job as head of the Council on Wage and Price Stability. Indeed he managed to achieve little more success in it than had his predecessor, Robert Strauss. As administrator of a voluntary control program, the chief inflation fighter had few weapons. Within the administration, Kahn had to vie for influence with other heavyweights: Treasury Secretary Michael Blumenthal, White House domestic policy chief Stuart Eizenstat, Council of Economic Advisers Chairman Charles Schultze, and Office of Management and Budget Director James McIntyre, Jr. Several of these rivals had been administration insiders since Carter's inauguration. Even within his own council, Kahn had to compete for influence with Director Barry Bosworth. For months, a freeze on new federal hiring frustrated Kahn's attempts to recruit even a small staff to assist him.[160]

In office, Kahn continued to receive a good press, but the politics of his position made it impossible to avoid costly struggles. Almost immediately, he became embroiled in disagreements with AFL-CIO chief George Meany, who argued that the administration's economic program favored business at the expense of labor. On another occasion, when Kahn suggested that consumers might boycott stores whose price increases exceeded the guidelines, he came under severe attack in the business press. Journalists continued to praise his forthrightness, but noted that this very quality caused "teeth-gnashing" within the administration.[161]

In the 1970s, Kahn had been very good at pointing out areas in which industry-specific protectionist arrangements were promoting inflation and costing consumers money. As chief inflation fighter, he continued his campaign against inappropriate regulation in particular industries; the Carter Administration's program for trucking deregulation, for example, was effectively managed from Kahn's office. But for the country at large, the control of inflation represented a special macroeconomic problem surrounded by a good deal of uncertainty. No rigorous theory of inflation existed, at least none comparable to the long-tested theories of price and entry that guided Kahn's CAB policies. The idea of wage-and-price guidelines seemed to contradict the very reliance on market mechanisms that had formed the basis for his great campaigns at both the CAB and the New York Public Service Commission. Success for Kahn in the role of chief inflation fighter was just not in the cards. He acquitted himself well, but the odds defeated him as they had defeated Strauss and others.[162]

Kahn's Achievement

Kahn had gone from Cornell to the New York Public Service Commission in 1974 and had remained at that post for a little less than three years. He arrived in Washington in 1977 and held the CAB chairmanship for about a year and a half. The four and a half years of his agency chairmanships is still too recent to allow for mature historical perspective. The utility and the airline stories are far from over. Each industry has been powerfully affected by subsequent events, especially by the absence of general economic prosperity in the years after Kahn's departure.

He had left both the New York PSC and the CAB, for example, prior to the Iranian revolution and the "second oil crisis" of 1979. These events shook the world economy and contributed to the start of another prolonged recession, which in turn struck hard at both electric utilities and airlines. For utilities, the recession meant diminished demand for electricity. This was not entirely bad news, given the industry's upward-shifting marginal-cost curve. But the decline in demand growth was so unusual that utilities actually began canceling construction projects long underway, thereby accepting writeoffs of hundreds of millions of dollars. Around America, abandoned construction sites stood as silent reminders of unrealistic assumptions about growth as the natural order of things—ghost towns of a lost prosperity.

In such a situation, marginal-cost principles assumed even greater significance than they had during Kahn's tenure in New York. The nationwide movement toward the right kinds of price signals had begun even before the second oil shock, and in that movement Kahn's pioneering played an important role. His generic rate hearings were copied in several other states, as intervenors and commissions sought to educate companies and consumers about the potential benefits from marginal-cost rate structures.

Of particular importance was the Public Utility Regulatory Policies Act of 1978, which Congress passed partly to induce companies and state commissions to use marginalist principles in rate-making. The staff of the New York Public Service Commission directly influenced the content of this legislation, and the commission's own position, of course, derived from Kahn's earlier tenure in Albany. The act imposed a statutory deadline (November 1981) by which all fifty states must follow certain standards in setting rates. One of these standards prohibited a utility from using declining-block rates unless it could demonstrate that its costs declined as its customers' consumption increased, a provision identical to one Kahn had imposed on New York utilities during his PSC chairmanship. Even though national progress toward implementing marginal principles lagged and the 1981 deadline was not universally met, the revolution in utility pricing went forward. All over the country in the early 1980s, rate hearings began to recapitulate the New York experience. Few innovative principles emerged that had not been anticipated by Kahn in the generic rate hearings of 1975–76. Again, the real question was whether state regulatory bodies could adapt quickly enough: whether they could look beyond their own inclination to discipline utilities by reflexive denials of requests for rate increases. As the industry entered one of the most critical stages in its history, some observers began to predict serious power shortages by the late 1980s.[163]

In the airline industry, the post-Kahn era did not appear to be so ominous, but still it was full of uncertainty. The prosperity of the 1977–78 period hardly lasted beyond Kahn's departure, as the oil crisis hit the airlines, doubling fuel prices and making existing fleets uneconomical. The companies had purchased aircraft designed under assumptions of low fuel costs, and the jump in price upset all cost estimates. A new generation of fuel-efficient airplanes would have to be designed and built. But in a period of general economic recession—which always affects this industry in an exaggerated way—where were the airline companies to find the money to pay for the new equipment?[164]

Despite such problems, the early returns on deregulation looked very favorable. Even during the recession, passenger traffic held fairly steady, drawn by special rates. Overall rate levels climbed in response to spiraling costs—particularly of fuel—but this had nothing to do with deregulation. An authoritative early study, produced by the Harvard Faculty Project on Regulation, found that the overall results of deregulation remained strongly positive through 1980, the cutoff date for the study. Later investigations, including an intensive analysis by the CAB itself (carried through the year 1982), confirmed the same result. In all studies, only two classes of "losers" could be identified: small cities not yet served by new commuter airlines and business travelers who received poorer service than they wanted and were willing to pay for (because of higher load factors, congested airports, and new classes of passengers).[165]

One major airline, Braniff, declared bankruptcy, but by common agreement Braniff's troubles derived from having overextended itself in an attempt to take advantage of deregulation. Under the open-entry provisions of the act of 1978, Braniff attempted to fly dozens of new routes for which it was ill equipped. In its effort to win traffic from competitors, Braniff slashed its rates, only to see other carriers match the cuts. At that point, as one Wall Street analyst remarked, "It became a bleeding contest. And Braniff bled to death faster." Kahn had predicted this kind of outcome. Poor management decisions and bankruptcies, he had argued, were routine occurrences in business. Competitive wars separated good managers from bad and afforded the opportunity for even established companies to make poor decisions. The only way to avoid all business failures was for the government to neutralize all competitive advantages, including superior management, by protecting participants and barring new entrants. Again, Kahn had been one of the few advocates of airline deregulation to engage this question openly. In the years before his arrival in Washington, fear of bankruptcies had imposed a major barrier to deregulation. Even Kahn's free-market-minded predecessor as CAB chairman, John Robson, had been reluctant to liberalize fare competition and route awards to the point that a major company might fail. Kahn himself, when Jimmy Carter's envoys urged him in 1977 to accept the CAB chairmanship, specifically asked, "What if Eastern Airlines goes bankrupt? Is the president going to pretend then that he doesn't know me?" For Kahn knew that, sooner or later, some important companies would perish. Under a system of free competition, mistakes by management could prove fatal; and, even with good management, the heavily unionized trunk carriers would be pressed hard by upstart airlines that employed nonunion labor.[166]

Still, during his tenure as CAB chairman, Kahn never had the unpleasant duty of explaining such an actual failure. It is clear in retrospect that he came to Washington at an unusually opportune moment. Arriving in the midst of a stalled deregulation movement but with overall economic prosperity still running high, he found the setting ideal for his purposes. No airline would likely plunge into bankruptcy, at least for a while. Kahn himself saw with remarkable clarity how fortunate his timing had been: "I came into the airline situation at precisely the perfect time—with demand recovering sharply relative to capacity, with a large number of empty seats simply begging to be priced at marginal costs, with the whole political atmosphere ripe for a relaxation of unnecessary protectionist and cartelist restrictions, and I have simply been doing what, I think, is the logical thing." The same point might be applied to the timing of his earlier experience in New York. Had Kahn attempted to institute time-of-day pricing in, say, 1954 or 1964 instead of 1974, it is difficult to see how he could have succeeded.[167]

Yet good timing in no sense diminishes the importance of his contributions. In regulatory strategy as in other types of business and political strategy, timing often does determine success or failure. Adams had proved that in the 1870s, and so had James Landis in the 1930s. Kahn's triumph, like theirs, was to see the opportunity clearly and to take advantage of it, acting with full commitment and conviction.

CHAPTER 8

Regulation Reconsidered

I F THIS WERE A BOOK of pictures rather than words, it would contain three different types of photographs. The biographical sections on Adams, Brandeis, Landis, and Kahn would be detailed closeup portraits, each showing a single strategist who succeeded or failed in making regulation work. The short connecting chapters would appear as medium-range photographs depicting a regional or national landscape that was undergoing slow but significant change, such as the change through the seasons from spring to winter. Now, in this final section of the book, I want to add a third perspective: a satellite photograph of the broad regulatory scene, expressed in a few general conclusions about the history of regulation. Most of these have been foreshadowed earlier in the book; others make explicit what has so far been only implied. I bring them together here to form a brief panoramic commentary on the significance of the regulatory experience in America.

As the historical record shows, the regulatory tradition has been adapted to many different ends and purposes. Regulation has served as a versatile tool whose handle has been seized at different times by reformers, business managers, bureaucrats, and lawyers—and manipulated as often for the particular interests of one of these special groups as for the general interest of the American public.

Over time, regulation has performed not only economic tasks, but political, legal, and cultural ones as well. Among the many particular functions that regulation has been used to serve are the functions of:

(a) disclosure and publicity (SEC, Adams' sunshine commission);
(b) protection and cartelization of industries (ICC, FCC, CAB before Kahn);
(c) containment of monopoly and oligopoly (FPC, FTC, Antitrust Division, state utility commissions);
(d) promotion of safety for consumers and workers (Consumer Product Safety Commission, Occupational Safety and Health Administration);
(e) legitimization of the capitalist order (SEC, Environmental Protection Agency).

Obviously such a list could be longer or differently stated. The general point is that regulation has served a variety of purposes, some of which (such as items b and c above) have been mutually inconsistent.

In view of these diverse and sometimes contradictory functions, all overarching theories and heroic generalizations about "Regulation" (with a capital R) run an extremely high risk of being in error. No single theory from any academic discipline can predict precisely which industries will be regulated and which will not. Some industries that in other market economies tend toward cartelization are, in America, regulated—but not all. Some regulated industries in America have social-overhead functions and are "affected with a public interest"—but not all. Some are "natural monopolies," with sharply declining costs to scale—but not all. Much of the American transportation industry is regulated—but not all of it.

Like the application of regulation to industries, the behavior of regulatory commissions, once they have been created, shows no clear single pattern. All agencies do not follow a standard "life cycle," for example, going from youthful exuberance to middle age, then finally to geriatric decrepitude. Instead, young agencies sometimes behave sluggishly (as did the early FTC) and old ones vigorously (the CAB under Alfred Kahn). No stage-by-stage evolution, nor any other assured expectation of agency behavior, can be predicted on the basis of actual regulatory history.[1]

The single constant in the American experience with regulation has been controversy. Here the reason why is not hard to find. Many of the diverse functions assigned to regulatory commissions were regarded by legislatures as essential tasks, but very difficult for existing governmental institutions to perform. Because legislators did not wish to burden themselves with such duties, they passed the responsibility to specialized agencies. But whatever agency received the assignment was also forced to accept the intrinsic controversy that had created each task in the first place. Almost by definition, therefore, controversy became attached to regulation like a Siamese twin. For the same reason, issues common to regulatory agencies are unlikely ever to be settled, once and for all, so long as the United States remains an open, democratic society.

As in so many other aspects of American politics, the fundamental controversy underlying the history of regulation has been an ongoing need to work out the inevitable tradeoffs between the good of the whole society, on the one hand, and the rights of the individual, on the other. In regulation, these tradeoffs have appeared most clearly as ways of relieving the persistent tension between the forces seeking to implement economic efficiency for the broad benefit of American society, and those dedicated to guaranteeing the observance of legal due process for every individual member of that society. At different times in our history, each party to these fundamental tensions has established a clear advantage over the other. On balance, however, it seems clear that the concern about legal process has controlled the outcome of regulation more often than has the concern about the substance of economic efficiency. In economists' language, this means that the concern for equity has generally triumphed over the quest for efficiency. In lawyers' terms, it means that in regulation the judicial model has usually triumphed over the legislative and administrative model. In cultural terms, it means that the concern for fairness and for the protection of the diverse interests of all affected individuals has most often won out over the concern for overall growth in the national economy. More generally in political terms, it means that regulation is best understood as a political settlement, undertaken in an effort to keep peace within the polity.

Overall, the conclusion appears inescapable that regulation in America has more often functioned as a protective device rather than as a promotional or developmental one. Of course, protection was not always inappropriate. By holding in check socially destructive forms of behavior, protective regulation often cushioned the impact of rapid industrial change. In America, in contrast to older societies, so many other forces consistently acted to promote pell-mell economic growth that regulation can hardly be condemned for not always doing so.

Because the appropriate balance between economic efficiency and legal due process has seldom been self-evident, individual persons and particular ideas have mattered a great deal in regulatory history. Thus, most of this book has explored the roles of particular persons, and I rest that part of my case on the biographies of Adams, Brandeis, Landis, and Kahn. The more general role of ideas in the history of regulation, however, deserves some additional comment. As the political scientist James Q. Wilson has written, "We must be struck at every turn by the importance of ideas. Regulation itself is such an idea; deregulation is another . . . To the extent [that] an agency can choose, its choices will be importantly shaped by what its executives learned in college a decade or two earlier."[2]

Ideas about regulation, as Wilson implies, vary with time. During the 1930s, national policymakers generally held the powerful conviction that market mechanisms left to themselves would produce widespread injustice and even inefficiency. Hence they believed that an active federal government was essential for the protection of the public interest. So these political activists created a broad portfolio of new, independent agencies: the SEC, the FCC, the CAB, and so on. A few decades later, during the 1960s and 1970s, a new generation of policymakers embraced a very different idea. Rather than applauding the old activism, they became convinced that many of the independent commissions created during the 1930s had since been captured by the very interests that these agencies had been set up to regulate.

Partly as a result of the capture idea, there arose during the 1960s a curious two-pronged reform movement: pointing, on the one hand, toward deregulation and, on the other, toward a new wave of large-scale social and environmental regulation. These new rules were to be enforced not by independent commissions of the 1930s variety, which usually administered brief general statutes designed to give broad discretion to a group of commissioners acting collegially; but rather by an entirely different type of agency, with a single executive at its head (who could be held individually responsible for success or failure) and an agenda set in advance by the explicit provisions of extremely detailed legislation. New laws such as the Clean Air Act and the Occupational Safety and Health Act, often running to scores of pages in length, were calculated to minimize administrative discretion and to close all possible loopholes. Meanwhile, on the other prong, the deregulation movement—whose basic intellectual premise was that economic markets *do* work well—also advanced, simultaneously but contradictorily, gaining momentum alongside the companion movement toward growth of regulation in the areas of social and environmental policy.

The result, by the 1980s, presented a most peculiar spectacle. In an ironic historical example of the ways in which ideas can move policymakers in opposite directions, significant deregulation had been instituted for such industries as airlines, trucking, railroads, financial markets, and telecommunications. At the same time, additional social and environmental regulation had become firmly embedded in the structure of state and federal government in such a form as to make any capture by regulated interests very difficult, if not impossible.

The movement of ideas alone, of course, had not produced this ironic result. Despite the power of thought in the history of regulation, ideas in themselves could not determine concrete outcomes. Instead, ideas had to interact with particular economic and political circumstances to form a reciprocal relationship in which one or both might be altered. Nor, in any absolute sense, did the ideas themselves have to be demonstrably true in order to exert strong influence. We have seen, for instance, how Louis Brandeis' flawed idea of competition moved the hearts of his contemporaries. To cite a second example, the disparate sets of ideas underlying the initial imposition of regulation in airlines and trucking during the 1930s, and the later deregulation of these same industries in the 1970s and 1980s, could not both have been correct, in the absolute sense. Yet both sets of ideas became institutionalized. What had changed was the historical context in which opposing ideas about the legitimacy and actual performance of economic markets were defined.

During the 1930s, a period not only of depression but also of economic *de*flation, policymakers searched for some way to stabilize prices, as a means of preventing further economic decline. By the 1970s, however, deflation no longer provided the historical filter; indeed, it had become almost inconceivable as a problem for policy to solve. Instead, *in*flation was now the pressing issue, and thus the same protectionist regulations that had been applied in the 1930s to combat deflation now seemed inappropriate to the new economic context. Both ideas remained alive, but a different time meant a different choice for public policy. To state the same point in a more general sense, it is clear that in American history both the producer-oriented protectionist tradition, on the one hand, and the consumer-oriented anticartelist tradition on the other have remained hostage to immediate economic conditions. The strengths of each tradition have ebbed and flowed in response to several external forces: the business cycle, the different degrees of maturity reached by different product markets, and the conditions of international war and peace.

In speculating about the future, it is difficult to foresee with much additional precision what new historical contexts for regulation might develop. But if the past is any guide, a good deal of caution is in order. What I have called in this book the "economist's hour" of the 1970s and 1980s, for example, represents a phenomenon of unpredictable duration. Certainly the economist's hour in the history of regulation came relatively late, long after other notably different hours during which the muckraker and the lawyer alternately held center stage. This history makes it seem unlikely that any single approach to regulation will ever triumph. Therefore, although we may live in the golden years of regulatory economics and its practitioners, we should be in no hurry to crown the economist as permanent king of the regulatory hill.

Economic analysis, however, will always remain directly relevant to regulatory policy. This is true because every industry, whether regulated or not, does possess a certain underlying economic structure: characteristics that make it different from other industries and that help to shape the internal conditions for regulatory opportunities and constraints. *More than any other single factor, this underlying structure of the particular industry being regulated has defined the context in which regulatory agencies have operated.* Sometimes the differences between industry structures can be radical: the railroad industry, with its huge fixed costs and enormous scale economies, could hardly differ more fundamentally from the securities industry, with its paper assets and labor-intensive structure. In other cases the differences can be more subtle, as in the contrast between center and peripheral firms, and the related distinction between tight and loose forms of horizontal combination.

Because the underlying characteristics of the industry so often shape the limits of governmental action, the industry may be regarded as the dog, the regulatory agency only as the tail. Yet many students of regulation have assumed that tails wag dogs and, further, that one standard type of tail can wag whatever breed of dog may be attached. Such observers, by focusing primarily on the similarities of regulatory commissions (most of which were bipartisan, appointed by the executive, expert in their fields, and so on), have missed a larger truth: the industries that these similarly-structured commissions regulated were extremely diverse. Thus these observers have duplicated the errors made historically by many regulators themselves, who often paid more attention to legal processes and administrative procedures than to the greater task of framing strategies appropriate to the particular industries they were regulating. For all parties who seek to understand regulation, the most important single consideration is the appropriateness of the regulatory strategy to the industry involved.[3]

The process of fitting regulatory strategies to particular industries is a difficult task, partly because industrial structures, like regulatory ideas, can change over time. The railroad industry represented a true natural monopoly when the Interstate Commerce Commission first emerged to regulate it during the 1880s. But several decades later, this natural monopoly status of railroads had disappeared before the rise of alternative modes of transportation—the automobile, truck, and airplane. Clearly, by the 1930s, some central assumptions behind the whole scheme of national railroad regulation needed to be revised, and regulatory policy adjusted accordingly. Yet until the 1970s little was done, as assumptions remained those of the 1880s. In the meantime, the Interstate Commerce Commission kept rates inflexible, prevented industry rationalization by blocking truck-rail mergers, and delayed for years the widespread application of unit-train technology. The ICC took so much time to recognize the revolutionary changes in the transportation industries that regulatory policy lagged badly behind market reality, causing unintended injury to the very railroad industry the commission was trying to protect.

Elsewhere, a similar process of unacknowledged change occurred in the communications industries. When Congress created the Federal Communications Commission in 1934, legislators acted on an assumption, valid at the time, that the electromagnetic spectrum (what physicists used to call the "ether") was finite. The lawmakers reasoned that if too many stations used the ether at once, radio signals would become garbled and communication would be impossible. Thus competitors had to be limited in number, through regulatory allocation of different parts of the spectrum to different broadcasting stations. Later on, however, new technology completely altered the situation. Through the use of satellite communications and dish receivers, community television companies in effect created vast new amounts of ether, thereby accommodating dozens of additional broadcast stations. When that occurred, the market power of the three major television networks diminished rapidly, and television broadcasting as an industry began to drift away from center status and toward peripheral.

To cite still another example, a situation of natural monopoly prevailed for many years in long-distance telephoning, based on the once-valid principle that a single set of transcontinental wires could most economically serve consumers' needs. But in the 1960s and 1970s, a technological revolution in microwave communication destroyed that premise and ended the natural monopoly in long-distance telephoning. As the significance of this technological shift became clear, new companies emerged to compete for long-distance telephone business, and just as quickly a movement to deregulate the telephone industry began. By 1984, the giant Bell System, once the most conspicuous natural monopoly in America, had divided itself into a number of much smaller companies. What had been a thoroughgoing center industry (telephoning) now became part center (local telephone service, heavy equipment manufacturing) and part peripheral (long-distance service, high-technology research and development, and light manufacturing). As a result of these seismic changes in industry structure, the regulation of telecommunications became during the 1980s one of the most publicized and controversial problems of state and federal government.[4]

For scholars, the evolution of both the telephone industry and television broadcasting provided outstanding examples of the protean nature of industrial organization. Not since the early emergence of center firms out of the advanced production technology of the late nineteenth century had there appeared such clear instances of the relationship between scientific change and subsequent shifts in the structure of existing industries. Traditionally,

such shifts had been from peripheral to center status, but the communications revolution showed how the movement could work in
the opposite direction as well. The implications for regulators
were profound, and the task of framing effective regulatory strategies, always one of the most difficult of governmental arts, became
in these industries still more challenging.

In thinking about the future of regulation, whether in broadcasting, telephones, or any other industry, it is important to keep in
mind the ambiguous record of the past. Even though much of regulatory history is tinged with apparent failure, regulation cannot
properly be said either to have "failed" or "succeeded" in an overall historical sense. Instead, individual regulatory experiments and
episodes must be judged against a standard true to the particular
historical moment. Many observers hold a contrary view and insist
on a single overriding verdict of failure. Because of this prevailing
opinion in our time, it becomes useful to speculate about ways in
which the same judgment might be applied to other parts of government. Can it be said with equal justice, for example, that legislation in general has failed historically, or that the court system
has failed, or that the office of the presidency has failed—without
specifying exactly which legislation, which court on what case,
and which president on what issue? Although the answer might
seem self-evident, the fact remains that in popular perceptions
over the last three decades regulation has been regarded as a syn-
onym for failure. Even in some of the best scholarship on regulation, failure has often been applied not merely as a conclusion but
also as a premise, a tacit assumption hidden behind apparently
scholarly explanations presented in theoretical forms: the theories
of capture, of public choice, of taxation by regulation, and several
others.[5]

To weigh against these multiple theories premised on failure,
we have only one premised on success. But it is a very useful one:
the theory of "public use of private interest." According to this
idea, regulators should always exploit the natural incentives of
regulated interests to serve particular goals that the regulators
themselves have carefully defined in advance.[6] And, in fact, the
historical record suggests that regulation in America has succeeded best when it has respected these incentives instead of ignoring them; when it has based its strategies less on some idealized

vision of what the economy should do and more on a clear understanding of what the economy actually is doing. Regulatory strategies framed in ignorance or disregard of real economic conditions
and market incentives—and the number of such attempts has been
legion—have usually led only to unfortunate results. By contrast,
strategies framed with these conditions and incentives in mind
have often produced strikingly successful outcomes, as the stories
of Adams, Landis, and Kahn demonstrate so clearly.

7. Adams, *Autobiography*, p. 170.

8. U.S. Bureau of the Census, *Historical Statistics of the United States: Colonial Times to 1970* (Washington: Government Printing Office, 1975), II, 739–740, 1102–1103; Alfred D. Chandler, Jr., ed., *The Railroads: The Nation's First Big Business* (New York: Harcourt, Brace and World, 1965), pp. 3–18; Henry Adams, *The Education of Henry Adams: An Autobiography* (Boston: Houghton Mifflin, 1918), p. 240.

9. Massachusetts *First Annual Report of the Board of Railroad Commissioners* (Boston: Wright & Potter, 1870), p. 43; Thoreau, *Walden*, J. Lyndon Shanley, ed. (Princeton: Princeton University Press, 1971), pp. 117–118.

10. See Chandler, *The Railroads;* George Rogers Taylor, *The Transportation Revolution, 1815–1860* (New York: Holt, Rinehart, 1951); John F. Stover, *American Railroads* (Chicago: University of Chicago Press, 1961); and Edward Chase Kirkland, *Men, Cities, and Transportation: A Study in New England History, 1820–1900* (Cambridge: Harvard University Press, 1948).

11. *Historical Statistics of the United States: Colonial Times to 1970,* II, 732.

12. Adams, *Autobiography,* p. 9; Mrs. Wendell Garrett, "The Published Writings of Charles Francis Adams, II (1835–1915): An Annotated Checklist," *Proceedings of the Massachusetts Historical Society,* 72 (October 1957–December 1960), 238–293.

13. Adams, "The Reign of King Cotton," *Atlantic Monthly,* 7 (April 1861), 450–465.

14. Adams to Wells, January 14, 1869, Wells Papers, Manuscript Division, Library of Congress, Washington, D.C.; Kirkland, *Adams,* pp. 34–37; Adams, letter to *The Nation,* 32 (April 28, 1881), 295.

15. Henry Adams, *The Education,* p. 240; John G. Sproat, *"The Best Men": Liberal Reformers in the Gilded Age* (New York: Oxford University Press, 1968); Stow Persons, *The Decline of American Gentility* (New York: Columbia University Press, 1973); John Tomsich, *A Genteel Endeavor: American Culture and Politics in the Gilded Age* (Stanford: Stanford University Press, 1971). Geoffrey Blodgett has delineated a career pattern in many ways similar to Adams' in "Frederick Law Olmsted: Landscape Architecture as Conservative Reform," *Journal of American History,* 42 (March 1976), 869–889. Parallels with Adams' economic thought are evident in the cases of David A. Wells, Edward Atkinson, Carroll D. Wright, and Francis A. Walker; see Daniel Horowitz, "Genteel Observers: New England Economic Writers and Industrialization," *New England Quarterly,* 48 (March 1975), 65–83.

16. These themes are synthesized from the following articles by Adams: "The Railroad System," *North American Review,* 104 (April 1867), 476–511; "Legislative Control over Railway Charters," *American Law Review,* 1 (April 1867), 451–476; "Boston," *North American Review,* 106 (January 1868), 1–25 and 106 (April 1868), 557–591; "The Erie Railroad Row," *American Law Review,* 3 (October 1868), 41–86; "Railroad Inflation," *North American Review,* 108 (January 1869), 130–164; "A Chapter of Erie," *North American Review,* 109 (July 1869), 30–106; "Railway Problems in 1869," *North American Review,* 110 (January 1870), 116–150; "Railway Commissions," *Journal of Social Sci-*

Notes

1. Adams and the Sunshine Commission

1. Thomas B. Adams, "A Word Worth Remembering," *Proceedings of the Massachusetts Historical Society*, 72 (October 1957–December 1960), 237.

2. Adams' achievements "in many paths" are reflected in the substantial body of scholarly studies of him in different roles. The standard biography is Edward Chase Kirkland, *Charles Francis Adams, Jr., 1835–1915: The Patrician at Bay* (Cambridge: Harvard University Press, 1965). Adams told his own story in *An Autobiography, with a Memorial Address delivered November 17, 1915, by Henry Cabot Lodge* (Boston: Houghton Mifflin, 1916), hereafter cited as Adams, *Autobiography*. Tributes and recollections of associates were published in *Proceedings of the Massachusetts Historical Society*, 48 (October 1914–June 1915), 383–423; see also "Three Views of Charles Francis Adams, II," ibid., 72 (October 1957–December 1960), 212–237, by three descendants. The most insightful dissertation is Helen Rena Upson, "Order and System: Charles Francis Adams, Jr., and the Railroad Problem," University of Iowa, 1969. On Adams as historian, see Arthur Herbert Auten, "Charles Francis Adams, Jr., Historian: An Appraisal," diss., Western Reserve University, 1965; and Robert L. Beisner, "Brooks Adams and Charles Francis Adams, Jr.: Historians of Massachusetts," *New England Quarterly*, 35 (March 1962), 48–70. Adams is compared with his brothers in William F. Dowling, Jr., "The Political Thought of a Generation of Adamses," diss., Harvard University, 1950. See also Richard Colton Lyon, "Charles Francis Adams, Jr., and the Age of Steam," diss., University of Minnesota, 1964; and L. Moody Sims, "Charles Francis Adams, Jr., and the Negro Question," *New England Quarterly*, 41 (September 1968), 436–438.

3. Adams, *Autobiography*, pp. 4, 19, 21–24, 31, 37; Kirkland, *Adams*, pp. 1–13; Charles's image of his father is confirmed by Martin Duberman, *Charles Francis Adams, 1807–1886* (Stanford: Stanford University Press, 1968).

4. Adams, *Autobiography*, pp. 13–15, 30–60, 124; Kirkland, *Adams*, pp. 13–20; Francis E. Parker to Otis Norcross, June 24, 1869, in Miscellaneous File No. 18 (1864–1885), Massachusetts Historical Society, Boston.

5. Adams, *Autobiography*, pp. 60–113; Kirkland, *Adams*, pp. 21–22; Duberman, *Adams*, chaps. 18 and 19.

6. Adams, *Autobiography*, pp. 13, 114–167; Worthington Chauncey Ford, ed., *A Cycle of Adams Letters, 1861–1865* (Boston: Houghton Mifflin, 1920), II, 261–262, 264–265; Kirkland, *Adams*, pp. 22–31.

ence, 2 (1870), 233–236; "The Government and the Railroad Corporations," *North American Review,* 112 (January 1871), 31–61. In addition to these pieces, Adams published several short items in *The Nation,* anonymously in most cases. Anonymity characterized a few of the listed articles as well, but the Boston circles Adams was trying to impress knew the author's identity.

17. Adams, "The Railroad System," p. 484. Sociologists and historians will note the similarity of this analysis to the "community-society" model associated with Ferdinand Tönnies and exploited by such historians as Robert H. Wiebe and Samuel P. Hays.

18. Ibid., p. 495.

19. Adams, "Railroad Inflation," pp. 144–149; Adams, "The Railroad System," p. 485.

20. Adams, "Railway Commissions," p. 234; emphasis in original (here and later).

21. Ibid. There is a vast literature on monopoly and its enemies in America. A convenient summary and analysis is in Arthur P. Dudden, "Antimonopolism, 1865–1890," diss., University of Michigan, 1950. See also Richard Hofstadter, "What Happened to the Antitrust Movement? Notes on the Evolution of an American Creed," in Earl F. Cheit, ed., *The Business Establishment* (New York: Wiley, 1964), pp. 113–151; and Ellis W. Hawley, *The New Deal and the Problem of Monopoly: A Study in Economic Ambivalence* (Princeton: Princeton University Press, 1966), pp. 3–16. See also Chapters 2–4 of the present book.

22. Adams, "The Railroad System," p. 508; Adams, "Railroad Inflation," p. 159. In the latter article Adams proposed an experiment with a contract system of railroad control, with private operation renewable after new biddings conducted by an expert tribunal (a commission, in other words), on behalf of the state.

23. Adams, "The Railroad System," pp. 496–502; Adams, "Railroad Inflation," pp. 150–154; Adams, "Railroad Legislation," pp. 18–32.

24. Adams, "Legislative Control over Railway Charters," pp. 473–474; Adams, "Railroad Legislation," pp. 25–28; see also Stephen Salsbury, *The State, the Investor, and the Railroad: The Boston & Albany, 1825–1867* (Cambridge: Harvard University Press, 1967).

25. Adams, "Railroad Legislation," p. 28.

26. Ibid., p. 32; see also Adams, "The Railroad System," pp. 497–499.

27. Adams, "Railroad Inflation," pp. 137–139. On the English experience, see Henry Parris, *Government and the Railways in Nineteenth-Century Britain* (London: Routledge and Kegan Paul, 1965).

28. Adams, "Railroad Inflation," pp. 137–140, 143–144.

29. Ibid., pp. 150–157.

30. Ibid., pp. 158, 163–164; Adams, "The Railroad System," pp. 497–499; Adams, "Boston," pp. 16–18, 24–25, and 558–559; Adams, "Railway Commissions," pp. 235–236.

31. Adams, Manuscript Diary, entry of May 12, 1869, Charles Francis Adams, Jr., Papers, Massachusetts Historical Society; Adams, "A Chapter of Erie," pp. 30–106; see also Adams, "An Erie Raid," *North American Review,*

112 (April 1871), 241–291. These items, together with other works by Charles and Henry, were anthologized as *Chapters of Erie and Other Essays* (New York: Henry Holt, 1886).

32. Adams, "A Chapter of Erie," p. 53.

33. Ibid., p. 103.

34. The early chapters of Kirkland, *Adams*, provide additional detail on Adams' malaise about his career during this period.

35. Kirkland, *Men, Cities, and Transportation*, II, 233–237.

36. Ibid., pp. 237–238; William A. Crafts (secretary of the Board of Railroad Commissioners), "Ten Years' Working of the Massachusetts Railroad Commission," in *State Railroad Commissions* (New York: Railroad Gazette, 1883), pp. 3–29; Crafts, "The Massachusetts Railroad Commission," *Engineering Magazine*, 10 (November 1895), 286–294; *Boston Daily Advertiser*, May 13 and 14, June 5, 8, 9, 19, and 30, 1869.

37. Adams, Manuscript Diary, dates noted.

38. Adams, Manuscript Diary, March 17, March 23, May 13, May 28, June 19, June 21, June 22, June 25, 1869; Francis E. Parker to Otis Norcross, June 24, 1869; Clement Hugh Hill to Norcross, June 21, 1869 ("Mr. Adams as you know has paid great attention to this whole subject of railroads and takes great interest in it; and I believe drafted the act creating the Board . . . I think that his appointment will be very serviceable to the City and the State.") Both of these letters are in Miscellaneous File No. 18 (1864–1885), Massachusetts Historical Society. The Parker letter is doubly interesting because Adams wrote years later that he would still like to know "what the keen-sighted, incisive Parker thought of me and my proceedings" (Adams, *Autobiography*, p. 42).

39. Massachusetts *Acts and Resolves*, Chap. 408 (1869), pp. 699–703.

40. "The law creating the board and defining its field of action was clumsily drawn," Adams wrote in 1878, "and throughout it there was apparent a spirit of distrust in its purpose . . . In fact, however, the law could not have been improved. Had it not been a flagrant legislative guess, it would have been an inspiration." See Adams, *Railroads: Their Origin and Problems* (New York: Putnam's Sons, 1878). But cf. *Autobiography*, pp. 172–174, and the evidence cited above of Adams' own draftsmanship of the act.

41. Massachusetts *Acts and Resolves*, Chap. 408 (1869), pp. 699–703; Adams, *Railroads: Their Origin and Problems*, p. 138; Adams to Charles S. Osgood, chairman of the Committee on Railroads of the Massachusetts General Court, February 20, 1879 (*Massachusetts House Document 225*, 1879), p. 3.

42. Leonard D. White, "The Origins of Utility Commissions in Massachusetts," *Journal of Political Economy*, 29 (March 1921), 177–197; Irston R. Barnes, *Public Utility Control in Massachusetts* (New Haven: Yale University Press, 1930), pp. 1–19; Frank Hendrick, *Railway Control by Commissions* (New York: Putnam, 1900), pp. 120–139; Kirkland, *Men, Cities, and Transportation*, II, 247–250; Adams, Manuscript Diary, February 3, February 16, February 24, February 25, March 2, March 10, March 15, April 5, April 30, May 2, June 3, June 13, 1870; the same pattern of contacts with the governor and legislature persist throughout the 1870s, as revealed in Adams' diary. See, e.g.,

March 7, 1871: "This living six months of each year under a legislative harrow is simply execrable,—it destroys all ones nerve."

43. *Massachusetts House Document 225* (1879), pp. 10–11. The budgets of each year are set forth in detail in the *Massachusetts Annual Report of the Board of Railroad Commissioners,* 1870–1880. The budget of 1874 was typical: $3152.52, plus $1640 for the printing of reports, plus salaries (*Fifth Annual Report,* pp. 62, 153).

44. Adams, Manuscript Diary, August 2, August 9, September 25, December 6, 1869; on the report, Dec. 10–13: "I came in prepared to face my colleagues with the draft of my report,—to my surprise they took it very kindly—indeed very well,—and so my views may be considered as successfully lanched [sic]." On the Appleton case, see diary entry for May 2, 1871: "My colleague Appleton, has settled his hash by calmly acknowledging to the habit of receiving fees from railroads."

45. Adams, Manuscript Diary, entries for December through February, 1869–1878; Adams to John D. Long, January 2, 1878, Long Papers, Massachusetts Historical Society; the "winter work" quotation is in a diary entry dated November 1, 1878.

46. Adams, Manuscript Diary, November 19, 1870 and passim; the variety of hearings conducted by the board is evident from the tabulations in the *Annual Reports.*

47. Adams, Manuscript Diary, December 12, 1873; Garrett, "The Published Writings of Charles Francis Adams, II," pp. 239–240; Adams to Schurz, October 31, 1878, Schurz Papers, Manuscript Division, Library of Congress.

48. In a letter to the chairman of the legislature's committee on railroads, Adams explained the policy: "In dealing with railroads as between railroads and individuals, it is futile to talk about law, declaratory and penal, and the usual process of the courts. Except in extraordinary cases, the remedy through this process is too slow and too expensive, while the power and wealth of the corporations, as compared with individuals, is too great. It is altogether different in proceedings before this commission. There are here no technicalities, or forms of procedure. The investigation takes place at once and upon the spot, and a conclusion is reached with no unnecessary delay." *Massachusetts House Document 225* (1879), p. 4.

49. See Carl McFarland, *Judicial Control of the Federal Trade Commission and the Interstate Commerce Commission 1920–1930* (Cambridge: Harvard University Press, 1933); Henry J. Friendly, *The Federal Administrative Agencies: The Need for Better Definition of Standards* (Cambridge: Harvard University Press, 1962); James M. Landis, *Report on Regulatory Agencies to the President-Elect* (U.S. Senate Committee on the Judiciary, 86th Cong., 2nd sess., 1960); and Richard B. Stewart, "The Reformation of American Administrative Law," *Harvard Law Review,* 88 (June 1975), 1667–1813.

50. Adams, *Notes on Railroad Accidents* (New York: Putnam's Sons, 1879), pp. 3–6.

51. Kirkland, *Men, Cities, and Transportation,* II, 353–354.

52. Massachusetts *Third Annual Report of the Board of Railroad Commissioners* (1872), pp. xciii–cxlv.

53. Ibid.; see also *Report of the Committee of the Directors of the Eastern Railroad Company, Appointed to Investigate the Causes of the Accident at Revere, on the Evening of August 26, 1871* (Boston, Eastern Railroad Company, 1872), copy in Corporation Records, Baker Library, Harvard University Graduate School of Business Administration.

54. Adams, *Notes on Railroad Accidents,* pp. 138–140.

55. *Railroad Gazette,* September 2 and 9, 1871; Adams, *Notes on Railroad Accidents,* p. 142.

56. Adams, Manuscript Diary, entries for August 28–September 7, 1871; Massachusetts *Third Annual Report of the Board of Railroad Commissioners* (1872), pp. cii–ciii.

57. Adams, Manuscript Diary, October 18, 1871; Massachusetts *Third Annual Report of the Board of Railroad Commissioners* (1872), pp. cvi–cvii, ccl–cclxiv; *Report of the Committee of the Directors of the Eastern Railroad Company,* passim.

58. *Rules and Regulations for Operating Railroads, as Agreed to by the Committee of Railroad Officers, Appointed Sept. 19, 1871* (Boston: Wright & Potter, 1872); Massachusetts *Third Annual Report of the Board of Railroad Commissioners,* pp. cvi–cvii, ccl–cclxiv; Adams, *Notes on Railroad Accidents,* p. 238.

59. The following pamphlets, all located in Baker Library, Harvard University Graduate School of Business Administration, show the effects of the commission's work with the committee of executives: *Rules and Regulations for the Management of the Boston and Providence Railroad* (Boston: Superintendent's Office, 1872); *Regulations Governing Employees upon the Main and Branch Lines of the Boston & Maine Railroad* (Boston: The Company, 1872); *General Rules and Regulations of the Eastern Railroad Company, for the Government and Information of Employees Only* (Boston: The Company, 1878); for influence outside Massachusetts, see *Proceedings of the Second Quarterly Meeting of the Western and Southern Railway Association* (Indianapolis: The Association, 1872), copy in Albert Fink Papers, Manuscript Division, Library of Congress.

60. Massachusetts *Third Annual Report of the Board of Railroad Commissioners* (1872), pp. cxix, cxliii–cxliv; Kirkland, *Men, Cities, and Transportation,* II, 368–376.

61. Ibid.; Adams' statements about juries, however, begged the difficult question of ever reaching a jury. As the history of liability insurance and workmen's compensation in America shows, corporations did everything in their power to avoid the vicissitudes of tort cases before juries. The evolution of the response of public policy to such doctrines as the "fellow-servant rule" and "contributory negligence" may be traced in Carl A. Auerbach, et al., *The Legal Process: An Introduction to Decision-Making by Judicial, Legislative, Executive, and Administrative Agencies* (San Francisco: Chandler, 1961).

62. Massachusetts *Seventh Annual Report of the Board of Railroad Commissioners* (1876), I, 2; Massachusetts *Thirtieth Annual Report of the Board of Railroad Commissioners* (1899), p. 14; Kirkland, Men, Cities, and Transportation, II, 269–273.

63. Massachusetts *Twelfth Annual Report of the Board of Railroad Commissioners* (1881), pp. 4–16.

64. Massachusetts *Second Annual Report of the Board of Railroad Commissioners* (1871), pp. cxv–cxx; Massachusetts *Fourth Annual Report of the Board of Railroad Commissioners* (1873), pp. 55–64; *Massachusetts House Documents 266, 284, 285* (1873) Massachusetts *Fifth Annual Report of the Board of Railroad Commissioners* (1874), pp. 36–44; *Massachusetts Senate Document 60* (1875); see also Massachusetts *An Index-Digest of the Reported Decisions, Precedents, and General Principles Enunciated by the Board of Railroad Commissioners From 1870 to 1904, Inclusive* (Boston: Wright & Potter, 1905).

65. Massachusetts *First Annual Report of the Board of Railroad Commissioners* (1870), pp. 59–60; Massachusetts *Third Annual Report of the Board of Railroad Commissioners* (1872), pp. clxx–clxxiv; Massachusetts *Fourth Annual Report of the Board of Railroad Commissioners* (1873), pp. 55–64. This last source responded to a specific inquiry by the General Court "to consider the subject of regulating railroad fares and freights by law, and report in the form of a bill or otherwise."

66. Massachusetts *Third Annual Report of the Board of Railroad Commissioners* (1872), pp. ccxix–ccxx; *Railroad Gazette*, September 2, 1871.

67. Massachusetts *Third Annual Report of the Board of Railroad Commissioners* (1872), pp. ccxxi–ccxxii.

68. Ibid., xxiii–lxxxvi; Adams, Manuscript Diary, entry of December 6, 1871.

69. Adams used these figures somewhat loosely. He may have had in mind prospective reductions and savings, but the amounts mentioned applied to the preceding year, which included the few months prior to the issuance of the circular letters. Massachusetts *Third Annual Report of the Board of Railroad Commissioners* (1872), pp. xxiv, xxxii, xxxiv.

70. Adams, "A Novel Scheme for Securing Railroad Competition," *The Nation*, 12 (January 12, 1871), 21–22 (this was an even earlier yardstick proposal); Adams, *The Regulation of All Railroads Through the State-Ownership of One, Speech on Behalf of the Massachusetts Board of Railroad Commissioners, Made Before the Joint Standing Legislative Committee on Railways, February 14, 1873* (Boston: Osgood, 1873); Adams, Manuscript Diary, February 14, 1873. For the complete story of the Hoosac Tunnel, see Kirkland, *Men, Cities, and Transportation*, I, 387–432.

71. Thomas K. McCraw, *TVA and the Power Fight, 1933–1939* (Philadelphia: J.B. Lippincott, 1971).

72. Average freight rates per ton mile, in cents, for Massachusetts roads:

1861	3.8¢	1885	1.59¢
1865	4.6	1890	1.45
1870	3.9	1895	1.28
1875	2.5	1900	1.22
1880	1.84		

Bulk coal rates per ton mile, distance between 40 and 60 miles, in cents:

	1869	1876	1884–85
Boston and Providence Railroad	3.65¢	3.1¢	2.34¢
Old Colony Railroad	4.23	3.1	3.125
Fitchburg Railroad	5.60	4.0	2.8
Boston to Worcester	4.09	2.05	1.8

Passenger fares per mile, in cents, various categories:

	Average all fares	Through	Single local	Commutation	Season
1861	2.61¢	–	–	–	–
1870	2.7	2.1(1871)	2.99(1871)	–	1.02
1880	2.05	1.94	2.45	–	0.91
1890	1.82	2.06	1.932	1.544	0.725
1900	1.75	1.973	1.836	1.168	0.625

See Kirkland, *Men, Cities, and Transportation*, II, 273, 274, 278, 291.

73. Boston and Albany Railroad, *Eighth Annual Report* (Springfield, Mass.: The Company, 1876), p. 7; *Ninth Annual Report* (1877), pp. 6–7; *Tenth Annual Report* (1878), p. 6, Corporation Records, Baker Library, Havard University Graduate School of Business Administration. Adams' similar interpretations of the decline in rates may be traced in his attacks on the Granger Laws of the upper Middle West. See, for example, Adams, "The Granger Movement," *North American Review*, 120 (April 1875), 394–424.

74. Massachusetts *Second Annual Report of the Board of Railroad Commissioners* (1871), pp. xx, cx. The legislature modified the language slightly; see Kirkland, *Men, Cities, and Transportation*, II, 283.

75. This paragraph and the following five paragraphs are based on *Massachusetts House Document 102* (1877), pp. 1–10; Massachusetts *Ninth Annual Report of the Board of Railroad Commissioners* (1878), pp. 41–49; and Adams, "The Brotherhood of Locomotive Engineers," *The Nation*, 24 (March 15, 1877), 158.

76. Adams, "The Brotherhood of Locomotive Engineers," p. 158; Massachusetts *Ninth Annual Report of the Board of Railroad Commissioners* (1878), p. 50; Adams, *Autobiography*, p. 174.

77. Massachusetts *Ninth Annual Report of the Board of Railroad Commissioners* (1878), p. 49; *Massachusetts House Document 102* (1877), pp. 11–12, 17.

78. Adams, "The Brotherhood of Locomotive Engineers," *The Nation*, 24 (March 22, 1877), 173.

79. Adams persisted in his views long after the Boston & Maine affair. See Adams, "The Prevention of Railroad Strikes," *Scribner's*, 5 (April 1889), 424–430; and Adams, *Investigation and Publicity as Opposed to "Compulsory Arbitration"—A Paper Read before the American Civic Federation at Its Meeting in New York, Monday December 8, 1902* (Boston: n.p., 1902).

80. Adams, Manuscript Diary, entry of February 20, 1877.

81. See, especially, Marver H. Bernstein, *Regulating Business by Independent Commission* (Princeton: Princeton University Press, 1955).

82. Adams, letter to *The Nation*, 32 (April 28, 1881), 295.

83. Adams, Manuscript Diary, entry of April 28, 1869; Alfred D. Chandler, Jr., *Henry Varnum Poor, Business Editor, Analyst, and Reformer* (Cambridge: Harvard University Press, 1956).

84. Adams, Manuscript Diary, 1869–1872, passim; Adams, *Autobiography*, p. 187 ("I have continually attempted too much—always had too many irons in the fire").

85. Adams, Manuscript Diary, 1872–73, passim. Part of Adams' relaxed mood toward the commission derived from the latter's very success and acceptance, as the following diary entries show:

February 28, 1870: "Things are working at the State House,—"

March 5, 1870: "This is a great victory for me;—our influence is now secure until we make a mistake."

February 7, 1873: "In the evening a hearing before the r.r. com*ee* about connecting roads;—it makes me laugh to see the difference between the standing of the com*n* now before the com*ee* and what it was two years ago."

February 19, 1874: "To town and busied myself at Commi*ss* office and at the Leg*e* Com*ee* room,—oh! what a contrast it all is to three years ago!—now it is such very smooth sailing!—"

86. See Kirkland, *Adams*, chap. 3. One could argue that a significant shift in the separation of public and private affairs took place during the Gilded Age, and that one of the meanings of the period was its transitional nature from the easy interweavings of the pre-1850 era to the more rigid divorcement of the twentieth century. The hearings and committee report on the behavior of Adams' commission colleague Albert D. Briggs shed much light on this issue. Briggs was an engineer who continued his consultations on behalf of several railroads after his appointment to the board, with no sense of wrongdoing as his firm built bridges for such corporations as the Boston & Providence Railroad. Adams recognized Briggs's poor judgment but argued strongly (and successfully) for his retention, in part because Briggs was one of the best qualified and most dedicated colleagues he had had on the board. See the 178-page *Massachusetts House Document 324* (1876), *Report of the Committee on Railroads on the Investigation of Albert D. Briggs, One of the Board of Railroad Commissioners.*

87. Adams to Garfield, October 1, 1873, and January 18, 1877, Garfield Papers, Manuscript Division, Library of Congress; Adams to Schurz, March 17, May 21, July 11, December 18, 1876; June 30, July 7, 1877, Schurz Papers, Library of Congress; Adams to John D. Long, January 2, January 8, 1878, Long Papers, Massachusetts Historical Society; Adams, Manuscript Diary, November 1876–February 1877.

88. Adams, *Autobiography*, pp. 174–175; Adams, Manuscript Diary, January 29, February 9, 1877.

89. Again, the transition can be observed vividly in Adams' diary:

March 28, 1877: "My strike legislation was defeated yesterday, quite a disappointment to me. Began a hearing to-day on the New York & New England R.R.,—dull and dreary. Out at 4 o'cl and in evening finished my chapter on the Antinomian controversy." [This latter endeavor was ultimately published in Adams' *Three Episodes of Massachusetts History: The Settlement of Boston Bay; The Antinomian Controversy; A Study of Church and Town Government* (Boston: Houghton Mifflin, 1892).]

January 14, 1879: "Another panic today, just six months from last,—this time slight, over my Comn being legislated out of office. Have I hung on just too long?"

90. Bureau of Railway Economics, "Albert Fink, October 27, 1827–April 3, 1897. A Bibliographical Memoir of the Father of Railway Economics and Statistics in the United States," unpublished manuscript (1927), copy in Library of Congress; Ellen Fink Milton, *A Biography of Albert Fink* (Rochester: Commercial Controls Corporation, 1951).

91. Fink, "Cost of Railroad Transportation," *Journal of The Railway Association of America*, 1 (October 1874), 46–73; D. T. Gilchrist, "Albert Fink and the Pooling System," *Business History Review*, 34 (Spring 1960), 29.

92. See Ann F. Friedlaender, *The Dilemma of Freight Transport Regulation* (Washington: Brookings Institution, 1969); Thomas G. Moore, *Freight Transportation Regulation: Surface Freight and the Interstate Commerce Commission* (Washington: American Enterprise Institute, 1972); and Ari and Olive Hoogenboom, *A History of the ICC: From Panacea to Palliative* (New York: Norton, 1976).

93. See, for example, Fink, "Cost of Railroad Transportation"; Fink, *The Railroad Problem and Its Solution. Argument of Albert Fink Before the Committee on Commerce of the U.S. House of Representatives in Opposition to the* [Reagan] *Bill to Regulate Interstate Commerce, January 14, 15, & 16, 1880* (New York: Russell Brothers, 1882). Excerpts from two of Fink's best pieces are reprinted in Chandler, *The Railroads*, pp. 108–117 and 172–176.

94. Gilchrist, "Albert Fink and the Pooling System," pp. 24–40; Massachusetts *Ninth Annual Report of the Board of Railroad Commissioners* (1878), pp. 68–70 and 81–94; William Z. Ripley, *Railroads: Rates and Regulation* (New York: Longmans, Green, 1912), pp. 367–368; Adams, *Railroads: Their Origin and Problems*, pp. 173–178.

95. This is a speculative point that hinges on the ability of the pool to inhibit new entrants and simultaneously keep prices close to marginal costs. Cartel theory suggests that the latter requirement would not easily follow. For a survey and analysis of the historical controversy over pooling, see Albro Martin, "The Troubled Subject of Railroad Regulation in the Gilded Age—A Reappraisal," *Journal of American History*, 61 (September 1974), 339–371.

96. Adams, Manuscript Diary, entries of June 24 and November 22, 1878; January 28, April 28–30, May 2, May 5, and May 9, 1879; Adams, *Railroads: Their Origin and Problems*, pp. 186–194. Significantly, Fink's title in the Trunk Line Association was "Commissioner," and Adams' diary habitually refers to the New York offices of the Association as "the commission." Adams clearly regarded the aims of the Trunk Line Association as congruent with those he had been promoting in Massachusetts. For evidence of cooperative pricing arrangements in Massachusetts, see Onslow Stearns (president of the Old Colony Railroad) to William T. Hart (president of the New York and New England),

June?, 1877, in Old Colony Records, Manuscript Department, Baker Library, Harvard University Graduate School of Business Administration.

97. Adams to Fink, May 5, 1879, copy in David A. Wells Papers, Library of Congress; Adams to Wells, May 9, 1879, Wells Papers.

98. Gilchrist, "Albert Fink and the Pooling System," pp. 36–49; Adams to Wells, June 24, July 3, 1880, and February 11, 1881, Wells Papers; Adams, *Autobiography,* p. 191; Kirkland, *Adams,* pp. 59–62; though Adams' friend Wells was one of his colleagues on the Board of Arbitration, the other was John A. Wright, a Pennsylvania Railroad man whom Adams thought "a thick witted lunk-head" (Manuscript Diary, May 5 and 9, 1879).

99. See Chandler, *The Railroads,* pp. 161–162 and 177–181 for a brief explanation of this complex sequence.

100. Adams, *Autobiography,* p. 190.

101. Adams to Richard Watson Gilder, January 31, 1906, in Adams Family Collection, Miscellany, Library of Congress; Adams, "Reflex Light from Africa," *Century,* 72 (May 1906), 101–111; L. Moody Sims, "Charles Francis Adams, Jr., and the Negro Question," *New England Quarterly,* 41 (September 1968), 436–438. On Adams' response to the war, see the epilogue by Worthington Chauncey Ford in Adams, *Autobiography,* pp. 216–217; Kirkland, *Adams,* p. 220; and Adams' letter to Lord Newton, October 21, 1914, published as "A Voice from America—Mr. Charles Adams on the War," *Spectator,* 113 (November 7, 1914), 633–634.

2. State to Federal, Railroads to Trusts

1. An immense body of good historical scholarship exists on the subject of state railroad regulation in the late nineteenth century. In general, see Lee Benson, *Merchants, Farmers, and Railroads: Railroad Regulation and New York Politics, 1850–1887* (Cambridge: Harvard University Press, 1955); Edward Chase Kirkland, *Industry Comes of Age: Business, Labor, and Public Policy 1860–1897* (New York: Holt, Rinehart and Winston, 1961), chaps. 3–6; Robert E. Cushman, *The Independent Regulatory Commissions* (New York: Oxford University Press, 1941), chap. 2; Morton Keller, *Affairs of State: Public Life in Late Nineteenth Century America* (Cambridge: Harvard University Press, 1977), pp. 422–430; and Stephen Skowronek, *Building a New American State: The Expansion of National Administrative Capacities, 1877–1920* (Cambridge, Eng.: University Press, 1982), chap. 5.

For contemporary analyses, see Charles Francis Adams, Jr., *Railroads: Their Origin and Problems* (New York: Putnam's Sons, 1878); Frank Hendrick, *Railway Control by Commissions* (New York: Putnam's Sons, 1900); Arthur T. Hadley, *Railroad Transportation: Its History and Its Laws* (New York: Putnam's Sons, 1886); Balthasar Henry Meyer, *Railway Legislation in the United States* (New York: Macmillan, 1903); and William A. Crafts, et al., *State Railroad Commissions* (New York: Railroad Gazette, 1883).

2. For the Granger commissions, see Charles Francis Adams, Jr., "The Granger Movement," *North American Review,* 120 (April 1875), 394–424; Charles R. Detrick, "The Effects of the Granger Acts," *Journal of Political*

Economy, 11 (March 1903), 237–256; Mildred Throne, "The Repeal of the Iowa Granger Law, 1878," *Iowa Journal of History,* 51 (April 1953), 97–130; William L. Burton, "Wisconsin's First Railroad Commission: A Case Study in Apostasy," *Wisconsin Magazine of History,* 45 (Spring 1962), 190–198; and— most useful of all—George H. Miller, *Railroads and the Granger Laws* (Madison: University of Wisconsin Press, 1971).

3. The rise of public utility commissions may be traced in Eli Winston Clemens, *Economics and Public Utilities* (New York: Appleton-Century-Crofts, 1950; Martin G. Glaeser, *Public Utilities in American Capitalism* (New York: Macmillan, 1957); and Forrest McDonald, *Insull* (Chicago: University of Chicago Press, 1962). For contemporary surveys, see National Civic Federation, *Municipal and Private Operation of Public Utilities* (New York: National Civic Federation, 1907); Clyde Lyndon King, ed., *The Regulation of Municipal Utilities* (New York: Appleton, 1912); and the symposium "State Regulation of Public Utilities," *Annals of the American Academy of Political and Social Science,* 53 (May 1914).

4. Massachusetts Department of Public Utilities summary (memorandum), May 8, 1963, department files, Boston, Massachusetts.

5. For the evolution of utility regulation in some states besides Massachusetts, see Mansel Griffiths Blackford, "Businessmen and the Regulation of Railroads and Public Utilities in California During the Progressive Era," *Business History Review,* 44 (Autumn 1970), 307–319; Robert F. Wesser, *Charles Evans Hughes: Politics and Reform in New York 1905–1910* (Ithaca: Cornell University Press, 1967); and Stanley P. Caine, *The Myth of a Progressive Reform: Railroad Regulation in Wisconsin 1903–1910* (Madison: State Historical Society of Wisconsin, 1970). For alternative proposals to state commission regulation, see David Nord, "The Experts Versus the Experts: Conflicting Philosophies of Municipal Utility Regulation in the Progressive Era," *Wisconsin Magazine of History,* 58 (Spring 1975), 219–236.

6. Rate of return regulation and its shortcomings are explained in detail in all textbooks on utility regulation. Some of the best are Clemens, *Economics and Public Utilities* (a good, if now dated, institutional analysis, cited in note 3 above); Paul J. Garfield and Wallace F. Lovejoy, *Public Utility Economics* (Englewood Cliffs: Prentice-Hall, 1964); and Alfred E. Kahn, *The Economics of Regulation,* 2 vols. (New York: Wiley, 1970–71).

7. For useful discussions of rate hearings, see the textbooks listed in note 6 above; and Douglas D. Anderson, *Regulatory Politics and Electric Utilities: A Case Study in Political Economy* (Boston: Auburn House, 1981), pp. 62–66.

8. Alfred D. Chandler, Jr., ed., *The Railroads: The Nation's First Big Business* (New York: Harcourt, Brace and World, 1965), parts 5 and 6; Gabriel Kolko, *Railroads and Regulation, 1877–1916* (Princeton: Princeton University Press, 1965), chaps. 1 and 2.

9. The *Wabash* case is 118 U.S. 557 (1886). Within the large literature on the origins of the ICC, especially useful studies include: Benson, *Merchants, Farmers, and Railroads,* chaps. 8–10; Ari and Olive Hoogenboom, *A History of the ICC: From Panacea to Palliative* (New York: Norton, 1976), chap. 1; Gerald D. Nash, "Origins of the Interstate Commerce Act of 1887," *Pennsylvania*

History, 24 (July 1957), 181–190; Edward A. Purcell, Jr., "Ideas and Interests: Businessmen and the Interstate Commerce Act," *Journal of American History*, 54 (December 1967), 561–578; and Albro Martin, "The Troubled Subject of Railroad Regulation in the Gilded Age—A Reappraisal," *Journal of American History*, 51 (September 1974), 339–371.

10. I. Leo Sharfman, *The Interstate Commerce Commission: A Study in Administrative Law and Procedure* (New York: Commonwealth Fund, 1931–1937).

11. For the early history of the ICC, the most useful primary sources include the commission's own *Reports* and the extremely revealing private papers of Thomas M. Cooley and of ICC statistician Henry Carter Adams, both of which are located in the Michigan Historical Collections, University of Michigan, Ann Arbor. The best secondary sources include the thorough and painstaking dissertation by John Horace Churchman, "Federal Regulation of Railroad Rates, 1880–1898," University of Wisconsin-Madison, 1976; Albro Martin, *Enterprise Denied: Origins of the Decline of American Railroads, 1897–1917* (New York: Columbia University Press, 1971); Paul W. MacAvoy, *The Economic Effects of Regulation: The Trunk-Line Cartels and the Interstate Commerce Commission Before 1900* (Cambridge: MIT Press, 1965); K. Austin Kerr, *American Railroad Politics, 1914–1920* (Pittsburgh: University of Pittsburgh Press, 1968); Sharfman, *The Interstate Commerce Commission*, vols. 1–4; Bernard Axelrod, "Railroad Regulation in Transition, 1897–1905: Walker D. Hines of the Railroads v. Charles A. Prouty of the ICC," diss., Washington University, 1975; and Thomas S. Ulen, "The Market for Regulation: The ICC from 1887 to 1920," *American Economic Review*, 70 (May 1980), 306–310.

12. These points about the ICC's political relations are made especially clear for the period 1914–1920 by Kerr in *American Railroad Politics*; and, for the 1930s, by William Ralph Childs, "Trucking and the Emergence of Federal Regulation, 1890–1940: A History of the Interactions of Technology, Business, Law, and Politics," diss., University of Texas at Austin, 1982. See also the voluminous papers of long-time ICC members Balthasar H. Meyer (at the State Historical Society of Wisconsin, Madison), and Joseph B. Eastman (at the Library of Amherst College, Amherst, Massachusetts).

13. Hoogenboom and Hoogenboom, *The ICC*; John R. Meyer, Merton J. Peck, John Stenason, and Charles Zwick, *The Economics of Competition in the Transportation Industries* (Cambridge: Harvard University Press, 1959); George W. Hilton, "The Consistency of the Interstate Commerce Act," *Journal of Law and Economics*, 9 (October 1966), 87–113; Ann F. Friedlaender, *The Dilemma of Freight Transport Regulation* (Washington: Brookings Institution, 1969); and George Wilson, *Economic Analysis of Intercity Freight Transportation* (Bloomington: Indiana University Press, 1980).

14. Alfred D. Chandler, Jr., *The Visible Hand: The Managerial Revolution in American Business* (Cambridge: Harvard University Press, 1977), parts 1–4; see also Glenn Porter, *The Rise of Big Business, 1860–1910* (New York: Crowell, 1973); and, for a contemporary view, John Moody, *The Truth About the Trusts* (New York: Moody, 1904).

15. *Historical Statistics of the United States: Colonial Times to 1970*

(Washington: Government Printing Office, 1975), p. 731. The best estimates about the annual rate of increase in total factor productivity are that it remained remarkably steady at roughly 0.3 percent for most of the nineteenth century, but rose very sharply to a rate of 1.7 percent for the period 1889–1919. This was almost a *six-fold increase*. Capital invested per worker in American manufacturing grew from about $700 in 1869 to about $2000 in 1899 (constant dollars). Total capital invested in manufacturing multiplied from $2.7 billion in 1879 to $8.2 billion in 1899, and to $20.8 billion in 1914 (current dollars). During the same period, prices dropped significantly worldwide. For these figures, and discussion of their meaning, see Paul Uselding, "Manufacturing," in Glenn Porter, ed., *Encyclopedia of American Economic History* (New York: Scribner's, 1980), pp. 409–411; John W. Kendrick, "Productivity," ibid., pp. 157–166; and *Historical Statistics*, pp. 200–201, 224.

16. Smith, *The Wealth of Nations*, Random House Modern Library (New York, 1937), p. 128.

17. See the following essays, all in Norbert Horn and Jürgen Kocka, eds., *Law and the Formation of the Big Enterprises in the 19th and Early 20th Centuries* (Göttingen, West Germany: Vanednhoeck & Ruprecht, 1979): William R. Cornish, "Legal Control over Cartels and Monopolization 1880–1914. A Comparison," pp. 280–303; Leslie Hannah, "Mergers, Cartels, and Concentration: Legal Factors in the U.S. and European Experience," pp. 306–314; and Morton Keller, "Public Policy and Large Enterprise. Comparative Historical Perspectives," pp. 515–531.

18. Ibid. (all three articles); for the figures on government employment, see *Historical Statistics*, p. 1103.

19. Arthur P. Dudden, "Men Against Monopoly: The Prelude to Trust-Busting," *Journal of the History of Ideas*, 18 (October 1957), 587–593; Sanford D. Gordon, "Attitudes Towards Trusts Prior to the Sherman Act," *Southern Economic Journal*, 30 (October 1963), 156–167; William Letwin, *Law and Economic Policy in America: The Evolution of the Sherman Antitrust Act* (New York: Random House, 1965).

20. A brief discussion of productive efficiency may be found in Robert H. Bork, *The Antitrust Paradox: A Policy at War with Itself* (New York: Basic Books, 1978), pp. 91, 104–6, and chap. 11. In Bork's somewhat overwrought language, "productive efficiency is a simple, indispensable, and thoroughly misunderstood concept. Not one antitrust lawyer in ten has a remotely satisfactory idea on the subject, and the proportion of economists who do, though surely higher, is perhaps not dramatically so. The situation has deteriorated so badly that one can hear it hotly denied that efficiency has anything to do with antitrust" (p. 104).

21. Phillip Areeda, *Antitrust Analysis: Problems, Text, Cases* (Boston: Little, Brown, 1974), pp. 6–9. Among economists, maximized allocative efficiency is also called "Pareto optimality." Additional discussion of the principles of allocative efficiency and consumer welfare may be found in almost any elementary or intermediate textbook on microeconomics.

22. Nearly all of the huge literature on trusts, monopolies, oligopolies, mergers, and consolidations applies in large part to horizontal combination. A

series of relevant articles and a thorough 29-page bibliography of recent work in the field may be found in Eleanor M. Fox and James T. Halverson, eds., *Industrial Concentration and the Market System: Legal, Economic, Social and Political Perspectives* (American Bar Association Press, 1979). See also Harvey J. Goldschmid, et al., eds., *Industrial Concentration: The New Learning* (Boston: Little, Brown, 1974); Bork, *The Antitrust Paradox*, chaps. 8, 10, 13; Frederick M. Scherer, *Industrial Market Structure and Economic Performance* (Boston: Houghton Mifflin, 1980); Edwin Mansfield, ed., *Monopoly Power and Economic Performance: The Problem of Industrial Concentration*, fourth edition (New York: Norton, 1978); and Yale Brozen, *Concentration, Mergers, and Public Policy* (New York: Macmillan, 1982).

23. Chandler, *The Visible Hand*, chap. 10; Willard F. Mueller, *A Primer on Monopoly and Competition* (New York: Random House, 1970).

A great deal of historical evidence suggests that tight horizontal integration was often followed by vertical integration, and that these two organizational changes often produced exceptional productive efficiencies. For example, between 1882 and 1885, Standard Oil, after absorbing other firms in horizontal acquisitions, concentrated production in the 22 most efficient of its 53 refineries, closing the least efficient 31. This "rationalization" of production facilities helped to reduce the company's average cost of refining a gallon of oil by two thirds, from 1.5¢ to 0.5¢. Similarly, American Tobacco, after its various consolidations and rationalizations, reduced the average wholesale price of its cigarettes from $3.02 per thousand in 1893 to $2.01 per thousand in 1899. See Harold F. Williamson and Arnold R. Daum, *The American Petroleum Industry: The Age of Illumination, 1859–1899* (Evanston: Northwestern University Press, 1959), pp. 474–475 and 483–484; U.S. Bureau of Corporations, *Report of the Commissioner of Corporations on the Tobacco Industry*, pt. 3 (Washington: Government Printing Office, 1915), pp. 158–160. Between 1893 and 1899, American Tobacco's *costs* dropped from $1.74 per thousand to $0.89.

24. The phrases "center firms" and "peripheral firms" are used in Robert T. Averitt, *The Dual Economy: The Dynamics of American Industry Structure* (New York: Norton, 1968). Other authors have invented their own nomenclature to denote phenomena similar to center firms: "the megacorp" in Alfred S. Eichner, *The Megacorp and Oligopoly: Micro Foundations of Macro Dynamics* (New York: Cambridge University Press, 1976); the "multiunit business enterprise" in Chandler, *The Visible Hand*; and, simply, "Big Business" in Porter, *The Rise of Big Business*. John Kenneth Galbraith's "technostructure," used in *The New Industrial State* (Boston: Houghton Mifflin, 1967), is a related concept. In each case, the author's purpose is specifically to distinguish the phenomenon from its antecedents: the single-function, labor-intensive firm without sufficient resources or power to affect the behavior of other firms.

25. Center firms and their managerial innovations were not peculiar to the United States. See Alfred D. Chandler, Jr., and Herman Daems, eds., *Managerial Hierarchies: Comparative Perspectives on the Rise of the Modern Industrial Enterprise* (Cambridge: Harvard University Press, 1980).

26. See the works cited in note 24 above and the brief bibliography in Averitt, *The Dual Economy*, pp. 202–204. Other sources on the idea of indus-

trial dualism—that is, the concept of a center (or "core") sector versus a peripheral one—include Suzanne Berger and Michael J. Piore, *Dualism and Discontinuity in Industrial Societies* (Cambridge, Eng.: University Press, 1980); E. M. Beck, Patrick M. Horan, and Charles H. Tolbert II, "Stratification in a Dual Economy: A Sectoral Model of Earnings Determination," *American Sociological Review*, 43 (October 1978), 704–720; Beck, Horan, and Tolbert, "The Structure of Economic Segmentation: A Dual Economy Approach," *American Journal of Sociology*, 75 (March 1980), 1095–1116 (on page 1109 of this article appears a quantified listing of particular industries, arrayed on a spectrum from peripheral to center or "core"); Beck, Horan, and Tolbert, "Industrial Segmentation and Labor Market Discrimination," *Social Problems*, 28 (December 1980), 113–130; Gerry Oster, "A Factor Analytic Test of the Theory of the Dual Economy," *Review of Economics and Statistics*, 61 (February 1979), 33–39; Michael J. Piore, "Labor Market Segmentation: To What Paradigm Does It Belong?" *American Economic Review*, 73 (May 1983), pp. 249–253.

27. For critical analyses of the concept of dualism, see Randy D. Hodson and Robert L. Kaufman, "Circularity in the Dual Economy: Comment on Tolbert, Horan, and Beck," *American Journal of Sociology*, 86 (January 1981), 881–887, with rejoinder from Tolbert, Horan, and Beck, ibid., 887–894; Robert L. Kaufman, Randy Hodson, and Neil D. Fligstein, "Defrocking Dualism: A New Approach to Defining Industrial Sectors," *Social Science Research*, 10 (March 1981), 1–31; and Randy Hodson and Robert L. Kaufman, "Economic Dualism: A Critical Review," *American Sociological Review*, 46 (December 1982), 727–739. All of these authors, whether pro or con on the subject of dualism, agree that industries should be segmented, conceptually, into something like the center versus peripheral model. The point I wish to emphasize in the present discussion is a very simple one, and all scholars of the subject would probably be inclined to agree with it: *center firms are peculiar to certain types of industries and are almost never found outside these industries.*

28. For elaborations of this problem, together with suggestions for remedying it, see Richard E. Caves, "Industrial Organization, Corporate Strategy and Structure," *Journal of Economic Literature*, 18 (March 1980), 64–89; and Oliver Williamson, *Markets and Hierarchies* (New York: Free Press, 1975). For a pioneering attempt to engage the question, see Alfred S. Eichner, *The Emergence of Oligopoly: Sugar Refining as a Case Study* (Baltimore: Johns Hopkins Press, 1969). Other relevant studies include Burton H. Klein, *Dynamic Economics* (Cambridge: Harvard University Press, 1977); and Michael E. Porter, *Competitive Strategy* (New York: Free Press, 1980).

29. *New York Review of Books*, February 8, 1978, p. 36 (emphasis added).

30. These data will appear in Chandler's forthcoming book on the growth of large firms worldwide. I am very grateful to him for permission to use them here. The data show greater divergence in some other industries, e.g., from 20 chemical firms in 1917 to 29 in 1973; from 29 primary metals companies in 1917 to 19 in 1973; and from 5 electrical machinery firms in 1917 to 13 in 1973.

31. Chandler, *The Visible Hand*, pp. 320–344; see also Leslie Hannah, "Mergers," in Porter, ed., *Encyclopedia of American Economic History*, pp.

649–650 (pp. 650–651 of the Hannah essay contain a helpful bibliography on the topic of mergers).

32. These data will appear in Chandler's forthcoming book on the growth of large firms worldwide.

33. Keller, *Affairs of State*, pp. 431–438; Letwin, *Law and Economic Policy in America: The Evolution of the Sherman Antitrust Act;* the text of the Sherman Act is in 15 U.S. Code, 1–7.

34. Walton Hamilton and Irene Till, *Antitrust in Action*, Temporary National Economic Committee Monograph No. 16 (Washington: Government Printing Office, 1940), pp. 135–143; Phillip Areeda, *Antitrust Analysis: Problems, Text, Cases* (Boston: Little, Brown, 1974), pp. 44–46 and chap. 2. For an excellent case study, see Mary Yeager, *Competition and Regulation: The Development of Oligopoly in the Meat Packing Industry* (Greenwich, Conn.: JAI Press, 1981). See also Ellis Hawley, "Antitrust," in Porter, ed., *Encyclopedia of American Economic History*, pp. 772–787. For shifts in the view of big business as reflected in the periodical press, see Louis P. Galambos, *The Public Image of Big Business in America, 1880–1940: A Quantitative Study in Social Change* (Baltimore: Johns Hopkins Press, 1975).

3. Brandeis and the Origins of the FTC

1. William E. Cushing to Mrs. B. M. Cushing, March 17, 1878, quoted in Edward F. McClennen, "Louis D. Brandeis as a Lawyer," *Massachusetts Law Quarterly*, 33 (September 1948), 5. A slightly different version of this letter appears in Alpheus Thomas Mason, *Brandeis: A Free Man's Life* (New York: Viking, 1946), p. 3.

2. The standard works on Brandeis include Mason, *Brandeis: A Free Man's Life;* Mason, *Brandeis: Lawyer and Judge in the Modern State* (Princeton: Princeton University Press, 1933); Alfred Lief, *Brandeis: The Personal History of an American Ideal* (New York: Stackpole, 1936); Felix Frankfurter, ed., *Mr. Justice Brandeis* (New Haven: Yale University Press, 1932); Samuel J. Konefsky, *The Legacy of Holmes and Brandeis: A Study in the Influence of Ideas* (New York: Macmillan, 1956); A. L. Todd, *Justice on Trial: The Case of Louis D. Brandeis* (New York: McGraw-Hill, 1964); Melvin I. Urofsky, *A Mind of One Piece: Brandeis and American Reform* (New York: Scribner, 1971); Urofsky, *Louis D. Brandeis and the Progressive Tradition* (Boston: Little, Brown, 1981); Nelson Lloyd Dawson, *Louis D. Brandeis, Felix Frankfurter, and the New Deal* (Hamden, Conn.: Archon Books, 1980); and Lewis J. Paper, *Brandeis* (Englewood Cliffs: Prentice-Hall, 1983).

Responsible Brandeis revisionism began with Richard M. Abrams' insightful article, "Brandeis and the New Haven-Boston & Maine Merger Battle Revisited," *Business History Review*, 36 (Winter 1962), 408–430; see also Abrams, "Brandeis and the Ascendancy of Corporate Capitalism," introduction to Abrams, ed., Louis D. Brandeis, *Other People's Money and How the Bankers Use It* (New York: Harper & Row, 1967), pp. vii–xliv; and Janice Mark Jacobson, "Mr. Justice Brandeis on Regulation and Competition: An Analysis of His Economic Opinions," diss., Columbia University, 1973.

Critical evaluations followed in the 1980s with Allon Gal, *Brandeis of Boston* (Cambridge: Harvard University Press, 1980); David W. Levy and Bruce Allen Murphy, "Preserving the Progressive Spirit in a Conservative Time: The Joint Reform Efforts of Justice Brandeis and Professor Felix Frankfurter, 1916–1933," *Michigan Law Review*, 78 (August 1980), 1252–1304; and Bruce Allen Murphy, *The Brandeis/Frankfurter Connection: The Secret Political Activities of Two Supreme Court Justices* (New York: Oxford University Press, 1982).

3. Gal, *Brandeis of Boston* (1980), made the first use of papers from Brandeis' law firm. The extensive Brandeis papers at the University of Louisville were microfilmed and made widely available in 1980. Still another useful project is Abram L. Sachar and William M. Goldsmith, eds., *A Microfilm Edition of the Public Papers of Louis Dembitz Brandeis in the Jacob and Martha Goldfarb Library of Brandeis University* (Cambridge: General Microfilm Company, 1978).

4. Melvin I. Urofsky and David W. Levy, eds., *Letters of Louis D. Brandeis* (Albany: State University of New York Press, 1971–78), hereafter cited as Brandeis *Letters*. Together with the editors' careful annotations, the *Letters* come to about 3200 pages.

5. See reviews of the *Letters* by Jerold S. Auerbach in *American Journal of Legal History*, 17 (January 1973), 88–91; and by Alfred H. Kelly in *Journal of American History*, 58 (December 1971), 781–783.

6. Laski to Oliver Wendell Holmes, November 30, 1930, in Mark DeWolfe Howe, ed., *Holmes-Laski Letters: The Correspondence of Mr. Justice Holmes and Harold J. Laski, 1916–1935* (Cambridge: Harvard University Press, 1953), II, 1298–1299 (I am indebted to Lewis L. Gould for this quotation); for the editors' comment, see Brandeis *Letters*, I, xxxiii.

7. Brandeis to Warren, May 30, 1879, Brandeis *Letters*, I, 35. Brandeis wrote this letter to Warren from St. Louis, to which he had moved and begun his law practice and from which he was anxious to return to Boston; see Burton C. Bernard, "Brandeis in St. Louis," *St. Louis Bar Journal*, 77 (Winter 1964), 53–68.

8. Brandeis to Amy Brandeis Wehle, January 20, 1877 and January 2, 1881; to Charles Nagel, July 12, 1879; all in Brandeis *Letters*, I, 14, 39, 62.

9. Edward F. McClennen, "Louis D. Brandeis as a Lawyer," *Massachusetts Law Quarterly*, 33 (September 1948), 3.

10. Brandeis to William Harrison Dunbar, February 2, 1893, Brandeis *Letters*, I, 107–109. The Brandeis Papers at the University of Louisville contain the scrapbooks, which are detailed and copious.

11. Brandeis memorandum and comment quoted in Mason, *Brandeis: A Free Man's Life*, p. 69; Brandeis to Dunbar, February 2, 1893, Brandeis *Letters*, I, 109.

12. Arthur Dehon Hill to Henry Cabot Lodge, January 31, 1916, Lodge Papers, Massachusetts Historical Society, Boston (I am indebted to Lewis L. Gould for this citation).

13. Gal, *Brandeis of Boston*, pp. 11–22; Brandeis, *Business—A Profession* (Boston: Small, Maynard, 1914), pp. 1–12; McClennen, "Louis D. Brandeis as a Lawyer," passim.

14. *Lochner v. New York*, 198 U.S. 45 (1905); *Muller v. Oregon*, 208 U.S. 412 (1908).

15. Supreme Court of the United States. October Term, 1907. No. 107. Curt Muller, Plaintiff in Error vs. State of Oregon. Brief for the Defendant in Error; Brandeis to Louis Brandeis Wehle, February 10, 1908 (plus editors' notes), Brandeis *Letters*, II, 77–78. See also editors' notes, Brandeis *Letters*, III, 364; Brandeis, "The Living Law," *Illinois Law Review*, 10 (February 1916), 461, 465; Mason, *Brandeis: A Free Man's Life*, pp. 245–252; and Mason, "The Case of the Overworked Laundress," in John A. Garraty, ed., *Quarrels That Have Shaped the Constitution* (New York: Harper & Row, 1966), pp. 176–190.

16. Published excerpts from the Brandeis brief, including the quoted passage, appear in Richard Hofstadter, ed., *The Progressive Movement, 1900–1915* (Englewood Cliffs: Prentice-Hall, 1963), pp. 61–65. A copy of the full brief may be found in *A Microfilm Edition of the Public Papers of Louis Dembitz Brandeis*, cited in note 3 above.

17. On the Ballinger-Pinchot affair, see Alpheus T. Mason, *Bureaucracy Convicts Itself: The Ballinger-Pinchot Controversy of 1910* (New York: Viking, 1941); Samuel P. Hays, *Conservation and the Gospel of Efficiency: The Progressive Conservation Movement 1890–1920* (Cambridge: Harvard University Press, 1959), pp. 165–174; and James L. Penick, Jr., *Progressive Politics and Conservation: The Ballinger-Pinchot Affair* (Chicago: University of Chicago Press, 1968). Other standard sources are listed in Penick, p. 199.

18. Hays, *Conservation and the Gospel of Efficiency*, p. 170: "For years to come as well as in 1910 the Pinchot-Ballinger controversy obscured rather than clarified conservation problems by reducing complex questions of resource management to simple matters of personal honesty."

19. Brandeis' fee from *Collier's* in the Glavis case was $25,000, an extraordinarily large sum in 1910. See Brandeis to Robert Joseph Collier, June 30, 1910, Brandeis *Letters*, II, 363.

20. Brandeis to various correspondents, January 1910–January 1911, Brandeis *Letters*, II, 307–399.

21. Brandeis to Alfred Brandeis, January 31 and March 27, 1910, Brandeis *Letters*, II, 315, 327–328.

22. Brandeis' opening and closing statements and brief to the joint investigating committee may be found in U.S. Congress, *Investigation of the Interior Department and the Bureau of Forestry*, (61st Cong., 3rd sess.), Senate Doc. No. 719 (1911), pp. 4903–4923, 5005–5021, 5041–5182. For his publicity effort and related matters, see Brandeis to various correspondents, Brandeis *Letters*, II, 338–343, 358, 379–380, 458–459. Of Brandeis' sincerity in attacking the Taft Administration there is little question. Toward the end of his life he remained of the opinion that Taft had been "guilty of the worst act ever done by any president"; see Brandeis *Letters*, V, 641.

23. Penick, *Progressive Politics and Conservation*, pp. 163–164.

24. Gal, *Brandeis of Boston*, pp. 46–49; in addition to his other reasons for taking the viewpoint of shippers, Brandeis had been involved since 1906 in a bitter dispute with the New Haven Railroad.

On the subject of size, in 1910 American railroads employed nearly 1.7

million persons, paid $1.144 billion in wages and salaries, took in operating revenues of $2.812 billion, and carried 972 million passengers and 1.026 billion tons of freight. Railroading was by far the nation's largest single industry at this time. See *Historical Statistics of the United States: Colonial Times to 1970* (Washington: Government Printing Office, 1975), pp. 728–740. A helpful but biased source on railroads in this period, including the episode of the advance rate case, is Albro Martin, *Enterprise Denied: Origins of the Decline of American Railroads, 1897–1917* (New York: Columbia University Press, 1971).

25. Brief on Behalf of Traffic Committee of Commercial Organizations of the Atlantic Seaboard, before the Interstate Commerce Commission, *In the Matter of Proposed Advances in Freight Rates by Carriers* (61st Cong., 3rd sess.), Senate Doc. 725, p. 4752; hereafter cited as ICC Brief.

26. ICC Brief, pp. 4759, 4765; Brandeis to Rudolph Gaar Leeds, November 9, 1910, Brandeis *Letters*, II, 383–385; to H. C. DeRan, February 12, 1912, ibid., 543.

27. ICC Brief, p. 4795; Martin, *Enterprise Denied*, pp. 161–162, 213–223. On the efficiency movement and Brandeis' role in popularizing it in the advance rate case, see Samuel Haber, *Efficiency and Uplift: Scientific Management in the Progressive Era 1890–1920* (Chicago: University of Chicago Press, 1964), pp. 52, 75–82, and chap. 5.

28. William J. Cunningham, "Scientific Management in the Operation of Railroads," *Quarterly Journal of Economics*, 25 (May 1911), 539–562. See also Martin, *Enterprise Denied*, pp. 214–221; Martin is extremely hard on Brandeis: "He does not seem, however, to have possessed the analytical mind of the economist or the statistician which, even in 1910, would have led him to see that Emerson's claims were pure hokum" (p. 222). On Brandeis' argument in the 1914 case, see U.S. Congress, *Arguments before the Interstate Commerce Commission, Hearings on 5% Rate Case* (63rd Cong., 2nd sess.), Senate Doc. 466, pp. 1–199, 5233–5266, 6328–6335.

29. K. Austin Kerr, *American Railroad Politics 1914–1920: Rates, Wages, and Efficiency* (Pittsburgh: University of Pittsburgh Press, 1968), chaps. 2–5; I. Leo Sharfman, *The American Railroad Problem* (New York: Century, 1921); Aaron Austin Godfrey, *Government Operation of the Railroads: Its Necessity, Success, and Consequences 1918–1920* (Austin, Texas: San Felipe Press, 1974); Walker D. Hines, *War History of American Railroads* (New Haven: Yale University Press, 1928); Martin, *Enterprise Denied*, chap. 12.

30. Brandeis to Edwin Doak Mead, November 9, 1895, Brandeis *Letters*, I, 121–122.

31. Lecture notes, pp. 320–321, Document 9 of *A Microfilm Edition of the Public Papers of Louis Dembitz Brandeis*.

32. Ibid., pp. 321–323.

33. Ibid., pp. 322–324.

34. Ibid.

35. Ibid., pp. 323–324.

36. Ibid., p. 334.

37. Ibid., pp. 324–333. The indirect promotion of tight combinations through the prohibition of loose ones is discussed in Chandler, *The Visible Hand*, p. 357, and—with more doubt—in Hans B. Thorelli, *The Federal Anti-*

trust Policy: Organization of an American Tradition (Baltimore: Johns Hopkins Press, 1955), pp. 604–606. See also the perceptive discussion in James Weinstein, *The Corporate Ideal in the Liberal State: 1900–1918* (Boston: Beacon Press, 1968), pp. 63–69.

38. Jesse Markham, "Survey of the Evidence and Findings on Mergers," in *Business Concentration and Price Policy* (Princeton: Princeton University Press, 1955), p. 144. See also Ralph Nelson, *Merger Movements in American Industry, 1895–1956* (Princeton: Princeton University Press, 1959); William Z. Ripley, *Trusts, Pools, and Corporations* (New York: Ginn, 1905); and Naomi Raboy Lamoreaux, "Industrial Organization and Market Behavior: The Great Merger Movement in American Industry," diss., Johns Hopkins University, 1979.

39. Chandler, *The Visible Hand*, pp. 315–344.

40. Brandeis testimony before Senate Committee on Interstate Commerce (the Clapp Committee, after its chairman, Senator Moses Clapp), U.S. Senate, *Report of the Committee on Interstate Commerce, Pursuant to Senate Resolution 98: Hearings on Control of Corporations, Persons, and Firms Engaged in Interstate Commerce*, 62nd Cong., 2nd sess. (Washington: Government Printing Office, 1912), hereafter cited as Brandeis Clapp Committee testimony (1911), p. 1148.

41. Ibid.

42. Ibid.

43. The Pullman Company was an integrated firm that manufactured and operated the sleeping cars, paying the railroads a fee for hauling them. It also enjoyed exclusive servicing contracts, which was an additional barrier to entry by potential competitors.

44. *Dr. Miles Medical Co. v. John D. Park & Sons Co.*, 220 U.S. 373 (1911).

45. The unpublished Brandeis papers at the University of Louisville contain voluminous files on this issue. Important letters to Brandeis include those of William H. Ingersoll dated May 22, May 28, June 18, June 19, July 23, September 16, September 23, September 26, October 2, October 25, November 8, November 17, November 24, and December 17, 1913; also February 26 and March 4, 1915; see also Edmond A. Whittier (secretary of the American Fair Trade League) to Brandeis, June 28, 1913; Gilbert H. Montague to Brandeis, January 10, February 18, and March 27, 1914. See also Brandeis to various correspondents during the period 1913–15 in Brandeis *Letters*, III, 89–90, 93–105, 111–113, 118–122, 125–129, 131–134, 138–139, 146–147, 152, 169–170, 173–174, 216–218, 225–226, 434, 446–448, 618–619.

46. Other important cases included *Bobbs-Merrill Co. v. Straus*, 210 U.S. 339 (1908), and especially *Bauer & Cie v. O'Donnell*, 229 U.S. 1 (1913); see Brandeis to John Rogers Commons, May 27, 1913; Brandeis to Robert Marion La Follette, May 27, 1913; Brandeis to William Cox Redfield, May 27, 1913; and Brandeis to Henry Robinson Towne, July 25, 1913, all in Brandeis *Letters*, III, 99–103, 152.

47. Brandeis testimony May 15, 1912, before the House Committee on patents, *Oldfield Revision and Codification of the Patent Statutes*, 62nd Cong., 2nd sess. (Washington: Government Printing Office, 1912), p. 4.

48. Brandeis to Hapgood, July 7, 1913, Brandeis *Letters*, III, 125; Ed-

mond A. Whittier to Brandeis, November 24, November 29, 1913; William H. Ingersoll to Brandeis, November 17, 1913; George Eastman to Brandeis, November 14, 1913, all in Brandeis Papers, University of Louisville.

The magazines in which "Competition that Kills" was excerpted include *World's Work, McCall's, Delineator, Designer, Good Housekeeping, Everybody's, Harper's Weekly, Woman's Magazine, Christian Herald, Leslie's, Country Life in America, Outlook, Scribner's, Review of Reviews, Garden Magazine, Cosmopolitan, Hearst's, Metropolitan,* and *Butterick Trio;* see Edmond A. Whittier to Brandeis, July 31, 1913, Brandeis Papers. The note introducing the reprints in these journals states: "This article is published by a number of the leading magazines in the belief that by giving wide publicity to the views of so noted a foe to monopoly as Mr. Brandeis the real interests of the enterprising individual manufacturer, the small dealer, and the public will be served."

49. Brandeis, "Cut-throat Prices: The Competition That Kills," *Harper's Weekly,* November 15, 1913, pp. 11–12; see also Brandeis, "On Maintaining Makers' Prices," *Harper's Weekly,* June 14, 1913, p. 6.

50. Brandeis testimony, U.S. Congress, House, Committee on Interstate and Foreign Commerce, *Hearings on Regulation of Prices,* 64th Cong., 1st sess. (Washington: Government Printing Office, 1915), pp. 39–41.

51. Ibid., pp. 45, 54.

52. Ibid., pp. 29–30.

53. Ibid., p. 53. In his widely distributed *Harper's Weekly* piece, Brandeis characterized the consumer as follows: "Thoughtless or weak, he yields to the temptation of trifling immediate gain; and selling his birthright for a mess of pottage, becomes himself an instrument of monopoly." See "Cut-throat Prices," p. 12.

54. *Hearings on Regulation of Prices,* pp. 55–57 and 63–64. Congress finally did pass fair-trade laws: the Miller-Tydings Act of 1937, strengthened by the McGuire Act of 1952. Both were repealed by the Consumer Goods Pricing Act of 1975. For details of the 1930s agitation for such legislation, see Federal Trade Commission, *Resale Price Maintenance* (Washington: Government Printing Office, 1945), and Ellis W. Hawley, *The New Deal and the Problem of Monopoly: A Study in Economic Ambivalence* (Princeton: Princeton University Press, 1966), pp. 254–258. A long and thorough exposition of the rise and fall of federal fair-trade laws may be found in Earl W. Kintner, ed., *The Legislative History of the Federal Antitrust Laws and Related Statutes* (New York: Chelsea House, 1978), pp. 457–982.

Economists and antitrust lawyers are not unanimous concerning the effects of resale price maintenance. For arguments that they are not horizontal but vertical relationships, and therefore do not harm consumer welfare, see Robert H. Bork, *The Antitrust Paradox: A Policy at War with Itself* (New York: Basic Books, 1978), pp. 32–33, 297; and Richard A. Posner, *Antitrust Law: An Economic Perspective* (Chicago: University of Chicago Press, 1976), pp. 147–166. Most scholars, however, would probably subscribe to the following characterization, jointly submitted to Congress in 1952 by a number of prominent economists and lawyers: "Resale price maintenance has no place in a society which depends on the competitive market as a major instrument for determining price and output. . . . The drive for price fixing by law comes from some groups of retailers who obtain their supplies through the older channels of wholesaler distribution. [That is, the restraints are horizontal, not vertical.] They want to sell in their local markets under monopolistic conditions—that is, free of price competition. Not only do they want to eliminate competition with each other. They also typically oppose the growth of chain stores, mail order houses, cooperatives, department stores, and other techniques of distribution which have over two generations greatly increased the degree of competition in, and reduced the costs of the distribution of consumer goods in almost every local market of the United States." The authors of this statement included, among many others, M. A. Adelman, John Kenneth Galbraith, Edward S. Mason, Fritz Machlup, Lloyd G. Reynolds, Carl Fulda, James Tobin, and George W. Stocking. The statement is printed in Kintner, *The Legislative History of the Federal Antitrust Laws and Related Statutes*, p. 850.

55. Brandeis Clapp Committee testimony (1911), p. 1226; Mason, *Brandeis*, pp. 432–435; Gal, *Brandeis of Boston*, chaps. 1–3 passim; see also Brandeis to Alfred Brandeis, June 18, 1907, Brandeis *Letters*, I, 584: "I am experiencing a growing conviction that the labor men are the most congenial company. The intense materialism and luxuriousness of most of our other people makes their company quite irksome."

56. Brandeis to Alice Goldmark, December 28, 1890, Brandeis *Letters*, I, 97.

57. Brandeis to H. W. Ashley, January 31, 1914, Brandeis *Letters*, III, 239; Brandeis to Felix Frankfurter, September 30, 1922, ibid., V, 70.

58. Brandeis to Frankfurter, September 30, 1922, Brandeis *Letters*, V, 70; Brandeis to George Henry Soule, April 22, 1923, ibid., 92.

59. Brandeis to Soule, April 22, 1923, Brandeis *Letters*, V, 92; Brandeis to Frankfurter, February 12, 1926, ibid., 207.

60. Brandeis Clapp Committee testimony (1911), p. 1234.

61. Ibid., p. 1170; Brandeis to Elizabeth Brandeis Raushenbush, November 19, 1933, Brandeis *Letters*, V, 527.

62. Brandeis Clapp Committee testimony (1911), p. 1167.

63. One of Brandeis' favorite presidents was Grover Cleveland, who exhibited great personal honesty and advocated sound money and minimal government. Surprisingly, in view of Brandeis' contemporary reputation as a radical, his votes in the early twentieth century went to such sober and conventional politicians as the Democrat Alton B. Parker (1904) and the Republican William Howard Taft (1908). Gal, *Brandeis of Boston*, pp. 22–28. See also Brandeis to Alfred Brandeis, November 4, 1908, Brandeis *Letters*, II, 213.

On Brandeis and La Follette, see Brandeis, "La Follette, a Constructor," *Boston Common*, September 23, 1911; Brandeis, "Protect Law-Abiding Business," *La Follette's Weekly*, January 27, 1912; Brandeis, "Are the Trusts Efficient?" *La Follette's Weekly*, February 3, 1912; and Brandeis to various correspondents, Brandeis *Letters*, II, 505, 523, 528–529, 539, 542, 568–569, 573, 585.

64. Brandeis to Norman Hapgood, July 3, 1912, Brandeis *Letters*, II, 633; see also other letters in July and August 1912 from Brandeis to Gifford Pinchot,

Alfred Brandeis, and Charles Zeublin, ibid., pp. 640–645, 648–649, 660–661.

65. Arthur S. Link, *Wilson: The Road to the White House* (Princeton: Princeton University Press, 1947), p. 489; Brandeis, "Shall We Abandon the Policy of Competition?" *Case and Comment* (February 1912), p. 494.

66. Brandeis to Wilson, September 30, 1912, Brandeis *Letters*, II, 688–694; Melvin I. Urofsky, "Wilson, Brandeis and the Trust Issue, 1912–1914," *Mid-America*, 44 (January 1967), 3–28.

67. Brandeis to Wilson, September 30, 1912, Brandeis *Letters*, II, 694.

68. Arthur S. Link, ed., *The Papers of Woodrow Wilson*, vol. 25 (Princeton: Princeton University Press, 1978), pp. 152, 368; "Notes of Interview of Louis D. Brandeis by Ray Stannard Baker," Baker Papers, Manuscript Division, Library of Congress; Brandeis *Letters*, V, 482.

69. Link, *Woodrow Wilson and the Progressive Era 1910–1917* (New York: Harper & Row, 1954), pp. 35–43.

70. Link, ed., *Wilson Papers*, vol. 27, pp. 8, 23, 71, 92–93, 108, 137–138; Gal, *Brandeis of Boston*, pp. 188–192; Mason, *Brandeis: A Free Man's Life*, pp. 385–397.

71. Brandeis to Wilson, June 14, 1913, Brandeis *Letters*, III, 113–116; Link, *Wilson: The New Freedom* (Princeton: Princeton University Press, 1956), pp. 212–219; Brandeis, *Other People's Money and How the Bankers Use It* (New York: Frederick A. Stokes, 1914).

72. Roosevelt's message was on March 29, 1933. See Bernard Schwartz, ed., *The Economic Regulation of Business and Industry: A Legislative History of U.S. Regulatory Agencies* (New York: Chelsea House, 1973), IV, 2573–2574.

73. On the diminished role of investment bankers, see Chandler, *The Visible Hand*, pp. 373–374: "If anything, there was a plethora of capital. Bankers, financiers, and speculators were eager to locate securities to sell. They did not discriminate between industries. They promoted enterprises as enthusiastically in those trades that remained competitive as they did in those that became concentrated. The wishes and decisions of financiers had little to do with the size of American firms and the structure of American industries."

The quoted passages in *Other People's Money* are from pp. 13, 110, 129, and 137.

74. Hans B. Thorelli, *The Federal Antitrust Policy: Origination of an American Tradition* (Baltimore: Johns Hopkins Press, 1955), chaps. 7 and 8; James Morison Russell, "Business and the Sherman Act, 1890–1914," diss., University of Iowa, 1966, pp. 116–181; Peter Hamilton Crawford, "Business Proposals for Government Regulation of Monopoly, 1887–1914," diss., Columbia University, 1963, chaps. 4–6; U.S. Congress, Temporary National Economic Committee, *Antitrust in Action*, TNEC Monograph No. 16 (Washington: Government Printing Office, 1940), and *A Study of the Construction and Enforcement of the Federal Antitrust Laws*, TNEC Monograph No. 38 (Washington: Government Printing Office, 1940).

75. Russell, "Business and the Sherman Act, 1890–1914," pp. 121 ff.

76. Ibid. Economic theory would have steered the Department of Justice to these associations of small firms because they were reducing allocative efficiency by controlling output and keeping prices high. For an analysis of lat-

ter-day motivations in the Antitrust Division, see Suzanne Weaver, *Decision to Prosecute: Organization and Public Policy in the Antitrust Division* (Cambridge: MIT Press, 1977).

77. Commenting on the American Tobacco dissolution, Brandeis said: "The independents are, if anything, worse off now than before; there are four great companies instead of one, each gunning for them." Here Brandeis appears to have been expressing a preference for monopoly over oligopoly on the grounds that it was likely to do less injury to small competitors. Such a thought typifies his uncertain reasoning on this subject. See Brandeis, "The Law and the Tobacco Trusts," *New York Times Financial Review for 1912*, p. 3, Document 127 in *A Microfilm Edition of The Public Papers of Louis Dembitz Brandeis;* and Brandeis, "An Illegal Trust Legalized," *The World Today*, 21 (December 1911), 1440–1441.

78. National Civic Federation, *The Trust Problem: Opinions of 16,000 Representative Americans* (New York: National Civic Federation, 1912); Gordon Maurice Jensen, "The National Civic Federation: American Business in an Age of Social Change and Social Reform, 1900–1910," diss., Princeton University, 1956, pp. 247–297; Crawford, "Business Proposals for Government Regulation of Monopoly, 1887–1914," pp. 478–501.

79. Quoted in *The Democratic Text-Book 1912* (New York: Democratic National Committee, 1912), pp. 9, 11.

80. Brandeis to Franklin Knight Lane, December 12, 1913, Brandeis *Letters*, III, 218–221; Crawford, "Business Proposals for Government Regulation of Monopoly, 1887–1914," chap. 6; Robert H. Wiebe, *Businessmen and Reform: A Study of the Progressive Movement* (Cambridge: Harvard University Press, 1962), pp. 137–141 of Quadrangle edition (1968).

81. Brandeis to Lane, December 12, 1913, Brandeis *Letters*, III, 219–221.

82. Quoted in Schwartz, ed., *Economic Regulation of Business and Industry*, III, 1731–1732; see also Urofsky, "Wilson, Brandeis and the Trust Issue," pp. 21–23.

83. Brandeis to Alfred Brandeis, Brandeis *Letters*, III, 236–237.

84. The so-called Hepburn bill of 1908, named for Representative William Hepburn (R., Iowa), provided for an expanded Bureau of Corporations that would register corporations and consider their proposals for combination and cooperation. The bill got nowhere, and in this sense it was less a precursor of the FTC than a reflection of uncertain support for a commission in 1908. Among legislators, the most persistent advocate of an interstate trade commission was Senator Francis Newlands (D., Nevada). The Newlands Papers at Yale University contain voluminous files on the evolution of legislative proposals for a commission.

On the Hepburn bill and early movements toward a commission, see George Cullom Davis, "The Federal Trade Commission: Promise and Practice in Regulating Business, 1900–1929," diss., University of Illinois, 1969, pp. 16–18. More generally, see ibid., chaps. 4 and 5; Link, *Wilson: The New Freedom*, pp. 417–427; Urofsky, "Wilson, Brandeis and the Trust Issue," pp. 23–26; and Gerard C. Henderson, *The Federal Trade Commission: A Study in Administrative Law and Procedure* (New Haven: Yale University Press, 1924), pp. 1–48.

85. Kintner, ed., *Legislative History of the Federal Antitrust Laws*, p. 1084. Clayton's legislation first appeared in three bills which were consolidated into one. The sum of the provisions of these bills still did not enumerate as many illegal practices as had the drafts (by Brandeis and others) of the La Follette-Lenroot antitrust bills introduced in 1912. See ibid., pp. 989–1023, 1974–1988; and Brandeis *Letters*, II, 435–436, 438–439, 442–443, 453–456, 495–496, 538, 688–693. Copies of the drafts are in the Brandeis Papers, University of Louisville.

86. Smith is quoted in Davis, "The Federal Trade Commission," p. 88.

87. The quotation from Wilson's speech is in Schwartz, ed., *The Economic Regulation of Business and Industry*, III, 1732.

88. William C. Redfield to Joseph P. Tumulty, April 18, 1914, Woodrow Wilson Papers (microfilm edition), series IV, case file 1339, reel 315; the businessman is quoted in Russell, "Business and the Sherman Act," p. 208. See also Link, *Wilson: The New Freedom*, pp. 433–436.

89. Russell, "Business and the Sherman Act," p. 231; Crawford, "Business Proposals for Government Regulation of Monopoly," pp. 478–503. The numbers in the Chamber of Commerce poll may have had a deceptive precision and should be taken as approximations. As Crawford points out, the phrasing of the questions may have unduly led the respondents.

90. The evidence in Brandeis *Letters*, III, 230–320, suggests that his primary concerns during this period were with the ICC case, the New Haven railroad fight (a long and for Brandeis obsessive battle at last nearing its conclusion), and zionist problems emerging from the onset of World War I.

91. Rublee Memoir, Columbia University Oral History Research Office, pp. 102–104. Rublee was also helping Brandeis in his battle for retail price fixing. See, on both points, Brandeis *Letters*, III, 216–217, 226–227, 236, 260, 320.

92. Rublee to Brandeis, July 18, 1912, Brandeis Papers; Rublee Memoir, pp. 102–115; the Hapgood letter is quoted in Link, *Wilson: The New Freedom*, pp. 437–438.

93. Rublee Memoir, pp. 110–115.

94. Schwartz, ed., *Economic Regulation of Business and Industry*, pp. 1734–1807; Link, *Wilson: The New Freedom*, pp. 433–444. The lobbying and legislative strategy for the FTC and Clayton acts may be traced through the hundreds of letters and memoranda on the subject in the Wilson Papers (microfilm edition), series II, reels 53–55, 60, and 62; series III, reels 136 and 138; and series IV, reel 307; and boxes 88–90 of the Francis Newlands Papers, Yale University.

95. The Federal Trade Commission Act of 1914 is 38 Stat. 719.

96. The text of the original act is printed in Schwartz, ed., *Economic Regulation of Business and Industry*, pp. 1723–1729, which also has a commentary.

97. Rublee, "Memorandum Concerning Section 5 of the Bill to Create a Federal Trade Commission, 22 pp., n.d. (July, 1914), copy in Wilson Papers (microfilm edition), series II, reel 60; see also Rublee, "The Original Plan and Early History of the Federal Trade Commission," *Proceedings of the Academy of Political Science*, 11 (January 1926), 115.

98. *Federal Trade Commission v. Gratz*, 253 U.S. 427 (1920).

99. Rublee had served as campaign manager for Representative Ray Stevens in Stevens' unsuccessful attempt to win a Senate seat in New Hampshire. The victorious candidate then used senatorial courtesy to block Rublee's confirmation as a member of the commission.

100. Chairman Joseph E. Davies was the lawyer-politician. Davies had headed the Bureau of Corporations under Wilson, but he was primarily a political operative. For a discussion of the early commission, see Davis, "The Federal Trade Commission," pp. 132–209; Henderson, *The Federal Trade Commission: A Study in Administrative Law and Procedure;* Thomas C. Blaisdell, *The Federal Trade Commission: An Experiment in the Control of Business* (New York: Columbia University Press, 1932); and Alan Stone, *Economic Regulation and the Public Interest: The Federal Trade Commission in Theory and Practice* (Ithaca: Cornell University Press, 1977), chaps. 1–3. For a view of the early FTC which differs almost altogether with these accounts (and with the interpretation in this book as well), see Gabriel Kolko, *The Triumph of Conservatism: A Reinterpretation of American History, 1900–1916* (New York: Free Press, 1963).

101. Ray Stannard Baker, interview with Brandeis, March 23, 1929, Baker Papers, Manuscript Division, Library of Congress.

102. Davis, "The Federal Trade Commission," pp. 177–209; Federal Trade Commission, *Annual Report* for the years 1915–1920 (Washington: Government Printing Office, 1916–1921). See also the plaintive letters from Rublee to Brandeis, February 25, April 3, and October 1, 1915, Brandeis Papers, University of Louisville; and Wilson to Representative John J. Fitzgerald, February 10, 1915, and Wilson to Senator Thomas S. Martin, March 1, 1915 (series IV, reel 307, Wilson Papers). On business-government relations during World War I, see Robert D. Cuff, *The War Industries Board* (Baltimore: Johns Hopkins University Press, 1973).

103. Henderson, *The Federal Trade Commission*, pp. 1–48; Davis, "The Federal Trade Commission," pp. 129–131; Wiebe, *Businessmen and Reform*, pp. 138–141; Link, *Wilson: The New Freedom*, pp. 438–444; and Crawford, "Business Proposals for Government Regulation for Monopoly," chaps. 5–6.

104. After passage of the Clayton and Federal Trade Commission acts in 1914, both the FTC and the Department of Justice were deluged with letters asking the limits of permissible business behavior. For typical negative or noncommittal responses, see Ernest Knaebel (Assistant Attorney General) to Austin Miller (Oklahoma Furniture Mfg. Co.), August 12, 1915; and Samuel J. Graham (Assistant Attorney General) to F. H. Burdick, August 5, 1916, Department of Justice Files (Record Group 60), National Archives, Washington, D.C. See also A. Freyer (?), Memorandum for Mr. Todd, May 10, 1915, ibid., a long internal Justice Department document arguing strenuously against advance advice.

105. The transcript of this discussion runs to 44 typed pages. It is reproduced as Document 163 of *A Microfilm Edition of the Public Papers of Louis Dembitz Brandeis in the Jacob and Bertha Goldfarb Library of Brandeis University;* hereafter cited as Brandeis FTC Interview.

106. Ibid., pp. 2–8.

107. Brandeis testimony of February 16, 1914, before the House Committee on the Judiciary, 63rd Cong., 2nd sess., *Hearings on Trust Legislation* (Washington: Government Printing Office, 1914), pp. 694–695.

108. The early administrative and judicial history of the FTC makes clear the troubles arising from the Act's ambiguity. See Davis, "The Federal Trade Commission," chaps. 7, 8, 10; and Henderson, *The Federal Trade Commission*, pp. 49–103. See also Raymond B. Stevens to Brandeis, June 22, 1915; Rublee to Brandeis, December 20, 1915; and Gilson Gardner to Brandeis, August 23, 1915 (with enclosures of critical newspaper editorials on the performance of the FTC), all in Brandeis Papers, University of Louisville. The strongest impression left by the FTC file in the Brandeis Papers is its thinness; Brandeis apparently cared much more deeply at the time about his legal cases and about such matters as retail price fixing and zionism than about the FTC.

109. On the SEC, see Chapter 5 of this book.

110. Brandeis FTC Interview, pp. 8–14.

111. Ibid., pp. 13–17.

112. Brandeis testimony of February 2, 1914, before the House Committee on Interstate and Foreign Commerce, 63rd Cong., 2nd sess., *Hearings on Interstate Trade Commission* (Washington: Government Printing Office, 1914), pp. 95–98; Brandeis to Franklin Knight Lane, December 12, 1913, Brandeis *Letters*, III, 219–221; Brandeis, *The Curse of Bigness*, pp. 137–142; Brandeis FTC Interview, p. 9.

113. Brandeis FTC Interview, generally.

114. Ibid., pp. 39–40.

115. Quoted in Mason, *Brandeis*, p. 489. A full examination of the confirmation fight is A. L. Todd, *Justice on Trial: The Case of Louis D. Brandeis* (New York: McGraw-Hill, 1964).

116. See the essays in Felix Frankfurter, ed., *Mr. Justice Brandeis* (New Haven: Yale University Press, 1932); and Samuel J. Konefsky, *The Legacy of Holmes and Brandeis: A Study in the Influence of Ideas* (New York: Macmillan, 1956).

117. This is the central conclusion of Janice Mark Jacobson, "Mr. Justice Brandeis on Regulation and Competition: An Analysis of His Economic Opinions," diss., Columbia University, 1973. Jacobson writes: "He never questioned the benefit to the consumer, in the form of lower prices, which might have resulted from large scale retail operation. Both as attorney for the people, and as justice, his concern was never primarily for the consumer, but rather for the small businessman" (p. 85); "Brandeis had characterized himself as a great foe of monopoly, while 'attorney for the people.' But his judicial opinions in this area present two major problems in the light of modern economic thought. First, his opposition to monopoly did not imply an equally strong commitment to competition. He consistently favored results which would protect the small, independent, and perhaps also inefficient producers, regardless of the effect of the result upon the consumer . . . Secondly, he had a very naive notion of monopoly power, if one examines his statements with the benefits of the hindsight of theories of monopolistic competition" (p. 255); see also pp. 7, 126–127, 211–212, 220, 324.

A brief analysis of three cases will illustrate Brandeis' position. In *American Column and Lumber Co. v. United States* (1921), Brandeis dissented from the court majority's ruling that the group's cooperative plan for "open competition" in fact amounted to an illegal cartel. Brandeis wrote that unless the lumber companies were permitted to cooperate, they might "be led to enter the inviting field of consolidation. And if they do, may not another huge trust with highly centralized control over vast resources . . . become so powerful as to dominate competitors, wholesalers, retailers, consumers, employees, and in large measure, the whole community?" (257 U.S. 419). Second, in *Quaker City Cab Company v. Pennsylvania* (1928), Brandeis again dissented from the court majority's decision that a state levy on corporate-owned taxicabs was illegal because no such tax applied to cabs owned by individuals. Brandeis argued that the Pennsylvania legislature had reasonable grounds to pass such a law because of the "evils incident to the accelerating absorption of business by corporations outweigh the benefits thereby secured" (277 U.S. 410–411). The third revealing case, *Liggett v. Lee* (1933), involved a discriminatory tax passed by the Florida legislature against chain stores. Again the court ruled the tax unconstitutional and, once more, Brandeis dissented: "They [the citizens of Florida] may have believed that the chain store, by furthering the concentration of wealth and or power and by promoting absentee ownership, is thwarting American ideals . . . it is sapping the resources, the vigor and the hope of the smaller cities and towns" (288 U.S. 568–569).

118. James Willard Hurst, *The Growth of American Law: The Law Makers* (Boston: Little, Brown, 1950), pp. 249–375; Lawrence M. Friedman, *A History of American Law* (New York: Simon and Schuster, 1973), pp. 265–292, 525–595. See also Daniel J. Boorstin, *The Americans: The Democratic Experience* (New York: Random House, 1973), pp. 53–64; Maxwell Bloomfield, *American Lawyers in a Changing Society, 1776–1876* (Cambridge: Harvard University Press, 1976); and Jerold S. Auerbach, *Unequal Justice: Lawyers and Social Change in America* (New York: Oxford University Press, 1976).

Perhaps the most revealing index of the prominent role of lawyers in American culture is their much lower number in other major market economies. In 1977 lawyers per one million population were:

Japan	89
West Germany	449
United Kingdom	588
Canada	703
United States	1,981

Source: *New York Times*, May 17, 1977. Nor is the statistical preponderance in the U.S. a recent phenomenon. There was one lawyer per 704 persons in the United States in 1900, one per 744 in 1970 (calculated from *Historical Statistics of the United States* (Washington: Government Printing Office, 1975), pp. 12, 140. The dramatically disproportionate presence of lawyers in the United States, as measured by crossnational comparisons, might be taken as symptomatic of many different characteristics of American culture. One is that entry into the legal profession has been open, without the guildlike restrictions that prevail in some other countries. Another is that many American lawyers do not in fact practice law but instead go into politics, manage businesses, teach, and engage in a variety of other pursuits. Law as a career in America has been a way of keeping one's options open. Whatever else it may signify, however, the dominance of lawyers means almost by definition that Americans have been more litigious than citizens of other countries. They have been less likely to resolve differences through informal processes of consensus. They have been alive to and insistent on their rights as individuals. They have been sensitive to due process and formal procedures and fond of pursuing their grievances or appeals to courts of last resort. This deep trait of American culture has had profound effects on the history of regulation in the United States.

119. Florence Ann Heffron, "The Independent Regulatory Commissioners," diss., University of Colorado, 1971, p. 189. The calculations are based on possession of LL.B.s by commissioners from the founding of the agency through the end of the Johnson Administration in 1969. The numbers are slightly understated, since J.D. degrees were held by an additional 3 percent of the ICC commissioners, 7 percent of the FTC, 9 percent of the FPC, 11 percent of the SEC, 5 percent of the FCC, and 16 percent of the CAB. Some of these J.D.s were post-LL.B. degrees but others the equivalent of the LL.B., reflecting the shift at most law schools in the name of the degree. For additional corroborating data, see E. Pendleton Herring, *Federal Commissioners: A Study of Their Careers and Qualifications* (Cambridge: Harvard University Press, 1936); Clarence A. Miller, "The Interstate Commerce Commissioners," *George Washington Law Review*, 5 (March 1937), 580–700; Gale Eugene Peterson, "President Harry S. Truman and the Independent Regulatory Commissions, 1945–1952," diss., University of Maryland, 1973; and U.S. Senate Committee on Commerce, 94th Cong., 2nd sess., *Appointments to the Regulatory Agencies: The Federal Communications Commission and the Federal Trade Commission (1949–1974)* (Washington: Government Printing Office, 1976), p. 422.

120. Huston Thompson, memorandum of a talk with Wilson, December 1, 1916, Thompson Papers, Manuscript Division, Library of Congress. Wilson went on to say that the ICC was plagued with this problem and that the procedures of American courts seemed unwieldy in comparison with the expedited procedures of British courts.

121. Senator John D. Works, quoted in Bruce Allen Murphy, *The Brandeis/Frankfurter Connection*, p. 29.

122. Brandeis, "Using Other People's Money," *New York American*, November 28, 1911; Brandeis, "Efficiency and the Trusts," address before the Town Criers, Providence, Rhode Island, October 7, 1912, p. 16, Document 142A of *A Microfilm Edition of the Public Papers of Louis Dembitz Brandeis*.

123. Brandeis Clapp Committee testimony (1911), p. 1156.

124. I do not mean to suggest here that the center-periphery concept is an entirely satisfactory framework for understanding business developments that have occurred during the years since Brandeis' appointment to the Supreme Court in 1916. In fact, the center-periphery split becomes a good deal more complicated when applied to business consolidations and other arrange-

ments that have developed in recent years. In particular, the diversification movement within American business; the rise of the conglomerate form, beginning in the 1960s (in which companies from both center and peripheral industries are mixed loosely within a large enterprise, as components of a conglomerate); and the spread of franchising (in which peripheral industries such as restaurants and drycleaners are often locally owned but are also affiliated with national chains that control important policies)—all have made the center-periphery notion somewhat less useful. The concept is not so much less valid now as it is simply less complete as a way of understanding very recent developments—compared with its utility in clarifying the evolution of business organizations during Brandeis' time.

125. Hartz, *The Liberal Tradition in America: An Interpretation of American Political Thought Since the Revolution* (New York: Harcourt, Brace, 1955), p. 232.

126. Van Hise to Hapgood, September 28, 1912, copy in Brandeis Papers, University of Louisville.

127. Ibid. Van Hise supported Theodore Roosevelt in 1912, and part of the disagreement with Brandeis was political.

128. Hovey to Brandeis, n.d. (received September 25, 1911), Brandeis Papers, University of Louisville.

129. Lippmann, *Drift and Mastery: An Attempt to Diagnose the Current Unrest* (first published 1914), Spectrum edition (Englewood Cliffs: Prentice-Hall, 1961), pp. 42–43.

130. Ibid., pp. 40–41.

4. Antitrust, Regulation, and the FTC

1. See, in general, Robert F. Himmelberg, *The Origins of the National Recovery Administration: Business, Government, and the Trade Association Issue, 1921–1933* (New York: Fordham University Press, 1976); Louis Galambos, *Competition and Cooperation: The Emergence of a National Trade Association* (Baltimore: Johns Hopkins Press, 1966); and Ellis W. Hawley, "Herbert Hoover, the Commerce Secretariat, and the Vision of an 'Associative State,' 1921–1928," *Journal of American History,* 61 (June 1974), 116–140.

2. *United States v. United States Steel Corporation,* 251 U.S. 417 (1920).

3. Richard A. Posner, "A Statistical Study of Antitrust Enforcement," *Journal of Law and Economics,* 13 (October 1970), 366; see also Walton Hamilton and Irene Till, *Antitrust in Action,* Temporary National Economic Committee Monograph No. 16 (Washington: Government Printing Office, 1940), pp. 135–141, which shows slightly different figures. For the years following those cited in the text, the number of cases instituted was as follows:

1930–1934	30
1935–1939	57
1940–1944	223
1945–1949	157
1950–1954	159

1955–1959	195
1960–1964	215
1965–1969	195

Posner, "A Statistical Study of Antitrust Enforcement," pp. 366–419, finds no significant correlation between political party in power and antitrust prosecutions. The salient trends are a rapidly stepped-up program beginning at the very end of the 1930s, with Thurman Arnold's tenure as chief of the Antitrust Division; an extraordinary rise in private antitrust cases beginning in the late 1940s; and no consistent economic rationale within the Antitrust Division for the cases selected for prosecution. For a stimulating discussion of the shifts in antitrust thought over time, see Richard Hofstadter, "What Happened to the Antitrust Movement? Notes on the Evolution of an American Creed," an Earl F. Cheit, ed., *The Business Establishment* (New York: Wiley, 1964), pp. 113–151.

4. These numbers are based on rough calculations of cases as described in the "Bluebook" of antitrust: *The Federal Antitrust Laws, with Summary of Cases Instituted by the United States, 1890–1951* (Chicago: Commerce Clearing House, 1952).

5. Posner, "A Statistical Study of Antitrust Enforcement," p. 411.

6. *Maple Flooring Manufacturers' Association v. United States*, 268 U.S. 563, 587 (1925); see also *Cement Manufacturers' Protective Association v. United States*, 268 U.S. 588 (1925).

7. *United States v. Trenton Potteries Company*, 273 U.S. 392 (1927). A good discussion of these trends in antitrust appears in Morton Keller, "The Pluralist State: American Economic Regulation in Comparative Perspective, 1900–1930," in Thomas K. McCraw, ed., *Regulation in Perspective: Historical Essays* (Boston: Harvard Business School, 1981), pp. 78–85.

8. Hamilton and Till, *Antitrust in Action*, p. 23; for a later period, see Suzanne Weaver, *Decision to Prosecute: Organization and Public Policy in the Antitrust Division* (Cambridge: MIT Press, 1977).

9. Himmelberg, *Origins of the National Recovery Administration*, chaps. 1–6; Ellis W. Hawley, *The Great War and the Search for a Modern Order, A History of the American People and Their Institutions, 1917–1933* (New York: St. Martin's Press, 1979), p. 103. The files of the Department of Justice in the National Archives for this period make clear the relatively lenient attitudes of the attorneys toward business associationalism.

10. See, generally, Robert D. Cuff, *The War Industries Board: Business-Government Relations during World War I* (Baltimore: Johns Hopkins University Press, 1973).

11. Ibid., chap. 10.

12. Himmelberg, *Origins of the National Recovery Administration*, chaps. 1–2.

13. Hawley, "Herbert Hoover, the Commerce Secretariat, and the Vision of an 'Associative State' "; see also Hawley, "Three Facets of Hooverian Associationalism: Lumber, Aviation, and Movies, 1921–1930," in Thomas K. McCraw, ed., *Regulation in Perspective*, pp. 95–123.

14. Ibid. (both articles); see also Himmelberg, *Origins of the National Recovery Administration,* chaps. 6–11.

15. George Cullom Davis, "The Federal Trade Commission: Promise and Practice in Regulating Business, 1900–1929," diss., University of Illinois, 1969, chaps. 10–12.

16. Ibid., chaps. 7–9; see also Gerard C. Henderson, *The Federal Trade Commission: A Study in Administrative Law and Procedure* (New Haven: Yale University Press, 1925).

17. Ibid. (both sources); see also Thomas C. Blaisdell, *The Federal Trade Commission: An Experiment in the Control of Business* (New York: Columbia University Press, 1932); and Carl McFarland, *Judicial Control of the Federal Trade Commission and the Interstate Commerce Commission, 1920–1930* (Cambridge: Harvard University Press, 1933). The correspondence of FTC Commissioners Victor Murdock and Huston Thompson, contained in their collected papers at the Manuscript Division, Library of Congress, reflects the frustration these regulators experienced during the 1920s, from adverse judicial review, inconsistent internal policies, and uncertain political support. The same point is abundantly evident in the *Minutes* of the FTC during the 1920s, contained in Record Group 122, National Records Center, Suitland, Maryland.

18. On trade-practice conferences, see generally Federal Trade Commission, *Trade Practice Conferences* (Washington: Government Printing Office, 1929); Himmelberg, *Origins of the National Recovery Administration;* and the speeches, memoranda, and correspondence on the subject in the William E. Humphrey Papers, Manuscript Division, Library of Congress.

19. Humphrey to Pinchot, n.d. (1928); for another example of extremely provocative and unbridled language, see Humphrey to Representative Tom Connally, n.d. (1928), Humphrey Papers, Manuscript Division, Library of Congress.

20. This conclusion is based on the overall judgment of Davis, "The Federal Trade Commission" (1969), Henderson, *The Federal Trade Commission* (1925), and especially Blaisdell, *The Federal Trade Commission* (1932). A perceptive analysis of the later FTC is Alan Stone, *Economic Regulation and the Public Interest: The Federal Trade Commission in Theory and Practice* (Ithaca: Cornell University Press, 1977).

21. William E. Leuchtenburg, "The Case of the Contentious Commissioner: Humphreys' Executor v. U.S.," in Harold M. Hyman and Leonard W. Levy, eds., *Essays in Honor of Henry Steele Commager* (New York: Harper & Row, 1967), pp. 276–312.

5. Landis and the Statecraft of the SEC

1. Rayburn to James Landis, May 14, 1940, Landis Papers, Manuscript Division, Library of Congress, Washington, D.C.; the cited study of the federal bureaucracy was the Hoover Commission Report, quoted in Louis Loss, *Securities Regulation,* 2nd ed. (Boston: Little, Brown, 1961), p. 1878.

2. Florence Ann Heffron, "The Independent Regulatory Commissioners,"

diss., University of Colorado, 1971, p. 188. These rankings were based on the author's evaluation of existing scholarship.

3. U.S. Senate, Committee on Government Operations, 95th Cong., 1st sess., *The Regulatory Appointments Process* (Washington: Government Printing Office, 1977), I, 270; SEC Transition Team, "Final Report," December 22, 1980, I, 9.

4. Morris Hadley to William A. Lockwood, May 8, 1936, quoting Shun Suzuki to Hadley, June 1, 1935, Landis Papers, Library of Congress. The best sources for Landis' life and career are his own verbal memoir (the typescript of which exceeds 700 pages), done in 1963 and 1964 for the Columbia University Oral History Research Office (cited hereafter as Landis Memoir); and Donald A. Ritchie, *James M. Landis: Dean of the Regulators* (Cambridge: Harvard University Press, 1980), an excellent biography.

5. Landis Memoir, pp. 1–11; Ritchie, *Landis*, chap. 1; "The Legend of Landis," *Fortune*, 10 (August 1934), 44–45; "James McCauley Landis," *Current Biography, 1942* (New York: H.W. Wilson, 1942), p. 481.

6. Landis manuscript diary, May 12, 13, 14, 16, and November 17, 1917; Paul Byrley to Landis, June 27, 1937, both in Landis Papers, Library of Congress; Landis Memoir, pp. 20–26; Gerhard P. Van Arkel, "James McCauley Landis '21," *Princeton Alumni Weekly* 36 (December 6, 1935), 237–238. One of the jobs Landis did for money was to create outlines for Princeton courses and sell them at high prices to his fellow students.

7. Jean P. Smith, "Frankfurter's Apprentice" (unpublished memoir), Landis Papers, Harvard Law School, p. 1; Lilienthal, *The Journals of David E. Lilienthal, V: The Harvest Years, 1959–1963* (New York: Harper & Row, 1971), p. 494. See also Ritchie, *Landis*, chap. 1. Landis reminisced on his law school experiences in a short piece he did for the Harvard Law School *Record* in 1947; see Landis to Jerome Shestack, March 4, 1947, Landis Papers, Library of Congress. The article Landis wrote while still an undergraduate was "The Commerce Clause as a Restriction on State Taxation," *Michigan Law Review*, 20 (November 1921), 50–85.

8. Landis to Jean P. Smith, November 1, 1924; see also Landis to Smith, October 1 and 10, 1924, Landis Papers, Harvard Law School; Landis Memoir, pp. 127–128; Landis, "Labor's New Day in Court," *The Survey*, 53 (November 15, 1924), 175–177; Landis, "The Fall-Doheny Verdict," *New Republic*, 49 (January 19, 1927), 239–242; Felix Frankfurter and Landis, "Bankers and the Conspiracy Law," *New Republic*, 41 (January 21, 1925), 218–220; Landis, "By the Artificial Reason of Law," *The Survey*, 54 (May 15, 1925), 213–214.

9. The law review articles were collected in the book by Frankfurter and Landis, *The Business of the Supreme Court: A Study in the Federal Judiciary System* (New York: Macmillan, 1928). See also "The Legend of Landis," *Fortune*, pp. 44–47; Ritchie, *Landis*, chap. 2; Landis Memoir, p. 97; and Landis to Jean P. Smith, January 8, February 5, and February ?, 1925, Landis Papers, Harvard Law School.

10. Landis to Jean P. Smith, June 30, July 15, 1925, Landis Papers, Harvard Law School; Landis Memoir, pp. 35–36; Landis to Ernst Freund, November 27, 1929; Henry J. Friendly to Landis, April 7, 1928, Landis Papers,

Library of Congress. When Landis became Frankfurter's colleague on the Harvard Law faculty, he grew less sanguine about their joint research: "I have the feeling that he is often jealous of someone else's ideas . . . The want of mutual cooperation in the basic hard work, and the knowledge that the credit and the formulation of the text will be his, acts as a drag on my own ambition" (Landis manuscript diary, October 5 and 9, 1928, Landis Papers, Library of Congress).

11. Landis, "Mr. Justice Brandeis: A Law Clerk's View," *Publications of the American Jewish Historical Society*, 936 (June 1957), 2–7; Landis Memoir, pp. 37–41, 64, and 71; Landis to Jean P. Smith, January 11, February ? and March 11, 1926, Landis Papers, Harvard Law School; Ritchie, *Landis*, chap. 2; Frankfurter to Brandeis, September 30, 1925, Brandeis Papers, University of Louisville; Brandeis to Frankfurter, January 1, 1926, quoted in Melvin I. Urofsky and David W. Levy, eds., *Letters of Louis D. Brandeis*, 5 vols. (Albany: State University of New York Press, 1972–78), V, 201n6.

12. Landis manuscript diary, 1928–1929 passim, Landis Papers, Library of Congress; Landis Memoir, pp. 136–137; Ritchie, *Landis*, p. 35.

13. Landis to Philip E. Wheelwright, May 8, 1930, Landis Papers, Library of Congress; Morton White, *Social Thought in America: The Revolt Against Formalism* (New York: Viking, 1949), chap. 5; Arthur Sutherland, *The Law at Harvard: A History of Ideas and Men, 1817–1967* (Cambridge: Harvard University Press, 1967), pp. 239–299. On the related theme of legal realism, see Edward A. Purcell, Jr., "American Jurisprudence Between the Wars: Legal Realism and the Crisis of Democratic Theory," *American Historical Review*, 75 (December 1969), 424–446.

14. Landis, "The Study of Legislation in Law Schools: An Imaginary Inaugural Lecture," *Harvard Graduates' Magazine*, 39 (June 1931), 433–442; Landis to Salvatore Galgano, October 3, 1928; Landis to Alpheus T. Mason, May 5, 1930; Landis to Guido Gores, December 10, 1929; Landis manuscript diary, 1928–1929 passim, all in Landis Papers, Library of Congress; Landis, "Statutes and the Sources of Law," in *Harvard Legal Essays Written in Honor of and Presented to Joseph Henry Beale and Samuel Williston by Their Colleagues and Students* (Cambridge: Harvard University Press, 1934), pp. 213–246.

15. Landis Memoir, p. 145; Landis, "The Legislative History of the Securities Act of 1933," *George Washington Law Review*, 28 (October 1959), 33.

16. For introductions to the securities industry, see George L. Leffler, *The Stock Market* (New York: Ronald Press, 2nd ed., 1957), a textbook, Vincent P. Carosso, *Investment Banking in America: A History* (Cambridge: Harvard University Press, 1970), a work of thorough scholarship; Cedric B. Cowing, *Populists, Plungers, and Progressives: A Social History of Stock and Commodity Speculation 1890–1936* (Princeton: Princeton University Press, 1965), a lively survey; John Brooks, *Once in Golconda: A True Drama of Wall Street, 1920–1938* (New York: Harper & Row, 1969), a popular history; Robert Sobel, *The Big Board: A History of the New York Stock Market* (New York: The Free Press, 1965), another popular history; Poyntz Tyler, ed., *Securities, Exchanges and the SEC* (New York: H.W. Wilson, 1965), a collection of useful articles;

Sidney Robbins, *The Securities Markets: Operations and Issues* (New York: The Free Press, 1966), an analysis based on the author's role in the Special Study of Securities Markets conducted by the SEC in the early 1960s; and Peter Wyckoff, *Wall Street and the Stock Markets: A Chronology, 1644–1971* (Philadelphia: Chilton, 1972), a book of useful statistics.

17. Carosso, *Investment Banking in America*, chaps. 1–2; Wyckoff, *Wall Street and the Stock Markets*, pp. 6–35.

18. The Dow-Jones Averages were separated into Industrials and Rails in 1897; the company had quoted rail-dominated averages since 1884; see Wyckoff, *Wall Street and the Stock Markets*, pp. 31–43. See also Alfred D. Chandler, Jr., ed., *The Railroads: The Nation's First Big Business* (New York: Harcourt, Brace, 1965), pp. 43–70; and Thomas R. Navin and Marian V. Sears, "The Rise of a Market for Industrial Securities, 1887–1902," *Business History Review*, 24 (June 1955), 105–138.

19. *Historical Statistics of the United States: Colonial Times to 1970* (Washington: Government Printing Office, 1975), p. 1007; David F. Hawkins, "The Development of Modern Financial Reporting Practices Among American Manufacturing Corporations," *Business History Review*, 37 (Autumn 1963), 145.

20. Jonathan Lurie, *The Chicago Board of Trade, 1859–1905: The Dynamics of Self-Regulation* (Urbana: University of Illinois Press, 1979), p. 75; Wyckoff, *Wall Street and the Stock Markets*, pp. 150–151. In the nineteenth century, a seat on the Chicago Board of Trade brought as much as $10,000. In the flush days of 1929, a seat on the New York Stock Exchange was selling for $625,000; this figure dropped to $17,000 in 1942. (The prices listed for the New York Stock Exchange were for the high of 1929 and the low of 1942; by way of comparison, the low for 1929 was $350,000 and the high for 1942 $30,000.)

21. Robbins, *The Securities Markets*, pp. 107–123; Sobel, *The Big Board*, passim; Hawkins, "The Development of Modern Financial Reporting Practices," pp. 149–151.

22. Lurie, *The Chicago Board of Trade*, p. 8; Robbins, *The Securities Markets*, pp. 107–123; on the efforts of the states to meet the problem, see Gerald D. Nash, "Government and Business: A Case Study of State Regulation of Corporate Securities, 1850–1933," *Business History Review*, 38 (Summer 1964), 144–162.

23. The OTC market is described in the following pamphlets: National Association of Securities Dealers, Inc. (NASD), *Over-the-Counter Trading Handbook* (Washington: NASD, 1960); NASD, *OTC* (Washington: NASD, n.d.); Commodity Research Bureau, Inc., *Understanding the Over-the-Counter Securities Market* (New York: Commodity Research Publications, 1960); and National Security Traders Association, *OTC* (New York: OTC Market Information Bureau, 1967).

24. Ibid. See also Leffler, *The Stock Market*, pp. 464–480; and Louis Loss, *Securities Regulation* (Boston: Little, Brown, 1951), pp. 709–715.

25. Hawkins, "The Development of Modern Financial Reporting Practices," pp. 136–140.

26. Quoted in ibid., p. 141.

27. Carosso, *Investment Banking in America*, chaps. 1–4.

28. Paul B. Abrahams, ed., "Brandeis and Lamont on Finance Capitalism," *Business History Review*, 47 (Spring 1973), 72–94.

29. Hawkins, "The Development of Modern Financial Reporting Practices," pp. 145–162.

30. *Historical Statistics of the United States*, pp. 135, 1005–1007, 1009; Wyckoff, *Wall Street and the Stock Markets*, p. 179.

31. Landis Memoir, pp. 155–185; Landis, "Legislative History of the Securities Act of 1933," pp. 30–34; Raymond Moley, *The First New Deal* (New York: Harcourt, Brace, 1966), pp. 306–315. A good history of the writing of the basic securities legislation is Michael E. Parrish, *Securities Regulation and the New Deal* (New Haven: Yale University Press, 1970), chaps. 3, 5; see also Ralph F. de Bedts, *The New Deal's SEC: The Formative Years* (New York: Columbia University Press, 1964), chaps. 2–3; and Joel Seligman, *The Transformation of Wall Street: A History of the Securities and Exchange Commission and Modern Corporate Finance* (Boston: Houghton Mifflin, 1982), chaps. 2–3.

32. Ritchie, *Landis*, chap. 4; Parrish, *Securities Regulation and the New Deal*, chaps. 3, 5, 6; Arthur M. Schlesinger, Jr., *The Coming of the New Deal* (Boston: Houghton Mifflin, 1958), pp. 441–445, 456–467; "The SEC," *Fortune*, 21 (June 1940), 92, 120, 123; Raymond Clapper, "Felix Frankfurter's Young Men," *Review of Reviews*, 93 (January 1936), 27–29; Felix Frankfurter, "The Young Men Go to Washington," *Fortune*, 13 (January 1936), 61–63; "Felix Frankfurter," *Fortune*, 13 (January 1936), 63, 87–88, 90; "Brain Rivalry: Growing Influence of Frankfurter and Harvard," *Business Week* (May 24, 1933), pp. 14–15.

33. Landis, "The Study of Legislation in Law Schools: An Imaginary Inaugural Lecture," pp. 437–439; Landis to Alpheus T. Mason, May 5, 1930, Landis Papers, Library of Congress.

34. These quotations may be found in Bernard Schwartz, ed., *The Economic Regulation of Business and Industry: A Legislative History of U.S. Regulatory Agencies* (New York: Chelsea House, 1973), pp. 2574, 2619; pp. 2549–2949 of this collection are devoted to securities and exchange regulation.

35. Ibid., pp. 2567–2571.

36. Ibid., p. 2614; Landis Memoir, pp. 155–185; Landis, "Legislative History of the Securities Act of 1933," pp. 40, 44–45, 47–48; Parrish, *Securities Regulation and the New Deal*, chaps. 3–4.

37. Landis Memoir, pp. 139–140 and 155 ff.; Landis, "Legislative History of the Securities Act of 1933," pp. 33–38.

38. Ibid. (both sources).

39. Ibid.

40. On the frequent failure of draftsmen and policymakers to match sanctions to problems, see Stephen Breyer, "Analyzing Regulatory Failure: Mismatches, Less Restrictive Alternatives, and Reform," *Harvard Law Review*, 92 (January 1979), 549–609.

41. Schwartz, *Economic Regulation of Business and Industry*, pp. 2606, 2609; Cohen to Landis, May 5, 1933, Landis Papers, Library of Congress; Frankfurter to Raymond Moley, April 15, 1933 (telegram); Rayburn to Frankfurter, May 26, 1933, both in Frankfurter Papers, Library of Congress.

42. *Annual Report of the Federal Trade Commission 1933* (Washington:

Government Printing Office, 1933), pp. 13–14; B. Bernard Greidinger, *Accounting Requirements of the Securities and Exchange Commission for the Preparation of Financial Statements* (New York: Ronald Press, 1939), chap. 2.

43. *Annual Report of the Federal Trade Commission 1934* (Washington: Government Printing Office, 1934), pp. 37–41. The first stop orders were issued against Speculative Investment Trust, Forth Worth, Texas; American Gold Mines Consolidation, Inc., New York; and Industrial Institute, Inc., Jersey City. See *FTC Annual Report 1933*, p. 15.

44. Landis to Frankfurter, January 27, 1934, Frankfurter Papers, Library of Congress.

45. Landis to Roosevelt, December 4, 1933 (not sent), Landis Papers, Library of Congress, pp. 10–11; Wyckoff, *Wall Street and the Stock Markets*, pp. 69–82; Schlesinger, *Coming of the New Deal*, pp. 456–488.

46. Landis to Frankfurter, March 6, 1934; Frankfurter to Landis, March 17, 1934, both in Frankfurter Papers; Ritchie, *Landis*, p. 74.

47. SEC Trading and Exchange Division, *Report to the Commission on the Problem of Multiple Trading on Securities Exchanges Nov. 20, 1940* (copy in Baker Library, Harvard University Graduate School of Business Administration), pp. 1–65.

48. Landis Memoir, pp. 195–206; Parrish, *Securities Regulation and the New Deal*, chaps. 5 and 8. The SEC Minutes (Record Group 66, National Archives, Washington, D.C.) throughout the 1930s reflect the continuing question of the New York Exchange as a particular problem.

49. This connection between the crash and the depression, though valid in the minds of New Dealers, has been challenged by modern scholars. See Peter Temin, *Did Monetary Forces Cause the Great Depression?* (New York: Norton, 1976); see also Parrish, *Securities Regulation and the New Deal*, pp. 111, 117–118; and Raymond Vernon, *The Regulation of Stock Exchange Members* (New York: Columbia University Press, 1941), pp. 12–57.

50. Schwartz, *Economic Regulation of Business and Industry*, pp. 2689–2690 and pp. 2746–2949 passim.

51. Ibid., pp. 2685–2686, 2692–2699, 2723–2725, 2735–2738.

52. Ibid., pp. 2684, 2728–2729, 2786, 2826–2827, 2830–2835, 2843–2848, 2851–2853, 2895–2899; Parrish, *Securities Regulation and the New Deal*, pp. 133–142; de Bedts, *The New Deal's SEC*, pp. 71–79; Ritchie, *Landis*, pp. 55–58.

53. Landis Memoir, pp. 188–191.

54. Ibid., pp. 190–191; Moley, *The First New Deal* (New York: Harcourt, Brace & World, 1966), pp. 517–520; Ritchie, *Landis*, pp. 59–61; Schlesinger, *Coming of the New Deal*, pp. 467–469.

55. Landis Memoir, pp. 190–193; Landis to Roosevelt, December 4, 1933 (not sent), Landis Papers, Library of Congress; Michael R. Beschloss, *Kennedy and Roosevelt: The Uneasy Alliance* (New York: Norton, 1980), pp. 85–95.

56. Kennedy address to Boston Chamber of Commerce, November 15, 1934 (Washington: Government Printing Office, 1934), p. 10.

57. Ibid., p. 1; Kennedy address to American Arbitration Association, New York, March 19, 1935 (Washington: Government Printing Office, 1935),

pp. 4–5; see also Kennedy addresses to the National Press Club, July 25, 1934, and to the Union League Club of Chicago, February 8, 1935, both published by the Government Printing Office. Copies of all four speeches are in Baker Library, Harvard University Graduate School of Business Administration.

58. Landis Memoir, pp. 225–227; SEC, *First Annual Report* (Washington: Government Printing Office, 1935), p. 38. The SEC had 692 employees at the time.

59. Landis to Pound, September 25, 1933, Landis Papers, Library of Congress; Landis to Frankfurter, January 27 and March 6, 1934, Frankfurter Papers; Landis to Rayburn, August 20, 1934, Landis Papers, Harvard Law School.

60. SEC, *First Annual Report*, p. 1; Ritchie, *Landis*, chap. 5; de Bedts, *The New Deal's SEC*, chap. 4. On Pecora's views, see his *Wall Street Under Oath* (New York: Simon and Schuster, 1939). On J. D. Ross, see Philip J. Funigiello, *Toward a National Power Policy: The New Deal and the Electric Utility Industry, 1933–1941* (Pittsburgh: University of Pittsburgh Press, 1973), pp. 194–209.

61. Landis, "The Securities and Exchange Commission: Its Origin, Personnel, and Objectives," *Yearbook of the Encyclopedia Britannica*, 2 (December 1934), 42.

62. *Journal of Accountancy*, 56 (December 1933), 409–410; see also Spencer Gordon, "Accountants and the Securities Act," ibid., pp. 438–451; and Robert Weidenhammer, "The Accountant and the Securities Act," *Accounting Review*, 8 (December 1933), 272–278.

63. This outreach to the profession began early; see Landis address to the New York State Society of CPAs, October 30, 1933, Landis Papers, Harvard Law School.

64. Landis, address to the New York State Society of CPAs, January 14, 1935, Landis Papers, Harvard Law School.

65. Special Committee on Cooperation with the SEC to Joseph P. Kennedy, July 8, 1935 (a 14-page letter), Landis Papers, Harvard Law School; *Journal of Accountancy*, 59 (February 1935), 81–82; ibid., 59 (March 1935), 161.

66. Albert J. Watson, "Practice Under the Securities Exchange Act," ibid., 59 (June 1935), p. 445; DR [sic] Scott, "Responsibilities of Accountants in a Changing Economy," *Accounting Review*, 14 (December 1939), 399.

67. In a speech of December 4, 1936 to the Investment Bankers Association, Augusta, Georgia, Landis said, "The impact of almost daily tilts with accountants, some of them called leaders in their profession, often leaves little doubt that their loyalties to management are stronger than their sense of responsibility to the investor" (Landis Papers, Harvard Law School).

On the cooperation between the SEC and CPAs, see Landis to George O. May, November 6, 1933, Landis Papers, Harvard Law School; Landis to John L. Carey (Secretary of the American Institute of Accountants), n.d. and November 13, 1935, Chairman's File, SEC Records (Record Group 66), National Archives, Washington, D.C.; John L. Carey, "Early Encounters Between CPAs and the SEC," *Accounting Historians Journal*, 6 (Spring 1979),

29–37; George C. Mathews, address before Illinois Society of CPAs, January 18, 1935, copy in Baker Library, Harvard University Graduate School of Business Administration; Mathews, "Accounting in the Regulation of Security Sales," *Accounting Review*, 13 (September 1938), 225–233; and Robert E. Healy, "The Next Step in Accounting," *Accounting Review*, 13 (March 1938), 1–9. Examples of SEC discussions pertaining to the Chief Accountant's role may be found in SEC Minutes of March 17, July 10 and 31, 1936; June 4 and November 16, 1937; and January 4 and February 12, 1938; and in William Werntz (Chief Accountant) to William O. Douglas, December 17, 1938, Chairman's File, SEC Records. See also Douglas, *Go East, Young Man: The Early Years* (New York: Random House, 1974), pp. 274–276.

68. C. Aubrey Smith, "Accounting Practice under the Securities and Exchange Commission," *Accounting Review*, 10 (December 1935), 325–332; William W. Werntz, "Some Current Problems in Accounting," ibid., 14 (June 1939), 117–126; Andrew Barr, "Accounting Research in the Securities and Exchange Commission," ibid., 14 (March 1940), 89–94; Carman G. Blough, "The Need for Accounting Principles," ibid., 12 (March 1937), 30–37; A.A. Berle, Jr., "Accounting and the Law," ibid., 13 (March 1938), 9–15.

69. B. Bernard Greidinger, *Accounting Requirements of the Securities and Exchange Commission* (New York: Ronald Press, 1939), p. v; editor's note, "Accounting Exchange," *Accounting Review*, 10 (March 1935), 102. As had often been the case in the history of regulation, the SEC's best opportunity for change came in the wake of a major scandal. In 1939, officials of the McKesson and Robbins Company, despite an independent audit by certified accountants, were shown to have overstated the corporation's assets by $20 million, to have embezzled several million dollars, and to have reported large profits from an imaginary drug business. In the aftermath of this sensational case, the SEC pushed through another reform program, which included a thorough overhaul of the rules of auditing. Again the agency worked through the accountants' own professional associations. Much as Charles Francis Adams' Massachusetts Board of Railroad Commissioners had done after the Revere train wreck, the SEC used this crisis to achieve permanent changes that it forced the accountants themselves to help design. On the McKesson and Robbins case and related matters, see Louis Loss, *Securities Regulation* (Boston: Little, Brown, 1951), pp. 231–236; Maurice C. Kaplan and Daniel M. Reaugh, "Accounting, Reports to Stockholders, and the SEC," *Accounting Review*, 14 (September 1939), 203–236; and SEC, *Report on Investigation, In the Matter of McKesson & Robbins, Inc.* (Washington: Government Printing Office, 1940).

One of the rigorous periods of oversight was the first thirteen years (1935–1947), when Carman G. Blough and William Werntz held the office of Chief Accountant. The tenure of Earle C. King and Andrew Barr (1947–1972) was noticeably less militant, but that situation changed abruptly with the appointment of John C. Burton, who served from 1972 to 1976. Burton was an aggressive reformer who believed the system needed restructuring. See William James Coffey, "Governmental Regulations and Professional Pronouncements: A Study of the Securities and Exchange Commission and the American Institute of Certified Public Accountants from 1934 through 1974," diss., New

York University, 1976, pp. 222–224 and passim. Coffey concludes that the co-operation has been close, that the institute's influence has been strong, and that the combined efforts have been salutary though the SEC on occasion might have taken more direct action. See also Andrew Barr and Elmer C. Koch, "Accounting and the S.E.C.," *George Washington Law Review*, 28 (October 1959), 176–193. For a dissenting view, see Robert Chatov, "The Collapse of Corporate Financial Standards Regulation: A Study of SEC-Accountant Interaction," diss., University of California, Berkeley, 1973. Chatov emphasizes the failures associated with conglomerate mergers in the 1960s, and he is especially provocative in detailing "the sociology of SEC-accountant interaction."

70. Calculated from *Historical Statistics of the United States: Colonial Times to 1970* (Washington: Government Printing Office, 1975), p. 140. The numbers, in thousands, are as follows:

	1930	1940	1950	1960	1970
Accountants and auditors	192	238	385	496	712
Physicians	163	174	198	233	282
Lawyers	161	182	184	218	273

71. All of these speeches are in the Landis Papers, Harvard Law School.

72. SEC, *First Annual Report* (1935), pp. 9–10, 35–37; SEC, *Second Annual Report* (1936), pp. 15–22; SEC, *Third Annual Report* (1937), pp. 72–75; SEC Minutes, January 3, February 15, March 5, 14, 21, 1935; February 17, September 21, October 18, November 18, 1936; March 5 and 15, May 26, 1937. See also "Douglas Over the Stock Exchange," *Fortune*, 17 (February 1938), 116, 119, and 122.

73. SEC, *Report on the Government of Securities Exchanges*, U.S. House, 74th Cong., 1st sess., Document No. 85 (Washington: Government Printing Office, 1935); Landis to Rayburn, February 4, 1935, Landis Papers, Harvard Law School; *Fortune*, "Douglas Over the Stock Exchange," pp. 116, 120.

74. Landis Memoir, p. 201; see also Brooks, *Once in Golconda*, chaps. 6–12, which covers Whitney's career (the quotation from Whitney is on p. 198).

75. Wyckoff, *Wall Street and the Stock Markets*, pp. 69–82, 176.

76. Landis' departure had nothing to do with the market slide. His appointment as dean had been announced eight months earlier. Roosevelt's letter accepting his resignation said, "You have brought the invaluable perspective of the scholar to the councils of those who have to make decisions in the administration of great affairs—and you leave behind you greater respect and appreciation for the scholar in Government," Roosevelt to Landis, September 14, 1937, Roosevelt Papers, Franklin D. Roosevelt Library, Hyde Park, New York.

77. Douglas to Roosevelt, April 12, 1939, Roosevelt Papers; Douglas, *Go East, Young Man*, pp. 269–276; *Fortune*, "Douglas Over the Stock Exchange," pp. 116–126; Parrish, *Securities Regulation and the New Deal*, pp. 181–182.

78. Brooks, *Once in Golconda*, pp. 242–245; Parrish, *Securities Regulation and the New Deal*, pp. 216–218; Loss, *Securities Regulation*, pp. 634–637;

"The SEC," *Fortune*, 21 (June 1940), 125–126; SEC Minutes, May 26, September 8, October 30, 1937. For several years, Paul Shields had already worked with the SEC on changing the NYSE's practices. In an April 3, 1935, telephone discussion with Landis, he had predicted that in the impending Exchange election, "That old group will be completely annihilated under this scheme. They will be shorn altogether" (memorandum, Landis Papers, Harvard Law School).

79. Joseph Alsop and Robert Kintner, "The Battle of the Market Place," *Saturday Evening Post*, 210 (June 25, 1938), 10–11, 78–82; *United States of America before the Securities and Exchange Commission in the Matter of Richard Whitney, et al.*, 3 vols. (Washington: Government Printing Office, 1938); Brooks, *Once in Golconda*, pp. 245–287. Douglas to Stephen A. Early (Memorandum on Whitney Report), October 27, 1938, Roosevelt Papers; Douglas to Early (Memorandum on Part II of Whitney Report), October 31, 1938, Chairman's File, SEC Records.

80. Douglas, *Go East, Young Man*, pp. 269–277; SEC Minutes, October 30 and November 23, 1937, February 9, 23, and 24, 1938. The SEC kept close watch on the elections to the Governing Committee of the New York Stock Exchange, familiarizing itself with all candidates and tracking the likely impacts of different mixes of representation on the 48-member board by bond dealers, trading specialists, trading specialists who also sold on commission, odd-lot dealers, floor brokers, and commission house brokers, the last named of whom the SEC further separated into five categories: large, medium, small, out of town, and underwriting. See Donald McVickar to Ernest Angell (SEC Regional Administrator for New York), memorandum, January 4, 1938, Chairman's File, SEC Records.

The negotiations between Douglas and Martin represented in microcosm the entire pattern of SEC regulation. For many months, the two men and their lieutenants held meeting after meeting in Washington and New York, during which they hammered out the details of the new system. As the unpublished records of these long conferences indicate, Douglas used the SEC's strong negotiating position to force the exchange to adopt genuine reform measures. Martin, for his part, raised the specter of direct SEC intervention to persuade his recalcitrant colleagues to accept the new system. In the end, the carefully orchestrated revolution achieved nearly every one of the common goals Douglas and Martin had in mind. Again, the SEC had used the circumstances of an evanescent crisis to work permanent change, insisting all the while that the exchange itself propose and adopt the new rules as its own. The commission kept the initiative throughout, by nurturing the indeterminacy of the situation and keeping its own future action unpredictable. The following excerpt from the unpublished minutes of an SEC commissioners' meeting of December 22, 1938 catches the essence of this drama, and of the larger SEC strategy: "Douglas reported that recent action of the New York Stock Exchange in refusing to proceed against certain members of the Exchange on charges growing out of the Commission's investigation of Richard Whitney and Co., had formed the basis of widespread rumors in the Street that a definite break had occurred in the cooperative program of the Exchange and the Commission.

Douglas presented the following statement which he recommended be authorized to the public, and the recommendation was adopted by the Commission: 'Mr. Martin and I have worked closely together and we are going to continue to do so. The action on the Whitney case has not caused a change in the cooperative program which we launched. It has placed, however, on the agenda of unfinished business a new item of importance, viz., the problem of better coordination and allocation of policing and disciplinary functions between the exchange and the Commission. That new item will be as objectively and constructively explored at the round table as have been the other items. What its solution will be I do not now know.' "

On these negotiations, see SEC Minutes, March 18, May 17, July 19, August 5, October 8 and 20, December 3, 14, 19, and 22, 1938, and March 10 and 21, June 26, July 14 and 27, August 28 and 29, September 9, 15, 20 and 22, 1939; memoranda of conferences between the SEC and officers of the New York Stock Exchange, May 18, June 3, 9, 16, 17, August 8, December 17, 1938; Milton Katz to Douglas, memorandum, April 13, 1938; Douglas to William McChesney Martin, Jr., December 27, 1938; Martin to Douglas, January 10, 1939; George C. Mathews to Martin, March 20, 1939, all in Chairman's File, SEC Records. See also Roosevelt to Douglas, November 18, 1937; and Douglas to Roosevelt, April 12, 1939, Roosevelt Papers. The process of constant consultation was not new, only more intense, during the Whitney scandal and the exchange reorganization. See *Report of the President* for 1936 (New York: Stock Exchange, 1936), pp. 3–4, and for 1937 (New York: Stock Exchange, 1937), pp. 1–5; copies in Baker Library, Harvard University Graduate School of Business Administration.

81. On the over-the-counter market and the National Association of Securities Dealers, see Loss, *Securities Regulation*, pp. 762–784; Marc A. White, "National Association of Securities Dealers, Inc.," *George Washington Law Review*, 28 (October 1959), 250–265; note, "Over-the-Counter Trading and the Maloney Act," *Yale Law Journal*, 48 (February 1939), 633–650; Homer V. Cherrington, "National Association of Securities Dealers," *Harvard Business Review*, 27 (November 1949), 741–759; A.R.W. (note), "The NASD—An Unique Experiment in Cooperative Regulation," *Virginia Law Review*, 46 (December 1960), 1586–1600; Richard W. Jennings, "Self-Regulation in the Securities Industry: The Role of the Securities and Exchange Commission," *Law and Contemporary Problems*, 29 (Summer 1964), 663–690; Howard C. Westwood and Edwin G. Howard, "Self-Government in the Securities Business," *Law and Contemporary Problems*, 17 (Summer 1952), 518–544; Parrish, *Securities Regulation and the New Deal*, pp. 214–216; and *National Association of Securities Dealers, Inc. Manual* (Washington: NASD, 1977), pp. 101–117.

82. See the sources cited in preceding note, especially the 1939 note in the *Yale Law Journal* and the 1964 article by Jennings in *Law and Contemporary Problems*.

83. Carosso, *Investment Banking in America*, pp. 384–388; Investment Bankers Code Committee, *Code of Fair Competition for Investment Bankers*,

with a Descriptive Analysis of Its Fair Practice Provisions and a History of Its Preparation (Washington: Investment Bankers Code Committee, 1934).

84. SEC Minutes, October 30, 1934, February 26 and April 10, 1935; Landis to Edward B. Raub, Jr., September 28, 1935, Chairman's File, SEC Records; Landis, address to National Association of State Security Commissioners, New Orleans, Louisiana, November 12, 1934, Landis Papers, Harvard Law School.

85. Carosso, *Investment Banking in America*, pp. 384–389.

86. SEC Minutes, April 8, May 3 and 24, June 3, September 19 and 23, November 15, 1935; January 29 and June 29, 1936; June 10, 1937; Landis to B. Howell Griswold, Jr., September 26, 1935 and June 29, 1936; Landis to Henry H. Hays, October 1, 1936, Chairman's File, SEC Records; Landis, address before the New England Council, Boston, November 22, 1935, p. 4, Landis Papers, Harvard Law School.

87. NASD, ". . . *A Symbol of Self-Regulation for Industry.* . . ," (Washington: NASD, 1943), p. 4; George C. Mathews, "A Discussion of the Maloney Act Program," address before the Investment Bankers Association of America, White Sulphur Springs, West Virginia, October 28, 1938, copy in Baker Library, Harvard University Graduate School of Business Administration; SEC Minutes, October 11, December 20, 1937, and January 28, February 28, June 28, 1938; William O. Douglas to Roosevelt, January 28 and May 19, 1938 (memoranda); Roosevelt to Douglas, February 1, 1938; Douglas to D.W. Bell, January 25, 1938; Bell to Roosevelt, January 29, 1938, all in Roosevelt Papers; Milton Katz to Healy (memorandum), March 7, 1938, Chairman's File, SEC Records.

88. See the general sources on the NASD cited in note 81 above. On the SEC's role, see SEC Minutes, June 18 and 28, July 6 and 30, October 6, November 29, and December 19, 1938; December 15, 1939; and December 3, 1940; see also B. Howell Griswold, Jr., to Douglas, February 13, 1939, and E.W. Pavenstedt to Ganson Purcell (memorandum), October 23, 1940, Chairman's File, SEC Records.

89. Note, "Over-the-Counter Trading and the Maloney Act," *Yale Law Journal*, p. 646; Loss, *Securities Regulation*, p. 784; Marc A. White, "National Association of Securities Dealers, Inc.," *George Washington Law Review*, 28 (October 1959), 265. The statistics on sanctions are from the *NASD Annual Report* for 1974 (p. 2); see also Louis Engel, *How to Buy Stocks*, 3rd ed. (Boston: Little, Brown, 1962), quoted in Poyntz Tyler, ed., *Securities, Exchanges and the SEC* (New York: H.W. Wilson, 1965), p. 73.

90. Homer V. Cherrington, "National Association of Securities Dealers," *Harvard Business Review*, 17 (November 1949), 756–757. In the late 1970s, the man who had been the most militant Chief Accountant in the SEC's history proposed that the NASD model be adapted for accounting regulation; see John C. Burton, "The Profession's Institutional Structure in the 1980s," *Journal of Accountancy*, 145 (April 1978), 63–69.

91. Interview with John C. Burton, August 1, 1979.

92. SEC, *Injunctions in Cases Involving Acts of Congress*, Senate Document No. 43, 75th Cong., 1st sess. (Washington: Government Printing Office, 1937), pp. 6–11; Landis Memoir, pp. 213–224; Douglas to Stephen Early

(memorandum), October 13, 1938, Roosevelt Papers; Parrish, *Securities Regulation and the New Deal*, pp. 145–178, 219–226; Funigiello, *Toward a National Power Policy*, chaps. 2–4.

93. Landis, address to Swarthmore Club, Philadelphia, February 27, 1937; address to Investment Bankers Association of America, Augusta, Georgia, December 4, 1936; address to the Economic Club of Chicago, April 29, 1936. All in Landis Papers, Harvard Law School.

94. Landis to Frankfurter, December 13, 1933; Frankfurter to Landis, January 10, 1934, both in Frankfurter Papers, Library of Congress. See also Landis to Archibald MacLeish, November 9, 1933; Auville Eager to ?, May 10, 1937; Eager to Landis, May 10, 1937, all in Landis Papers, Harvard Law School; and Ritchie, *Landis*, pp. 72–74.

95. "The Legend of Landis," *Fortune*, 10 (August 1934), 44–45, 118–120.

96. Ritchie, *Landis*, pp. 132–139; Arthur E. Sutherland, *The Law at Harvard: A History of Ideas and Men, 1817–1967* (Cambridge: Harvard University Press, 1967), pp. 300–312; Erwin N. Griswold, "James McCauley Landis—1899–1964," *Harvard Law Review*, 78 (December 1964), 315; Landis to James Rowe, Jr., June 6, 1940, Landis Papers, Library of Congress; Landis, "Morale and Civilian Defense," *American Journal of Sociology*, 47 (November 1941), 331–339; Landis, "Community War Cabinets," *Christian Science Monitor*, November 28, 1942; Landis, "Two Years of OCD," *New York Times Magazine*, May 30, 1943; Landis, "Anglo-American Co-operation in the Middle East," *Annals of the American Academy of Political and Social Science*, 240 (July 1945), 64–72.

97. Ritchie, *Landis*, chaps. 10–11.

98. Ritchie, *Landis*, chap. 11; Harry S. Truman, Memorandum for Robert E. Hannegan, February 7, 1946, Harry S. Truman Library, Independence, Missouri; Landis, address at Commencement Exercises of Brooklyn College, New York, June 15, 1947, Landis Papers, Harvard Law School; Landis, et al., sixth report of the Special Board of Inquiry on Air Safety to the President, December 29, 1947, Record Group 197, National Archives.

99. Ritchie, *Landis*, pp. 141–152; Landis to Senator Edwin Johnson, April 28, 1949, Landis Papers, Library of Congress; *The Air Line Pilot*, January 1948.

100. Landis, handwritten memorandum of interview with Truman, December 26, 1947; Henry J. Friendly to Landis, January 1, 1948; T. E. Braniff to Landis, December 31, 1947; Walton Hamilton to Landis, January 6, 1948, all in Landis Papers, Library of Congress; Felix Frankfurter, Diary, February 2, 1948, Frankfurter Papers, Library of Congress; Philip Murray to the President, December 29, 1947, Sam Rayburn to the President (telegram), December 30, 1947; David L. Behncke to the President (telegram), December 23, 1947, all in Harry S. Truman Library. See also Ritchie, *Landis*, pp. 152–155.

101. Ritchie, *Landis*, chap. 12; James Fayne to Landis (memorandum), August 22, 1951; John F. Kennedy to Landis, August 3, 1953; Landis to Joseph P. Kennedy (memorandum), January 21, 1953; Landis to John F. Kennedy, November 23, 1953, all in Landis Papers, Library of Congress. Boxes 50 and 51 of these papers contain a variety of material on Landis' relationship with the Kennedy family.

102. Ritchie, *Landis*, pp. 174–178; Landis, *Report on Regulatory Agen-*

cies to the President-Elect, U.S. Senate, Committee on the Judiciary, 86th Cong., 2nd sess. (Washington: Government Printing Office, 1960).

103. "Regulatory Agencies Panel," oral history interview with Alan S. Boyd, William L. Cary, Newton N. Minow, Joseph C. Swidler, and William Tucker, by Dan Fenn, Jr., August 18, 1964, Washington, D.C., John F. Kennedy Library, Boston; Ritchie, *Landis*, p. 187.

104. Ritchie, *Landis*, pp. 187, 192–197; Victor S. Navasky, *Kennedy Justice* (New York: Atheneum, 1971), pp. 378–390.

105. Ritchie, *Landis*, pp. 197–199.

106. Ibid., pp. 200–201; Henry J. Friendly to Frankfurter, August 12, 1963, Frankfurter Papers, Library of Congress.

107. Ritchie, *Landis*, pp. 201–202.

6. Ascent, Decline, and Rebirth

1. On the NRA, see Ellis W. Hawley, *The New Deal and the Problem of Monopoly: A Study in Economic Ambivalence* (Princeton: Princeton University Press, 1966); Bernard Bellush, *The Failure of the NRA* (New York: Norton, 1975); and Michael M. Weinstein, "Some Redistributive and Macroeconomic Impacts of the National Industrial Recovery Act, 1933–1935," diss., Massachusetts Institute of Technology, 1978.

2. Landis, *The Administrative Process* (New Haven: Yale University Press, 1938), p. 1. The invitation to give the Storrs lectures came in December 1935, but Landis delayed their delivery until his departure from the SEC.

3. Ibid., pp. 4–5.

4. Ibid., pp. 23–24; see also pp. 30–34.

5. Ibid., p. 24.

6. Ibid., p. 84.

7. Ibid., p. 85. The SEC issues several thousand no-action letters each year; for a survey of the method, accompanied by sample letters and commentary on advance advice, see William J. Lockhard, "SEC No-Action Letters: Informal Advice as a Discretionary Administrative Clearance," *Law and Contemporary Problems*, 37 (Winter 1972), 95–134.

8. Landis, *The Administrative Process*, pp. 154–155.

9. For a detailed and well-researched history of the SEC from its origins to the middle 1970s, see Joel Seligman, *The Transformation of Wall Street: A History of the Securities and Exchange Commission and Modern Corporate Finance* (Boston: Houghton Mifflin, 1982). On regulatory appointments, see Gale Eugene Peterson, "President Harry S. Truman and the Independent Regulatory Commissions, 1945–1952," diss., University of Maryland, 1973. A good picture of federal regulation from the 1930s to the 1950s may be gleaned from the extensive papers of longtime FPC Commissioner Leland Olds, at the Franklin D. Roosevelt Library, Hyde Park, New York.

10. On the issue of capture, see Thomas K. McCraw, "Regulation in America: A Review Article," *Business History Review*, 49 (Summer 1975), 162–183.

11. Landis himself contributed to both Hoover Commission reports. In the first Hoover report (1949), the section on regulation was drafted by Landis (on behalf of commission member Joseph Kennedy), then revised by others to suit Hoover and additional commission members. See Landis to Robert R. Bowie, September 27, 1948; Landis to Joseph P. Kennedy, January 5, 1949; Landis to Herbert Hoover (enclosing 17-page draft of report on Independent Regulatory Commissions), January 24, 1949; Landis to James Rowe, January 27, 1949; Landis to James M. Douglas, January 27, 1954; Landis to Reginald Heber Smith, February 17, 1954, all in Landis Papers, Library of Congress. See also, on evaluations of regulation from the 1930s to the 1950s, Carl McFarland, "Landis' Report: The Voice of One Crying in the Wilderness," *Virginia Law Review*, 47 (April 1961), 374–376.

12. Huntington, "The Marasmus of the ICC: The Commission, the Railroads, and the Public Interest," *Yale Law Journal*, 61 (April 1952), 467–509; Jaffe, "The Effective Limits of the Administrative Process: A Reevaluation," *Harvard Law Review*, 67 (May 1954), 1105–1135; Bernstein, *Regulating Business by Independent Commission* (Princeton: Princeton University Press, 1955); Landis, *Report on Regulatory Agencies to the President-Elect*, U.S. Senate, Committee on the Judiciary, 86th Cong., 2nd sess. (Washington: Government Printing Office, 1960).

13. Landis, *Report on Regulatory Agencies*, pp. 5–6, 10, 22–24, and 54.

14. Ibid., pp. 11, 66–68, 85–87.

15. Ritchie, *Landis*, pp. 178–186; "Regulatory Agencies Panel," oral history interview with Alan S. Boyd, William L. Cary, Newton N. Minow, Joseph C. Swidler, and William Tucker, by Dan Fenn, Jr., August 18, 1964, Washington, D.C., John F. Kennedy Library, Boston.

16. Landis himself anticipated this trend in his *Report on Regulatory Agencies*, pp. 19–21. He argued, for example, that in transportation there existed a "lack of any policy as to the nature of the competition that should exist as between forms of transportation and also as between the carriers themselves"; and he insisted that what was good for one agency or industry might not be good for another, primarily because of economic reasons: "the agencies have to be shaped internally for the functions that they are intended to serve." One of the most important harbingers of the coming revolution in regulatory thought appeared in a book written by a group of economists: John R. Meyer, Merton J. Peck, John Stenason, and Charles Zwick, *The Economics of Competition in the Transportation Industries* (Cambridge: Harvard University Press, 1959).

7. Kahn and the Economist's Hour

1. Garry Wills, *Nixon Agonistes: The Crisis of the Self-Made Man* (Boston: Houghton Mifflin, 1970), p. ix.

2. Kahn, *The Economics of Regulation: Principles and Institutions*, 2 vols. (New York: Wiley, 1970, 1971). The Chicago position is summarized in George J. Stigler, *The Citizen and the State: Essays on Regulation* (Chicago:

University of Chicago Press, 1975). For a critique of Stigler's argument, see Thomas K. McCraw, "Regulation, Chicago Style," *Reviews in American History*, 4 (June 1976), 297–303.

3. Ralph Blumenthal, "Off and Running Against Inflation," *New York Times Magazine*, January 14, 1979, p. 62; Lora S. Collins, "The Sayings of Chairman Kahn," *Across the Board*, 16 (April 1979), 57; "Yes, We Have No Bananas," *Time*, December 11, 1978, p. 84.

4. Blumenthal, "Off and Running Against Inflation," pp. 62–63; Collins, "The Sayings of Chairman Kahn," p. 61; *People*, October 2, 1978, pp. 71–74; "Big Kahn Job," *Barron's*, February 19, 1979, p. 16; Ernest Holsendolph, "The Rulings of Alfred E. Kahn, C.A.B. Chairman, Have Fueled the Competitive Fires," *New York Times*, April 23, 1978, sec. 3, pp. 1, 5.

5. Kahn, "Route Awards and Airline Scheduling Practices," statement prepared for conference of Civil Aeronautics Board and Federal Aviation Administration, March 2, 1978, CAB Records, Washington, D.C.

6. Kahn, "The Economics of Regulation," remarks at 54th National Conference of Regulatory Utility Commission Engineers, Hershey, Pennsylvania, June 23, 1976 (the illustration about meat prices came originally, Kahn noted, from Professor William Vickery of Columbia University); Kahn, "Electricity Costs, Pricing and Use: A Regulatory Evaluation," address at 43rd Annual Convention of Edison Electric Institute, Denver, Colorado, June 3, 1975. Both speeches are in the files of the New York State Public Service Commission, Albany. I am indebted to Douglas D. Anderson for providing me with copies.

7. *Current Biography Yearbook* (New York: H. W. Wilson, 1979), pp. 198–201; see also sources cited in notes 3 and 4 above.

8. Kahn, "Fundamental Deficiencies of the American Patent Law," *American Economic Review*, 30 (September 1940), 485.

9. Kahn, *Great Britain in the World Economy* (New York: Columbia University Press, 1946). This book received very favorable reviews: by W. F. Stolper in *Annals of the American Academy of Political and Social Science*, 244 (March 1946), 215–216; and by Arthur I. Bloomfield in *Journal of Political Economy*, 54 (December 1946), 559–560.

10. Kahn, "Palestine: A Problem in Economic Evaluation," *American Economic Review*, 34 (September 1944), 538–560; "The British Balance of Payments and Problems of Domestic Policy," *Quarterly Journal of Economics*, 61 (May 1947), 368–396; "The Burden of Import Duties: A Comment," *American Economic Review*, 38 (December 1948), pp. 857–866; "Investment Criteria in Development Programs," *Quarterly Journal of Economics*, 65 (February 1951), 38–61. The information on Kahn's thoughts about going to law school came from my interview with him on August 4, 1983.

11. Lilienthal, *Big Business—A New Era* (New York: Harper, 1953); Galbraith, *American Capitalism, The Concept of Countervailing Power* (Boston: Houghton Mifflin, 1952).

12. Joel B. Dirlam and Alfred E. Kahn, *Fair Competition: The Law and Economics of Antitrust Policy* (Ithaca: Cornell University Press, 1954), chaps. 1–2.

13. Ibid.; see also Kahn, "Standards for Antitrust Policy," *Harvard Law Review*, 67 (November 1953), 28–54; Dirlam and Kahn, "Antitrust Law and

the Big Buyer: Another Look at the A & P Case," *Journal of Political Economy*, 60 (April 1952), 118–132, and "A Reply," ibid., 61 (October 1953), 441–446; A.D.H. Kaplan and Kahn, "Big Business in a Competitive Society," *Fortune*, 47 (February 1953), sec. 2 (insert), pp. 1–14.

14. Dirlam and Kahn, *Fair Competition*, pp. 17–18. The authors were quoting in this passage some phraseology from Vernon Mund, *Government and Business* (New York: Harper, 1950), p. 63.

15. Dirlam and Kahn, *Fair Competition*, p. 20.

16. Ibid., pp. 27, 267–268, 284.

17. Ibid., p. 265. The quoted review is by John S. McGee in *American Economic Review*, 45 (June 1955), 452–454; for less harsh treatment, see Sigmund Timberg in *Columbia Law Review*, 55 (November 1955), 1088–1092.

18. Kahn was no stranger to hostile reviews or to what he liked to call "pugnacious" comment on the work of others. See his own harsh remarks in "Discussion of Report of the Attorney General's Committee on Antitrust Policy," *American Economic Review*, 46 (May 1956), 498, 500; "Discussion of Antitrust and Patent Laws: Effects on Innovation," *American Economic Review*, 56 (May 1966), 314; and "Economic Theory as a Guideline for Government Intervention and Control," *Journal of Economic Issues*, 8 (June 1974), 304.

19. Kahn to Barry Brooks, editor of *The Daily Texan* (University of Texas, Austin), March 9, 1978, records of CAB, Washington.

20. James M. Landis, *Report on Regulatory Agencies to the President-Elect*, Senate Committee on the Judiciary, 86th Cong., 2nd sess. (Washington: Government Printing Office, 1960), p. 54.

21. The evolution of Kahn's thinking about the regulation of oil and gas may be traced through Melvin de Chazeau and Kahn, *Integration and Competition in the Petroleum Industry* (New Haven: Yale University Press, 1959); Kahn, "Regulation of Crude Oil Production in the United States and Lessons for Italy," *Banca Nazionale Del Lavoro Quarterly Review*, 8 (June 1955), 67–79; Kahn, "Economic Issues in Regulating the Field Price of Natural Gas," *American Economic Review*, 50 (May 1960), 506–517; Kahn, "The Depletion Allowance in the Context of Cartelization," *American Economic Review*, 54 (June 1964), 286–314; and Kahn, *The Economics of Regulation*, I, chaps. 3–4. The quotation in this paragraph is from my interview with Kahn, August 4, 1983.

My understanding of the oil and gas issue from the 1950s through the 1970s, including the two-tier system, has been greatly enriched by conversations with my colleague, Richard H. K. Vietor.

22. Louis B. Schwartz in *Antitrust Bulletin*, 17 (Winter 1972), 1151–1169 (review appeared originally in the January 1972 issue of *University of Pennsylvania Law Review*); George Eads in *Bell Journal of Economics and Management Science*, 2 (Autumn 1971), 678–682; Francis X. Welch in *Public Utilities Fortnightly*, 87 (January 21, 1971), 4–8, and ibid., 88 (August 5, 1971), 53–55.

23. Kahn, *The Economics of Regulation*, I, vii.

24. Ibid., p. 15.

25. *Economic Report of the President 1980* (Washington: Government Printing Office, 1980), calculated from data on pp. 205, 207, 208, 278.

26. Richard F. Hirsh, "Conserving Kilowatts: The Electric Power Indus-

try in Transition," paper delivered at Conference on Energy in American History, Mountain Lake, Virginia, October 1, 1982.

27. As Kahn liked to point out, the impact of the OPEC shock of 1973 and 1974 was higher in the eastern United States than elsewhere because most oil for this region was imported and therefore subject to the full "world price" imposed by the OPEC cartel. See Kahn, "Balancing the Energy Future of New York State," address before Syracuse Press Club, March 21, 1975, files of New York Public Service Commission.

28. Murray L. Weidenbaum, "Variation in Public Utility Regulation," *Public Utilities Fortnightly*, 94 (October 24, 1974), 30; see also Leonard S. Hyman, "Rate Cases in 1970–74: A Quantitative Examination," ibid., 96 (November 6, 1975), 22–30.

29. See also Charles J. Cicchetti, "Electricity Price Regulation: Critical Crossroads or New Group Participation Sport," *Public Utilities Fortnightly*, 94 (August 29, 1974), 13–18.

30. Thomas K. McCraw, *TVA and the Power Fight, 1933–1939* (Philadelphia: Lippincott, 1971), pp. 60–62; Eli Winston Clemens, *Economics and Public Utilities* (New York: Appleton-Century-Crofts, 1950), pp. 622–624. After the consumption of 1400 kilowatt-hours, a TVA residential customer's rate went from .40¢ to .75¢. This reflected a conviction that only extremely wealthy households could use more than 1400 and that the rich should enjoy no increasing benefit.

31. McCraw, *TVA and the Power Fight*, pp. 60–62, 74–76; McCraw, "Triumph and Irony: The TVA," *Proceedings of the Institute of Electrical and Electronics Engineers*, 64 (September 1976), 1376.

32. Kahn, "The Graduated Fair Return: Comment," *American Economic Review*, 58 (March 1968), 172; McCraw, *TVA and the Power Fight*, pp. 60–62; Clemens, *Economics and Public Utilities*, pp. 603–628.

33. Clemens, *Economics and Public Utilities*, pp. 603–628; other information from TVA Technical Library, Knoxville, Tennessee.

34. Harvey Averch and L. L. Johnson, "Behavior of the Firm Under Regulatory Constraint," *American Economic Review*, 52 (December 1962), 1052–1069; William J. Baumol and Alvin K. Klevorick, "Input Choices and Rate-of-Return Regulation: An Overview of the Discussion," *Bell Journal of Economics and Management Science*, 1 (Autumn 1970), 162–190.

35. Kahn, "Inducements to Superior Performance: Price," in Harry M. Trebing, ed., *Performance Under Regulation* (East Lansing: Graduate School of Business Administration, Michigan State University, 1968), p. 92.

36. Kahn, "Between Theory and Practice: Reflections of a Neophyte Public Utility Regulator," *Public Utilities Fortnightly*, 95 (January 2, 1975), 33. To take a specific example of this remarkable trend, residential customers of the TVA paid 2.11¢ per kilowatt-hour in 1940, but only 0.89¢ in 1967. Had electricity followed the consumer price index, they would have paid not 0.89¢ but 5.02¢, or between five and six times as much. Data for these calculations are in McCraw, "Triumph and Irony: The TVA," p. 1376; and *Economic Report of the President, 1980*, p. 239.

37. Kahn, "Economic Theory as a Guideline for Government Interven-

tion and Control: Comment," *Journal of Economic Issues*, 8 (June 1974), 301, 307.

38. See National Association of Regulatory Utility Commissioners, *Annual Report on Utility and Carrier Regulation* (Washington: NARUC, 1975), a compendium of information on state commissions prepared by their trade association. Hereafter cited as NARUC *Annual Report*.

39. Over the last 75 years, the general reputation of state regulatory commissioners has never been high, as almost any written or oral source will show. NARUC *Annual Report* (all years) contains short biographies of incumbent commissioners in all states, and a perusal of these biographies will suggest both the predominance of lawyers and the otherwise wide range of background and training typical of state commissioners.

40. NARUC *Annual Reports*, passim.

41. For federal commissioners, see Florence Ann Heffron, "The Independent Regulatory Commissioners," diss., University of Colorado, 1971, p. 189; E. Pendleton Herring, *Federal Commissioners: A Study of Their Careers and Qualifications* (Cambridge: Harvard University Press, 1936); Clarence A. Miller, "The Interstate Commerce Commissioners," *George Washington Law Review*, 5 (March 1937), 580–700; and U.S. Senate Committee on Commerce, 94th Cong., 2nd sess., *Appointments to the Regulatory Agencies: The Federal Communications Commission and the Federal Trade Commission (1949–1974)* (Washington: Government Printing Office, 1976), p. 422; and for the state commissions, biographies in NARUC *Annual Reports*.

42. NARUC *Annual Reports*, passim.

43. Douglas D. Anderson, *Regulatory Politics and Electric Utilities: A Case Study in Political Economy* (Boston: Auburn House, 1981), p. 86; NARUC *Annual Report*, section on New York commission.

44. *New York Times*, April 3, 1975.

45. Ibid., January 30, 1977.

46. Quoted in Anderson, *Regulatory Politics and Electric Utilities*, p. 98.

47. Ibid., p. 101.

48. Ibid., pp. 101–102.

49. New York State Public Service Commission, *Annual Report, 1974* (Albany, 1975), pp. 1–2.

50. Ibid., pp. 2–3; see also Kahn, address at 3rd Annual Symposium on Problems of Regulated Industries, Kansas City, Missouri, February 14, 1977, files of New York Public Service Commission.

51. The discussion that follows in this section owes a great deal to Douglas D. Anderson's fine book, *Regulatory Politics and Electric Utilities*, especially chap. 4. Professor Anderson has been of great assistance to me in understanding this story, not only through his book but also in conversations and in his generous sharing of his collection of addresses by Kahn as a member of the New York Public Service Commission.

52. The Madison Gas & Electric case pioneered systematic testimony in the benefits of marginal-cost pricing. The case was not on the same scale of the LILCO case in New York because the Wisconsin company was not so large as LILCO, because the potential savings from marginal-cost pricing were not so

great, and because the Madison utility had a significantly higher load factor and lower industrial and commercial consumption. The case was, nevertheless, an important foreshadowing of both the generic rate hearing in New York and the LILCO rate case. Kahn himself comments on the Madison case as follows: that a key role was played by the consulting firm of economists (National Economic Research Associates), "whose president, Irwin M. Stelzer, had been a student of mine, and that embarked on a campaign to convince utility companies that marginal cost pricing was in their interest as well as the public's— Madison Gas was their client. I remember expressing dismay that because of their efforts—and the educability and courage of Dick Cudahy—then Chairman of the Wisconsin Public Service Commission and now a judge of the U.S. Circuit Court of Appeals—Wisconsin beat me in issuing *the* pathbreaking marginal cost pricing decision." Kahn to author, July 13, 1983.

53. Anderson, *Regulatory Politics and Electric Utilities*, pp. 90, 113–114.

54. New York Public Service Commission, *Annual Report, 1975*, pp. 13, 17; Anderson, *Regulatory Politics and Electric Utilities*, pp. 113–115.

55. Quoted in Anderson, *Regulatory Politics and Electric Utilities*, p. 98.

56. Quoted in ibid., p. 99.

57. Kahn speech to Smith Barney Electric Utility Conference, New York, January 15, 1976, files New York Public Service Commission; *New York Times*, January 22 and May 18, 1975.

58. Anderson, *Regulatory Politics and Electric Utilities*, p. 115.

59. Ibid., pp. 115–123; *New York Times*, December 14, 1975.

60. Anderson, *Regulatory Politics and Electric Utilities*, pp. 123–124.

61. Ibid.; *New York Times*, January 6 and 11, March 19, 1976.

62. Anderson, *Regulatory Politics and Electric Utilities*, pp. 126–127.

63. A table of the new rates is listed in ibid., pp. 128–130; for background, see also *New York Times*, December 14, 1975 and January 6 and 11, 1976. The 12:1 ratio is described in Kahn, "Route Awards and Airline Scheduling Practices," a statement prepared for a dual conference between the Civil Aeronautics Board and the Federal Aviation Administration, March 2, 1978, CAB Records, Washington, D.C.

64. New York Public Service Commission, *Annual Report, 1975* and *1977; New York Times*, April 3 and August 30, 1975; Kahn testimony to Senate Committee on Finance in connection with the Energy Conservation and Conversion Act of 1975, Washington, D.C., July 18, 1975, files of New York Public Service Commission; Kahn, "Utility Rate Regulation: Applications of Economics," address before American Economic Association, Atlantic City, New Jersey, September 17, 1976, files of New York Public Service Commission.

65. New York Public Service Commission, *Annual Report, 1974*, passim; *1975*, pp. 13–14. See also *New York Times*, December 16, 1976.

66. Kahn, "Utility Rate Regulation: Applications of Economics," address before American Economic Association, Atlantic City, New Jersey, September 17, 1976, files of New York Public Service Commission; *New York Times*, March 18, 1975.

67. Kahn, "Utility Rate Regulation," address before American Economic Association; Kahn, speech at Smith Barney Electric Utility Conference, New

York, January 15, 1976, files of New York Public Service Commission; *New York Times,* January 30, 1977.

68. Kahn, "Utility Rate Regulation," address to American Economic Association; *New York Times,* August 23, 1975, and April 11, 1976.

69. *New York Times,* May 10, 1977; Kahn to author, July 13, 1983; Kahn interview with author, August 4, 1983.

70. Enzo Angelucci, *Airplanes from the Dawn of Flight to the Present Day* (New York: McGraw-Hill, 1973); Edward V. Rickenbacker, *Rickenbacker* (Englewood Cliffs: Prentice-Hall, 1967).

71. *Historical Statistics of the United States: Colonial Times to 1970* (Washington: Government Printing Office, 1975), II, p. 769.

72. Ibid.

73. Stephen Breyer, *Regulation and Its Reform* (Cambridge: Harvard University Press, 1982), pp. 198–199. For an overview of the onset of airline regulation, see Bernard Schwartz, ed., *The Economic Regulation of Business and Industry: A Legislative History of U.S. Regulatory Agencies* (New York: Chelsea House, 1973), IV, 2983–3078.

74. Kahn illustrated the nature of airline markets well in a presentation he gave on May 4, 1978, before a symposium on international air commerce at Georgetown University: "There is no large domestic market for air transportation in the sense that there is for computers or color television sets. There are, rather, hundreds of individual city-pair markets just as there are throughout the world" (copy in CAB Records). The numbers quoted are from Breyer, *Regulation and Its Reform,* p. 199. See also, for airline regulation in general, Richard Caves, *Air Transport and Its Regulators—An Industry Study* (Cambridge: Harvard University Press, 1962), which was the first important book-length critique of the CAB's policies by an economist; William A. Jordan, *Airline Regulation in America: Effects and Imperfections* (Baltimore: Johns Hopkins Press, 1970); Theodore Keeler, "Airline Regulation and Market Performance," *Bell Journal of Economics and Management Science,* 3 (Autumn 1972), 399–424; and George W. Douglas and James C. Miller III, *Economic Regulation of Domestic Air Transport: Theory and Policy* (Washington: Brookings Institution, 1974).

75. John Newhouse, *The Sporty Game* (New York: Knopf, 1982), pp. 8–9; Breyer, *Regulation and Its Reform,* pp. 198–199.

76. CAB, *Annual Report, 1977* (Washington: Government Printing Office, 1978), pp. 140–143. The figures for 1977 are for the fiscal year; others are for calendar years; the numbers cited pertain to all route carriers. See also *Historical Statistics of the United States: Colonial Times to 1970* (Washington: Government Printing Office, 1975), pp. 767–774.

77. At the time of Kahn's arrival in Washington, the trunkline companies divided their part of the American domestic market as follows:

Company	Rev. passenger miles	Market share	Load factor
United	31,227 million	22.7%	60.0%
American	20,849	15.2	57.4
Delta	18,051	13.1	56.1

Eastern	16,238	11.8	54.6
TWA	15,843	11.5	55.9
Northwest	8,058	5.9	46.8
Western	7,712	5.6	56.6
Continental	6,309	4.6	55.4
Braniff	5,831	4.2	51.4
National	5,436	4.0	45.6

Source: CAB, *Annual Report, 1977,* p. 127. The numbers are for the year ending September 1977.

78. U.S. Congress, *Civil Aeronautics Board Practices and Procedures,* Report of Subcommittee on Administrative Practice and Procedure of the Senate Committee on the Judiciary, 94th Cong., 1st sess. (Washington: Government Printing Office, 1975), pp. 31–33. Hereafter cited as *CAB Practices and Procedures.*

79. Ellis W. Hawley, "Three Aspects of Hooverian Associationalism: Lumber, Aviation, and Movies, 1921–1930," in Thomas K. McCraw, ed., *Regulation in Perspective: Historical Essays* (Boston: Harvard Business School, 1981), pp. 108–115. The quoted representative was James J. Wadsworth (D., N.Y.); see Schwartz, ed., *Economic Regulation of Business and Industry,* p. 2984.

80. Schwartz, ed., *Economic Regulation of Business and Industry,* pp. 3062–3063.

81. Ibid., pp. 3064–3065.

82. When Kahn arrived at the board, United Airlines had just begun to break ranks with the other trunk carriers and move toward a deregulation stance. For general discussions of the CAB's rate regulation policies, see the works by Caves, Breyer, Jordan, and Keeler cited in note 74 above.

83. Again, see the works by Caves, Breyer, Jordan, and Keeler cited in note 74 above; also Kahn, *Economics of Regulation,* II, 209–217.

84. Landis, *Report on Regulatory Agencies to the President-Elect,* submitted by Subcommittee on Administrative Practice and Procedure to Senate Committee on the Judiciary, 86th Cong., 2d sess. (Washington: Government Printing Office, 1960), p. 41.

85. Ibid., pp. 41–44.

86. On the subject of CAB proceedings, Judge Henry J. Friendly, himself a former counsel to several airlines, wrote in 1962: "My quarrel is with the decisional process and the opinion writing. If most airline executives and lawyers thought that the Board had no standards as to the grant or denial of competitive [routes], that the elaborate hearings had almost no effect on the outcome, that the factors truly motivating decisions were quite other than those stated, that as was later to be said by one of the wisest of airline counsel 'instead of the decision of a case being based upon the findings of fact and determination of policy disclosed in the agency opinion, the findings and determinations are based on the decision,' the two [route case] opinions [under discussion] amply warranted such views." Quoted in William E. Fruhan, Jr., *The Fight for Competitive Advantage: A Study of the United States Domestic Trunk Air Carriers*

(Boston: Harvard Business School, 1972), p. 160. See also the general discussion of this issue, ibid., pp. 159–161.

87. *CAB Practices and Procedures*, pp. 92–93; Robert Burkhardt, *CAB— The Civil Aeronautics Board* (Dulles International Airport, Virginia: Green Hills Publishing Company, 1974), p. 157.

88. *CAB Practices and Procedures*, p. 93. One CAB member who resigned for this reason was Harmar D. Denny; see Burkhardt, *CAB—The Civil Aeronautics Board*, photo section following p. 86.

89. Kahn, *Economics of Regulation*, II, 209–217; *CAB Practices and Procedures*, pp. 84–90. Fruhan, *The Fight for Competitive Advantage*, is a thorough study of the problem of overcapacity induced by regulatory policy.

90. The situation of airline regulation in the middle 1970s is concisely described in Breyer, *Regulation and Its Reform*, chaps. 11 and 16. For additional background, see John R. Meyer and Clinton V. Oster, Jr., eds., *Airline Deregulation: The Early Experience* (Boston: Auburn House, 1981), pp. 3–37.

91. Breyer, *Regulation and Its Reform*, chap. 16.

92. *CAB Practices and Procedures*, pp. 40–42. The fare quoted in the table for Houston-San Antonio was an offpeak (nights and weekends) fare not strictly comparable with the quoted fare for Boston-New York. The latter was $19 offpeak, but the relative use of offpeak rates was much greater in the Texas markets.

93. Ibid., pp. 45, 47.

94. Michael E. Levine, "Is Regulation Necessary? California Air Transportation and National Regulatory Policy," *Yale Law Journal*, 74 (July 1965), 1416–1447; Kahn, *Economics of Regulation*, II, 216–220.

95. Cited in Meyer and Oster, eds., *Airline Deregulation*, p. 54.

96. *Washington Post*, May 13 and July 11, 1977; Rush Loving, Jr., "The Pros and Cons of Airline Deregulation," *Fortune*, August 1977, pp. 209–217.

97. On the gala, see *Airline Reports*, May 26 and June 27, 1977. Kahn's interview was in *New York Times*, August 21, 1977.

98. *Airline Reports*, March 31, 1977; *Washington Star*, April 27, 1977; *Aviation Daily*, August 24, 1977; *New York Times*, September 22, 1977 (editorial).

99. *Airline Reports*, April 4, 1977.

100. *Wall Street Journal*, April 4, 1977 and May 9, 1978.

101. *Washington Star*, April 3, 1977; *Washington Post*, April 11, 1977; *Air Line Pilot*, June 1977 (editorial).

102. Kahn to Professor Harvey Levin, August 16, 1977, CAB Records.

103. Kahn memorandum to Bureau and Office Heads, Division and Section Chiefs, June 16, 1977, CAB Records; *Washington Post*, June 7, 1977; Kahn to Wallace Lovejoy, June 21, 1977, CAB Records.

104. See, for example, the four drafts of Kahn to Dave Pritchard, September 22, 1977; and the two of Kahn to J. Robert Barlow, September 23, 1977. See also Kahn interviews in *New York Times*, August 21, 1977; and Kahn letters to Sally Reithlingshoefer, August 10, 1977, to Congressman John J. La Falce, July 29, 1977, and to Nancy Cheney, June 30, 1978, all in CAB Records.

105. *Travel Weekly*, June 1977 (editorial); transcript of MacNeil-Lehrer television program, January 10, 1978.

106. Kahn to Paul Tierney, August 31, 1977; Kahn testimony before House Budget Committee Task Force on Tax Expenditures, Government Organization, and Regulation, July 14, 1977, both in CAB Records.

107. Kahn interviews in *Travel Trade*, July 11, 1977, and in *National Journal*, January 14, 1978; Kahn address to New York Society of Security Analysts, February 2, 1978, all in CAB Records.

108. Kahn interview in *Travel Weekly*, November 10, 1977; Kahn, address to Symposium on International Air Commerce, Georgetown University, May 4, 1978; Kahn, paper at *Financial Times* Conference on International Transport, London, October 4, 1978; transcript of MacNeil-Lehrer television program, January 10, 1978.

109. *Airline Reports*, April 21, May 12 and 23, 1977; *Aviation Daily*, April 30, May, 3, 5, and 11, and August 10, 1977; *Washington Star*, May 10, 1977, and January 24, 1978; *Washington Post*, April 19, May 1, and August 6, 1977; *Chicago Tribune*, May 7, 1977.

110. *Aviation Daily*, May 26 and July 12, 1977; *Washington Post*, July 26, 1977.

111. Kahn to Herman Roseman (National Economic Research Associates), August 19, 1977; see also Kahn to Charles Warren (Council on Environmental Quality), September 30, 1977, both in CAB Records.

112. Kahn to D. S. Caverly, September 2, 1977, CAB Records; CAB organization charts are published in every *Annual Report* of the Board, and such a chart for this period is reproduced in Thomas K. McCraw, "Regulatory Agencies," in Glenn Porter, ed., *Encyclopedia of American Economic History* (New York: Scribner's, 1980), II, 800.

113. CAB, *Annual Report, 1977*, pp. iii, 70–72, and *1978*, pp. iii, 55; *Washington Post*, May 6, 1978.

114. Kahn to Alan K. Campbell (Civil Service Commission), September 2, 1977; Kahn to Pat McCann (Congressional Budget Office), December 23, 1977; Kahn to Irwin Stelzer, September 13, 1978, all in CAB Records.

115. *Airline Reports*, December 19, 1977; *Washington Post*, January 12, 1978. According to Kahn himself, other key CAB managers included the managing director, Dennis Rapp, whom Kahn brought from the Office of Environmental Planning of the New York Public Service Commission; and Don Farmer, head of the Office of International Aviation, whom Kahn hired from the Antitrust Division of the Department of Justice. Kahn to author, July 13, 1983.

116. *Washington Post*, January 12, 1978.

117. CAB, *Annual Report, 1977*, p. 21.

118. Ibid., and ibid., *1978*, p. 21; *Washington Post*, February 3, 1978; Kahn to Stu Eizenstat (White House), November 9, 1977, CAB Records.

119. CAB, *Annual Report, 1978*, pp. 114–115. Amounts are in current dollars not adjusted for inflation.

120. Kahn, paper at *Financial Times* Conference on International Transport, London, October 4, 1978, CAB Records.

121. Kahn, address to New York Security Analysts, February 2, 1978, CAB Records; *Washington Post*, September 22, 1977.

122. Kahn to Andrew W. Brainerd, January 31, 1978; Kahn to Nina Cor-

nell (Council of Economic Advisers), February 14, 1978, both in CAB Records.

123. Kahn to Andreas F. Lowenfeld, June 30, 1978, CAB Records.

124. Kahn to Barry Goldwater, September 11, 1978; Kahn to Irwin Stelzer, September 13, 1978, both in CAB Records.

125. Kahn, "Applications of Economics to an Imperfect World," address to American Economic Association, Chicago, August 26, 1978, CAB Records.

126. Kahn, address at Northwestern University, November 6, 1977, CAB Records.

127. Ibid.

128. Kahn, "Applications of Economics to an Imperfect World," August 26, 1978.

129. Ibid.

130. Ibid.; *Chicago-Midway Low Fare Route Proceeding*, CAB Docket 30277, Orders 78-7-40, July 12, 1978, and 78-8-203, August 31, 1978; Kahn to Irving Kahn, September 1, 1977, CAB Records.

131. *Oakland Service Investigation*, CAB Docket 30699, Order 78-4-121, May 30, 1978; Kahn, "Applications of Economics to an Imperfect World," August 26, 1978; Kahn, address to American Association of Airport Executives, Cincinnati, May 22, 1978; *New York Times*, May 31, 1978; Kahn to Alan Cranston, December 14, 1977; Kahn to William G. Shepherd, July 24, 1978, CAB Records; CAB, *Annual Report, 1978*, pp. 8–13.

132. Kahn to Irving Kahn, September 1, 1977; Kahn to Robert A. Anthony (Administrative Conference of the United States), August 28, 1978, both in CAB Records.

133. A good capsule commentary on administrative procedure may be found in Stephen Breyer, *Regulation and Its Reform*, pp. 378–381. See also the textbook by Breyer and Richard B. Stewart, *Administrative Law and the Regulatory Process* (Boston: Little, Brown, 1979).

134. A good discussion of these developments is in Richard B. Stewart, "The Reformation of American Administrative Law," *Harvard Law Review*, 88 (June 1975), 1669–1813.

135. Kahn, address to New York Security Analysts, February 2, 1978.

136. Discussions of sunshine practices and other procedural matters may be traced in Kahn to D. S. Caverly (Environmental Assessment Board, Toronto), September 2, 1977; Kahn to Senator Lawton Chiles (Subcommittee on Federal Spending Practices and Open Government), September 7, 1977, and April 7, 1978; Kahn to John W. Dregge (North Central Airlines), September 8, 1977; Kahn to James T. McIntyre (Office of Management and Budget), December 27, 1977; Kahn to Congressman Glenn M. Anderson (Subcommittee on Aviation), January 24, 1978; Kahn to Richard L. Garwin (IBM), February 8, 1978; Kahn to Robert A. Anthony (Administrative Conference of the United States), March 23, 1978; and Kahn to David Cohen (Common Cause), April 11, 1978, all in CAB Records.

137. Kahn, "A Paean to Legal Creativity," talk before the American Bar Association, New York, August 8, 1978, CAB Records. Kahn received help in drafting this important speech from "my superb Executive Assistant, a lawyer, Mike Roach." Kahn to author, July 13, 1983.

138. Ibid.

139. Kahn, paper at *Financial Times* Conference on International Transport, London, October 4, 1978, CAB Records. Kahn cited a study done by the Council on Wage and Price Stability for the period 1970–1977, which found average pay increases of 9.34 percent in tightly regulated industries, compared with 7.20 percent in unregulated. Even assuming that persons in each type of industry began with the same salary, say, $10,000 in 1970, by 1977 the regulated-industry workers would be earning $18,683, or 15 percent more than the unregulated, at only $16,269.

140. Kahn to Dennis DiDonna, June 26, 1978, CAB Records.

141. Kahn to George T. Jehn, August 16, 1978, CAB Records.

142. *Washington Post*, September 15, 1977; Kahn interview in *National Journal*, January 14, 1978; AP news dispatch, December 22, 1977; transcript of MacNeil-Lehrer television program, January 10, 1978.

143. Kahn to Jimmy Carter, March 13 and May 15, 1978, CAB Records; *Washington Post*, March 30, 1978; *Aviation Daily*, March 30, 1978; *Air Transport World*, April 1978; *New York Times*, March 24, 1978.

144. Kahn to Hamilton Jordan, January 27, 1978, CAB Records.

145. Kahn to James T. Gamill, Jr., and Diana Rock (White House), April 21, 1978, CAB Records.

146. Kahn to Tim Engel (Ad Hoc Committee for Airline Regulatory Reform), March 8, 1978, CAB Records.

147. *Air Transport World*, December 1977.

148. Kahn to Congressman Silvio Conte, March 16, 1978, CAB Records; see also *New York Times*, April 24, 1978.

149. *Washington Post*, February 8 and March 7, 1978; *Wall Street Journal*, May 10, 1978; Kahn to Senator Howard Cannon, October 2, 1978, CAB Records.

150. Kahn to Senator John Melcher, July 27, 1977; Kahn to Senator Jacob Javits, June 29, 1978, CAB Records.

151. Kahn to Congressman Matthew McHugh, July 5, 1978, CAB Records.

152. Kahn, address to Commuter Airlines Association Conference, New Orleans, November 15, 1977, CAB Records.

153. Kahn to all senators, April 14, 1978; see also Kahn to Congressman Elliott Levitas, October 4, 1977; Kahn to Senator Barry Goldwater, December 22, 1977; Kahn to Congressman Robert Sikes, March 7, 1978; Kahn to Congressman Dan Glickman, March 15, 1978; Kahn to Congressman Robert Duncan, April 6, 1978; Kahn to Senator Ted Stevens, March 10, 1978; Kahn to Senator James Allen, March 14, 1978; Kahn to Senator Edward Kennedy, April 19, 1978; Kahn to Senator George McGovern, August 28, 1978; Kahn to Congressman Harold T. Johnson, September 11, 1978; Kahn to Senator Harrison Schmitt, September 12, 1977; Kahn to Congresswoman Helen Meyner, November 11, 1977; Kahn to Congressman Elliott Levitas, April 5, 1978, all in CAB Records.

154. Kahn to Karl Bopp, April 13, 1978, CAB Records; see also *Business*

NOTES TO PAGES 293-298

Week, October 30, 1978; *Airline Reports,* May 25, 1978; *Wall Street Journal,* July 3, 1978.

155. *Aviation Daily,* June 15, 1978; Kahn to Harold J. Maves, September 12, 1978, CAB Records.

156. The Airline Deregulation Act is Public Law No. 95-504, 92 Stat. 1705 (1978). An explanation and description of its provisions may be found in *New York Times,* November 7, 1978. The remark about the Supreme Court was made by Kahn to the author, July 13, 1983.

157. *The Regulators* (typescript report, Washington newsletter), September 20, 1978.

158. *Aviation Week and Space Technology,* November 20, 1978, p. 15.

159. Kahn to Edward Zorinsky, October 26, 1978; Carter to members and staff of the Civil Aeronautics Board, October 25, 1978, both in CAB Records.

160. *New York Times,* December 4, 1978.

161. *Washington Post,* November 30, 1978; *New York Times,* December 13, 1978; *Business Week,* December 25, 1978, p. 186; *National Journal,* January 14, 1978.

162. Kahn to author, July 13, 1983; Kahn interview with author, August 4, 1983; Kahn, "The Political Feasibility of Regulatory Reform: How Did We Do It?" in LeRoy Graymer and Frederick Thompson, eds., *Reforming Social Regulation: Alternative Public Policy Strategies* (Beverly Hills: Sage Publications, 1982), pp. 247–263. See also Milton Friedman's column in *Newsweek,* November 20, 1978, p. 94.

163. On the Public Utility Regulatory Policies Act in general, see U.S. Department of Energy, *Annual Report to Congress,* DOE/RG-0034-1 (Washington: DOE, May 1980), vol. 1. For reports of progress in particular state cases, see *Public Utilities Fortnightly,* issues of October 25, 1979, pp. 52–54; January 21, 1982, p. 63; March 18, 1982, p. 80; April 18, 1982, p. 72; and April 29, 1982, p. 69. For an updated analysis of the difficulties of implementation, see A. Scott Rothey and Samuel C. Randazzo, "Marginal Cost Electric Rate Making: Some Realities," *Public Utilities Fortnightly,* July 8, 1982, pp. 34–38.

164. Newhouse, *The Sporty Game.* The author of this account of competition among aircraft manufacturers believes deregulation to have been a bad idea because airlines "are a public utility" (p. 228). But his real interest is in promoting a national industrial policy for the United States as a means of improving American international competiveness in the aircraft industry.

165. John R. Meyer, et al., *Airline Deregulation: The Early Experience* (Boston: Auburn House, 1981), chap. 12; see also Douglas W. Caves, Laurits R. Christensen, and Michael W. Tretheway, "Airline Productivity under Deregulation," *Regulation,* 6 (November–December 1982), 25–28. The most thorough official study of the effects of deregulation is David R. Graham and Daniel P. Kaplan, *Competition and the Airlines: An Evaluation of Deregulation,* staff report by the CAB's Office of Economic Analysis (Washington: CAB, December 1982), which concurs with the favorable analyses of the other two studies cited in this note.

166. Meyer, *Airline Deregulation,* p. 271; *Wall Street Journal,* May 14, 1982. Robson's comment was made to the author in 1977, at a seminar of the Harvard Faculty Project on Regulation.

167. Kahn to Paolo Baffi (governor of the Bank of Italy), August 3, 1978, CAB Records. The same point about Kahn's experience in the New York Public Service Commission is made by Douglas Anderson in *Regulatory Politics and Electric Utilities*, pp. 130–132. For a good general analysis of this point with respect to the CAB (as well as a good analysis of the CAB's overall policies before and during the Kahn era), see Bradley Behrman, "Civil Aeronautics Board," in James Q. Wilson, ed., *The Politics of Regulation* (New York: Basic Books, 1980), pp. 75–120.

8. Regulation Reconsidered

1. The most useful models of agency behavior tend to be based on medium-range generalizations. See, for example, the classifications by James Q. Wilson around the themes of concentration and diffusion of costs and benefits: "The Politics of Regulation," in James W. McKie, ed., *Social Responsibility and the Business Predicament* (Washington: Brookings Institution, 1974), pp. 135–168.

2. James Q. Wilson, ed., *The Politics of Regulation* (New York: Basic Books, 1980), p. 393; see also Alfred E. Kahn, "The Political Feasibility of Regulatory Reform: How Did We Do It?" in LeRoy Graymer and Frederick Thompson, eds., *Reforming Social Regulation: Alternative Public Policy Strategies* (Beverly Hills: Sage Publications, 1982), pp. 249–251.

3. My point here overlaps but is not identical with the central argument made by Stephen Breyer in *Regulation and Its Reform* (Cambridge: Harvard University Press, 1982). Whereas Breyer quite properly points out the need to match specific regulatory responses to the type of problem at issue, I am emphasizing the need to tailor regulatory strategies to industry structures and behaviors. On the relationship between structural and behavioral models in modern economic scholarship, see the collection of essays edited by John V. Craven, *Industrial Organization, Antitrust, and Public Policy* (Boston: Kluwer-Nijhoff, 1983), particularly the essays by Alfred E. Kahn and Oliver E. Williamson.

4. On the breakup of the Bell System, see Paul W. MacAvoy and Kenneth Robinson, "Winning By Losing: The AT&T Settlement and Its Impact on Telecommunications," *Yale Journal on Regulation*, 1 (1983), 1–42.

5. For discussions of regulatory theories, see George J. Stigler, "The Theory of Economic Regulation," *Bell Journal of Economics and Management Science*, 2 (Spring 1971), 3–21; Richard Posner, "Theories of Economic Regulation," ibid., 5 (Autumn 1974), 335–358; Richard B. Stewart, "The Reformation of American Administrative Law," *Harvard Law Review*, 88 (June 1975), 1669–1813; Thomas K. McCraw, "Regulation in America: A Review Article," *Business History Review*, 49 (Summer 1975), 159–183; McCraw, "Regulation, Chicago Style," *Reviews in American History*, 4 (June 1976), 297–303; Barry Mitnick, *The Political Economy of Regulation* (New York: Columbia University Press, 1980); Paul Quirk, *Industry Influence in Federal Regulatory Agencies* (Princeton: Princeton University Press, 1981); Douglas Anderson, *Regulatory Politics and Electric Utilities: A Case Study in Political*

Economy (Boston: Auburn House, 1981); Peter Navarro, "Theories of Government Regulation: A Survey and Synthesis," unpublished manuscript, Harvard University, 1981; and William Gormley, *The Politics of Public Utility Regulation* (Pittsburgh: University of Pittsburgh Press, 1983).

6. See, especially, Charles L. Schultze, *The Public Use of Private Interest* (Washington: Brookings Institution, 1977).

Acknowledgments

My greatest debts, intellectual and otherwise, are to Susan McCraw. Nearly every part of this book has been improved by her sharp legal skills, her genius at organization, and her fine editorial hand. I also owe much to Alfred Chandler, who showed me how to analyze economic organizations; to James Willard Hurst, who taught me how to think about legal institutions; and to Paul Glad, who convinced me that the interaction between ideas and behavior not only must be taken seriously, but should be studied directly as a subject in itself. All four of these persons, by the example of their dedication and craftsmanship, have provided me with a large measure of inspiration over many years, in addition to their help with this book.

I received invaluable research assistance from Gerald Berk and William Childs, both of whom are tireless diggers in archives and walking storehouses of knowledge about the history of regulation. I was fortunate in receiving editorial help from Michael Aronson, Joyce Backman, Max Hall, Earl Harbert, and Erica Liederman. Useful opportunities to test the ideas in this book came not only in my own classes at the Harvard Business School, but also in a variety of other forums: the Federal Trade Commission, the United States Regulatory Council, the Harvard Faculty Project on Regulation, the Senior American Historians at Harvard group, the Charles Warren Center, the Organization of American Historians, the Social Science History Association, the Conference on the History of Public Policy at the Harvard Business School, and the summer seminar at the University of Wisconsin, Research in American Legal History.

Parts of the manuscript were read and criticized by numerous colleagues at the Harvard Business School: Douglas Anderson, Kenneth Andrews, Joseph Auerbach, Joseph Badaracco, James Baughman, Joseph Bower, Colyer Crum, Ronald Fox, Richard Hirsh, George Lodge, Jesse Markham, Albro Martin, Gale Merseth, Glenn Porter, Helen Rochlin, Michael Rukstad, Bruce Scott, Richard Tedlow, Raymond Vernon, and particularly Richard Vietor. I am very grateful for their generosity and their insights.

Any scholar who tries to examine four different periods of American history in some detail, as I have done in this book, must rely for help on experts in those periods. I am much indebted to friends and colleagues outside my own school who provided this kind of specialized assistance: Geoffrey Blodgett of Oberlin College, Robert Cuff of York University, Christopher DeMuth of the Kennedy School of Government, Arthur Donovan of Virginia Tech, Louis Galambos of Johns Hopkins, Lewis Gould of the University of Texas, Ellis Hawley of the University of Iowa, Thomas Parke Hughes of the University of Pennsylvania, Alfred Kahn of Cornell, Barry Karl of the University of Chicago, Morton Keller of Brandeis, David Levy of the University of Oklahoma, Daniel Pope of the University of Oregon, Robert Reich of the Kennedy School of Government, Donald Ritchie of the U.S. Senate Historian's Office, Joel Seligman of the George Washington University Law Center, Richard Stewart of the Harvard Law School, and John Whitworth of the New York bar.

Finally, I want to express my gratitude for the indispensable help I received from librarians and archivists at all of the repositories listed in the notes of this book; and for the generous financial support provided by the National Endowment for the Humanities, the Newcomen Society in North America, and especially the Division of Research of the Harvard Business School.

Index